The publisher gratefully acknowledges the generous support of the Jewish Studies Endowment Fund of the University of California Press Foundation, which was established by a major gift from the S. Mark Taper Foundation.

The publisher also gratefully acknowledges the generous support of the Humanities Endowment Fund of the University of California Press Foundation.

Cumin, Camels, and Caravans

CALIFORNIA STUDIES IN FOOD AND CULTURE

Darra Goldstein, Editor

Cumin, Camels, and Caravans

A Spice Odyssey

Gary Paul Nabhan

UNIVERSITY OF CALIFORNIA PRESS
Berkeley · Los Angeles · London

University of California Press, one of the most
distinguished university presses in the United States,
enriches lives around the world by advancing scholarship
in the humanities, social sciences, and natural sciences.
Its activities are supported by the UC Press Foundation
and by philanthropic contributions from individuals and
institutions. For more information, visit www.ucpress.edu.

University of California Press
Berkeley and Los Angeles, California

University of California Press, Ltd.
London, England

Compositor: BookMatters, Berkeley
Indexer: Thérèse Shere
Cartographer: Paul Mirocha
Printer and binder: Maple Press

Library of Congress Cataloging-in-Publication Data

Nabhan, Gary Paul.
   Cumin, camels, and caravans : a spice odyssey / Gary
Paul Nabhan.
     pages   cm. — (California studies in food and
culture ; 45)
   Includes bibliographical references and index.
   ISBN 978-0-520-26720-6 (cloth : alk. paper) — ISBN
978-0-520-95695-7 (e-book)
   1. Spice trade. 2. Spice trade—History. I. Title.
II. Series: California studies in food and culture ; 45.
   HD9210.A2N33   2014
   382'.456645—dc23
                                    2013032714

Manufactured in the United States of America

22
10 9 8 7 6 5 4 3

To three mentors who showed me how the Old World and New World are deeply connected culturally: Agnese Haury, Juan Estevan Arellano, and Michael Bonine

Contents

Illustrations

MAPS

Recipes

*The recipes in this book open a window onto the people and commu-
nities who made and still make these foods. Even the varied names of
the dishes give some sense of the paths they have taken over the centuries. The recipes also record the cultural diffusion of spices as they pass
from one place to another: a chicken mole that fuses elements of the
Persian, Arabic, and Moorish kitchens; tharīd, a bread-and-broth soup
from the Arabian Peninsula that gave rise to açorda soup in Portugal,
gazpacho in Spain, and perhaps even sopa de tortilla in Mexico; and
mansaf, one of the oldest recipes in the world, a Mesopotamian stew
seasoned with a mix of cumin, turmeric, and cassia cinnamon, which is
still being made today.*

Spice Boxes

The spices profiled in this book embrace an eclectic assortment of herbs, incenses, gums, fruits, musks, and teas. Some are esoteric, such as frankincense and mastic, while others are familiar and beloved, like cumin and chocolate. Some might come as a surprise, since they are not widely thought of as spices, like pomegranate, caper, and Damascus rose. But what all of these have in common is that they were in high demand throughout history as flavorings, fragrances, and pharmaceuticals. Because many aromatics were specific to certain geographic areas, they had to be traded for rather than produced locally. These valuable commodities gave their names to the roads by which they were traded, which became collectively known as the Spice Routes. The spice profiles give an overview of the vernacular names, folk uses, medicinal applications, and local lore surrounding each of these global travelers.

Introduction

The Origin of "Species":
Trading Spices to the Ends of the Earth

Perhaps my lifelong love of aromatics—from allspice to *za'atar*—served as the genesis of this reflective inquiry. But somewhere along the line, I realized that one could not truly love spices without conceding that their use is never politically, economically, or even culturally neutral. It is impossible to reflect on the significance of aromatics and their history without acknowledging that imperialism, cultural competition and collaboration, religious belief, and social status are embedded in every milligram of cardamom, cinnamon, or cumin.

And so, this book is less the story of any single spice or spice trader and more about the cultural, economic, and political factors that propelled spices across the face of the earth, depleting some species while causing others to proliferate. It is a multilayered narrative that is as much about alchemy as it is about chemistry, cultural history as it is about natural history, and culinary imperialism as it is about transcontinental and multicultural collaboration. In short, the history of the spice trade is an object lesson in how, step by step, globalization has developed and sealed off other formerly prevalent options for business and cross-cultural negotiation among the world's diverse peoples.

If this story line occasionally strays away from the trajectory that particular incenses, gums, and culinary and medicinal herbs took as they traveled around the world, so be it, for I am ultimately trying to answer a series of much larger questions. When, where, how, and through whose hands did the process of globalization begin? What have we gained and what have we lost by entering into this Faustian bargain? And finally, how has globalization irrevocably changed the human condition? How has that thirteen-letter word come to be perhaps the most pervasive expression of the current cultural tendency to trade a place-based existence for one that is essentially placeless?

I was encouraged to ponder this issue after reading "The Dawn of the Homogenocene," a fascinating essay by the deeply thoughtful environmental historian Charles C. Mann.[1] Mann, like another fine contemporary writer, David Quammen, likes to use ecologist Gordon Orians's term *homogenocene,* which refers to the present era in geological history, one in which the world's biota has become blandly uniform in place after place due to "recent" biological and cultural invasions on every continent. In his essay, Mann suggests that the roots of globalization and homogenization can be traced back to 1493 and the Casa Almirante (Admiral's House) of Cristóbal Colón (our Christopher Columbus) on the island of Hispaniola.

Indeed, the initiation of the Columbian exchange of plants, animals, and microbes between the Old World and the New World was a benchmark in the onset of "ecological imperialism" that not only reshaped life in the Americas but on all other continents as well.[2] It is a "rupturous" moment in history that I have elsewhere referred to as the Great Colónoscopy.[3]

Nevertheless, I believe that while Mann understands and writes eloquently of the socioeconomic and ecological processes associated with globalization, he has grossly erred in dating its onset. So has Felipe Fernández-Armesto in his lovely *1492: The Year Our World Began.*[4] It certainly did not emerge from humanity's economic endeavors as late as 1493 CE, nor even as late as 1493 BCE. Depending on what we might use to date the earliest evidence of spice (or copper) trade occurring between regions or continents,[5] Fernández-Armesto, Mann, and I would likely agree that the initial phases of the inexorable process that led toward ever more pervasive globalization occurred at least as early as thirty-five hundred years ago.

I would argue that the same mentalities, skills, and economic drives that led to the colonization of the Americas were already well articulated by the time the inhabitants of the Middle East colonized regions of Africa, Asia, and southwestern Europe. After 1492, they simply extended their base of operations to two other continents, using many of the same entrepreneurial and political strategies employed first to capture transcontinental trade in spices from the New World and then to expand their hegemony over other arenas of economic activity. And although none of us would necessarily grant its "invention" to an Italian-born immigrant such as Christopher Columbus, I believe that we could agree that Semitic peoples such as Phoenicians, Nabataeans, Arabs, and Jews left legacies of navigation, geographical exploration, culinary imperialism, and globalization that clearly informed Columbus.

For almost anyone who has lived on earth over the last four millennia, it is difficult to imagine a world without extra-local herbs, spices, incenses, infusions, and medicines next to our hearths or in our homes. It is as if their fragrances have *always* been wafting into the culturally constructed spaces where our saints and sinners, prophets and prodigal sons come together to be healed or to celebrate a communal meal. The aromas of leafy herbs, dried fruits, crushed seeds, ground roots, and droplets of tree gums lodge deeply in our memories. Although we have difficulty verbally describing what distinguishes one fragrance from another, the most memorable of them nevertheless insinuate themselves into the holiest of oral histories and the most sacred of ancient scriptures we have shared as a species.

The words *species* and *spices* come from the same roots in Latin, *spec* (singular) and *species* (plural), which referred to kinds, forms, or appearances of items within a larger assortment. But according to etymologist Walter W. Skeat, by the time Middle English was in use, *spis*, *spyses*, or *species* more particularly denoted different kinds of aromatic plants or drugs in trade.[6] Following Skeat, our current usage of the Modern English term *species* seems to have evolved out of the need to speak collectively of cinnamon, cloves, nutmeg, and saffron, and then to be able to distinguish among them as distinctive aromatics; only later was this sense of species extended to other non-aromatic plants and to animals. Thus, the origin of *species* as a construct within English may very well be rooted in the economic or aesthetic need to discern various kinds of spices from one another. Spices and our own species have certainly traveled together and shaped one another as far back as our surviving mythic narratives reach.

In the Hebrew scriptures, a Jew named Joseph is sold off to a caravan carrying spices out of Palestine into the ancient Egyptian cities along the Nile. In the Christian scriptures, in the part known as the godspel among Christian speakers of Old English, we hear the "good news" that three traders of incense came from the East to encounter another Joseph, his young wife, Mary, and their newborn baby, Yeshu, one winter night when the stars were bright. In the Qur'an, we learn that before receiving his call to be the Prophet, Muhammad assisted his uncle Abu Talib and his own first wife, Khadijah, with their spice caravans, riding dromedaries from Mecca to Damascus and Aleppo. They became used to guarding from pirates and competitors their camel-hair bags burgeoning with herbs, dates, frankincense, and other exotic aromatics long enough to sell them for higher prices when they envisioned that such opportunities would soon emerge, leading to our current practice of speculation. A spice speculator was considered a visionary, someone who could anticipate when a new story (or market) was emerging and help to shape it.

Whenever I hear such stories, I come away from them sensing that these visionaries on their spice odysseys were also quite worldly, for they navigated through tangible perils as they crossed barren deserts, war-torn borders, and tumultuous seas. Their stories inevitably retain meaning for us today, for they reveal some of the earliest recorded efforts to race into "undiscovered" or contested space, to globalize trade, and to forge new fusion cultures and cuisines.

Despite the relevance these tales hold for us, we have been left with little understanding of what it was like to make one's living trading spices on a daily basis. We have only a few fragments, like those from the eleventh century found among the sacred trash of Arabized Jews in the Cairo Geniza,[7] which give us a fleeting glimpse into the lives of the *tajir,* or "big-time merchants," who reshaped life in the Mediterranean basin.

I myself have briefly made a meager portion of my living hauling wild chiles and Mexican oregano across the United States–Mexico border, but until recently, I had seldom thought much of my own activity as a trader in relation to the lifelong (and sometimes multigenerational) commitment made by most spice traders. Is cross-cultural trade in aromatics a rarified and inherently risky activity fitting for only a few overly adventurous polyglots? Did most spice traders have the money-thirsty mindset of Marco Polo's father Niccolò and uncle Maffeo, who left their families for years on end in order to profit from exotic treasures from distant lands? Or were some of these pilgrims spiritually motivated, like those mysterious Magi who allegedly followed stars from one place to the next in search of a new voice on earth?

In most cases, the lens through which we view the historic spice trade has long been obscured by romance and fogged by clichés. Each of us may recall when we first saw those nineteenth-century lithographs or Persian rug designs with scenes depicting merchants arriving at caravansaries within the fortified gates of port towns. There, they would ceremoniously dismount from their dromedaries, which had carried vast quantities of aromatic cargo into souks nearby. Those marketplaces would be crowded with buyers and sellers of spices from the Molucca Islands, Malabar Coast, or Zanzibar and incense that had come across the Horn of Africa or the Empty Quarter of the Arabian Peninsula.

Unequivocally, the strongest and most lingering images we have of the spice trade come from the Mediterranean shores of the Middle East, where the Oriental and Occidental worlds met, competed, and intermingled. Turks, Persians, Portuguese, Berbers, Sogdians, Gujaratis, Chinese, Greeks, and Romans have clearly had their hands in spice bags, baskets, and barrels. And yet, it seems that those of the Semitic language family—Arabs and Jews, Phoenicians and Nabataeans—have played peculiarly pivotal roles in the development and control of the global spice trade.

To validate the impression that spice merchants, especially those of Arab and Jewish descent, were among those who played a disproportionately important role in efforts to globalize trade across continents, we must look for evidence beyond the souks clustered at the crossroads of the Middle East. To be sure, Arabs and Jews did not act alone but interacted with Persians, Sogdians, Berbers, Uighurs, Gujaratis, Han Chinese, Spaniards, Portuguese, Italians, and Dutch at these crossroads. We must go to the ends of the line—to the farthest corners of the earth—where the Silk Road, the Frankincense Trail, the Spice Route, and the Camino Real of Chile and Chocolate become no more than rustic footpaths climbing up into the hinterlands.

It is at the ends of these lines that we might truly fathom how the spice trade contributed to today's globalization and how pervasive the culinary influences of Arabs and Jews have become.

For our immediate purposes, imagine the ends of one line for trading spices to be Ulaanbaatar, Mongolia, and Quanzhou and Xi'an, China, on the east and the montane hinterlands of Taos, Santa Fe, and Las Vegas, New Mexico, on the west. Let us begin in Ulaanbaatar's precursor, historically known as Yihe Huree (literally "Great Camp"), which stood not far from where the most far-flung of all Arab contributions to global cuisines was once recorded. From 1328 to 1332 CE, the country from Xi'an northward into Mongolia was ruled by the emperor Tutemur, who suffered chronic health problems during his brief reign. These maladies were severe enough to prompt him to seek dietary advice from a medical doctor who had vast knowledge of medicinal and culinary herbs in use in Persia and Arabia.

The man chosen to be the imperial physician, Hu Szu-hui, was most surely of Hui Muslim ancestry and had widely traveled in Central Asia, Asia Minor, and the Arabian Peninsula before settling in north-central China. Hu Szu-hui encouraged the emperor's kitchen staff to favor healthful Persian, Arabic, and Turkish recipes heavily laden with certain dried spices that were already becoming popular in China and Mongolia. In essence, he worked with the emperor's chefs to craft China's first dietary manual. It was a valiant but ultimately unsuccessful attempt to keep Tutemur, a descendant of Kublai Khan, alive, in good health, and in power for several years longer.

Although the emperor soon died, the Hui doctor's recipes lived on in a medieval manuscript, *Yin-shan cheng-yao*, recently translated by food historian Paul Buell and ethnobotanist Eugene Anderson. One of Hu Szu-hui's recipes curiously resurfaced in a place halfway around the world from where the Hui and Mongolians had traded spices.[8]

At a meeting of ethnobiologists in May 2013, Gene Anderson recounted to me the story of how, while rummaging through used books in a shop in Silver City, New Mexico, he noticed a recipe for lamb stew in a 1939 booklet called *Potajes Sabrosos*. He showed the recipe to Paul, and they quickly realized that it was nearly identical to a recipe that Hu Szu-hui had left behind in China some seven hundred years earlier—one that Gene and Paul had translated for *Yin-shan cheng-yao*. Both recipes were for a lamb and garbanzo bean stew. The Spanish version by Cleofas Jaramillo that appeared in *Potajes Sabrosos*—later translated as *The Genuine New Mexico Tasty Recipes*[9]—lacked only one ingredient that appeared in the Arabic-Persian stew recorded by Hu Szu-hui. That single missing ingredient was mastic, a gum from a wild pistachio tree relative that was used as a thickening agent in the Mediterranean. Hispanic New Mexicans apparently found their own local surrogates for such gummy thickeners.

The similarities between these two recipes are so uncanny that some sort of cultural diffusion makes more sense to food historians than independent invention does. Had the same core knowledge of what spices to pair with lamb and beans independently diffused to different corners of the earth? How in the name of heaven had the same recipe landed at one end of the line as well as at another halfway around the world, when both of these places were equally remote from the Middle East, the heartland of Arabic and Jewish spice trade?

❧ HARIRA ❧ CARNE DE CORDERO EN LA OLLA
Lamb and Garbanzo Bean Stew

This ancient dish may have emerged at different times in multiple places, but it clearly spread with Arab and Persian influence as far east as Mongolia, and with Jewish and Arab-Berber influence as far west as the Hispanic communities of northern Mexico. Currently, its most widely acclaimed expression is in the many variations of *harira* and *chorba* prepared in Morocco and other parts of the Maghreb, where they are traditionally eaten at sundown each day during Ramadan. In this particular recipe, I have based the ingredient list and cooking instructions on the Hispanic culinary traditions documented in Arroyo Hondo, New Mexico, by Cleofas Jaramillo in 1939, then elaborated on them through attention to Paula Wolfert's records on the various types of *harira* in Morocco. Following Wolfert, I suggest that the garbanzos be soaked and then peeled, a step not done in all places where such a stew has diffused, but one that allows for a softer texture. In a pair of *harira* recipes, she illustrates two different thickeners, a mixture of semolina flour and water in one and beaten eggs in the other. To enhance this rich culinary melting pot, I have used mastic here in the same role, a soup ingredient included in the medical dietary recommendations known as *Yin-shan cheng-yao* by Hu Szu-hui, published in the early 1300s. Look for mastic, sometimes labeled gum mastic, in food shops specializing in Greek, Turkish, or Middle Eastern ingredients or online.

Serve with a flat bread, such as Lebanese or Jordanian *za'atar* bread, focaccia, or even a whole wheat tortilla. A small salad of romaine lettuce hearts, watercress, or purslane leaves tossed with dried mint, lemon juice, and olive oil complements this stew, as well. *Serves 4.*

⅓ cup dried garbanzo beans

1½ cups water

1 teaspoon fresh lemon juice

¼ cup olive oil or *smen* (Moroccan fermented salted butter)

1 pound boneless lamb from the shoulder, cut into 1-inch cubes

1 large white onion, finely chopped

4 plum tomatoes, finely chopped

1 teaspoon finely crushed mastic

Salt and white or black pepper

½ cup fresh cilantro leaves, minced

1 teaspoon freshly ground cassia cinnamon

½ teaspoon peeled and minced fresh ginger

½ teaspoon peeled and minced fresh turmeric
½ teaspoon freshly ground cumin seeds
¼ teaspoon freshly grated nutmeg
Pinch of saffron threads
2 lemons, cut into wedges

In a bowl, cover the garbanzo beans with the water and stir in the lemon juice. Allow to soak for 8 to 24 hours in a warm spot or, if preferred, in the refrigerator. Drain, rinse, and then rub the beans between your fingertips to release their skins. Set the beans aside.

In a heavy pot, heat the olive oil over medium-low heat. Add the lamb and brown the meat on all sides. Using a slotted spoon, transfer the lamb to a plate. Add the onion to the oil remaining in the pan and sauté over medium-low heat until translucent, 4 to 5 minutes. Add the tomatoes and cook, stirring occasionally, for a couple minutes to release their juices.

Return the lamb to the pan, add the garbanzos and mastic, season with salt and pepper, and stir well. Add water to a depth of 2 to 3 inches, raise the heat to medium-high, and bring the mixture to a boil. Lower the heat to a gentle simmer and cook uncovered, stirring occasionally, until the beans are nearly tender, about 45 minutes. Add water as needed to cook the beans properly and to maintain a good stew consistency.

Add the cilantro, cinnamon, ginger, turmeric, cumin, nutmeg, and saffron, stir well, and continue to simmer until the garbanzos are tender, about 20 minutes longer.

Ladle the stew into individual bowls and serve. Pass the lemon wedges at the table for guests to squeeze into their bowls as desired.

Buell, Paul D., and Eugene N. Anderson, eds. *A Soup for the Qan: Chinese Dietary Medicine of the Mongol Era as Seen in Hu Szu-hui's Yin-Shan Cheng-yao.* London and New York: Keegan Paul International, 2000.
Jaramillo, Cleofas M. *New Mexico Tasty Recipes.* Layton, UT: Gibbs Smith, 2008, p. 2.
Wolfert, Paula. *Couscous and Other Good Food from Morocco.* New York: Harper & Row, 1973, pp. 58–61.

Mastic is one of the names given to the sun-dried resinous droplets of a gum that flows from the wounds of the cultivated *Pistacia lentiscus* var. *chia* tree, a close relative of the tree that yields pistachio nuts. Although the tree can be found throughout the Mediterranean basin and its many islands, the resinous gum with the sweetest fragrance and most distinctive *terroir* comes from only one area on the Greek island of Chios, in the Aegean Sea. There, the clear nectarlike resin that weeps from the wounds inflicted on the leafy shrublike tree is called the Tears of Chios and is carefully harvested and dried into a hard, translucent mass that looks like peanut brittle. When chewed or dissolved over heat in a saucepan, the resin softens and becomes pliant once more, turning a pearly white and taking on an opaque luster.

All of the production of high-quality mastic occurs on limestone ridges around the medieval villages in the Mastichochoria region of Chios, where the resin has been granted denomination of origin status and a local cooperative oversees the harvest and its sale. Although the Lebanese cultivate this same species for its nutlike fruits to flavor sausages and for its mastic, they cannot legally sell the latter as true mastic in food and beverage markets. There is also a Bombay mastic harvested from *Pistacia atlantica* ssp. *cabulica*.

The English term *mastic* is borrowed from the Greek *mastiha*, which is etymologically related to the ancient Greek and Phoenician word *mastichan*, "to chew." Mastic has been casually used as a chewing gum, a breath freshener, a perfume, a varnish, a medicine, and a digestive for at least twenty-four hundred years. Over time, Mediterranean cultures identified additional culinary and enological uses for the versatile gum, so that today most of the Chios production is used in liqueurs, pastries, and candies.

Mastic is an essential ingredient in many anise-flavored distilled beverages, including Greek ouzo and Turkish and Cretan raki. In addition to using *mastiha* in their own ouzo, the residents of Chios also make a sweet-smelling liqueur called *mastichato*. Growing up in a Lebanese American family in a Greek American neighborhood where ice-cold water was always added to fine arak and ouzo to make them milky and sweet, I had wondered whether mastic was the magical ingredient that caused white crystals to condense and color the drink. The true cause, however, is simpler than that: anethole, the essential oil in aniseeds, is soluble in alcohol but not in water. The Greeks also use *mastiha* in two refreshing summertime drinks: *soumada*, a mix of mastic, cane sugar, almond milk, and the potent liquor *tsipouro*; and *hypovrihio* (submarine), which consists of mastic, honey, and cold water.

Some teetotalers may have ingested mastic and savored its flavors when sampling the famous confection called *loukoumia*, or Turkish delight, found throughout the Middle East. Mastic is also used to flavor and thicken puddings, candies, sweet pastries, ice creams, jams, and cheeses, and it can be added to rubs for baked or fried poultry and seafood to give them a distinctive crust. If these uses sound exclusively secular compared with those of gums such as frankincense and myrrh, remember that followers of the Greek Orthodox faith celebrate scores of sacred feasting and fasting days each year. It is therefore not surprising that *mastiha* is ritually used in Greek festival breads such as *vasilopita* (St. Basil's bread). Mastic was also a key ingredient in the lamb and garbanzo bean stew that Hu Szu-hui recommended to his Mongolian emperor, as recorded in *A Soup for the Qan,* the classic food history of the Silk Roads. I have been known to keep a few lumps of mastic on the top of my desk, to chew on whenever I need to project my imagination into the eastern Mediterranean.

Davidson, Alan, ed. *The Oxford Companion to Food.* Oxford: Oxford University Press, 1999.
Green, Aliza. *Field Guide to Herbs and Spices.* Philadelphia: Quirk Books, 2006.
Katzer, Gernot. "Gernot Katzer's Spice Pages." http://gernot-katzers-spice-pages.com/engl/index.html. Accessed May 8, 2013.
Sherman, Deborah Rothman. "The Magic Tree." *Epikouria Magazine of Fine Food and Drink from Greece* 1 (2005). www.epikkouria.com.
Sortun, Ana, with Nicole Chaison. *Spice: Flavors of the Eastern Mediterranean.* New York: Regan Books, 2006.

When Cleofas Jaramillo was a budding folklorist for the Federal Writers' Project during the Depression, she became intent on collecting recipes and other lore from the villagers of the Rio Arriba watershed of northern New Mexico. Those Spanish speakers pointedly referred to their ancestry as Hispanic, not Mexican, and certainly not as Jewish or Arabic. A few may have known that some of their Spanish-speaking ancestors who had accompanied Hernán Cortés from Spain to Veracruz, Mexico, in 1519 did not want to linger very long in central Mexico, where echoes of the Spanish Inquisition had already begun to reach. They linked their cultural identity to "new beginnings" in the Rio Arriba in the 1590s, when Gaspar Castaño de Sosa and Juan de Oñate recruited emigrants from Spain to join them in the colonization of the northern highlands now known as New Mexico. It seems that many of the people who joined Oñate and the others for the journey were at first thought to be conversos—newly confirmed Catholics from historically Jewish (or perhaps some former Muslim) families—who had recently fled from Andalusia, the Canary Islands, or Portugal. And yet it may well be that they were conversos in name only, and that they continued to practice their former faiths and associated culinary traditions clandestinely. Although historian Stanley Hordes and sociologist Tomás Atencio have referred to these people as crypto-Jews, their colleague Juan Estevan Arellano has suggested that there may have been crypto-Muslims among the earliest "Spanish" colonists of New Mexico, as well.

The descendants of these original Spanish-speaking inhabitants still reside in the remote uplands of northern New Mexico, where they remain quick to distinguish themselves from recent Mexican immigrants in language, appearance, and custom. Curiously, among the culinary customs that many of these Hispanos juxtapose with those of more recent immigrants from Mexico is their abhorrence of pork and their predilection for lamb, as well as their breaking of fasts with *capirotada* (bread pudding) and *pan de semita* (a bread made with bran, sesame, or nuts, originally unleavened but today also leavened). They do not see such observances practiced among the Spanish-speaking newcomers to the arid, windswept reaches of the Rio Arriba, and for good reason.

We now know that many of the descendants of those original "Spanish" and "Portuguese" inhabitants of New Mexico, when genetically fingerprinted, test positive for Semitic roots, Sephardic Jewish, Arabic, or both. Thanks to the groundbreaking work of Hordes, Atencio, and Arellano, we are able to confirm that both bloodlines and cultural practices of Semitic communities from the Middle East reached one of their most remote outposts in northern New Mexico during their worldwide diaspora. The crypto-Jews, crypto-Muslims, and true conversos had arrived at "the ends of the earth" in 1591, less than a hundred years after the Great Colónoscopy of the New World had begun.[10]

But let us return to consider that recipe-catching folklorist Cleofas Jaramillo. The surname Jaramillo, like many others in northern New Mexico, such as Robledo, Martinez, Gómez, Oñate, Salas, and Medina, now appears to be one that was commonly attached to Jewish or Muslim families escaping to less populated areas of the Americas to avoid the Mexican Inquisition. Genealogical and historical evidence suggest that among the first sheepherders, garbanzo bean growers, and spice traders in New Mexico were crypto-Jews and crypto-Muslims who outwardly behaved as conversos in their Catholic-dominated communities but maintained many of the religious and culinary traditions of Sephardic Jews, Arabs, and Moors within the confines of their homes.

When Cleofas Jaramillo visited with her brother's neighbors in the

Rio Arriba village of Arroyo Hondo, New Mexico, in 1938, she was ostensibly collecting nineteenth-century Hispanic culinary traditions. But both the direct and indirect roots of their cultural and culinary practices can be traced far deeper than that. The Arabic, Sephardic Jewish, and even Phoenician influences on "Spanish" cuisines were centuries if not millennia old, perhaps dating back to the twelfth century BCE in Spain. Given the status of historical research during her career, it would not have been possible for Cleofas Jaramillo or anyone else of her upbringing during that era to extricate those Arabic and Sephardic subtleties from other influences on the culinary traditions of New Mexico, Mexico, or even Spain itself.

Perhaps that inextricability is due in part to certain advances in the Spanish culinary arts initiated by the Phoenicians, who arrived in Cádiz, Spain, around 1100 BCE. These arts became even more deeply indebted to Persian and Arabic influences in 822 CE, when an enigmatic figure named Ziryab arrived in Córdoba, Spain. As we will discover later, Ziryab not only revolutionized Spanish farming and cookery but also sent Spanish table manners, seasonal dress, and chamber music on altogether fresh trajectories. Of course, one of his principal contributions to Spanish cuisine was the delicate mixing of rather pungent, aromatic spices in a manner already popular in the courts and kitchens of Damascus and Baghdad.

In the late 1970s in Santa Fe, I had the good fortune to walk down a side street into a marketplace then known as Roybal's General Store. There, among hundreds of bags and bins of culinary and medicinal spices, I found the same herbs that Cleofas Jaramillo had earlier recorded in her recipes for lamb and garbanzo stew. Roybal's store reminded me in many ways of the stores that my Lebanese uncles first tended when they arrived in America, for they were much like spice stands in the souks of Lebanon and Syria. Some of the spices there, such as cumin and coriander seeds, had clearly been transplanted from the Mediterranean landscapes of the Middle East and North Africa. But was the Roybal family that ran the store aware that its own roots may have extended back to Ignacio Roybal of Galicia, Spain, who married a crypto-Jew by the name of Francisca Gómez Robledo in Santa Fe in 1694?

A half century after Cleofas Jaramillo recorded a recipe that was a dead ringer for an Arabic or Sephardic Jewish one—and a quarter century after I first bought Middle Eastern spices in Roybal's General Store—many New Mexican Hispanics began to acknowledge a secret long held within their families: that they had maintained Jewish or

Muslim customs, including food taboos and formulas for mixing spices, sometimes without being able to put a name on them, in an unbroken chain that reached across centuries.

It was at the end of that line—one that had reached across the Atlantic Ocean into the New World—that the pervasiveness of the Arab and Jewish spice-trading legacy had been revealed to me. This discovery does not diminish the culinary contributions made by many other cultures along the line, and it may in fact enhance their significance.

It is a long way from Muscat, Mecca, Mar'ib, Jerusalem, Damascus, Aleppo, or Alexandria to Ulaanbaatar in Mongolia and Xi'an and Quanzhou in China at one end and Arroyo Hondo, Santa Fe, and Taos, New Mexico, on the other. And yet, around the time of the 9/11 disasters in 2001, I decided that I needed to trace the story of how Arabs and Jews had both collaborated and competed for centuries in the spice trade from one end of the earth to the other. I sensed that such a journey would tell me much about who we have been, where we have gone wrong (or stayed steady), and what we have become through the process of globalization. If that were correct, my journey would also shed light on the cryptic and unheralded influences now found in virtually every cuisine on the planet. Some of those influences clearly delighted those who shared recipes and ingredients with one another, but such exchanges rarely occurred on a level playing field; most were ushered in through the processes of culinary imperialism.

Although aromatic herbs, gummy exudates from thorny trees, and roots extracted from dry desert soils are among this story's many characters, the story line is more about imperialist politics and the hegemonic economics of cross-cultural exchange than it is about plants. It is perhaps a parable about the origins and consequences of globalization and a morality play that may help us to discern the difference between what Slow Food founder Carlo Petrini calls "virtuous globalization" and its more capitalistic, conniving, and crass counterparts.

Of course, most spices embody the essence of mobility—high value in its most featherweight forms—and so this tale is inherently a cross-cultural odyssey, one that will take us to the far reaches of the earth.

And yet, there is another kind of moral to this story, one that forces us to recognize that for centuries, if not millennia, many communities of Arabs and Jews worked collaboratively to move spices all the way across their known worlds. This is not to pretend that they did not compete economically or suffer atrocities at the hands of each other in cer-

tain places at certain times, but it also does not ignore long periods of
the coexistence that Américo Castro first labeled *convivencia* in the late
1940s. Although this term has been used in a rather romantic and naïve
manner in the last decade by some social scientists, what has become
clear is that the comingling of Jewish and Muslim cultural traditions did
occur peaceably at times, while at other times it was an uneasy if not
ugly truce at best.[11] In a historical moment when both Arab Muslims
and Sephardic Jews are among the most maligned peoples in the world,
and the subject of a rising frequency of hate crimes, it would do well for
the rest of humanity to acknowledge our collective debt to these peoples,
however complex and conflicted that legacy may be. (Whether or not
you "like" globalization is an altogether different issue; perhaps for us, it
is the equivalent of asking a fish whether it "likes" water.) More important, perhaps, it is time that we remember the elements of *convivencia*,
such as cross-cultural civility, that showed what humans are capable
of, rather than assuming that we must be locked into the kinds of violence that later tore at the once-shared fabric of their lives. Not only in
Andalusia but also in historic Fez, Alexandria, Cairo, Jerusalem, Beirut,
Damascus, Baghdad, Aleppo, Smyrna, Constantinople, Thessaloniki,
Bukhara, Turpan, Chang'an (Xi'an), and Zayton (Quanzhou), such *convivencia* was for centuries the custom rather than the exception. Was
cooperation among most spice traders along a five-thousand-mile caravan route once the norm, or was subtle or not-so-subtle coercion and
domination always there? Why do the descendants of those same traders today live in a world where hatred and violence keep the holiest of
cities, Jerusalem, a divided, desperate shadow of what it once was?

Although I will not give you direct answers to those questions at the
moment, I will give you a hint: if you come far enough with me along
the spice trail that opens up in the next few pages, the answer will come
wafting toward you like the purifying aroma of burning frankincense.

But where will I be going? I will be traveling sections of the spice
roads that played pivotal historical roles in shaping the processes of
globalization that now affect each one of us every day of our lives. In
particular, I will be visiting the historically significant souks, *mercados,*
bazaars, and harbors where these processes were first field-tested before
being applied and extended to countless other landscapes. I will stay
in caravansaries, *pensiones,* hostels, hotels, and haciendas where landmark negotiations have been made and debts have been paid, so that I
might listen to the ways in which "spicers" trade across currencies and
cultures, with or without a shared language. I will relate the essence of

these conversations back to you, as I have captured them in field journals or on the edges of paper napkins. Over the course of twelve years, these inquiries have taken me to markets in Afghanistan, Bali, China, Egypt, Ethiopia, Israel, Lebanon, Mexico, Morocco, Oman, Palestine, Portugal, Spain, Syria, Tajikistan, Turkey, and the United Arab Emirates.

To be sure, many of the modes of spice commerce have changed over the centuries. Recently, much of the great market of Aleppo, Syria, has been destroyed by civil war, while others, such as the Souk al-Attarin in the Old City of Jerusalem, have been made into touristic facades of their former selves. To understand what once went on in these places, it has been necessary to dip into private archives, public libraries, and nearby museums. In some cases, traces of the former activities of these historic markets still linger around the corner, and there ancient fragrances and flavors, the modes of cooperation and elements of conflict or colonization, may still prevail.

And so, this narrative will weave at least two strands together again and again: the ancient practices that can be discerned from history, archaeology, ethnobotany, and linguistics of how spices were gathered, traded, and diffused into various cuisines and my own descriptions that bear witness to the remnants of those practices that remain in place. In fact, many of those customs retrace my own Arab ancestors' participation in the spice trade or in cross-cultural cooperation and conflict. Yes, both personal and scholarly motives have driven me to undertake these journeys; I have wanted to decipher my own family's historical role in developing the processes of globalization that inevitably affect my own behaviors, values, and consumption patterns. I have questions to ask of my ancestors and perhaps of yours as well. As an itinerant British geographer suggested in 1625, "Let our Merchants answer, [for they] owe their spices to Arabia."

CHAPTER I

Aromas Emanating from the Driest of Places

I am tracking a scent across the desert. I meander up a slope between boulders of limestone almost too hot to touch, dodging dwarfed trees and bushy shrubs, all with spiny branches twisted and punctuated with greasy but fragrant leaflets. A few spindly milkweeds with toxic sap cling to the cliff face beside me.

As I stop for a moment to catch my breath, I let my eyes scan the arid terrain rolling high to the south of me, up the mountain plateau called Jabal Samhan. I am witness to a stark and largely unpopulated landscape. It is not totally barren, yet most of the world's farmers and city dwellers would declare it empty. By that, they might mean that it is marginally arable, barely habitable, or is incapable of offering much of value to humankind today.

But they are wrong if they presume that this landscape lacks any value to our common heritage. Over millennia, something of exceptional value came out of this arid landscape that, when combined with other forces, changed the course of human history. The question is whether we value what grows in and is harvested from this landscape in any profound way today.

I have come here on a pilgrimage to seek an answer to that question. I have climbed into the Dhofar highlands, a plateau that sits some two thousand feet above the Arabian Sea. It is home to a scatter of semi-nomadic herding and foraging Jabbali tribes known as the people of the Shahri, the ones who "make mountain talk."

I hear no kind of talk at this moment. All is quiet. There is no wind. I gulp down hot air. My nostrils flare and I pick up a distinctive fragrance, subtle but inviting.

The smell prompts me to remember that ancient Greek geographers called this odoriferous country Eudaimôn Arabia, or "Arabia, the Blessed." One of them, Herodotus, noted that "the whole country exhales an odor that is marvelously sweet."[1] Later this land came to be known to the wider world as Arabia Felix, a vortex of happiness amid much hardship and struggle. At first, it offered nothing more than a few fragrant desert plants and animal substances that were known collectively to the Greeks as *aromatikos*. Such aromatic substances have long been perceived by many cultures as having the capacity to generate a sense of happiness, healing, well-being, and harmony within the world.

As I make my way up the switchbacks of a goat trail, I wonder how long the "happy" slopes of Jabal Samhan have baked in the torrid sun. My feet kick up dust in the wake of my walking. It has not rained here for weeks. This is a land of heat and drought.

Scientists who call themselves chemical ecologists suggest that the aridity that results from these two conditions has helped rather than hindered the evolution of aromatic plants, which they define as those having compounds containing benzene rings.[2] Over millennia, the deserts of the Arabian Peninsula developed into prime habitat for the most powerfully aromatic plants in the world. What these desert plants lacked in productivity, they often made up in fragrance, flavor, and mythic potency.

Perhaps that is because the leaves of many of them exude aromatic oils that help them resist heat, drought, and damage from herbivores. Such aromatic but highly volatile, fleeting chemicals are more concentrated in the floras of arid climes than anywhere else.

Although much of the Dhofar region has limited agricultural potential and an uneven distribution of useful wild plants, Arabia Felix could aptly be called the birthplace of the global trade in aromatics. Like Aladdin's magic ring, when properly rubbed, this landscape opens up to reveal a psychotropic world of incenses, culinary spices, perfumes, and curative herbs to delight and refresh the weary.

Despite its scarcity of vegetation, Arabia Felix is full of highly pungent scents and flavors. It has wild crocuses akin to saffron, barks reminiscent of cinnamon, wild fennel, leeks, garlic and onions, aromatic gums, and resins galore. When mixed into a paste with dates and plastered onto pit-roasted mutton or goat, an Omani selection of these plants provides the taste portfolio called *khall al-mazza.*[3] If you crave currylike flavors in savory stews, you will be satisfied with an even more complex mix of herbs and spices called *bizar a'shuwa,* which has long been used across the Arabian Peninsula.

The term used for this herb-rich rocky habitat in Dhofar is *nejd,* from the ancient Semitic languages of "mountain talkers," the tribes of al-Kathiri, al-Qara, and al-Mahra. The highland cultures of Jabal Samhan share a history and preference for landscapes markedly different from those of the better-known Bedouins of the Arabian sands. The striking contrast in plant composition between these adjacent landscapes is what ecologists call "beta diversity,"[4] a pronounced dissimilarity in the herbs that a plant collector might find between localized floras as he or she moves from one patch of desert to the next. In general, deserts exhibit high rates of "species turnover" from one arid landscape to another, so that few of the favored food and medicinal plants of one desert mountain range can be found in another just a day's walk away. Thus, for as long as we know, plants have been traded from one place to another and savored beyond their place of origin.

Off to the southeast, the windward slopes of Jabal Samhan dive toward the cooler, breezier, more humid coast of Yemen. To the west, in the domain of the truly nomadic Bedouin, lies the infamous Empty Quarter, the austere sea of sand known to Arabic speakers as the Rub' al-Khali. For centuries, it has been the stretch of the Arabian Peninsula least frequented, even by the hardiest of nomads. Even the Bedu, the most competent nomads who frequented the sandier stretches of the Arabian Peninsula, are wary of its paucity of water and the perils of its drifting sands.

Here in the Dhofar highlands, at least enough *terra rossa* exists among the limestone to support a scatter of low shrubs, some far-flung patches of wiry grass, resinous bushes of rockrose, and withered but bristly stalks of thistles. This desert-scrub vegetation is seasonally browsed by a few goats and camels, the hardiest of livestock breeds. In fact, they sometimes seem to be the only creatures tenacious enough to inhabit the *nejd,* but by no means do they comprise the sum total of the fauna there.

The small caves I spot along the rocky crest on the western horizon occasionally shelter the stick-gathering hyrax and rock-climbing lizards. I have also noticed larger caves and ledges below the cliffs that protect the meager harvests of spices gathered by al-Qara foragers and herders, their baskets and bundles left there in the shade.

❧ MARAK MINJ ☙
Green Lentil Curry with Frankincense, Ginger, and Omani Spices

Nowadays, frankincense is seldom used in the kitchen, but it and other aromatics were once highly regarded for their culinary as well as their medicinal and spiritual value. To this day, however, Omanis like to infuse both main dishes and desserts with incenses, rose water, and bright spices such as saffron and *shouranah,* saffron's aromatic wild relative on the Arabian Peninsula. In this recipe, I combine the warm, rich middle notes of frankincense and the fine, high notes of ginger and turmeric with the complex flavors of the curry-like spice mixture known as *bizar a'shuwa* in a traditional lentil dish enjoyed at the dinner tables of the al-Wusta region of central Oman. It uses the succulent leaves of purslane, which can be found throughout the world as a field green and in domesticated form primarily in Europe, the Middle East, Mexico, and much of Asia (with large leaves nearly the size of those of watercress in the Middle East). Purslane, which has a rich flavor and is high in omega-3 fatty acids, can be found at farmers' markets and specialty-food stores in the United States, or it can be gathered in the wild in the summertime. I have adapted the recipe of Lamees Abdullah Al Taie to include the frankincense of Dhofar to the south.

Serve with rice and a fruit chutney or with a fruit salad of mangoes, apricots, figs, and plums sliced into crescents and dressed with lime juice. *Serves 2 to 4.*

    1   cup green lentils
  1½   teaspoons fresh lemon juice
    2   cups water
   ¼   cup olive oil
    1   teaspoon finely chopped green (young) fresh ginger, peeled and
        finely chopped mature fresh ginger, or peeled and finely chopped
        fresh turmeric
        Leaves from 1 bunch cilantro, chopped
    1   pound purslane leaves (stripped from stems), chopped
    1   teaspoon frankincense, ground and soaked in 2 cups water
   ½   teaspoon sea salt
    1   tablespoon *bizar a'shuwa* (see note)
    2   tablespoons fresh kaffir lime juice or finely shredded kaffir lime zest
    2   tablespoons coconut milk

In a bowl, combine the lentils with water to cover and stir in the lemon juice. Allow to soak at room temperature for about 7 hours. Drain, rinse, and transfer to a saucepan. Add the water, place over medium heat, and bring to a simmer. Turn down the heat to low and cook uncovered, stirring occasionally and adding more water if needed to prevent scorching, until the lentils are tender, 30 to

60 minutes. Remove from the heat. At this point, very little water should remain in the pan; drain off any excess. Set the lentils aside.

Meanwhile, in a frying pan, heat the olive oil over medium-low heat. Add the ginger, cilantro, and purslane leaves and sauté just until the purslane is tender, 3 to 5 minutes. Remove from the heat.

In a blender or food processor, combine the reserved lentils, frankincense water, and salt and puree until smooth. Return the mixture to the saucepan in which you cooked the lentils, add the purslane mixture and *bizar a'shuwa,* and stir well. (If not serving right away, transfer the mixture to a covered container and refrigerate.)

To serve, place over low heat and heat gently until hot. Transfer to a serving bowl and stir in the lime juice. Drizzle the coconut milk over the top and serve hot.

> NOTE: To make the *bizar a'shuwa* spice mix, combine 1 teaspoon each toasted and ground cumin seeds, coriander seeds, and cardamom seeds; 1/2 teaspoon each coarsely crushed black peppercorns, fennel seeds, and either *mahlab* seeds (from a species of cherry) or dried Aleppo chile pepper; and 1/2 teaspoon each ground cinnamon and turmeric. Mix the spices with 2 cloves garlic, crushed, and a sprinkle of distilled white vinegar to make a thick paste. Measure out 1 tablespoon to use for this dish. Refrigerate the remainder in a tightly capped glass container for up to 2 weeks and use as a rub for lamb or other meat or to flavor a braise or stew.

Al Taie, Lamees Abdullah. *Al-Azaf: The Omani Cookbook.* Muscat: Oman Bookshop, 1995, p. 49.

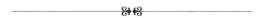

No one would call the Dhofar highlands a landscape of bounty. On the whole, most of its habitats lack much fertility, fecundity, productivity, or diversity. If the inhabitants do not take advantage of the brief spurts of plant growth that follow occasional rains, they could easily go hungry. And within Dhofar, the *nejd* is one of the most intensely arid habitats. But it also holds a singular treasure, a desert plant that emits an extraordinary fragrance.

Long ago, that particular treasure catapulted some Semitic-speaking nomads out of the desolation of the southern reaches of their peninsula, propelling their descendants toward all corners of the globe. They began to trade their aromatic herbs, incenses, and spices to others in better-watered climes. They exchanged their fragrances, flavors, and cures for staple foods and other goods that their arid homeland could not consistently provide. They understood that all habitats are not created equal in terms of the natural resources found within them.

So early on in their history, these Semitic tribes realized they should not remake one place to resemble another but rather trade the most unique goods of each to those who lacked them. They made an asset out of one of the inherent weaknesses of their homelands: its inequitable distribution of plant and animal productivity. In doing so, they built an economic model for trade between regions that initially redistributed both wealth and wonder among the inhabitants.

Later on, that model changed, for the spice trade triggered an economic and ecological revolution that rippled out to every reach of the human-inhabited world. It is the revolution that we now call globalization. And yet, it has been difficult for many of us to imagine its origins, for we live and breathe within it unconsciously, as if it has always existed and will always continue to exist as it does today.

As I ponder that thought, ahead of me I spot the destination—a precious part of the origin of that revolution—that initially motivated me to travel nine thousand miles from my home. I am now far enough up the slope finally to touch, for the first time in my life, the very spark that may have jump-started the engine of globalization.

I reach my hand out and gingerly lay it on the limber branches of a tree that is about as tall as I am. It has a voluptuous trunk covered in a jacket of ashy-hued bark. I reach farther into its canopy and grasp a thicker branch around its girth, as if I am feeling the bulging biceps of an iron-pumping friend. These sinuous branches are laden with small clusters of slightly crumpled but highly aromatic leaflets. I notice that the trunk is indelibly marked with scars, scorings in the bark made by intentional slashes with a knife, and on these scars are dried droplets of a pale white resin that forms perfect tears.

Just beneath the bark are microscopic tear-duct-like structures that can be stimulated to shed their resin by scoring, the very same means used by our primate ancestors to obtain acacia gum, gum tragacanth, mastic, or myrrh from other woody plants. Like them, this resin has long been valued as a medicine, vermifuge, flavorant, spice, and incense.

But that is where the comparisons among gummy incenses stop. For close to four millennia, this particular gum has been regarded as the highest-quality incense in the world. It was once the most economically valuable and most widely disseminated plant product on the globe: frankincense, food of the gods.

Even the stuffiest of scientists begrudgingly acknowledge the sacredness of this tree every time they recite its scientific name, *Boswellia sacra.* I have some familiarity with its distant relative, the elephant tree of the Americas, for I have often collected the copal incense from its trunk. And many winter days, when I suffer from inflammation and pain from an old horseback-riding injury, I rub my muscles with the salve of *B. serrata,* the so-called Indian frankincense, or *salai.*

I dip beneath the canopy of the gnarly tree and pull a small but recently crystallized lump of gummy sap from a scar on its central trunk. It looks as if in the spring prior to my arrival the trunk's bark had been scarified in two or three places, probably by a Somali migrant harvester. He likely slashed at the bark with a *mingaf,* a short-bladed tool that looks much like a putty knife, then came back a month later and cleaned the wound. At the end of spring, he did so a second time as well, and then the wound wept for several more weeks.

The milky sap flowing out of the tree's phloem has already begun to congeal into a semiliquid resinous latex. Frankincense tappers call the creamy sap "milk," or *lubān* in Arabic, *shehaz* in mountain talk. But this is the sweetest, whitest, and milkiest of all frankincense, the internationally acclaimed *hojari fusoos.* Its quality is found nowhere in the world except here, in the highlands of Dhofar.

During the height of its use in the Roman Empire, more money was spent on acquiring this superlative form of frankincense than was spent on any other aromatic—incense, spice, or herb—whether traded long distances by land or sea. In Babylon, those rich enough to afford it would bask in its smoke, purifying and imbuing their bodies with its fragrance prior to bouts of lovemaking.

When I find another bit of sap that has begun to harden, I pinch the viscous substance until it pulls away from the trunk like taffy. I hold it in my hand and let the sun shine on the dried globule, which has turned amber. It shines dully back at the sun, a cloudy droplet of oleoresin resembling a freshly made curd of goat cheese. A bluish hue is hidden deep in the sap's pearly clouds, as if shards of fallen sky are waiting to be sent up to join the rest of the heavens.

For millennia, people have been doing just that: they have made a burnt offering of the sacred milk so that its smoke can rise beyond this world. Believers say that smoke from the best frankincense forms a single white column that flows straight into the sky. If its vapor trail is strong enough to ascend into the heavens, this gift will inevitably reach, nourish, and delight the Creator, the Prophet, or particular saints— whoever is meant to receive these fragrant prayers.

Timidly, I place a tiny piece of the sap in my mouth and gnash it between my teeth as I might do with any chewing gum. Hints of honey, lime, verbena, and vanilla well up and spread through the juices of my mouth. I smile as I remember that pregnant Bedu women also chew on frankincense gum, hoping that it will encourage the child in the womb to live an intellectually and spiritually elevated life. Both Shahri and Somali harvesters chew on this gum while they "milk" more *lubān* from one tree after another, depositing their harvests into two-handled baskets woven from the fronds of date palms.

I quickly warm to this world of incense, camels, and date palms, for it seems vaguely but deeply familiar to me. I belong to a bloodline that traces its origins back to Yemeni and Omani spice traders of the Banu Nebhani tribe. It is plausible that my own ancestors wandered these same hills more than fourteen hundred years ago, before they spread north across the Arabian Peninsula and beyond. This possibility alone suggests why I have felt motivated—even destined—to come to one of the driest and most remote parts of the world. But frankly, I am after something far larger than that.

I have come here to dig for the roots of globalization, if the roots of such an ancient and pervasive phenomenon can be traced at all. I wish to track them back to the very first bartering for tiny quantities of aromatic resins like mastic, bdellium, frankincense, and myrrh; for the stone-ground seeds of cumin and anise; for the fragrant musk extracted from the glands of deer; for the bitingly sharp leaves of mint or oregano; for the bark of cassia from China and true cinnamon from Sri Lanka; for the sun-dried skins of kaffir limes; for the shavings carved off the egg-shaped seed of the nutmeg tree; for the withered orange-red stigma of the saffron flower; for the willowy pods of the vanilla vine and the pungent ones of a myriad of chile plants.

Collectively, these various plant and animal products are ambiguously referred to as "spices" in English, just as they were rather coarsely lumped together as *aromatikos* by the ancient Greeks. Perhaps these references build on the ancient Arab concept of *shadhan*, a term used to describe a particularly pungent herb, but one that can also jointly refer to strongly fragrant and flavorful substances of both plant and animal origin. A related word, *al-shadw*, is used to comment on the intensity of pungency in a pepper, a piece of cinnamon bark, or a lump of the *hojari fusoos* grade of frankincense.

A third Arabic word, *al-adhfar,* relates to any pungent smell, from musk to human sweat.[5] Indeed, some scholars have suggested that musk, pungent ointments, and rose waters have been routinely used in hot climes to mask the odor of human sweat, which would otherwise be the most pervasive smell in desert camps and cramped cities much of the year.

Historian Patricia Crone once offered this litany to circumscribe the many faces and fragrances of aromatics: "They include incense, or substances that gave off a nice smell on being burned; perfumes, ointments, and other sweet-smelling substances with which one dabbed, smeared or sprinkled oneself or one's clothes; things that one put into food or drink to improve their taste, prolong their life, or endow them with medicinal or magical properties; and they also included antidotes."[6]

By the early fourteenth century, the Italian merchant Francesco di Balduccio Pegolotti documented the arrival of at least 288 varieties of spices into Europe, mostly through Semitic merchants who sometimes referred to their origin in particular Arabian, African, or Asian landscapes. These spices ranged from asafetida to *zedoary* and included everything from gum Arabic to manna to the madder of Alexandria.[7]

Such spices are the sensuous signposts that can tell us where the trails and rustic roads of globalization first ran and remind us why we have been so engaged with these aromatic products in the first place. And so a quest to understand the semiotics of globalization must begin with reading spices as signs of deeper desires or diseases that have been embedded in certain segments of humankind for millennia.

For many years now, I have been preoccupied if not altogether consumed with finding out why some individuals, communities, or cultures have been content with staying home and savoring what immediately lies before them, while others have an insatiable desire to taste and see or even possess that which comes from afar. I have wondered why certain peoples culturally and genetically identified as Semitic—Minaeans and Nabataeans, Phoenicians and other Canaanites, Quraysh and Karimi Arabs, Radhanite and Sephardic Jews—have played such disproportionately large roles in globalized trade, not merely over the short course of decades or centuries but over the long haul of many millennia.

As I stand on the dry ridge, panting and sweating my bodily fluids into thin air, I remind myself why I have decided to begin this journey on this particular ridge in southern Oman, even though it is one that bears a name known only by a handful of tribesmen living in the region of Jabal Samhan. It is because some 250 acres here have been set aside as a frankincense reserve by the Omani government of Sultan Qaboos— 250 acres that in my mind loom far larger.

This spot is the perfect launching pad for a spice odyssey, one that will take us to the ancient port of Zayton on the China Sea, to the Turpan Depression that edges the Gobi Desert below the Tian Shan range on the border between China and Kazakhstan, to the Panj River that separates the Hindu Kush of Pakistan from the Pamirs of Tajikistan, to the coastal ports of Oman, Egypt, Turkey, and Mexico, to the slot canyons of Petra in Jordan, and to the sprawling souks, *çarşısı*, bazaars, and *mercados* of Syria, Ethiopia, Egypt, Turkey, Morocco, Portugal, Spain, and Mexico. We will wander down the Incense Trails of the Middle East, the Silk Roads of Asia, the Spice Trails of Africa, and the Camino Real of Central and North America. It will take us back in time, and possibly, it may launch us into considering our future.

But first we must pay homage to the spindly frankincense tree here in its primordial *nejd* habitat, for it was once the most expensive and widely traveled cargo in the world, its antiseptic, culinary, medicinal, and magico-religious uses well regarded by dozens of cultures.

How odd it is that the unforgettable fragrance of frankincense comes not from its flowers or fruits but from its wounds, as if it were one more saint like Francis of Assisi or Jesus of Nazareth with stigmata that drip with blood, sweat, and tears. Whether wounded by the whipping of branches during seasonal windstorms, bruised by the browsing of camels, or cut open by the crude *mingaf* knives of Omani, Yemeni, and Somali harvesters, this injured bush offers up a few grams of gum as its only useful product. If it is too badly injured or too frequently milked by greedy tappers, the bush will succumb to a premature death. These stunted perennials already struggle to survive on sun-scorched scree where rainfall is scant; it does not take very much additional stress to hasten their demise.

For that reason, and because there are few other lucrative products that can be derived from the *nejd* barrens in the Dhofar highlands, frankincense stands have been traditionally owned, carefully protected, and diligently managed for millennia. In his great *Naturalis Historiae,* Pliny the Elder wrote descriptively of the frankincense groves that he called "the forests of Arabia Felix": "The forest is divided up into definite portions, and owing to the mutual honesty of the owners, is free from trespassing, and though nobody keeps guard over the trees after an incision has been made, nobody steals from his neighbor."[8]

Although an aromatic incense can be gathered from the trunks of several species in the genus *Boswellia*, it is the milky resin, or *lubān*, of *B. sacra* from Yemen and southern Oman that has long commanded the highest prices for any incense in the world. Carrying the aromas of pine resin, vanilla, and Heaven itself, the smoke of the best frankincense soars straight up into the air. Frankincense is derived from a syrupy latex that does not become accessible unless the small tree is wounded by weather or livestock, or intentionally scored by harvesters. The slow-flowing latex begins to dry into a gummy resin below the wound on the bark, and then hardens into amber droplets the size of tears. In essence, the plant weeps when wounded.

The fragrance and flavors of frankincense are so evocative spiritually and emotionally that this aromatic is mentioned at least 140 times in the Bible, yet its value is conspicuously absent from the Qur'an. Once it had been introduced to the Babylonians, Greeks, Romans, and Egyptians, it became a symbol of purity, immortality, and access to wealth. It was used to fumigate the bodies of the dead and of suitors on the verge of lovemaking, and was omnipresent in Greek and Roman temples, synagogues, mosques, and cathedrals.

By the time frankincense had traveled by camel caravan northward to reach Roman and Greek brokers, its price per volume had risen manyfold. During the Roman Empire, a shipment of Yemeni frankincense cost five times what a farmer or artisan made in a year in the eastern Mediterranean. Of course, it was the Minaeans,

---

Outside of Dhofar, I listen to an Omani forest steward explain to me that his job is much like that of a game warden. His task, he says, is to "keep watch over what is precious."

His name is Ali Salem Bait Said. He comes from a family and Jabbali tribe that functioned as traditional owners of a particular frankincense gathering ground until the late 1960s. All such historically controlled lands were divided into parcels called *menzelas*. When the paternal bloodline inheritance of the right to manage and harvest a grove, or *menzela*, of frankincense finally broke down, it terminated a centuries-old land tenure tradition. But Ali Salem Bait Said still remembers his family's stories of how to care for a productive stand of frankincense properly: "In the past, [my] people thought of themselves as friends of the tree. They don't scratch down to the bone. They go and cut closer to the bark—not deep—so that they will not hurt the tree. Now [with the

Nabataeans, and Phoenicians who did the lion's share of transporting, carrying as much as three thousand tons of frankincense annually along three major transport routes to Babylon and the Mediterranean. Just as there was no single Silk Road, there was no single Frankincense Trail.

Today, frankincense has four primary uses. First, the people of the Hadhramaut and Dhofar highlands continue to use it as fumigant, air freshener, and traditional medicine to stop bleeding. It remains important as a church incense, particularly in Eastern Orthodox and certain Buddhist rites. It is distilled into an essence used in perfumes, facial cosmetics, and aromatherapy products. Finally, it has become a historical curiosity, sold to tourists and employed in novel ways by culinary artists in high-end restaurants around the world to flavor candies and baked goods. After several millennia of prominence, frankincense may no longer be the most valuable commodity in the world, but it still evokes a certain level of mystery and sanctity for many whenever its name is spoken.

Farah, Mohamud Haji. "Non-Timber Forest Product (NTFP) Extraction in Arid Environments: Land-Use Change, Frankincense Production and the Sustainability of *Boswellia sacra* in Dhofar (Oman)." PhD diss., University of Arizona, 2008.

Musselman, Lytton John. *Figs, Dates, Laurel, and Myrrh: Plants of the Bible and the Quran*. Portland, OR: Timber Press, 2005.

Shackley, Myra. "Frankincense and Myrrh Today." In *Food for the Gods: New Light on the Ancient Incense Trade*, edited by David Peacock and David Williams, 141–47. Oxford, UK: Oxbow Books, 2007.

suspension of traditional ownership] there is no one to take care of the trees. And so there are people who come here that think of them as wild [not managed] and milk them for all they can give, until the trees dry up. [Those migrant harvesters] may not even know the traditional songs for *lubān*, the ones which we sang in celebration of God."

Ali points out trees that have had branches broken by feral camels and others that he believes have been milked too frequently. He suggests that at least in his tribe such occurrences would have been uncommon when the centuries-old practices of *menzela* management were still intact.

Later, I have the opportunity to learn about more ancient frankincense gathering and management traditions from a remarkable field scientist and observer of frankincense culture, Mohamud Haji Farah, who received his doctorate in desert studies from the same University

FIGURE 1. An Omani forester approaches a frankincense tree near Sohar, a port of departure for the Arabic spice trade. (Photo by the author.)

of Arizona program where I obtained mine. Although Somali by birth, Dr. Farah has spent several years near Dhofar documenting how indigenous Omani tribal herders and migrant Somali harvesters work with frankincense. Ironically, he focused on Jabal Samhan, the same area that I was fortunate enough to visit. Of slight build and quiet voice, Farah speaks and writes with discerning authority on the indigenous traditions that have evolved around this much-revered spiritual and economic resource. Among his observations is that "frankincense trees are presumed to possess or house supernatural powers associated with both good and evil spirits. . . . [And so, it was] a sacred commodity, and its harvesters worked under ritualistic constraints."[9]

I had heard that harvesters were not allowed to sleep with their wives or eat certain foods during the harvest season. Farah neither confirms nor denies this for me. Instead, he notes how the chanting of prayers and the burning of incense are still enacted at the beginning of the tapping season. Some harvesters believe that frankincense trees could not survive, thrive, and yield incense in such harsh and desolate arid environments if they did not have sacred powers.[10]

The rituals, Farah surmises, are means of showing respect to the trees and perhaps even pacifying them. He has found that such beliefs were widespread among Arab harvesters, not only in Oman but in Yemen and Saudi Arabia as well. Farah and other scientists who have surveyed the persistence of these traditions guess that such beliefs and rituals promote self-constraint among harvesters. It seems that they discourage would-be trespassers from entering someone else's *menzela* patch in order to milk their trees clandestinely.

In listening to both Ali Salem Bait Said and Mohamud Farah, I am struck by just how vulnerable frankincense is on its home ground, and yet how long the harvesting of its incense has persisted—perhaps four thousand years—without widespread decimation of its populations. I wonder whether the ritual constraints and the prayerful gathering of its precious resins have somehow kept frankincense populations from being overexploited, even though the incense has been in transcontinental trade for thousands of years.

Or perhaps the harvesters in Yemen, Oman, and Saudi Arabia recognize that if they eliminate their most valuable resource, they would have few other desert plants, animals, or minerals to trade for food. Especially during times of drought or political disruption, the trading of frankincense has been one of the few hands they could play. Yet another reason for the longevity of frankincense was suggested to me by a second Omani forester, who explained, "It would not be right to fail to protect this plant, for it is the source of our history."

I begin to think about other desert dwellers I have known, especially herders and hunter-gatherers who have not had the food crops produced in irrigated oases to fall back on during the worst of times. Having a mythical medicine, spice, or incense to trade was perhaps all that kept them from starvation during the harshest periods.

The nomadic Seri Indians with whom I have lived and worked in Mexico's deserts offer such an example.[11] As soon as European missionaries arrived on the edge of their traditional territory, the Indians opportunistically engaged these Jesuit priests in unwittingly supporting two of their economic strategies. First, the Seri obtained food by trading incense such as copal, medicines such as jojoba, and spices such as oregano to the priests to send back to Europe. Then, once they knew what the outsiders had in store, they would clandestinely raid their trading partner's pantries for additional food and drink.

As I leave the highlands of Jabal Samhan for the port town of Salalah, I take a handful of frankincense beads along with me to burn ritually that night. They are modest in size and sit lightly in my palm. And yet I have heard that they command respectable prices in the souks and tourist shops along the Omani coast of the Persian Gulf and Arabian Sea, perhaps as high as fifty dollars per kilogram, or twenty to twenty-five times what a harvester might be paid in the desert for the same quantity. I decide to go into a souk to see if this is true.

When I enter the souk, I realize that there is one secret of frankincense commerce that I have already surmised: such a little thing, as diminutive and nearly as weightless as a single grain of wheat, is the perfect commodity to trade over long distances. Of course its economic and mythic value must be made to loom larger than the trade item itself, as well. This, I guess, has been the trade secret shared by most spice traders over the last four millennia: if you can, carry to the far corners of the earth something as light as a feather that can linger in one's memory forever, but eschew anything as dull and as heavy as lead. In other words, whenever feasible, trade in potent fragrances and flavors, for they are the tangible corollaries of visions and dreams. They are intermediaries between the physical and spiritual domains, reminding us that there is more to the world that what we can absorb through our eyes.

These elusive things become deeply rooted in our imaginations, far more so than most material goods. For at least thirty-five hundred years, and perhaps for as long as fifty-five hundred years, incense, spices, and herbs have captured the human attention and imagination.[12] They have not only been worth trading for, for some they have been worth dying for.

As the most protected harbor close to the Dhofar highlands, Salalah was one of those historic places where individuals lived for and occasionally died for frankincense. Its ruins sit on the edge of the coastal plain overlooking the Arabian Sea, sprawling over the site of the ancient trade center of Zhafar. Because it is just a short camel drive of eighteen miles from the highlands to this naturally protected harbor, the ports here have long attracted professions in addition to those of sailor and shipper. They have welcomed incense graders, incense makers, incense mixers, and carvers of incense smokers or censers called *midkhān,*[13] as well as camel drovers and mule skinners of the kind that have brought aromatic goods in from the desert to the sea for upward of thirty-five hundred years.

Once I arrive in the city, it does not take me long to find Salalah's largest souk, where all matter of things sacred and profane can be bought and sold, but where frankincense has long been the featured attraction. How could it not be? Once I approach the dozen or so shops that are constantly sending smoke up toward the heavens and out toward their prospective customers, I could hardly resist lingering there for a while.

The shops are small and rather gaudy and glitzy, but they are far more elegant than most spice shops in other Middle Eastern souks. Incense burns while some scratchy recordings of Arabic music play on loudspeakers. I had assumed that one could only purchase frankincense here, but myrrh, sandalwood, and musk are also on sale. In fact, I count dozens of kinds of incense, native perfumes, and aromatic herbs being offered, not merely to tourists but to Omanis as well.

It may be a leap for a Westerner to make, but in the southern reaches of the Arabian Peninsula, incense is regarded as a form of nourishment. There are recipes for over two dozen incense mixtures and herbal scents included in *Al-Azaf,* the most popular Omani cookbook in shops and marketplaces.[14] Those recipes bring together *oud* (aloe wood) oil with black musk, ambergris with sandalwood, saffron with snails, cloves with rose water, blending them into various divinely fragrant concoctions. But among all of the aromatics sold in the souk, frankincense is the one that they let stand alone. A soloist, its olfactory melody is too heavenly for Omanis to ever want it to be overdubbed.

Synesthesia. As I walk in and out of incense shops that share the same open corridor, I begin to feel as if I am stoned, for my senses are being bombarded with a mix of images unlike anything they had ever experienced before. This is literally a land of smoke and mirrors. The mirrors are placed to make the shops appear larger, to multiply the colored lights, and to catch the whirls of smoke rising from clay incense burners. Nearly every incense shop is stocked with fashionably shaped aspirators and decanters of perfumes, censers and smokers, rustic bags of dried incense, and bowls with glistening samples of both. But added to that is the harmonic intensity of oud music, voices speaking a dozen languages, and the memorable profiles of women in brilliantly colored silk gowns, dazzling jewelry, and gorgeous scarves. As half a dozen kinds of smoke from incense gradually fill my lungs, the world glimmering before me begins to seem like an illusion.

An elderly Somali Omani shopkeeper, her hands and lower arms aflame with intricate patterns inscribed with henna, notices my befuddlement. She smiles and with a fine British accent invites me into her little shop. She beckons me to come and sit so that I might learn to distinguish the five grades of *lubān* from one another. She says that she will show me how to vaporize them properly over glowing coals in a traditional clay incense burner rather than "burning away" much of their potency.

She explains that the differences among grades may at first seem too subtle to the uninitiated tourist, but that they are worth recognizing. The top grade, *hojari fusoos,* commands prices three to four times higher than that of the next level of quality, the *nejdi.* The trick of the shopkeeper is to discern quickly how much—or really, how little—a visitor actually knows about frankincense.

Feigning alarm, her almond-shaped eyes magnified by the delicate lines of kohl drawn around them, she notes how some of her competitors display low-grade "ore" that is roughly the same color and texture as *hojari.* In a whisper, she confides in me that there might even be some unscrupulous merchants who will try to market their nuggets of *nejdi,* or even lower-quality *shazri,* as *hojari fusoos.*

"They are out to take the shirt off of your back for a few pebbles of frankincense," she frowns. She then swears to me that she has never perpetrated such an impropriety, and that I can place my trust in her henna-colored hands.

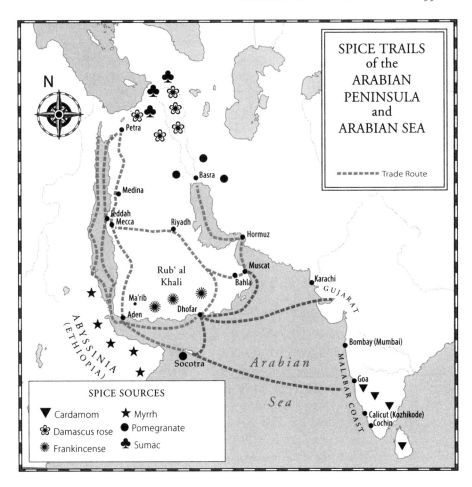

MAP 1. Spice trails of the Arabian Peninsula and Arabian Sea

I begin to daydream then, not fully hearing the rest of her sales pitch, but instead remembering little fragments of what historians had compiled about frankincense and spices in the ancient economies.

The best frankincense, *hojari fusoos,* or some comparable grade from the region of Yemen, cost the ancient Romans 6 denarii per pound. That was roughly the same as ginger, more than black pepper, and twice the price of cardamom. Myrrh was twice the price per volume at that time because it would dehydrate and thus shrink; however, it was never used in the quantities that the Romans transported and consumed frankincense. In late Roman times, the cost of transporting a camel-load of frankincense from the southern Arabian Peninsula to the Mediterranean was 680 to 1,000 denarii, more than five times the cost of living a year in Palestine during the same era. In exchange for frankincense, each year, goods worth close to 10 million denarii would flow back the seventeen hundred miles from the shores of the Mediterranean, or from Persia and India.[15]

For a desert region where less than one-thousandth of the land's surface could be used to grow crops, it was frankincense that stimulated the flow of goods from better-watered regions in to Dhofar and the Hadhramaut. The Semitic tribes of Arabia Felix would trade their *lubān*, which the Romans called *olibanum*, for a range of material items that were beyond their capability to produce: silk sashes, muslin sheets, medicinal ointments, dry white wines, emmer wheat, copper vessels, and silver plates. Of course, small irrigated oases were scattered across Arabia Felix that provided most of the tribes with their dates, cereals, and some other cultivated foods, but trade in frankincense was what leveraged access to them for the nomads.

Until Arab and Phoenician seafarers gained a certain competence in maritime navigation, transport of frankincense and other goods over such long distances could be done only by camel. Dromedary camels appear to have been domesticated in the coastal settlements of eastern Arabia not far from present-day Salalah. They may have been initially managed as a wild resource for the medicinal value of their milk, which fends off microbial infections of the eye—just as frankincense offered its antiseptic *lubān* to treat irritations, cancers, and tumors in the eyes of the Semitic tribes there long before the era of Abraham. Clay figurines of camels made in Yemen close to three thousand years ago suggest that these creatures soon assumed the status of a keystone species in the Arab economy and an icon in its spirituality, for camels provided not only milk but also wool, meat, flammable dung, medicinal urine, leather, and transportation. Because a single adult camel can shoulder as much as 130 pounds of loaded goods and still cover twenty-two miles of desert a day, no other beast of burden could possibly hold its own against it when crossing windswept sands. Their convex backs enable camels to carry far more than horses over short distances, with loads of 650 pounds not uncommon.[16]

It is not surprising that the first appearance of frankincense well beyond its native range—in Egypt between three thousand and thirty-five hundred years ago—was about the time that camels were tamed and reliably used for long-distance transport. Among the nine hundred or so terms relating to camels in the Arabic language, one can find some wonderful metaphors that treat them as companions, gifts from Allah, and sailing vessels. Throughout much of their historical range, they were likened to "ships of the desert," capable of navigating vast seas of sand like no other animal. Camels, spice caravans, and incense trade not only shared a common history but also launched the Semitic tribes onto a shared economic trajectory. No wonder prints of camel caravans and miniature replicas of dromedaries are scattered throughout the souks of Salalah.

The elderly Somali shopkeeper taps me on the shoulder. "Excuse me, kind sir. Are you . . . ? You looked as though you were falling asleep. Do you want to purchase something from me before you go off to rest?"

I try to shake myself awake. I decide to purchase a quarter pound of *hojari fusoos* and a crudely decorated incense smoker from her, in part to avoid embarrassing myself any further.

"Please excuse me," I reply, "I am tired. I have come a long way to be here," I add, as I pay for the dreamy scent of frankincense.

I have been lucky enough to see where frankincense is found in the wild, how its resins are collected, and how it is still sold in souks in the very same port where it has been traded for millennia. It is clear that a little of the harvest could be bartered or sold for much more in the outer world, and this fact alone propelled the mountain talkers to engage in extra-local spice trade just as others began to do the same during pre-historic eras in other landscapes around the planet.

But the frankincense trade immediately changed into something larger and more pervasive than what happened with the nearly three hundred other spices that were traded globally. It established an insatiable desire for "the other," the exotic or extra-local, to propel some people out of the humdrum ordinariness of their daily lives. It stimulated them to imagine something beyond the here and now, something with which they wanted to connect. And that initial stimulus that may have led inexorably toward globalization in all its dimensions began more than three thousand years ago in remote arid landscapes where Semitic peoples wandered.

It has made me even more tired to try and fathom it all. Weary, I return to my boarding room, where I begin to vaporize a few tears of *hojari fusoos* over small coals in the simple clay incense smoker. As I lay down on the bed, I realize that traveling nine thousand miles through space has not been enough. I must figure out a way to travel back in time. I close my eyes. The ethereal smoke of the frankincense carries me away.

CHAPTER 2

Caravans Leaving Arabia Felix

Following the trail of smoke rising from the tears of frankincense and myrrh, I leave the Arabian Peninsula, cross over to the Horn of Africa, and put my feet back on the lava-strewn earth along the volcanic rim of the Blue Nile Gorge. Near the seven-hundred-year-old monastery of Debre Libanos, I smell a mix of spices being shared on ancient market grounds beneath a gigantic tree within sight of the Abay River, a tributary of the Blue Nile. A clamor of brilliant color and strange sounds welcomes me as I enter the grounds where merchants from near and far have come for the morning spice market.

I continue to follow my nose. It picks up an earthy, mustardy smell. I have a hunch that it is emanating from turmeric *(Curcuma longa),* a gingerlike rhizome. It is used around the world to reduce inflammation among the tired and the elderly and to stimulate the immune systems of children after they have been sick.

Searching for the source of this pungent fragrance, I wander up and down the crowded aisles of the makeshift bazaar. It seems more like a motley swap meet or picnic than a formal marketplace. I spot a young black woman gesturing toward me and giggling at the out-of-place stranger in the midst of the bazaar.

My eyes focus on her and what she is selling. She is seated on the ground, wearing a blue-and-gray gown decorated with crescent moons and six-pointed stars. Her eyes peek out from beneath a long piece of purple cloth draped over her head. She is beckoning me to pause and

A cousin to ginger and galangal, turmeric is an intriguing source of sharp, earthy aromas and pleasantly bitter flavors. The pale green, pencil-thin rhizomes of young *Curcuma domestica* (also known as *C. longa*) dry to a yellow-orange and are even more richly colored beneath their skin. Clearly of South Asian origin, most turmeric used today is grown in India. Early on, its trade beyond the Indian subcontinent utilized overland caravans to reach the Assyrians and Sumerians of Asia Minor.

By the eighth century CE, turmeric was being traded westward across the Indian Ocean and Arabian Sea in dhows, reaching both Yemen and East Africa, including the Mascarene Islands of Mauritius, Réunion, and Rodrigues. It was transported across Sub-Saharan Africa along caravan routes controlled by Berber, Bedouin, and Jewish traders. Dhows had also carried it eastward to China by the seventh century, where both its cultivation and use spread. Marco Polo saw it growing not only in China but on Sumatra and along India's Malabar Coast, as well.

There appears to be a different route for the diffusion of the names for turmeric, however, one that likely involves Ashkenazi Jews in its journey along more northerly routes. Terms cognate with the Hebrew *kurkum* appear in Yiddish, Greek, Italian, Bulgarian, Russian, Ukrainian, Korean, Finnish, Norwegian, German, Estonian, Czech, Croatian, Dutch, Breton, Catalan, Spanish, and even Korean. The notion that the English term *turmeric* comes through French from the Latin *terra merita*, or "meritorious earth," because of the visual resemblance of turmeric powder to precious minerals seems to me to be apocryphal. Turmeric and *kurkum* are likely related etymologically by their reference to the yellow root, as terms for this plant in other languages signify.

Green, Aliza. *Field Guide to Herbs and Spices*. Philadelphia: Quirk Books, 2006.

Hill, Tony. The *Contemporary Encyclopedia of Herbs and Spices*. Hoboken, NJ: John Wiley and Sons, 2004.

Katzer, Gernot. "Gernot Katzer's Spice Pages." http://gernot-katzers-spice-pages.com/engl/index.html. Accessed May 8, 2013.

Sortun, Ana, with Nicole Chaison. *Spice: Flavors of the Eastern Mediterranean*. New York: Regan Books, 2006.

taste what looks like a heap of gold dust piled up on a towel before her. I bend down and take a pinch, lick my index finger, and warm to the earthy, peppery, slightly bitter, somehow brilliant flavor that it offers. It is the turmeric that I have been seeking.

Suddenly, I feel connected to traditions of trading that stretch out far beyond my own life span. Spices, incenses, medicinal teas, and other aromatics that have been harvested nearby have also been traded, bartered, bought, and sold in this place for upward of ten thousand years. And yet, their time-tried value in cross-cultural exchanges persists to this day. Some, like ginger and turmeric, originally came from far away, before they found their way into dooryard gardens. Today, the locals consider them theirs, as if these aromatic roots had always been available to their ancestors.

This weekly spice exchange is held among Amharic-speaking Ethiopians who live in clusters of huts nestled in the slopes above the Abay River. The river at the bottom of the barranca is known to the outside world as a major tributary of the Blue Nile. The spice traders congregate on the hard-packed earth in the shade of a giant wild fig that teeters on the edge of the Blue Nile Gorge. The women here live within walking distance of Debre Libanos, the Coptic monastery of the "Lebanese Brothers." Once a week, they load up their shawls with freshly harvested goods, hike to the tree, and spread out their wares in front of their laps, placing them on handmade cloths or in woven baskets.

I tiptoe among the various vendors, for there is so little room around their piles of chile peppers, turmeric powder, ginger, myrrh, and fenugreek. I can smell the subtly bitter butterscotch aroma of roasting fenugreek seeds nearby. The Ethiopians whom I have met like to roast and grind fenugreek seeds to add to many of their foods. This roasted *abesh* is destined for their crepelike *injera,* a flat bread made of fermented teff flour.

As I look around at the mulling of hundreds of people under the branches of the massive fig, I sense that this open-air market has been going on ever since mankind first began to boil potherbs in clay pots and to exchange stories as well as foods around the campfire. The umbrella-like canopy of the old tree that arches above the traders may just be the fabled "tree where man was born."[1]

How can something this ancient still be so animated and engaging, not just to me as an accidental participant but to most of the locals as well? Is it something deeply wired in our genes that make us want to taste the exotic, the pungent, the aromatic? Somehow, exchanges such as this, replete with mounds and mountains of spices, incenses, green coffee beans, grains, pulses, poultices, and teas, seem to have always been the primary means of bringing diverse peoples together from neighboring valleys, gorges, and mountain ranges.

Something new began to happen to these localized spice exchanges around thirty-five hundred years ago, although minute changes in many locally isolated economies had been gradually accumulating for some forty-eight hundred years. Perhaps it first occurred on the eastern reaches of Africa, or somewhere along the southern coast of the Arabian Peninsula. I do not presume to know the first place in which it occurred, or among whom it emerged. But when this phenomenon spread, it shifted the trajectory of the world's economies and ecologies.

While still in southern Oman, I had a chance to visit one of the many earliest spice-trade centers on the peninsula, where this shift presumably occurred during early prehistoric times, irrevocably changing the nature of the marketplace as we know it today. This particular spot was on a gentle rise above the Arabian Sea, with a small estuarine inlet edged by volcanic outcrops. That inlet, which had been selected by people who knew how to choose sites for both their beauty and their utility, formed the most naturally protected harbor I had ever seen.

When I arrived there many millennia after its first settlement, boats were no longer coming into the harbor. Instead, the inlet had become a refuge for herons, egrets, and buzzards that were perhaps attracted to many of the same features that had drawn the earliest human inhabitants. A hyena ran from the edge of the estuary up onto one of the volcanic ridges and disappeared into a cave, nook, or cranny. The harbor offered an abundance of shellfish and finfish, as well as comfortable shelter and easy but protected entry from the sea. Feral dromedaries came near, looking for freshwater in pools near the coast. This remarkable spot once functioned as the harbor of Zhafar, which served the prehistoric port town of al-Balid. The ancient name Zhafar gave rise to that of the province of Dhofar, contemporary Oman's southernmost trading hub. Just a few miles away I had bought my supply of *hojari fusoos*.

As sunset cast its lemon-and-rose-colored light over the sea that evening, I wandered through the al-Balid ruins where caravans of camels once met seaworthy dhows, just as the great pilgrim-writer Ibn Battuta had seen during the fourteenth century. The dhows would then sail away with frankincense and other aromatics, taking them beyond their natural ranges, across gulfs and seas to other continents.

FIGURE 2. The ruins of al-Balid, one of the earliest ports for transcontinental trade across the Indian Ocean. (Photo by the author.)

The name al-Balid was an early Arabic term for a permanent town, something altogether different from the seasonal camps that preceded it. It is not surprising that archaeologists have confirmed that this 160-acre site was indeed a major population center four thousand years ago.[2] At that time, Oman was called the Land of Magan. It was already known in the wider world for trading copper northward to the prosperous city-state of Dilmun, an ancient trade center in a fertile agricultural valley not far from Qalat al-Bahrain, in the present-day island nation of Bahrain.

Remarkably, the ancient cuneiform texts found at al-Balid have been partially deciphered, and they confirm that long-distance trade of tons of staple foods had begun by 2800 BCE. Sumerian and Akkadian inscriptions from the same period report maritime trade from Mesopotamia to the north, on to the island of Dilmun; southward to Magan, on the Arabian Peninsula; and then eastward across the waters to Melukhkha. This latter place name may have referred to the legendary Spice Islands, now known as the Moluccas.[3]

Indeed, some of these Sumerian and Akkadian inscriptions may be the earliest written records of long-distance globalized trade. They indicate that the Semitic tribes of Magan were exchanging copper, and perhaps incense medicines or spices as well, for hundreds of tons of barley. Those enormous quantities of cereal grain traveled down the coast of the Persian Gulf southward past the Straits of Hormuz and along the shores of the Arabian Sea as far as Zhafar harbor.[4]

Minds were traveling as well. Perhaps the traders' minds leapt to consider the possibility that asafetida from one land might be as valuable as their own fine *zedoary,* and so a complete alphabet of comparable values for totally dissimilar substances could potentially come into play.

Simply put, Semitic tribes from the driest of lands had learned how to trade the few precious metals, gems, and potent plant products they had—resins, seeds, cinnamon-like bark, colorful stigmas of flowers and their bracts or buds, aromatic herbs, gums—for the surpluses of staple foods produced in better-watered pockets of the world.

Let me speculate for a moment on the significance of the phrase "learned how to trade." As spice traders gained rudimentary marketing skills, perhaps they came upon psychological strategies to convince a farmer that he needed a copper bell for his wife's necklace or an anti-inflammatory for the pain in his back as much as he needed enough teff or millet to keep his family from starving during the coming season of hunger. Could it be that people became willing to imagine that someone in another part of the world had something as desirable, potent, and worthwhile as the finest product they could harvest or produce on their own home ground? Perhaps this was the first moment that they sought out staples that they themselves could not easily grow: sorghum, barley, wheat, and teff, as well as fava beans, garbanzo beans, and lentils. They found these grains and beans on islands of irrigated lands in the middle of a desert sea. There, oasis dwellers expressed a desire to acquire spices that might break up the monotony of consuming the same old staples every day and thus brighten an otherwise dull meal.

Dates and goat meat, goat meat and millet, millet and dates. Sorghum and goat meat, mutton and sorghum. Cracked wheat and quail meat, quail eggs and garbanzo bean stew. What might have a certain *shadhan,* that is, an irrepressible pungency or unforgettable flavor that could provide some pleasurable relief to an otherwise unrelenting sequence of staples? What could break up the dietary monotony and the drudgery of processing, preparing, and eating nearly the same stuff every day?

We can now imagine that there might be a psychological risk to asking such questions on a regular basis. Could it be that such questions made people more apt to be dissatisfied by what lay before them and

Nomads of the Arabian Desert were opportunistic in their foraging for foods, looking for windfalls or unanticipated bumper crops that they could harvest, dry, and store for use over the lean months that would inevitably follow. The food had to be compact and nonperishable, for it would ride in a camel saddle-bag for months. It was often traded for staple cereals grown by oasis dwellers such as the Minaeans.

The following recipe combines the locust recipe in the compilation made by Ibn Sayyār al-Warrāq, identified by Lilia Zaouali as the author of one of the oldest surviving Arabic cookbooks, with the ancient practice of kneading locusts into date pulp. I have incorporated spices that have been found on the Arabian Peninsula or obtained through trade with India for millennia, in particular, fennel and asafetida. Chef Ana Sortun finds that the addition of fennel seeds imparts a sweet, warm, almost mintlike flavor to fruits and vegetables. According to Tony Hill of World Spice Merchants, the ground powder of asafetida (a member of the parsley family) emanates an unbelievably strong sulfurous odor until exposed to heat, which transforms it into a curiously complex set of onion and garlic flavors. For this recipe, wild dates are historically preferable, though Medjools or many other widely available domesticated varieties will do. Avoid the more perishable types, such as the Black Sphinx, for this dish. If you cannot find a swarm of locusts (or are wary of capturing it if you do), you can substitute salted roasted grasshoppers, which are available as *chapulines* in some Mexican American spice shops importing their supplies from Mexico City.

Accompany with hot mint or iced hibiscus tea. *Serves 6 to 8.*

    4 cups live locusts
    4 cups water
    ¼ cup sea salt
    2 tablespoons coriander seeds
    2 tablespoons fennel seeds
    2 tablespoons ground asafetida

    For the Brine Solution
    5 quarts plus 1 cup water
    3 cups rose water
    6 tablespoons salt

    8 cups Medjool dates, pitted and chopped

Find a swarm of locusts resting after a long flight and gather them in a covered basket. Under the shade of a date palm, carefully pick out and discard the dead locusts. Place the live ones in a large bowl, add the water and salt to drown them, then drain off the water and return the locusts to the basket.

In a stone mortar, combine the coriander seeds and fennel seeds and grind together to a fine to medium-fine powder. Stir in the asafetida.

To make the brine solution, combine the water, rose water, and salt in a 6-quart container and stir to dissolve the salt. In a ceramic or other pottery dish, arrange the locusts in a layer ½ inch deep. Ladle 4 cups of the brine solution over the locusts and sprinkle 1 tablespoon of the spice mixture evenly over the top. Top the layers with a heavy plate, pressing down on the plate, and let stand for 10 minutes. Drain off the brine, then repeat the layers of locusts, brine solution, and spice mixture 5 more times, pressing down on the plate and letting the layers stand for 10 minutes each time. Each time you drain off the brine, it should be lighter colored. The final batch should be nearly clear. Transfer the drained locusts to a crock and seal the top so the container is airtight. Let the locusts ferment at room temperature for at least a few days or up to a couple weeks.

Transfer the locusts to a large bowl, add the dates, and knead them together with your hands until fully combined and a soft mixture has formed. Pat the mixture into disklike cakes about 2 inches in diameter and ¼ inch thick. Store in a saddlebag of camel leather.

Hill, Tony. *The Contemporary Encyclopedia of Herbs and Spices: Seasonings for the Global Kitchen.* Hoboken, NJ: John Wiley and Sons, 2004, pp. 42–43.

Sortun, Ana, with Nicole Chaison. *Spice: Flavors of the Eastern Mediterranean.* New York: Regan Books, 2006, pp. 72–73.

Zaouali, Lilia. *Medieval Cuisine of the Islamic World: A Concise History with 174 Recipes.* Translated by M.B. DeBevoise. Berkeley: University of California Press, 2007, p. 140.

prone to crave something that was almost out of reach? Semitic peoples, at least some of them, seem to have succumbed to a thirst that could *never* be quenched—the grass would always be greener on the other side of the desert. It could never be quenched because of one simple fact: they tended to create a psychological desert wherever they went and could therefore reach neither the "grass" nor the happiness.

Thus, like nomadic herders, the traders were motivated to travel far and wide, not only to bring in a larger set of foods to their larders but also to spice them up. As economic historians have recently confirmed, early Semitic traders did indeed find a marvelous way to adapt to the patchy distribution of agricultural and wild resources on the Arabian Peninsula. They became effective traders between or among the peoples living in dissimilar patches, redistributing diversity and wealth in the process.[5] To succeed, they appear to have adopted not only a certain kind of mobility but also a mindset that was, until then, rather uncommon elsewhere in the world.

I did not fully fathom the significance of what these early traders had done until I left the Dhofar region to visit the souks of northern Oman, well beyond the range of frankincense itself. At that time, my wife, Laurie, and I were traveling with a brilliant agricultural scientist, Sulaiman Al-Khanjari, who, like many Omanis, had family ties and roots in Zanzibar. Once we had arrived in the coastal metropolis of Muscat, Sulaiman asked if we wouldn't mind visiting yet another spice souk. "The products you'll see will be much like those in Salalah, but there is someone who may be working in this souk today whom I particularly want you to meet." Did I detect a certain twinkle in Sulaiman's eye as he mentioned this?

Once in the souk, we wander down its narrow aisles, past groups of Arab youths looking to purchase cloth, jewelry, electronics, watches, slippers, shoes, and, of course, spices. Laurie and I try to keep up with Sulaiman, but crowds of Omanis press in on us, wedge in between us, and leave us yards behind our friend and guide. When at last we catch up to him, Sulaiman pulls us into a close huddle to explain the next step. "I want to take a moment to look for an acquaintance, one who has a shop just up at the top of that little stairway. . . . Do you see? There, yes, that one. If he is up there, I will have a word with him, then wave to you to come up to join us."

I see Sulaiman wave to another man in a white *kandora* robe, white skull cap, and slipperlike shoes. Dressed identically, the two of them embrace for a moment and then speak quietly for a while. At last, Sulaiman waves for Laurie and me to come up to where they stand.

"Dr. Nabhan of Arizona in America, meet your long lost cousin, Mr. Nebhan, the frankincense trader of Muscat, Oman." Sulaiman grins. He then translates his words in English back into Gulf Arabic to the middle-aged man standing next to him. This man is shorter than I am, with a full head of black hair and with bags under his eyes that remind me of some of my closest relatives. His skin, like my father's, is olive colored.

"Al-hamdu lilah! [Praise be to God!]" The smiling spice and incense merchant hugs me, then grabs my hand and holds on to it. He beckons for Laurie to take a picture of us together. Then he offers us some of his frankincense as a gift. We begin to ask questions of each other, with Sulaiman kindly translating and adding his own commentaries to provide some context.

"Are there many of the Banu Nebhani clan here in Oman?" I ask.

The merchant nods. "Well, yes, he supposes so," Sulaiman explains. The merchant continues nonstop in Arabic while Sulaiman tries to listen, then paraphrases, "Your namesakes have been here a long time . . . maybe fifteen hundred years, maybe two thousand years. So that makes a lot of Banu Nebhani who have lived here . . . in some villages nearby." Sulaiman then adds some commentary that is clearly his own: "They are like the Smiths or Joneses in your country! They say that the Banu Nebhani came from Yemen with other al-Hadr tribes, I don't know how long ago."

My presumed distant cousin, the frankincense vendor, offers more commentary, which Sulaiman tries to translate a bit more literally: "Old tribe . . . clan of what do you call them? Big shots, you know? Many sheikhs." Our host then asks if there are many Banu Nebhani in my country, and if there are, where they sailed from.

As I answer, Sulaiman translates back into Gulf Arabic: "My grandfather, grandmother, and aunts were born in Lebanon, near the border with Syria. They sailed to America about a century ago, from Beirut to Marseilles and then on to New York. Others went to Mexico or to Brazil."

After Sulaiman finishes translating my answer, he and Mr. Nebhan banter back and forth for several more minutes. Sulaiman finally turns back toward Laurie and me and grins. "He wants to know what your family trades in your shops in America."

As I think about how to answer Mr. Nebhan, this Omani merchant, I remember that when the first members of my family came through Ellis Island to New York, some of them worked peddling spices, packaging spices, and retailing spices in corner grocery stores on Atlantic Avenue in Brooklyn.

I have paid my dues as well, digging up sassafras roots when I was young, and later harvesting wild chiltepin chiles and wild Mexican oregano with Native American friends in Sonora, Mexico, then serving as a middleman to get them into retail outlets. And now I grow two dozen kinds of peppers, mints, and oreganos on a small farm in the desert highlands of Arizona.

I look up and see that Mr. Nebhan and Dr. Al-Khanjari are still waiting for me to answer. I realize I cannot explain all of that in a manner that makes sense in Arabic, so I respond succinctly: "Well, yes, my family has traded spices in America, but I am a teacher . . . and a farmer." I ask Sulaiman to explain this to our host. "First, my grandfathers and then my uncles did so. I myself have harvested *fulful* [peppers] and *za'atar* [herbs] in America, and have driven truckloads of them from one country to another."

Mr. Nebhan, a trader of frankincense who has never left his motherland, knowingly smiles, as if he were now sure that I am indeed his distant cousin.

Without access to Arabic genealogies still housed in archives in Yemen, there is no easy way to learn the degree to which we are related, or how many generations ago his ancestors and mine in the Banu Nebhani tribe took up this profession—a predilection, really—of trading spices. All we know is that several thousand years ago some unprecedented developments had begun to affect how Semitic peoples behaved in the places where incense, herbs, musk, dyes, and spices were gathered.

First, traders began to use semidomesticated camels and small sailboats to take these goods far beyond their areas of origin. They moved across continents to cultures that spoke languages they had never previously heard. At first, they retained camels as their sole mode of travel, for they could cover twenty-two miles of roughly level ground a day. But the traders ultimately sought other means to move heavier loads of spices, incense, and herbs longer distances than were possible with their beasts of burden.

They began to build and equip small dhows to sail the open waters of the Arabian Sea and Indian Ocean. Their goal was to travel even farther each day than the strongest camel could, that is, if the winds were in their sails. Of course, by this time, many other cultures around the world had figured out how to navigate the shallow shoals along their open coasts and the backwaters behind nearby barrier islands. They employed boats of buoyant animal bladders and sown-together skins, bundles of reeds, or hollowed-out palms or tree trunks.

And yet, I imagine, the sailors from the southern and eastern reaches of Arabia began to do far more than that. They erected masts with broad, maneuverable sails on them that could be shifted with the direction of the winds. They set out to sail directly across a sea, using the seasonal winds to take their dhows back and forth. Soon, no longer content to navigate along the shores of a bay or shoals of a peninsula, they began to use distant landmarks and stars to maneuver their way over open waters.

Well over a half century ago, historian George Fadlo Hourani, himself the son of a Lebanese shipping merchant, began to wonder why Arabs were among the first people known to venture fully out across the seas.

FIGURE 3. Dhows such as this one in the seas near Lamu, Kenya, were essential seafaring vessels for early spice traders. (Photo by Karl Ragnar Gjertsen. Courtesy Wikimedia Commons.)

In his beautifully crafted classic, *Arab Seafaring in the Indian Ocean in Ancient and Early Medieval Times,* Hourani boldly proposed that

> geography favored the development of sailing from Arabian shores. A very long coastline bounds the peninsula on three sides, stretching from the Gulf of Suez round to the head of the Persian Gulf. Near these coasts lie the most fertile parts of Arabia: al-Yaman, Hadramawt, and 'Umūn; communication between them by sea was no more formidable than the crossing of the deserts and mountains which separated them on land. Commerce with neighboring countries was invited . . . so that across the enclosed waters of the Red Sea and the Persian Gulf the Arabs might be in contact with two of the most ancient centers of wealth and civilization—Egypt and Iran—not to mention Mesopotamia. . . . Most important of all, the Red Sea and the Persian Gulf, supplemented by the Nile, the Euphrates, and the Tigris, are natural channels for through traffic between the Mediterranean basin and Eastern Asia; the Arabs were astride two of the world's great trade routes.[6]

It is thus plausible that certain of the Semitic peoples of the southern and eastern reaches of the Arabian Peninsula were no longer satisfied with staying put, for they had come into more frequent contact with many other cultures through long-distance trade. This may be conjecture, but it seems that their belief systems soon departed from those of the many pantheistic and polytheistic place-based cultures of the era.

These restless souls probably became more cosmopolitan, but at the same time, more emotionally and morally displaced, or "placeless." The pioneering human ecologist Paul Shepard has suggested that the emergence of this peculiar Semitic mindset in the deserts of the Middle East marked a turning point in human history: "On the most ambitious scale in the history of the world, the ancestors of the Old Testament made virtue out of their homelessness. . . . In a Semitic storm god they found a traveling deity who was everyplace and therefore not bound by location."[7]

Curiously, perhaps because they chose to bring their God along with them wherever they traveled and even settled in other lands, the various Semitic tribes did not necessarily lose their cultural identity by moving away from home. That is, their identity appears to have become somewhat independent of where they actually lived, although many of them may have kept a nostalgic connection to the mythic place in which their ancestors were presumed to have lived.

Although not as cynical about this placeless tendency as ecologist Shepard was, the great Jewish theologian Abraham Joshua Heschel conceded that at some point, the core Semitic beliefs radically shifted away from those of other Near Eastern cultures. In their minds, Heschel maintains, several Semitic tribes began to reject the very notion "that the deity resides in space, within particular localities like mountains, forests, trees or stones, which are, therefore, singled out as holy places; [that] the deity is bound to a particular land."

Instead, Heschel himself conjectured that most Semitic religions gradually came to accept that "there is no quality that space [or a presumably sacred place] has in common with the essence of God."[8] If God could be found anywhere in space or time rather than in particular places, so could economic opportunities.

As if to establish that possibility as a fact, the seafaring Semitic tribes of Oman launched sixty- to seventy-day expeditions into lands where other people were eager to purchase their novelties. Journeys of one thousand to two thousand miles suddenly became commonplace. By thirty-two hundred years ago, written records in Mesopotamia were noting that loads of frankincense had been arriving from Oman or Yemen in an ever-increasing frequency and volume.

As a result of the new challenges posed by managing caravans and cargo ships for long-distance transport and cross-cultural exchange, a distinctive multilingual merchant class began to emerge. These business-people forged solutions to the logistical difficulties that were integral to caravanning or seafaring. But they became adept at learning different languages, as well, allowing them to tell others compelling stories about the potency of their products and the adventures that had occurred while in transit. They also began to negotiate for the sales of not just one cargo load but many.

Of course, some people are natural polyglots, and gifted storytellers have emerged in nearly every culture around the world. But Semitic spice merchants somehow prepared their youth to combine these two talents, in order that some stay-at-home members of a foreign cultural community in a distant land might be touched by the mythic dimensions of the merchants' peregrinations in the foreigner's own tongue. After all, the best spice merchants knew full well that they were not merely selling calories, cures, or scents but also the stories that came along with them that might magnify the value of each item.

One of the first of these merchant cultures that we can put a name to is that of the Minaeans from the land of Punt, the place name that certain Europeans used for the Sayhadic incense kingdoms that once spanned most of present-day Yemen and the Dhofar region of southern Oman. Punt is where Biblical scholars suggest that the legendary Queen of Sheba resided, though that particular incense kingdom is correctly referred to as Saba, not Sheba. Although most of the finest frankincense came from the Hadhramaut and Dhofar highlands, the Minaeans who lived to the west of these regions in their own kingdom of Ma'in were among the pioneers who moved it into broader trade. At first, they likely swapped frankincense for the cultivated food crops farmed in the irrigated oases closest to their seasonal camps. Later, they traded it for other products from the world at large.

Of course, little doubt exists that they and others had long been trading locally in wild fennel seeds, cinnamon-like barks, indigo dyes, and even myrrh, all items within a few days' reach of the more northerly encampments in the kingdom of Ma'in. These wildcrafted goods could be bartered for the grain, pulses, dates, and herbs grown in the oasis villages in the more southerly, better-watered kingdoms of Saba, Timna, and Shabwa. Leather goods and metals were also transported down various paths, not just one Frankincense Trail.[9] Most of the Minaeans lived deeper in the hinterlands, on the ecological boundary between Arabia Felix and Arabia Deserta.

For much of their history, the Minaeans controlled the last small, stone-walled oases where sedentary Arabs dwelled: Yathrib (later called Madinat Rasul Allah, or Medina) and Qarnaw. That was before their own caravans began to venture out to where nomads roamed the sand seas of the Rub' al-Khali or gathered gums in the groves of frankincense or myrrh on the edge of the *nejd*.

The Minaeans soon became the regular go-betweens that linked two very different worlds: that of the nomadic tribes who wildcrafted fragrant herbs, aromatic incenses, and potent medicines from the desert itself, and that of the sedentary tribes who cultivated millet, dates, sesame seeds, and flax and used saffron and indigo to brighten their lives.

Minaean storytellers developed countless ways to heighten the mystique of the nomadic cultures to the sedentary farmers, who seldom had time to explore beyond their irrigation ditches. Likewise, Minaean bards found ways to make the nomads envious of all of the wealth that the farmers accumulated in their permanent homesteads and villages. The Minaeans lived in both of these worlds, and they learned to play one against the other with relative ease.

It was this group of intermediaries who gradually but firmly took control of the early spice trade in the southern reaches of the peninsula from 1200 to 650 BCE. Although they never achieved the full expansion of their domain to the entire peninsula, they set the stage for lasting interregional trade. Historian Caroline Singer notes their pivotal presence even in the crossroad communities of the Hadhramis (at the Shabwa oasis) and the Sabaeans (at the Ma'rib oasis) and in Qana, the primary port for the maritime shipping of aromatics:

> The merchants themselves would probably not have been natives of Shabwa; there is no evidence for either Hadramites [Hadhramis] or Sabaeans acting as incense dealers. It appears instead that there was a very specific group of South Arabians who acted as long-distance traders, and who came from the kingdom of Ma'in. According to Pliny, the Minaeans [became] the best-known South Arabians in the Roman world. They took consignments of incense to Syria, Egypt and Assyria, as well as to the Greek and Roman world, and they established a dynamic network of traders, each under the supervision of a magistrate, in various key points along the route. There was a settlement of Minaean traders in the Qatabanian capital of Timna', in the Hadramite capitol Shabwa; in the [outlying] oasis of Dedan, and in various cities of Egypt, including Alexandria.[10]

Curiously, throughout the Arabian Peninsula, incense and spice traders like the Minaeans tended to keep their most valuable stores of incense away from port towns. Good ports were valuable, but they were also vulnerable, for they could be more easily raided by rakes and ramblers from the outside. Like the famous hidden city of Petra later populated by the elusive Nabataeans, the oases frequented by most spice merchants lay inland, where marauders would have had to cross difficult stretches of featureless desert to find the fortresses where the most precious caches were guarded. This held true for incense repositories located in what is now Oman, just as it was for such repositories in Yemen.

While still in Oman, Laurie and I were taken to Bahla Fort, one of the most representative and intact fortresses historically used by spice traders, including my own Banu Nebhani clan. This mythic fortified city was situated a considerable distance inland from the several ports where my clansmen once controlled the trade. We traveled back across barren coastal plains, then down dry gravel riverbeds and up and over low limestone ridges before we glimpsed the still-stunning site of Bahla. It edged a steep-rising limestone plateau, Jabal al-Akhdar, where many of my kinsmen took refuge once their hegemony over the fertile valleys ultimately declined. I first caught sight of a dense patch of towering date palms, and then saw other soaring profiles rising above the horizon, like a mirage in the blistering hot sun. Protected with ten linear miles of high stone walls, the castlelike fortress rose above the fields and groves.

Here was where the spices, incenses, dates, and precious metals were kept before they were taken to the coast by camel caravan during the cooler hours of the night. And here is also where the cinnamon and cardamom, the black and white peppercorns, the saffron and sandalwood—goods that had been purchased from sailors who had ventured as far as Socotra, the Malabar Coast of India, Sri Lanka, or Indonesia—were hoarded.

We spent much of the day wandering along the irrigation ditches that watered the plots of fava beans and hedges of roses, the groves of dates and the orchards of citrons, pomegranates, and figs. They had been nurtured by a *falaj,* an irrigation system of hydraulic structures that harvested and stored rainwater from the barren limestone slopes above the walled oasis. We visited stone-lined pools for prayers, pools for baths, and canals that meandered through a shady and verdant world that bore no resemblance to the sunbaked desert beyond the walls.

Later, when we arrive at the souk in nearby Nizwa and enter the marketplace where vegetables and fruits are sold, we are joined by Ali Masoud al-Subhi, a local resident. Ali tells me that he may have some-

FIGURE 4. Bahla Fort served as an inland hub for trade out to the Strait of Hormuz, Gulf of Oman, and Indian Ocean. It is now a World Heritage Site. (Photo by the author.)

thing special to show me. He marches us right up to a produce vendor's booth where an old man is dozing—his face is partially hidden by a white *jalabiyah*—as if he has been unable to stay attentive to his customers during the midday heat. Before him on a white countertop is a two-foot-long palm raceme harboring a cluster of freshly harvested dates. "Try one," Ali whispers to me, "and don't worry about stealing. I will leave some coins for the old man to find when he awakens."

I pinch a few ripe dates off of the palm inflorescence and give one to Sulaiman, another to Laurie, and then take a third one for myself. My teeth cut through its dark chocolate skin and rich, sugary caramel-colored flesh. It is overwhelmingly sweet but delicious.

I look up. Ali has left a few coins on the counter and is now pinching another date off of the cluster. He holds it up between his index finger and thumb, as if it is a scientific specimen of some sort. "This, my friends, is called the Nebhani seedling date, and I believe it grows only here. Perhaps it exists in no other oasis. Perhaps it was named long ago for your family."

Of all of the irrigated date palm oases on the Arabian Peninsula, including Nizwa and Bahla, perhaps the one at Ma'rib on Wadi Adhanah, in north-central Yemen, has the greatest primal significance to the history of Arab peoples. Indeed, it is often considered to be the earliest

After saffron and vanilla, cardamom (*Elettaria cardamomum*) is the most expensive spice in the world. The essential oils terpinene, cineol, and limonene make it intensely aromatic. The twenty-five jet black seeds in each green-and-white lanternlike pod simultaneously conjure up the flavors of sassafras, eucalyptus, allspice, cloves, camphor, and pepper. It is amazing how their fragrance can be astringent and offer a delicate warmth at the same time.

This distant relative of ginger appears to have originated in the Kerala Hills in the Western Ghats of southern India, and references to it in ancient Sanskrit texts date back five thousand years to the Late Vedic period. It reached Babylon by 7000 BCE and arrived in Greece no later than 50 CE. Today, the cardamom shrub is widely cultivated from India to Guatemala. There is another variety with larger fruit from Sri Lanka as well.

Linguistically, we can trace the cardamom trade overland into Asia Minor, and by sea to the Arabian Peninsula and East Africa. The terms for cardamom in the Middle Eastern and East African languages are all quite similar: *habbu al-hayl* in Arabic; *hel* in Hebrew, Farsi, and Amharic; and *hil* in Azeri and Tigriniya. These cognates are derived from the ancient Sanskrit *eli, ela,* or *ellka,* which likely gave rise to the Hindi and Kashmiri *elaichi,* the Bengali *elach,* and the Gujarajati *elchi* or *ilaychi,* as well. Curiously, European terms, particularly those in the Romance languages, exhibit a total break with the terms from East Africa, the Middle East, and the Indian subcontinent. They all have their root in the ancient Greek *kardamomom,* which, according to spice scholar Gernot Katzer, is of uncertain and inexplicable origin. *Kardamomom* was often linked to a presently unidentified spice, *amomon,* as was cinnamon, or *kinnamomon.* One possible hypothesis is

exemplar of hydraulic civilizations, for when it was first built some four thousand years ago, it was the site of the greatest irrigation engineering achievement of its time, watering more than four thousand acres of food and fiber crops.

Historians claim that many of the cultural traditions now associated with irrigated agriculture throughout the world emanated from the Mar'ib, first to Oman and Mesopotamia, then across the Mediterranean to the West and to China in the East, and finally, to the Americas. Even the term *acequia,* widely used in the Spanish-speaking world for an irrigation ditch, has its root in the ancient Yemeni Arabic term *al-sāqiya,* a word that can mean any kind of conduit for water.

that *amomon* referred to *Amomum subulatum,* the large cardamom of Nepal and of Sikkim in northeast India, which may have dropped out of use in Europe after Roman times.

The use of cardamom by Bedouins on the Arabian Peninsula is ancient, but it has remained strong to this moment. In fact, many contemporary Bedouin nomads carry coffee pots that have a small chamber in their spouts for holding cardamom pods. Although my close Arab relatives in the Middle East are not Bedouins, they are no less attached to cardamom. When I am in any home in the Bekáa Valley of Lebanon, it seems as though cardamom has insinuated itself into every coffee cup, many rice puddings (*roz bi haleeb*), and even some morning *man'oushé* pastries. In fact, "regular," or *mazbûta,* coffee in Lebanon is typically served with a pinch of ground cardamom and a drop or two of orange blossom water.

Cardamom is a key ingredient in many of the great spice mixtures of the world, including Yemeni *zhoug;* Syrian, Turkish, and Iraqi *baharat;* Indian curry powders; blends for *chai* and *khorma;* and Malaysian masalas. Cardamom pods are once again finding their way into specialty gins, where they keep juniper berries and cassia bark company.

Gambrelle, Fabienne. *The Flavor of Spices.* Paris: Flammarion, 2008.

Green, Aliza. *Field Guide to Herbs and Spices.* Philadelphia: Quirk Books, 2006.

Hill, Tony. *The Contemporary Encyclopedia of Herbs and Spices.* Hoboken, NJ: John Wiley and Sons, 2004.

Karaoglan, Aida. *Food for the Vegetarian: Traditional Lebanese Recipes.* Beirut: Naufal Press, 1987.

Katzer, Gernot. "Gernot Katzer's Spice Pages." http://gernot-katzers-spice-pages.com/engl/index.html. Accessed September 1, 2011.

Ravindran, P. N., and K. J. Madhusoodanan. *Cardamom: The Genus Elettaria.* London: Taylor and Francis, 2002.

But when the Minaean culture was flourishing, it did so by forging a symbiotic relationship between the more sedentary al-Hadr tribes, engaged in irrigation agriculture, and the more nomadic Bedu and Jabbali tribes, which herded livestock or traded aromatics. While the oasis-dwelling farmers offered food security to all of the original tribes of Arabia Felix and many in Arabia Deserta, the camel drovers, incense gatherers, and spice traders offered both wealth and worldliness.

The Ma'rib dam was actually built in phases over thousands of years and ultimately irrigated more than ninety-five hundred acres of annual crops, orchards, and date palm groves.[11] Its ultimate span across the Wadi Adhanah plugged a six-hundred-yard gap in the Balaq Hills. When

FIGURE 5. The *sakieh,* an ancient form of water wheel, was a highly prized innovation from al-Hadr Arabs and Persians. Typically driven by oxen, these water wheels were used for irrigation throughout the Middle East and Egypt. (Photography Collection, Miriam and Ira D. Wallach Division of Art, Prints and Photographs, New York Public Library, Astor, Lenox and Tilden Foundations.)

its final phase was completed in 715 BCE by Sheikh Sumhu' Alay Yanuf and his son, the tightly fit stone and masonry blocks of its walls rose fifty feet above the original streambed of Wadi Adhanah. On the sides of the dam, sluice gates sent water down along twenty-five-foot-thick flood retention walls abutting the bedrock of the Balaq Hills. From there, mile-long "mother canals" channeled the stored floodwaters down to secondary and tertiary canals that entered the grain fields and orchard gardens of the Sabaean farmers.[12] These farmers then traded their agricultural goods with the Minaeans. In exchange for frankincense, fennel, myrrh, and wild medicinal herbs, the Minaean traders received the grains of a half dozen cereals, four kinds of legumes, a dozen kinds of tree fruits, and vine crops such as melons, watermelons, and cucumbers.

Most of these fruits and vegetables were eaten raw while still fresh; the rest were sun dried for later use. The grains and even the legumes were toasted and ground, then made into *harira,* which often combined wheat, garbanzo beans, and lentils in the same dish. Spices, onions, and wild greens might be added. Unleavened breads were baked on wood-fired ovens and used to mop up broths of grains, mutton, or goat meat, serving as precursors to dishes such as *tharīd* (a broth with bread, typically incorporating meat, but sometimes vegetarian) and *maqluba* (a boiled grain, meat and vegetable stew). Dates, fresh or pressed into thick pastes, were always available. This was desert peasant food at its most basic, and perhaps at its best.

The Minaeans would be offered cotton and flax for their weaving in exchange for Sabaean-tanned hides of camel, goat, and sheep. The wild desert world and its nomads found a certain synergy with the tamed and tended world of the Ma'rib oasis for upward of twenty-eight hundred years, with regional trade providing prosperity to both.

But then, some thousand years after Sumhu' Alay Yanuf and his workers had attempted to control desert nature, the Ma'rib dam burst, releasing floodwaters.[13] Overnight, the Sabaean Arabs witnessed the draining of the reservoir on which they had depended for more than forty generations. Their role in the world and that of their neighbors—the Minaean spice and incense traders—suddenly and irrevocably changed forever.

Although some Semitic-speaking tribes had long before migrated out of Arabia Felix into other reaches of the Arabian Peninsula, by the third century, refugees from the Ma'rib flood joined them in a diaspora of unprecedented proportions for its era. The great Arab historian Albert Hourani marks the out-migration of proto-Arab Semitic clans from Yemen during this time as one of the pivotal moments of Arab history.[14] Many of these clans left their southern motherland for good, fanning out across the peninsula and slowly transforming into the major Arab tribes that have dominated entire regions of the Middle East ever since. Some took the trails northward that had already been pioneered by the first mercantile caravans carrying frankincense to Mesopotamia, Syria, and Egypt. A number of their descendants later entered the spice trade themselves.

And yet, like certain groups of Jews after their departure from their Promised Land, the Arabs who left the well-watered oases of southern Yemen became a restless lot, relatively unattached to any place other than the mythic motherland from which their ancestors had come. Of course, they were intelligent enough and resilient enough to physically and economically make a new home nearly anywhere, but in doing so, they severed the psychic umbilical cord that attached them to their mother country. They were able to build houses, dynasties, and economies in many climes, but they could never go home anymore.

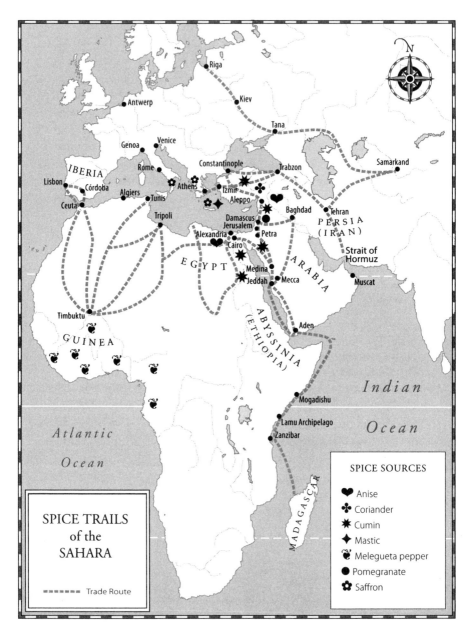

MAP 2. Spice trails of the Sahara

Many became listless drifters. Perhaps that is the inevitable personality profile for a spice trader.

In the sand seas of the Rubʿ al-Khali, they marked their ancient trails out of Yemen by leaving stone triliths as tall as a man. As their name suggests, the obelisklike stone cairns were three to a cluster, and were tall enough to rise above the drifts of sand that accumulated after storms. They marked the pathways that one might need to follow away from Arabia Felix and into the larger world.[15]

These weather-worn triliths can still be found today, their edges softened by centuries of sandstorms but standing exactly where they were originally erected. They serve as some of the earliest surviving evidence of one of the greatest mass migrations in history—that of Semitic tribes, of Minaean, Arab, Jewish, Phoenician, and Aramaic, away from Arabia Felix. Once the dam broke, they left their peninsular homelands in hot pursuit of the most pungent spices and potent incenses that money could buy anywhere . . . and everywhere.

I will follow them wherever their fragrant trails lead.

CHAPTER 3

Uncovering Hidden Outposts in the Desert

The desert shimmered before me, chimerical by its very nature. After days of visiting the spice souks of Alexandria and Cairo, Father Dave Denny and I were making our way across the Sinai with two Cairene van drivers in an old Volkswagen bus. It was the time of year when the Sinai is hot, dry, and desolate, with barely a cloud or a caravan in sight. For hours, we gazed out the window and saw sandy swales on the edges of hamadas, regs, and limestone ridges where it seemed as if every cobble was covered with a shiny black desert varnish. The sun's heat reradiated off of the sheen. The road ahead was drenched with mirages of water that suddenly pooled up before our eyes. As we approached one of the pools, we realized that it was not filled with recently fallen rain, but with inky black asphalt from the ancient beds of bitumen excavated near Gaza.

As the van bounced along its bumpy surface, I tried to read a coverless, out-of-print British guidebook to my old friend Dave. It noted how archaeologists had been deciphering inscriptions about the spice trade on a twenty-three-hundred-year-old sarcophagus found in Egypt. The inscriptions detailed a Minaean trader's account of following a route similar to the one on which we were traveling, but in the opposite direction. The trader was carrying perfumes and spices from the southern stretches of the Arabian Peninsula that were to be used in a prominent Egyptian temple.

Later, Callixenus of Rhodes recorded seeing one such caravan as it sought to go beyond the peninsula in search of better prices for its goods: "There marched three hundred Arab sheep and camels, some of which carried three hundred pounds of frankincense, three hundred pounds of myrrh, and two hundred of saffron, cassia, orris [an aromatic iris root], and all other spices."[1]

I glanced up from the book in time to see a few Bedu on camelback, heading toward the coast of the Red Sea. Soon, I was looking out over the beaches and coral reefs along the shoreline and across the waters of the Gulf of Aqaba to the northwestern edge of the Arabian Peninsula, where low coastal ranges seemed to waver and wriggle with the heat. The highway ran roughly parallel to the coast, sometimes nearer to the water, sometimes farther, for another hour. If this route seemed tiresome to me as I sat in a van that lacked air-conditioning, I wondered what the journey must have been like on the back of a camel, barely buffered from the desert sun?

And yet, for several centuries in the first millennium BCE, Minaean caravans had carried frankincense, myrrh, and spices along this route, northward from Hadhramaut in Arabia Felix, across the Arabia Deserta to the Gulf of Aqaba, and then up to Petra and Gaza, or across the entire Sinai to the Nile. Some of the caravans were lucky enough to avoid the raids known as *ghazw,* in which poor nomads captured food and other resources from richer tribes, thereby redistributing wealth. If a Minaean expedition was successful, its goods might reach Damascus and Jerusalem. Or they might find their way to Alexandria and Giza (near present-day Cairo) on the other side of the Nile. But whenever droughts or plagues affected the local nomads' capacity to raise livestock or forage for wild foods, they reverted to stalking the spice traders. To avoid losing all of the goods they carried in their caravan, the Minaeans often resorted to paying bribes or protection fees so that they might pass safely through the territories of poorer nomadic tribes.

I had become impressed by the tenacity and perspicacity of those prehistoric traders, but I was also getting road weary just thinking about the tediousness of their journeys across the open desert. The attitude that one must maintain to endure such a journey was well captured by explorer John Lloyd Stephens more than a century ago. After traveling in the company of Bedouins from the Red Sea toward Petra, he wrote, "We got through the day remarkably well, the scene always being precisely the same: before us, the long desolate, sandy valley, and on each side the still more desolate and dreary mountains. Towards evening we encamped; and after sitting for some time around a fire with my companions, I entered my tent [to sleep]."[2]

It may seem odd that the most expensive spice in the world comes from the tiny sexual parts of a small, lilac-colored flower with grass-like leaves, one that offers only a rather acrid, bitter, haylike aroma and a golden yellow colorant for which there are less expensive substitutes. But true saffron (*Crocus sativus*) remains the gold of the spice trade, with one kilogram of its threadlike red stigmata selling for more than a thousand dollars wholesale and ten thousand dollars retail. The harvest of saffron threads remains labor-intensive: one kilogram of threads requires handpicking the stigmata from 150,000 flowers. The production costs are also significant, as it takes a full acre of flowers to yield a single pound of dried threads. But the real reason for the exorbitant price of saffron may well be that no other spice looms as large in the imaginations and olfactory memories of the cultures that have traditionally relied on it.

Of course, none of saffron's surrogates have the magical mixture of crocin, safranal, and picrocrocin to give them the same brilliance and pungent punch. Saffron gets its bright gold color from crocin, a pigment-rich chemical compound. Its intense fragrance comes from the essential oil safranal, and its flavor from picrocrocin, a glucoside, which delivers its slightly bitter aftertaste and its medicinal qualities. It is one of the few water-soluble spices, and soaking the threads in water overnight will yield a sunny gold liquid by dawn. Combined with a color-stabilizing mordant, saffron has served as a golden dye for garments of many of the religious and political elite over the millennia, including Buddhist monks.

As a medicine, saffron's usefulness as an antispasmodic, sedative, and abortive has been documented in the treatment of scores of illnesses. In a highly concentrated form, it can be poisonous, but it would be an expensive way to die.

Because several *Crocus* species have been harvested historically for use as a spice, colorant, and medicine, it is difficult to attribute all of the ancient drawings and writings about saffron use to *C. sativus,* which is easily the mostly widely utilized and highly prized of all the crocuses today. Botanists have long debated the origins of this domesticated crop, since wild plants similar to it are not found in the natural habitats within the crop's geographic range. Recent studies have partially resolved this problem, however, establishing that *C. sativus* originated from the natural hybridization of two other *Crocus* species, one of which was *C. cartwrightianus,* a plant that grows on mainland Greece and some of its islands, among them Santorini, where it is still actively harvested for its saffron.

The other parent of *C. sativus* may be *C. thomasii,* which also occurred in the Mediterranean region, where it still survives in Italy and on islands in the Aegean Sea. Although it is likely that polyploid forms of C. *sativus* were first domesticated for saffron somewhere adjacent to the Aegean, another area of possible domestication is the arc running from Turkey, through Iraq and Iran to northwestern India. Archaeologists studying rock paintings in Iran have recovered fifty-thousand-year-old flower pigments from the *Crocus* genus, though these almost certainly were extracted from a wild species. Iran remains the largest producer of saffron for exports, but Fabienne Gambrelle claims that the best product is harvested from Kashmir.

Some historians have speculated that saffron-bearing plants were first cultivated on Crete, simply because there are three-thousand-year-old depictions of a crocuslike flower in the Palace of Minos at Knossos. But neither these images nor the famous fresco of saffron gatherers on one of the palace walls necessarily confirms early domestication. Alas, all the pieces of the puzzle regarding the origins of saffron have not yet been put into place. Much more remains for archaeologists and other history detectives to explore.

What strikes me wherever I travel is how strongly saffron is linked to the culinary identity of particular ethnicities. Whenever I have been invited for a homemade dinner among Indian immigrants to Europe or America, they proudly serve me saffron-infused rice. When my Spanish friend chef Francisco Pérez learned that I loved paella, he took a three-hour "Sunday break" from his professional duties to show me how to prepare his signature dish properly, producing enough to feed forty of our friends. But my favorite example of saffron being embedded in cultural identity comes from the Basque immigrants to the Great Basin of western North America. When I have gone to gatherings in the Basque country of Idaho, Nevada, or Utah, it is inevitable that the evening celebrations feature enormous quantities of paella colored and seasoned with the finest saffron that the hosts have been able to import from the Basque country in Spain. As I enjoy a savory plate of this paella, I have secretly wondered to myself what it means for saffron, mussels, clams, and shrimp to have been transported from the shores of the Iberian Peninsula to a dry, landlocked basin in North America thousands of miles away.

When Jewish and Muslim families were expelled from Spain beginning in the late fifteenth century, they took their grandmothers' recipes and spices with them as they fled to elsewhere in Europe and to North Africa, the Middle East, and the Americas. In the families of Sephardic Jews in particular, the practices of kosher cuisine were further blended with Arab influences to forge new traditions that reinforced their distinctive identity. Meatballs (*albóndigas*) in saffron sunset sauce is just one example of an Arab recipe adapted by Sephardic Jews who relocated to Venice. The Arabic name of the dish, *chems el aachi,* means "setting sun," because the golden color of the sauce is reminiscent of a glorious sunset in the Maghreb and Andalusia.

Gambrelle, Fabienne. *The Flavor of Spices*. Paris: Flammarion, 2008.

Goldstein, Joyce. *Saffron Shores: Jewish Cooking of the Southern Mediterranean*. San Francisco: Chronicle Books, 2002.

Green, Aliza. *Field Guide to Herbs and Spices*. Philadelphia: Quirk Books, 2006.

Grilli Caiola, Maria, and Antonelli Canina. "Looking for Saffron's (*Crocus sativus* L.) Parents." *Functional Plant Science and Biotechnology* 4 (2010): 1–14.

Musselman, Lytton John. *Figs, Dates, Laurel, and Myrrh: Plants of the Bible and the Quran*. Portland, OR: Timber Press, 2007.

Schneider, Sally. "From the Saffron Fields of Spain." *Saveur*, March 23, 2007. www.saveur.com/article/Travels/From-the-Saffron-Fields-of-Spain.

A flat tire and a half-hour pit stop on the barren side of the Sinai highway provided me with sufficient time to consider the wide ripple of influences that emanated from the doggedly determined Minaean traders who had preceded Stephens by two to three millennia. During the years that their trading culture flourished, their envoys had reached as far as the Greek island of Delos, the port of Alexandria, the oasis of Palmyra and settlements of Chaldea, and even to the ancient harbor of Keralaputra on the coast of present-day India. They had maintained a string of oasis outposts across the Arabian sands, including Najran and Timna. But after centuries of dominating trade in aromatics, the Minaeans began to falter in their efforts to control all spices, incenses, dye, and minerals flowing in and out of Arabia Felix. One possible reason for this waning was that the costs of bribes and protection fees simply became too great.

But a second possibility for their demise seems equally plausible: their competitors had learned to sail all the way to the southern port of Aden, both from the Red Sea on the west and the Arabian Sea on the east, thereby avoiding desert raiders.[3] Ultimately, the Minaeans lost their competitive edge and economic niche. By 100 CE, their peculiar Semitic language, the now-extinct Madhabic tongue, was no longer the lingua franca of globalized trade.

I was jogged out of my reverie on Minaean history by the driver revving up the engine of our Volkswagen bus. Now outfitted with a nearly bald but inflated tire, our aged vehicle limped into the Red Sea resort

❧ CASSIA CINNAMON ❧

Considerable confusion has surrounded discussions of the scientific identities and the cultural origins of various "cinnamons" found in the historical records of the spice trade. However, *Cinnamomum cassia* (formerly known as *C. aromaticum*) has a flavor and history distinctly different from the rest of its namesakes. Best known as cassia or Chinese cinnamon, there is no reason to refer to it in English as a "bastard cinnamon," as some have in the past, for it is in no way inferior to the others. Although many would agree that its array of flavors is a bit simpler than that of so-called true cinnamon, it is also more straightforwardly intense, due to the higher oil content in its reddish brown bark. Like other extracts derived from the tall cone-shaped evergreen trees of the genus *Cinnamomum*, its warm and savory notes are derived not from true wood but from the inner bark of the trees, where most of the potent aromatic oils are found.

An extremely high concentration of cinnamaldehyde in its essential oil is what gives cassia and most other cinnamons their spicy sweetness. But unlike true cinnamon from Sri Lanka, cassia also contains significant amounts of coumarin, a blood-thinning agent. Some Asian populations have genetically adapted to coumarin in their foods in beneficial ways, but particularly vulnerable individuals could suffer dangerous health effects if cassia is taken with other blood-thinning agents. Most people who consume cassia sparingly find it to be delicately, rather than cloyingly, sweet, with a pleasantly woody aftertaste.

Cassia cinnamon grows wild in a few southeastern Chinese provinces, such as Guangdong and Guangxi, although much of its production today is from managed cultural landscapes rather than truly natural habitats. But it is also native to Assam and Myanmar and has long been cultivated in Vietnam. When the trees reach harvestable age, a square of inner bark is massaged by harvesters before being incised. It forms a thick, scroll-like tube often referred to as a cork, which is then left to dry and age. The inner bark of cassia is thicker and rougher than the bark of other cinnamons and has a coarse, dark brown surface that exudes the slightly bitter aroma of camphor, though cassia, unlike Sri Lankan or Ceylon cinnamon, doesn't contain eugenol. Less commonly sought outside the areas in which the trees are grown are the caperlike floral buds, which echo the flavors of allspice and pepper in addition to cinnamon, and the leaves, the oils of which are distilled.

The original name for cassia in at least some of the many Chinese dialects may have been *kwei-shi*. In 216 BCE, the first emperor of the Qin dynasty, Qin Shihuangdi, renamed one of the most prized spots that he conquered for a cassia grove cultivated there, calling it Kweilin, or Guilin, the present capital of Guangxi Province.

The extra-local trade of cassia dates back to antiquity, when it was carried along certain routes predating the appearance of other cinnamon species. It is identifiable in herbals from the second and third century BCE, and it is likely that the cinnamon referred to in the Bible is cassia and not true cinnamon. According to *The Periplus of the Erythraean Sea,* written in Greek around the middle of the first century CE, cassia was being moved through Indian harbors and shipped past the Gulf of Aden to Somalia. But these maritime traders did not necessarily know where the cassia was harvested.

In time, Sogdian and Persian traders on the Silk Roads did become aware of the source of the spice and named it *dar-chin,* with the *chin* referring to China and the *dar* possibly meaning fragrant or spicy wood. The Uighur in western China still use the term *dar* as a generic reference to spices. Cassia is also referred to as *darchibi* in Bengali, *dal chini* in Hindi, *tarçin* in Eastern Turkic, *darichini* in Georgian, and *addarsin* in Arabic.

It appears that Jewish or other Semitic traders introduced cassia to Europe, for their Hebrew term *ketsiah* (also the name for Job's daughter) is echoed in the Greek *kasia,* as well as in terms found in most of the Romance languages. By the time cassia and other cinnamons had been traded through Central Asia and India to the West, their origins had been wonderfully mythologized. In *The History,* the very gullible Herodotus wrote that huge birds in Arabia used cinnamon quills to build their nests, and in order for the Arabs to secure the cinnamon for themselves, they would put big chunks of meat on the ground under the nests. The birds, tempted by the food, would carry it up to their homes, thereby forcing the nests to collapse under so much weight. As the nesting materials fell to the ground, the cinnamon would be

town of Taba, the easternmost settlement in all of Egypt. When it came to a stop, I paid the two Egyptian drivers in pounds, and they immediately began their return trip west. Without even purchasing a new tire or some food, they had chosen to hasten toward Cairo and the comforts of the Nile.

Father Dave and I checked into two rooms in a modest hotel built just above the shoreline, and I took time out to soak my bones in the hypersaline waters of the Gulf of Aqaba. When the heat began to dissipate an hour before sunset, we left the crowded beach and hiked back from the highway into the shadows of a side canyon, where we found an encampment of forty to fifty Tarabin Bedouins who had moved up from neighboring Nuweiba.

These Bedu had improvised shade shelters and storage sheds next to gathered by the ever-patient Arabs waiting below them. If that were not enough, Herodotus also believed that cassia grew in shallow lakes in Arabia, where it was protected by loud, pesky bats. Only Arabs fully covered in protective leather garb could shield themselves from the bats' wrath and collect sufficient cassia to make its transport to Europe worth the risk of having their eyes plucked out by the protective bats.

Cassia finds its way into many of the great spice mixtures of the world, from five-spice powder in China to *baharat* and *qalat daqqa* in the Middle East to moles and *recaudos* in Mexico. Most of my Lebanese kin prepare kibbe, *kefta,* and *lahem meshwi* by first seasoning the lamb with cassia. But my most frequent encounter with cassia is far from its home and mine, in Latin America. From the semiarid Mexican Altiplano all the way to Guatemala, there are local communities who cannot imagine drinking hot coffee unless it is laced with cassia. In fact, for them, cassia *is* cinnamon.

Gambrelle, Fabienne. *The Flavor of Spices.* Paris: Flammarion, 2008.
Green, Aliza. *Field Guide to Herbs and Spices.* Philadelphia: Quirk Books, 2006.
Hill, Tony. The *Contemporary Encyclopedia of Herbs and Spices.* Hoboken, NJ: John Wiley and Sons, 2004.
Katzer, Gernot. "Gernot Katzer's Spice Pages." http://gernot-katzers-spice-pages.com/engl/index.html. Accessed May 4, 2013.
Musselman, Lytton John. *Figs, Dates, Laurel, and Myrrh: Plants of the Bible and the Quran.* Portland, OR: Timber Press, 2007.
Weiss, E.A. *Spice Crops.* Wallingford, UK: CABI Publishing, 2002.

their tents and corrals. The structures were elaborated from the debris they had looted, retrieved, or rescued from construction sites along Taba's boulevard of resort hotels. I was greeted by a couple of Bedu boys and one girl who had been herding Nubian goats and fat-tailed sheep into the corrals for the night.

As soon as the sheep and goats were safe, the children walked me back to where their parents were camped. A middle-aged couple and an old man warmly welcomed me, then rolled out a carpet on the stony ground, sat me down, and not far from the carpet made a small wood fire on which to heat water. They prepared some *shai nana'a* (spearmint tea), offered us each a cup, and then poured cups for themselves. As we sipped our tea, the children came around to entertain us. When we got up to leave the campsite, the old man offered me a sandstone carving of a striped hyena consuming the head of a luckless tourist. I took it without question, giving him a few pounds and a couple of paisley bandanas in exchange.

Returning to our lodging just before dark, I realized that I could see the lights of Eilat, Israel, across the bay. Immediately to the right of them were the lights of Aqaba, Jordan. Long before these present-day resort towns illuminated the northern horizon from Taba, historic port towns had existed along the coast, where goods that had come from as far away as India were transferred to camel caravans for their trip into the desert.

The coastal ranges of Saudi Arabia across the gulf were also visible. From my vantage point, I could see how the northern reaches of the Red Sea are divided into four countries today. Twenty centuries ago, they were all part of one legendary nation of spice traders, a desert country with amorphous boundaries that the Jewish historian Josephus called the Nabatene kingdom, and whose itinerant traders were known from Ma'rib to Rome as the Nabatu. We call them the Nabataeans.

There was something about the Sinai's scrappy Tarabin Bedouins that echoed the little that I knew about the ancient Nabataeans. Although a Nabataean presence is first evident in the archaeological record at the start of the fourth century BCE, their small nomadic clans are hardly mentioned in written documents for another several hundred years. In 312 BCE, Hieronymus of Cardia offered one of the first recorded observations of them. He worked with them in the gritty business of mining bitumen from the near-sterile edges of the Dead Sea. The Nabataeans then loaded up camels with as much as they could carry and headed off across the barren desert toward the cities of Egypt, where they hoped to trade this asphalt for foods grown on the fertile floodplain of the Nile.[4]

The Nabataeans of that era forbid their own people to cultivate any crops and were said to abhor being engaged in any practice of agriculture other than herding. And yet, they had to eat, so they traded what they could, whether it was goat hides or wild medicinal plants. By the second century BCE, the Greek geographer Agatharchides reported that the growing Nabataean population had become so depauperate and desperate that they had switched from raiding the few caravans that came across their stretch of desert to preying on another kind of caravan, the fleets out in the sea.[5] In essence, the Nabataeans left the desert to become pirates who looted sailing ships throughout the Gulf of Aqaba, where they particularly enjoyed pouncing on hapless Egyptian sailors.

Ten thousand nomadic raiders strong, the early Nabataeans played the role of the bad boys of the Red Sea, accosting ships out in the gulf or caravans along its coast rather than practicing any farming or building their own fixed abodes. Some historians suggest that most of the Nabataeans of this time were descendants of the Bani Nabatu, one of the earliest recognized Semitic tribes of Arabia Felix. They were a people who had survived scarcity for centuries if not millennia, and they had become lean and mean in the process.

But as they gained a modicum of wealth, they worked hard to develop unprecedented modes of communication across desert landscapes. Both the Arabic alphabet and the Kufic calligraphy still used today for writing the Qur'an appear to be derived from their lovely ornamented cursive scripts.

Some scholars have suggested that the Nabataeans did not remain a single ethnic entity for very long, but became a heterogeneous community that absorbed other tribes.[6] Gradually they wove together many influences, including Roman, Greek, Egyptian, and Hebrew, into a larger cultural and economic fabric. Together, they created a distinctive "fusion cuisine" of *harira* and *chorba* (hearty stews), *murrī* (a salty fermented barley paste), and *kāmakh rījāl* (a somewhat rancid but sharp-tasting cheese spread made by keeping yogurt in an open vessel for several weeks).[7]

The ancient Nabataean names for these foods spread in Aramaic to nearby Arabic and Hebrew dialects and then became loan words in Persian, Greek, and Roman tongues. Over time, the Nabataean amalgamation harbored an eclectic mix of Aramaic, Hebrew, and Arabic speakers who joined together as bands of outlaws, "redistributing" all of the loot that could be had between Alexandria and Jerusalem. Diodorus, a Greek historian born in Sicily and active from about 30 to 60 BCE, thought them to be mostly Arab herders who turned opportunistically to the sea whenever they could easily retrieve some booty by raiding.

> A great number among them bring incense, myrrh and the most precious perfumes which they receive from Arabia Felix, via the ocean. . . . This tribe occupies a large part of the coast and not a little of the country which stretches inland, and it has a people beyond telling and flocks and herds in multitude beyond belief. Now, in ancient times these Arab men observed justice and were content with the food which they received from their flocks, but later, after the kings of Alexandria had made the ways of the sea navigable for their merchants, these Arabs not only attacked the shipwrecked, but fitted out pirate ships and preyed upon the voyagers. . . . After some years, however, they were themselves ambushed on the high seas by some larger ships and then punished for all their bad deeds.[8]

FIGURE 6. *Harira* stews became vehicles for introducing savory spices to a range of Persian, Arabian, and Berber populations. This lunch was offered by Berbers at Siwa Oasis in Egypt. (Photo by the author.)

Whatever their origins, the Nabataeans gradually shifted from looting others to trading. But they didn't trade in the way that their neighbors had. They sought to more systematically control the management of most, if not all, of the land and sea trade emanating from the incense kingdoms. By employing long caravans of camels along hard-to-trace routes supplemented by sophisticated ships equipped with oars and sails, they completely eclipsed the Minaeans in dominating the many Frankincense Trails. As observed by Walter Weiss, the Nabatene kingdom "was an unusually peaceful state geared solely to profit from trade, with no real borders, no taxation or social unrest and very few slaves. Its strength was that it consistently managed to keep a distance between the producers and consumers of the goods it transported."[9]

In essence, the Nabataeans became the first cultural community to be comprised largely of middlemen. They became spice, incense, and perfume brokers who developed, maintained, and controlled transcontinental trade networks. In fact, hardly any of the goods they moved along the Frankincense Trails were from their own lands. Their ecological niche was to serve as obligatory intermediaries in the trade of frankincense, myrrh, Indian spices, and other aromatics across the seas and between the continents.

To do so, most of them opted to live in the "empty space" between the grounds where the aromatics were gathered and the urban markets where they were destined to be used. For them, the desert and the sea had become little more than space to be crossed, for they no longer eked out a living directly from its local resources. What mattered most was their control of the caravansaries and other safe harbors that could serve as way stations on their journeys across such vastness.

Their "strength," as Weiss calls it, was their insistence that consumers have no direct contact with producers. As long as they kept harvesters clueless about who desired their goods, and never divulged to end users where the goods had actually come from, they controlled the value chain along the Frankincense Trails. This mandate allowed the Nabataeans to profit immensely from the spice trade, for all others in the supply chain had little means of understanding the value embedded in other links in the chain.

Pliny the Elder noted that while incenses, spices, and other products passed through Nabataean hands on their way from Arabia Felix to Gaza, their value accrued to a hundredfold of what it had been when the goods first entered their hands, whether hauled by camel caravan or shipped by coconut-wood dhows with lateen sails.

But the true genius of the Nabataeans may have been their capacity to keep the incenses, spices, salves, and silks destined for Europe, Africa, and Asia Minor imbued with a sense of wonder. They were marketing mystique as much as they were materials. Perhaps they had learned this strategy from the Minaeans who came before them. It was neither the caloric content nor the antiseptic value of the seeds, gums, leaves, and barks that sold cumin, cinnamon, frankincense, labdanum, or myrrh. Instead, sales depended on their compelling marketing of the mythic dimensions of these exotic goods. They essentially did what promoters of amaranth, extra-virgin olive oil, ginseng, and magic mushrooms continue to do today. Beyond the physical properties of the plant or fungus, they brokered the "placebo effect" to their own economic advantage.

For starters, the Nabataeans got the Europeans to believe that frankincense had to be expensive because of the stealth that it took to harvest it from the protected groves of southern Arabia. As the Greek historian Herodotus explained to his fellow Europeans, "When gathering frankincense, they burn storax [a resin of sweet gum trees] . . . and this storax raises a smoke that keeps away the small flying snakes. Great numbers of them keep guard over all the trees that bear the frankincense. Smoking them out with storax is the only way to get rid of them."[10]

Consider for a moment the paradox of those juxtapositions: to enjoy access to divine incense, one must use another smoky fragrance to snatch the sacred substance away from evil serpents that otherwise serve to protect it! Although this legend was possibly told to Herodotus by some Minaean spice trader in the fifth century BCE, the Nabataeans made sure that such stories continued to circulate for several more centuries in the countries remote from the spice kingdoms of Arabia Felix. No doubt the Nabataeans themselves generated equally luminous stories about the places and peoples from which their frankincense was obtained.

By this era, no outsiders were permitted to come near the places of origin of frankincense or myrrh, nor even enter the caravansary where they were temporarily stored. Even the heart of Petra, the temple and trade center that ranked among the greatest in the world by the end of the first century CE, was physically and metaphorically hidden away in the rock.

Petra was the perfect physical manifestation of how the Nabataeans went about their work: its power and beauty were cloaked in mystery until the last moment before arrival, and then they were suddenly revealed in a manner that could only generate awe. Oddly, virtually no archaeological remains of frankincense and other aromatics have been found anywhere near the temples carved into the cliff faces of Petra. Perhaps they were sequestered elsewhere, hidden in nearby slot canyons where foreign soldiers or raiders would be unlikely ever to find them.

For several centuries, Nabataean traders supplied Alexandria, Al 'Arīsh, Gaza, Jerusalem, Basra, and Damascus with most of their spices, dyes, gums, balms, incenses, and exotic herbs. They had a knack for working with other middlemen to obtain camel loads of silk and ginger from China, true cinnamon and pepper from Ceylon and India, aloe and dragon's blood from Socotra, and nutmeg from the Spice Islands. Although they did not necessarily visit all of these source areas themselves, they did deal directly with many of their harvesters of aromatics. For six centuries, the Nabataeans moved thousands of tons of goods out of Yemen and Oman, taking them across the Arabian sands and seas to their ports of Luce Come and Aila (later called Elath and then Eilat). From there, the precious cargo went overland to Syria, Canaan, Egypt, and beyond.

I had wanted to follow the Nabataean trade routes northward across the Negev, first to Jerusalem and later to Damascus. But the tense political realities of that moment made it impossible to move easily among these countries. Because I was a Lebanese American who had previously visited relatives in Lebanon and Syria on the same passport I was currently carrying, I was interrogated for three hours at the Israeli port of entry at Eilat. It did not help that I shared a surname with an al-Qaeda operative leader from Somalia. Customs officials told me that I could not enter if I was planning to go on to Syria, even though it was only to have an audience with a cousin who had become mother superior of a convent! I was told that I would have to leave Israel by the same port of entry and then return to Egypt before I could make my way into Jordan (toward Petra). Plus, Syria would not let me enter if my passport carried an Israeli stamp. It all seemed daunting, so Father Dave and I opted for the simplest solution: to focus exclusively on the trail to Jerusalem and reserve Jordan and Syria for other trips.

Once inside Israel, Father Dave and I were disappointed that there was little to see of the old Nabataean and Roman ports of Aila in present-day Eilat. When I later spoke with archaeobotanist Peter Warnock, he confirmed that neither the Nabataean port of Aila nor the hidden trade center of Petra has yet to render much evidence of the trade items that passed through them. This is in part due to poor archaeological preservation of the ground herbs, spices, and dyes recovered there, unlike the relatively rich evidence of grains and beans. Thousands of tons of incense and spices may have been carried through the Negev long ago, but they left not a trace.

Perhaps this is because the aromatics that were funneled into the Nabataean ports and caravansaries were slated to depart soon after their arrival. Spice traders seldom made much money holding on to their merchandise for very long, since the potency of aromatic oils fades with time. Instead, they learned to maximize the rapid turnover of goods. I have seen this where I farm near the largest port of entry for produce coming into the United States, mostly from Mexico. The bulk of the cilantro, cucumbers, peppers, and tomatoes reaching the brokerage houses along the border remains there for less than two hours before being whisked away by semitrucks that haul their cargo north-ward another five hundred to one thousand miles.

While still in Israel, I continued to puzzle over this paradox: here I was, traveling in the desert between two of the world's greatest prehis-toric spice trade centers, Petra and Aila, and no archaeologist or tourist guide could point to any remains of the aromatics that had made these two sites so famous. The fragrance of their perfumes had dissipated; the incenses had gone up in smoke.

With little to see in Eilat, Father Dave and I boarded a bus and headed for Jerusalem, hoping to catch a glimpse of the ancient des-ert homeland of the Nabataeans along the way and then to survey the Old City's souks for the spices and incense that are still traded today. I knew that the Nabataeans had once maintained an archipelago of water holes and way stations in the Negev like so many buoys bobbing in an open sea.

I had imagined spotting them from the highway as we rode along with conservatively dressed Hasidic Jews and Bedouins on the bus from Eilat to Jerusalem. Instead, I could see little from my speeding transport, which was fully packed with sun-tanned teenagers. We were surrounded by young Israeli Jews and by other "liberal" Jews visiting from Europe and America, all of them dressed in the latest beach fashion: designer-branded bikinis, Speedos, T-shirts, tank tops, and flip-flops. And yet it was not their dress that was unsettling; it was their social behavior, or lack of it. Most of them sat on their bus seats, silent, text messag-ing acquaintances on their mobile devices or listening to music through their headphones.

Like many youths from around the world, they could have been any-where doing the very same thing, because they were nowhere. In some two hours, I noticed only a single teenager even glancing out of the bus windows, as if the desert itself might be of some interest.

It was an odd way to spend my first few hours in the Negev, the legendary heartland of the Nabataean kingdom, a superficially barren stretch of land that spanned the entire distance from the Red Sea to the Dead Sea. While my fellow passengers listened to their reggae, rock, and hip-hop, I focused on the Negev itself, a desert perhaps as dry and for-midable as the *nejd* in southern Oman.

Except for a few remarkably verdant kibbutzim and date groves nourished by treated sewage effluent, the land was perhaps *more* barren than when the later eras of Nabataeans had known it.[11] To help me visu-alize this desert prior to the construction of Israel's resorts, I returned to the journals of Stephens, the first American explorer to reach Petra from the apex of the Gulf of Aqaba:

> Standing near the shore of this northern extremity of the Red Sea, I saw before me an immense sandy valley, which, without the aid of geological science, to the eye of common observation and reason, had once been the bottom of a sea or the bed of a river. . . . The valley varied from four to eight miles in breadth, and on each side were high, dark, and barren mountains, bounding it like a wall. On the left were the mountains of Judea, and on the right those of Seir . . . ; and among them, buried from the eyes of strangers, the approach to it known only to the wandering Bedouins, was the ancient capital of this kingdom, the [partially] excavated city of Petra . . . lay before me, in barrenness and desolation; no trees grew in the valley, and no verdure on the mountain tops. All was bare, dreary, and desolate.[12]

What Stephens could not see from the back of an Arabian horse— and what I could not spot from a speeding bus—was that the Negev lands north of Eilat were littered with petroglyph-inscribed boulders and pockmarked with a scatter of hidden cisterns and "chains of wells." The Nabataeans controlled the Frankincense Trails by virtue of the intimate knowledge of where the scant supplies of water might be found along the routes from southern Yemen to the Levant.

The Nabataeans and their Idumean neighbors were among the finest desert hydrologists and geomorphologists the world has ever known. The hidden waters of the desert seldom eluded them. Even in the seemingly hostile moonscape of Machtesh Ramon, the largest natural crater in the Nabataean kingdom, they found the artesian flows of Ayn Zaharan, the water source now known among the Jews as Ein Saharonim. If the Nabataeans could control access to freshwater, the most precious and scarce substance on the entire Arabian Peninsula, they knew that they would control its spice trade. They would have made good nanotechnologists, for they were fascinated by the little things that could leverage large gains in wealth.

Only through the use of aerial photography have archaeologists been able to realize how richly the Nabataeans had transformed the Negev into a network of signposts marking trade routes and outposts replete with freshwater reserves. The signposts take the form of isolated boulders and cliff faces where Nabataeans scratched their pale messages into the dark desert varnish that had accumulated over the millennia. These messages were mostly left in their Kufic-like script, but it appears that others were left in Safaitic, Thamudic, Aramaic, and even Greek alphabets, for perhaps they were used as "code languages" by Nabataean

FIGURE 7. Wells in extremely arid landscapes such as the Negev were critical to keeping Nabataean traders alive. (Courtesy Library of Congress Prints and Photographs Division, www.loc.gov/pictures/item/mpc2004005723/PP.)

polyglots. Some of their signs are directional, such as "Go east, over the ridge and into the wadi for water." Others document a missed rendezvous: *Sa'id ma shaf Sud* plaintively reports that "Sa'id didn't get to see his friend Sud" after all the work it took to arrange and attempt an ill-fated reunion.[13]

By 50 CE, these signposts also pointed to another, unprecedented set of developments in the Negev: islandlike vineyards, orchards, and flood-water fields of fodder and staple crops.

Yes, crops. As noted earlier, at first, all Nabataeans adhered to a taboo against cultivating the soil; instead, they traded, raided, herded, or reaped the wild harvests that the desert offered. Although they flourished because of their tenacious control of certain trade routes, it was perhaps inevitable that the Romans and others would try to capture or circumvent those routes. At some point during the first century CE, anticipating that the larger armies and arsenals of the Romans might bear down on their trade centers, the Nabataeans lifted their self-imposed ban on farming. They then used their extensive knowledge of water harvesting to grow crops in some of the driest places that agriculture has ever been practiced. To avoid domination by their Roman competitors, the Nabataeans began to target their agricultural production to provide the foodstuffs in scarcest supply throughout the Roman Empire. As archaeologist Douglas Comer has explained,

> Wealth from agriculture became more important as what had been a spectacular source of wealth from trade attenuated. For hundreds of years before the time of Christ, the Nabateans enjoyed a virtual monopoly on the trade of spices, incense and other precious goods from Southeast Asia and Africa, transporting them from the southern tip of the Arabian Peninsula to the Mediterranean, over which they were shipped to Rome. Only the Nabateans knew the routes across the Empty Quarter. But beginning with Pompey's war on the pirates in 66 BC, sea lanes were gradually made safer, finally breaking the hold that the Nabateans had on the transportation system of the Arabian Peninsula. . . . [And so, they turned to exporting transportable cereals.] Agricultural producers would have found a ready market in the Roman Empire, which suffered a shortage of grain that has been compared to the chronic shortage of oil throughout much of the developed world.[14]

The Nabataeans suddenly shifted from trade in wild spices and incense to the production and trade of agricultural commodities. They became some of the world's first cereal commodity brokers, holding or dumping grains into markets to profit from drought, plagues, famines, or inflation in one part of the empire or another. They not only offered the grains themselves to the Romans, Greeks, and Persians but also introduced certain cereal-based condiments, such as the fermented balls of barley dough that became widely known as *bunn*.[15]

In some ways, Nabataean grain traders played an economic role much like that of Glencore International, a multinational brokerage firm that today controls a quarter of the world's barley, rape, and sunflower-seed supply and a tenth of its wheat supply. Although Glencore is far from a household word, the transnational firm and its subsidiaries are valued at more than $60 billion and hold assets worth over $79 billion, including half of the world's available copper supply, a third of the aluminum supply, and a quarter of the thermal coal supply. When its shares went public on the London Stock Exchange in the summer of 2011, its chief executive officer made an estimated $9 billion in a matter of weeks. Without Glencore ever actually holding large stores of these commodities in its own facilities for very long, it is, according to Al Jazeera, "profiteering from hunger and chaos." As Chris Hinde, a mining industry analyst, told Al Jazeera's Chris Arsenault, "They are the stockbrokers of the commodities business [that operate] in a fairly secretive world. They are effectively setting the price for some very important commodities."[16]

The Nabataean shift in roles from desert traders, herders, and foragers to irrigation farmers ultimately transformed the desert in which they had lived, but the extent of that transformation was not realized until centuries later. Around 1870, the archaeologist E.H. Palmer began to map the thousands of intentionally shaped mounds of cobbles where grapes once grew—the enigmatic *tuleilat el-anab*.[17] They were moisture catchers, agrohydrological structures that were engineered to condense, capture, and deliver fog and dew to fuel the growth of the vines, wheat, and fruit trees. Not long after Palmer, others discovered lengthy alignments of cobbles that channeled the infrequent storm runoff from square miles of desert down into fertile terraced grain fields on the floodplains.

Just twenty-five miles north of where my bus sped out of Eilat, archaeologists noticed a series of round features on the ground near Ain Ghadian. They looked at first like bomb craters, and then like prayer beads strung on a necklace.[18] It took considerable effort by a desert-soil scientist who had once worked with hydraulic engineers to identify these features and definitively determine their function.

These later Nabataean innovations were clandestine water catchments linked through well-like shafts connected to a horizontal tunnel that tapped into groundwater and harvested rainwater and stored them both in underground cisterns. The scientist who discovered their efficacy and extent, Berel Aisenstein, referred to these ingenious Nabataean creations as "artificial springs."[19] These chains of wells were so effective in providing a steady flow of fresh drinking water that Nabataeans were able to survive in areas that received as little as a single inch of rainfall in a drought year! They are called *qanats* in several Semitic languages, and that term may be at the root of a tree of words now widely used in water management. The related words *canal, channel, cane,* and *alcantarilla* are in use around the globe.[20]

I knew that such water-harvesting techniques had also been employed by the Nabataeans some one hundred miles away from Eilat, in the canyons where their capital of Petra was wedged into a mountain range accessible only through a slot canyon. But just how could a prehistoric city of twenty thousand to thirty thousand inhabitants ever be supported by a climate this dry? Certainly, spices did not suffice. Man cannot live on cinnamon, saffron, or sage alone. The average annual rainfall recorded in the Negev varied from three to nine inches among sites, and from one to thirteen inches among years. As I considered the possibilities for self-sufficiency there from a farmer's perspective, I realized that was not much to work with to support a family, let alone a civilization.

Of course, the answer depends on what is meant by "support." The Nabataeans did indeed improvise some astonishing means of securing water and food from wadis that ran with floods only a few times each year, and they did so through hydraulic public works projects paid for by the profits from their spice trade. Perhaps with labor provided by the newcomers to their mercantile culture, they moved thousands of tons of stone, built water catchments, and hid their drinking water cisterns in ways that amazed travelers who accidentally stumbled on them.

After centuries of lucrative trading, they had gained enough wealth to employ countless workers to lay out rock alignments and construct check dams that harvested the runoff from the stony slopes of ridges, funneling it into their fertile floodplain fields, thereby "multiplying" the rainfall available to their plots of arable land. In these ways, they were apparently able to grow enough dates, stone fruits, figs, grains, and legumes to keep their camel drovers and warriors well nourished.

But they were also growing a highly stratified society, as most nations with a wealthy mercantile class have done since that time. Unfortunately, they had taken up fixed abodes and invested considerable infrastructure in certain caravansaries, which made them more vulnerable to forces competing for control of the spice and incense trade.

As with the Minaeans, it was not primarily their local food production that supported the development of their sophisticated culture. Instead, it was the wealth and bargaining power they accumulated as the preeminent traders in the entire Middle East during their era. They rigorously managed all spice trade along several routes, each with its own string of hidden outposts. Their franchises of protected caravansaries stretched from the oases of Yemen, down through Yathrib, and on to Gaza, Petra, and Mount Houran. Through them, for a moment in time, the Nabataeans gained control of the price of frankincense, labdanum, cumin, cinnamon, and other aromatics all the way up to Rome and Athens, despite some initially futile attempts by the Romans and Greeks to wrest control away from them.

Ultimately, when a well-equipped Roman army swarmed into the oasis of Egra on the Red Sea coast, the entire Nabataean army was devastated while attempting to fend off the invaders, and their trade monopoly was dissipated. By 80 CE, the Nabataeans had permanently lost their exclusive access to Yemen's bounty because they had become far too dependent on a single source of wealth. The Romans realized that they could easily establish alternative trade routes that altogether circumvented the Nabataean kingdom.[21] Within a matter of decades, the Romans had annexed Nabataea and Idumaea, and the Nabataean identity gradually withered and died. It is therefore quite remarkable that more than six centuries later, Persian cookbook writer Ibn Sayyār al-Warrāq attributed certain hearty stews of Syrian Christians to their ancestors among the Nabataeans, calling the recipes *nabātiyyāt*.[22]

But until that moment in time, the Nabataeans had greatly profited from the wealth developing in the city-states of Mediterranean Europe, just as today's Latin American cartels ultimately depend on drug addicts with access to the wealth of the north. The Roman elite had become obsessed with the fragrance of frankincense and other precious aromatics, squandering much of their gross metropolitan product on purchase. According to economic historian William J. Bernstein, the Romans wrapped up a considerable portion of their wealth in the conspicuous consumption of aromatics: "A significant part of the Roman booty went toward the purchase of incense. . . . Alongside the sacrificial altar, standing on a tripod, was the *acera* in which frankincense was placed. So central was the burning of this aromatic to Roman ritual that it was admitted into the empire duty-free, in contrast to the 25 percent duty on most other imports."[23]

Although many history books credit the Greeks and Romans with being the primary sculptors of Western civilization, perhaps it was really the Nabataeans who exercised the greatest control over the world trade of the era. They also influenced culinary practices and demonstrated a remarkable capacity to access the rest of the world's treasures. And yet, except for their graffiti casually left as petroglyphs on the boulders of the Negev's regs, we know very little about the private and spiritual lives of these Semitic spice traders. It can only be conjectured that the earliest-recognized Nabataeans worshipped multiple gods, including the sun god Dushara and the fertility goddess al-Lāt. Both of these deities were first recorded among the Arab tribe known as the Banu Thaqif. But as the Nabataeans became more conversant in the Aramaic language and its sensibilities, it appears that their religion was transformed into one that was more monotheistic.

They soon realized that their own practice of any religion could be linked to making social and political alliances that could then provide them with more economic opportunities. As their territory expanded into Idumaea and they established trade partnerships with the Jews, the Nabataeans converted to Judaism. Later still—after 70 CE and the fall

ᛥ NABĀTIYYĀT ᛤ
Nabataean Chicken, Pasta, and Garbanzo Bean Stew

As Charles Perry notes in the foreword to Lilia Zaouali's *Medieval Cuisine of the Islamic World*, *nabātiyyāt* literally refers to the soups, stews, and other dishes of the ancient Nabataeans, as passed down and refined by Arab and Persian chefs. Zaouali's text goes on to explain that this particular recipe was recorded by Ibn Sayyār al-Warrāq in the second half of the tenth century, but it clearly goes back to the Nabataean era between the fourth century BCE and the second century CE. Although the popular but erroneous assumption persists that pasta was introduced by Marco Polo from China to the Middle East and Europe, Iran-born cookbook author Najmieh Batmanglij observes that various forms of pasta appear to have been documented in Mesopotamia and Persia far earlier than that. Pasta then spread eastward into Central Asia and China.

The *itriya* pasta mentioned here was likely made from durum wheat (although emmer was probably used as well), which was cracked and then mixed with water, aniseeds, and salt into a thick paste. The paste was then extruded into thin strands, much like angel hair pasta, and the strands were twisted into nests before drying. Al Taie notes that this pasta is still made in Oman. A similar Italian pasta called *tria* survives in Calabria and Sicily, and an Egyptian one known as *treyya* is found in settlements along the Nile. The use of legumes and pasta together to thicken the broth reminds me of Moroccan *harira* and *chorba*. The true distinctiveness of this particular stew, however, is the addition of rose water in the final stages, which succeeds in ratcheting up all of its flavors several notches.

Spikenard, an aromatic herb from the Himalayas, was commonly used in Roman times as a culinary flavoring. Long pepper, which originated in India and was also a popular ingredient in the Roman kitchen, is sold as small dried whole fruits. Related to the common peppercorn, the fruits release piperine when ground, the same pungent alkaloid found in pepper. During the era in which this recipe emerged, the chicken would likely have been grilled over charcoal. To achieve a smoky flavor reminiscent of that traditional preparation, brown the chicken on your backyard grill, rather than on the stove top. To add additional flavor to this dish, once you have boned the chickens, make a broth from the bones and use it in place of the water added to the crushed beans and chicken.

Accompany the stew with a platter of spinach or mustard greens sautéed with pearl onions and porcini mushrooms in olive oil. *Serves 6 to 8.*

1 cup dried garbanzo beans
2 tablespoons fresh lemon juice
6 cups water
¼ cup olive oil

2 whole chickens, 7 to 8 pounds total weight, boned and cut into large pieces (or equivalent amount of chicken thighs)
1 white onion, chopped
1 cinnamon stick (not cassia)
½ teaspoon black peppercorns
½ teaspoon white peppercorns
½ teaspoon long pepper
1 teaspoon coriander seeds
1 teaspoon whole cloves
1 teaspoon sea salt
1 teaspoon freshly grated or ground nutmeg
1 teaspoon ground galangal, or 1/2-inch piece fresh galangal, peeled and finely chopped
1 teaspoon peeled and finely minced fresh ginger
¼ teaspoon culinary-grade spikenard oil, or 1 teaspoon fresh spikenard root, peeled and finely minced
2 cups rose water
3 to 4 ounces dried pasta nests such as anise-flavored *itriya, tria,* angel-hair pasta, or other herb-infused thin pasta noodles
5 eggs, hard boiled, peeled, and sliced
4 ounces pecorino or other aged sheep cheese, sliced

In a bowl, combine the garbanzo beans with water to cover and stir in the lemon juice. Allow to soak for 8 to 24 hours at room temperature or, if preferred, in the refrigerator. Drain, rinse, and transfer to a pot. Add the water, place over medium-high heat, and bring to a boil. Turn down the heat to medium-low and simmer gently, uncovered, until the beans are very tender and soft, 2½ to 3 hours. Drain the beans and crush with a metal or wooden spoon until a rough paste forms.

Pour the olive oil into a soup pot or Dutch oven and place over medium heat. When the oil is hot, working in batches, add the chicken pieces and brown on all sides. Using a slotted spoon, transfer to a plate. When all of the chicken is browned, add the onion to the oil remaining in the pot and sauté over medium heat until translucent, about 5 minutes. Add the crushed beans and cinnamon stick and return the chicken to the pot. Pour in just enough water to cover the chicken and beans and bring to a simmer. Adjust the heat to maintain a gentle simmer and cook until the chicken is tender, 30 to 45 minutes.

Meanwhile, in a mortar, combine the black and white peppercorns, long pepper, coriander, and cloves and grind finely with a pestle (or use a spice grinder). Stir in the salt.

When the chicken is tender, add the ground spices, nutmeg, galangal, ginger, spikenard, and rose water to the pot and stir well. Bring to a boil, toss in the noodles, stir just to combine, and cook until the noodles are al dente.

Using a large spoon, transfer the chicken and noodles to a deep-sided platter and pour the broth remaining in the pot over them. Arrange the egg and cheese slices around the edge of the platter and serve.

Al Taie, Lamees Abdullah. *Al-Azaf: The Omani Cookbook.* Muscat: Oman Bookshop, 1995, p. 48.

Batmanglij, Najmieh. *Silk Road Cooking: A Vegetarian Journey.* Washington, DC: Mage Publishers, 2002, p. 14.

Perry, Charles. Foreword to *Medieval Cuisine of the Islamic World: A Concise History with 174 Recipes,* by Lilia Zaouali. Translated by M.B. DeBevoise. Berkeley: University of California Press, 2007, p. x.

Zaouali, Lilia. *Medieval Cuisine of the Islamic World: A Concise History with 174 Recipes.* Translated by M.B. DeBevoise. Berkeley: University of California Press, 2007, 119–20.

of the Temple in Jerusalem—some of them became Christians, hoping perhaps that this change would facilitate their trade with the Catholic elite of Rome. And yet, as time went on, and their own language gradually returned to its Arabic roots, their writing and bartering in Aramaic were abandoned, and their descendants converted to Islam.

The Nabataeans had become shape-shifters, first nomadic herders and foragers, then pirates, then skippers of ships, then merchants, and then cereal commodity speculators and public-works administrators. Within a matter of centuries, they changed their beliefs from pantheism to polytheism to monotheism, perhaps to secure stronger social relationships with power brokers along their trade routes and their destination points. They learned and absorbed other languages and sequentially adopted Judaism, Christianity, and then Islam. Up until their final era, each time that they outwardly shifted religions, they gained opportunities to strengthen their intercontinental trade alliances.

They had learned to put a "spin" on the stories of the spices they marketed, and in doing so, perhaps they learned to do a makeover of their own lives and beliefs whenever it seemed needed. In fact, they may have been among the first great cultures on the planet to succumb to the mind games of economically driven spin doctors. Incense and other psychotropic plants were the medications they offered to placate the masses.

Those masses, for the most part, were situated in the coastal ports of the Mediterranean and the marshlands of Mesopotamia. I have been particularly struck by the abundance of archival documents from Rome and Athens that confirm that frankincense, pepper, and cinnamon were not merely the curios of the elite.[24] Nearly every household in these city-states regularly burnt incense, if only to disperse the horrendous scents that emanated from the bodies of the seldom bathed, the butcher shops, and the sewage reservoirs. Heavenly scents kept the masses from being constantly repulsed by the stench and stupor of their everyday labors. Just as the urban poor today may purchase cell phones or designer jeans as status symbols, whether they can afford them or not, the poor of the ancient Mediterranean sought out fragrances, flavors, and infusions to assert their worldliness even as these extravagances drained them of their little wealth.

It came to be understood, at least by a few, that trade can impoverish, just as surely as it can enhance or enrich. Julius Caesar himself attempted in vain to regulate the Roman culture of excess that was consuming his empire's wealth. He went so far as to send out SWAT teams of food and incense police into markets and private homes to ferret out those who were so fixated on conspicuous consumption that they were not only bankrupting themselves but the empire as well.[25]

Of course, I had arrived in this dry land far too late for a chance to speak to Nabataean traders about their notion of globalization, or to hear them articulate their marketing strategies for spices. But I could, through the glass darkly, see how their legacies have continued to spin in the souks of Jerusalem.

The bus had begun to climb up out of the Negev, past the Dead Sea, and into the better-watered hills of Jerusalem and Bethlehem. When it arrived at last in the so-called Holiest of Cities, Father Dave and I found a place to stay, and then I set out on foot to its oldest quarters, the ones that Nabataean traders had once frequented. At least eight hundred merchants still hawk their wares within the Old City.

The walls surrounding the Old City were completed in 1538, but some of the sections of cut stone were first put into place more than two thousand years ago. Walking through the Damascus Gate, the north-facing entrance to the Christian and Muslim quarters, I went down some stairs and along Souk Khan Ez-Zeit Street until I arrived at Souk al-Attarin, the market where spice trade had occurred in Jerusalem for the longest duration.

There were virtually no spices to be seen. The site had become populated by dry-goods vendors, with their stalls full of sneakers, sandals, satchels, and duffle bags.

I moved away from the stacks of factory-made materials and meandered down the crowded paths of the Christian Quarter until I spotted the Church of the Holy Sepulchre. Regaining my orientation, I turned toward the three stone arches forming the entry to Souk Aftimos, once reputed to be the largest spice emporium in Jerusalem.

I visited one stall after another of Armenian and Jewish spice merchants. They stood behind pyramidal piles of speckled brown *za'atar,* yellow turmeric, beige cumin, and red sumac powder. Some stalls offered thick chunks of incense, not only frankincense and myrrh, but jasmine and rose and specialty blends mixed on the spot to satisfy the customer's desire.

But these improvisational spice blenders were few and far between. Most of the vendors offered prepackaged "souvenirs" of three to four kinds of incense, hermetically sealed in cellophane or plastic bags and embedded in carry-on-the-plane boxes branded as "Jerusalem incense" or "gifts of the Magi." Needless to say, I could not smell a thing through all the layers of protective packaging. I noticed that most of the tourists took digital photos of the spice vendors and gave them cheap tips, but few took any spices and incense back home with them. Instead, they headed toward the Jewish Quarter, where the "real" souvenirs were: Dead Sea body-care products and olive oil soaps, Jesus sandals and Druse hand bags, anointing oils, postcards, and T-shirts. Most were made in China, but that did not seem to bother the shoppers. These were the items most sought after by the million or so "religious tourists" who venture into the Old City in the average year.

The only fresh "spice" I found in the Old City that day was growing on its ancient walls. A sprawling caper plant towered over all of the tourists, who rarely acknowledged its persistence.

Except for the next morning, when I had a joyful foraging excursion for capers, sage, sumac, mustard seeds, pine nuts, and wild pistachios in the Ben-Gurion Urban Forest with chef Moshe Basson, I felt a palpable tension wherever I went in Jerusalem. So I made my way to Bethlehem in the West Bank not so much for a change in scenery as for a break from the Old City's intensity. Although Bethlehem is merely six miles from the heart of Jerusalem, it took me nearly two hours to get through the traffic-riddled streets and the road blocks and checkpoints to reach the edge of the area's "other" sacred city.

It was there that I met Marwan, a Palestinian seed trader and nurs-

The primary product of the spiny, arid-adapted caper bush (*Capparis spinosa* var. *spinosa*) is an unopened flower bud, and a somewhat sharp, astringent, palate-punishing one at that. To rid the buds of their bitterness, they are cured in salt or pickled in a salt and vinegar brine. Once cured, the capric acid, quercetin, and kaempferol in the buds (the latter two are flavonoids) generate a powerful fragrance in the never-to-fully-bloom flowers.

The caper bush also yields berries, the mature fruits of the plant. Like the flower buds, the delicately ribbed, olive green, teardrop-shaped berries are cured to reduce their pungency and then used in many of the same ways. Both the buds and the berries are harvested on islands and along coastlines around the Mediterranean, but the berries have never experienced the demand beyond their home ground that the buds have enjoyed. The tiniest buds, despite their size and ephemeral nature, command the highest prices around the world. Italy, Morocco, Spain, and Turkey serve as the largest producers.

Capers appear in archaeological records from the Mediterranean to southern Russia, but their prehistoric use did not extend much farther east than Turkey and the Levant. It appears that the Arabic term *al-kabar,* or perhaps even an older form from some other Semitic language such as Phoenician or Nabataean, has become *the* loan word into most other languages in which these buds and berries are known. In Turkish, we hear *kapari;* in Hindi, *kobra* or *kabra;* in Japanese, *keipa;* in Italian, *cappero;* in Portuguese, *alcaparra;* and so on. There may have been direct diffusion of this semicultivated plant, its curing techniques, and its consumption from the earliest Semitic spice traders to the rest of the known world.

Capers love ruins. I have seen the bushes growing feral among the stones of Baalbek in the Bekáa Valley of Lebanon; in Jerusalem's Old City, twining up light posts outside the Arab Quarter; in Athens, crawling up the walls of the Parthenon; and in Andalusia, spreading along the garden walkways of the Alhambra. I was most surprised to find them in the ruins of the ancient city of Jiaohe in the Taklimakan Desert of western China, where they have become the most dominant plants within the nearly forgotten two-thousand-year-old metropolis.

ery manager who had some of the most desert-adapted traditional spice and vegetable seeds remaining in all of the Middle East. He called them seeds of the *biladi*—"of the country and its peasantry"—true heirlooms of the desert, passed down from hand to hand for generations. Marwan was a quiet man, more prone to speak of plant prop-

There is, in fact, an Asian caper that is recognized by botanists as a distinct variety (*C. spinosa* var. *mariana*). It is native to India, Pakistan, and Southeast Asia, but I am not familiar enough with it to know whether it is what I actually encountered in western China, or whether the Persians and Arabs had brought their own caper with them when they settled at the far eastern reaches of the Silk Roads.

I first saw caper vines being cultivated under fruit trees at food historian Mary Simeti's farm in central Sicily. There they grew scandent, that is, they had become shrublike at their bases, but then twined up the trunks of trees like true vines. Giuseppe Barbera, a Sicilian agronomist friend of Mary's, told me that capers had long been one of the most precious commodities shipped from Sicily to the rest of the world. No Sicilian American can visit the homeland without hiding a package of this high-priced delicacy in his or luggage on leaving, and so, I kid my Sicilian friends that long before their mafioso neighbors smuggled drugs, they smuggled capers! I remain envious of Mary's biodynamically grown caper bushes, for each time I have tried to transplant caper seedlings into the limestone soils of my own orchard, they have withered and died after a few weeks, perhaps for the lack of Mediterranean breezes and their humidity.

Capers are used in all kinds of sauces for meats, fish, and fowl, including *pescado a la veracruzana,* which speaks to Andalusian, Moorish, and Lebanese influences in colonial Mexico; the *picadillos* found throughout Latin America and Spain, *salsa puttanesca* in Italy, and the rémoulades found in Acadian, Cajun, and Creole cuisines. In France, capers flavor Montpellier butter, and in Slovakia, Hungary, and Austria, they join onions, herbs, and other flavorings in Liptauer cheese. In Greece, Crete, and Cypress, they seem to garnish nearly every kind of salad and are added to a wide range of sauces. In Lebanon and Palestine, they are ever-present among the many mezes, and if a cook there ever runs out of capers, he or she can simply go out to the closest stone wall and immediately retrieve a few for the next dish.

Green, Aliza. *Field Guide to Herbs and Spices.* Philadelphia: Quirk Books, 2006.
Katzer, Gernot. "Gernot Katzer's Spice Pages." http://gernot-katzers-spice-pages.com/engl/index.html. Accessed September 1, 2011.
Weiss, E.A. *Spice Crops.* Wallingford, UK: CABI Publishing, 2002.

agation than of geopolitics, but one topic inevitably spilled over into the other.

"These *biladi* seeds can grow with our scant rainfall. . . . Sure, I select them for quality, but they have been with us here for hundreds of years. It is necessary that they can grow without much irrigation, you know, because our water lines are regularly cut off by the Isray-eli soldiers. The groundwater has been pumped out from beneath us, and at most we are left to use sewage to keep our fruit trees and crop plants alive. But even if these seeds can survive on minimal water, I hardly have any customers anymore to buy them."

"No customers?" I asked. I looked at the beautiful quality of his seeds. "For good desert-adapted herbs and spices like these? Have all the farmers and gardeners left Palestine?"

Marwan looked tired. He was quiet for a moment. Then he replied with barely a whisper: "I am afraid you don't understand. Farmers still try but they don't make money. Even if their plants survive until the harvest with the little water we have, well . . . The farmers here would load them on their trucks early in the morning to take them toward the market in Jerusalem, but they would be stopped at the checkpoints . . . And they would sit there in the traffic, unable to move, waiting to move up to be inspected. Sit and sit, hardly moving . . . the salad greens, the herbs, they wither . . . "

He sighed, looking pained, then continued. "Sometimes the farmers have been forced to wait so long that their entire truckload of produce rots while they are in line. They come back discouraged. They give up on being farmers, and they no longer buy my seeds."

I said farewell to Marwan and left his seed shop and nursery saddened, humbled. I decided that I must see where Bethlehem's Church of the Nativity stands, for it is one of the oldest continuously operated Christian churches in the world. But in all the clutter of gift shops and bus parking lots, I found it hard to imagine what this place might have looked like some two thousand years ago, around 4 BCE, when some foreigners guided by a star—possibly magicians or astrologers who also carried incense—arrived on camels from some distant land to look for a newborn baby.

An ancient text recently translated from Syriac suggests that these Magi were not necessarily three Zoroastrian "wise men" from Persia, but an entire caravan of magicians or shamans originally from Shir, a land in the Far East, by the sea.[26] They came westward during the era of Herod the Great, an Idumaean Jew who had been born of a Nabataean mother. There are few clues about who these visitors to Herod's land actually were, but we have been left with a couple of recognizable names for them that were recorded in Syriac. One of them was called Gudaphar (or Gandapor), almost certainly from a surname long used within the Indo-Parthian kingdom on the northeast side of the Arabian

Sea. It was a country where Aramaic and Greek as well as Sanskrit and Pali were spoken over the centuries, and where both Zoroastrian and Buddhist influences spread along the southern routes of the Silk Road.

The Syriac text recently translated as *Revelation of the Magi* includes no mention of frankincense and myrrh being offered as gifts from the East. And yet, these aromatics were clearly in currency in northern reaches of the Arabian Sea, and perhaps as far east as the North China Sea during that era. Such aromatics would have been valued gifts of their day, whether brought by land or sea.

If they did indeed arrive in Bethlehem in 4 BCE, they arrived at a time when the trading of aromatics was spanning the far reaches of the known world, from China, Morocco, India, and Socotra to Zanzibar in present-day Tanzania and the Lamu Archipelago off the coast of Kenya. It was a moment in history when both land and sea trade in aromatics was ushering in an era of truly unprecedented globalization. Intercontinental trade had already become the norm, not the exception. It depended, in large part, on people's fascination with "the exotic" as a way to escape the drudgery and redundancy of their own increasingly domesticated lives. The spice trade had become a means to capitalize on a kind of psychic hunger that was developing within various civilizations scattered around the world, a craving that came less from an empty stomach and more from a dissatisfied mind.

CHAPTER 4

Omanis Rocking the Cradle
of Civilization

It is late spring, and I find myself on the shores of the Gulf of Oman, walking around Sohar Fort with my friend Sulaiman Al-Khanjari. I approach the fort's pale, stuccoed walls, which have been plastered with lime year after year over the centuries. They rise above me nearly as high as the date palms planted alongside them. It is a hot, sunny day and the brilliant sheen on both the sea and the snow white walls of the fort nearly blind me with their intensity.

Sulaiman must see that I am squinting. He beckons me to follow him, and so I walk down a cobblestone stairway to where he is standing in the shade of a wall covered with deep green bougainvillea vines punctuated with blood red flowers. I duck into the shade with him and turn to face a low stone wall surrounding a hole in the ground. I let my eyes adjust to the shadows, and then open them widely to take a look around.

A crowd has aggregated around an Arab historian who is waving his arms and pointing to a protected pit, explaining to a group of students that it is the site of an earlier archaeological excavation. "Come here and listen," Sulaiman whispers to me. "I'll try to translate what he is saying." I huddle near him, glad to be in the shade.

"If the Gulf of Oman is the ancient cradle of navigation, Sohar is one of the first ports from which our navigators departed. . . . The ancient stone-walled port was another two hundred yards out past the fort, but it was destroyed by the storms. By the tenth century, Muslim geographer al-Istakhri called it 'the greatest seaport of Islam,' for it was situated in the largest and wealthiest trading hub on the east coast of the Arabian Peninsula. Portions of the present Sohar Fort that we stand within were built by the people of Hormuz in the thirteenth or early fourteenth century to hold soldiers who would protect the now-destroyed harbor. But well before that—during the Nebhani dynasty—the harbor was used for trading copper and spices for wood for shipbuilding."

"The Nebhani dynasty?" I ask.

"It extended from the mid-twelfth century to the end of the fifteenth century. That's when your ancestors, you know, the Banu Nebhani, controlled this port, ruling this region. Of course, trade activity at this site preceded them, and probably even preceded the building of the first fort, around the first century CE. Let's listen."

"It seems that some seafarers . . . they began around here as early as 3000 BCE, with the boats at first hugging close to the coast. The earliest written manuscripts from this coast were from the era of King Abi Sin [who ruled from 2029 to 2006 BCE].[1] They document the trade of copper and incense from Magan [Oman] for wood from Mesopotamia and spices from India. Later on, maritime trade expanded to cross the gulf, the sea, the ocean. Here, right below us, in the lowest levels of later forts constructed on this site, they have found Chinese porcelain, perhaps carried from India. For centuries, not only Arab traders were harbored here but Jewish ones, as well. In fact, some of the names we think of as Muslim may have been Jewish to begin with, and then were modified slightly when the people converted to Islam."

"But the Omanis then, like now, didn't stay put."

Sulaiman smiles, clearly having shifted from translating to offering his own commentary. "My own family has roots in East Africa, where Omanis have been involved in the spice trade of Zanzibar for millennia. Others, like your Nebhani ancestors, settled in the Lamu Archipelago off the coast of Kenya. Omanis historically established their own colonies in India, Iran, Pakistan, Abyssinia, Zanzibar, and perhaps Madagascar. Yes, many were spice traders."

"Was frankincense traded up through ports this far north in Oman, or was it all through al-Balid in Dhofar Province to the south?"

"Well, if you look at old maps, there were several inland trade routes from the land of frankincense all the way up through what we now call northern Oman. Everyone thinks they know the Frankincense Trail, which they describe as running from Sanaa and Ma'rib in Yemen, up through Mecca and Yathrib to Petra, and then to Jerusalem or

FIGURE 8. These ruins of an ancient Omani trading center in the desert below the Jabal al-Akhdar plateau are reminders of the vagaries of trade-route use over centuries. (Photo by the author.)

Alexandria. But there were other routes for the caravans as well—many different routes—even ones that ventured across absolutely barren parts of the Rub' al-Khali. Here, we had one that ran somewhere up the east coast of the peninsula from Dhofar to Muscat and Nizwa—I'm not sure where exactly—and then it went on to Ibri and Yabrin and to Basra and Baghdad.

"I don't think it would run right along the coast, for fear of pirates. Instead, it was hidden back in the interior, so that the goods could be protected in fortified oases such as Bahla. Then, when they were ready to take their goods to sea, whether it was copper, leather, or *hojari* incense, they would caravan them out to ports like Sohar."

I close my eyes again, trying to make sense of all of this. Seafaring relatives. Inland hideaways. Ancestors with connections to islands off the coast of Africa. I am humbled by how little I know of the roots of my own bloodline.[2]

Although the Omani kingdom of Magan had its own indigenous Semitic tribes, including some that early on practiced a form of Judaism, it accommodated other Semitic peoples as well, mostly immigrants from

Yemen. These Yemeni Semites included those who had moved north-ward in droves after a breaching of the Ma'rib dam on Wadi Adhanah in the second half of the third century CE.[3]

It is possible that my own clan, the Banu Nebhani, may have been part of this diaspora, as they had first fled to the highlands of Jabal al-Akhdar to get as far above flood-prone ground as an Arab could possibly reach. It would be naive to assume that they had simply left Yemen of their own volition, for the entire balance among nomadic herders and incense foragers, traders and oasis farmers had convulsively and irrevocably shifted around them, prompting many tribes to flee at the same time. It appears that whenever the loose symbiosis between nomadic forager-herders and sedentary agriculturalists was stressed by natural or political pressures, something innovative and unusual began to emerge out of these demographic upheavals.

The breaching of the Ma'rib dam in the third century sent many of the original Arabic tribes out across the rest of the Middle East to find new homes or even new occupations.[4] These refugees included both nomadic herders and the more sedentary al-Hadr clans that once farmed the larger irrigated oases like those surrounding the agricultural hub of Ma'rib along Wadi Adhanah. The spread of irrigated agriculture across the Middle East and beyond is sometimes attributed to the diffusion wrought by these al-Hadr tribes, who, from the late fourth millennium onward, had been constantly refining their techniques for using canals to water crops.

Once these people left their ancestral homelands in Yemen for good, it is clear that they kept on moving, and they did not restrict their movements to land masses. As soon as they mastered marine navigation, they stepped out into the wider world and seldom returned to their natal grounds. The harbors of Oman became their springboards, and the shipping of aromatics became their mostly widely celebrated trade.

While the Phoenicians had perfected their navigation skills in the Red Sea and the Mediterranean before venturing farther, the seafaring Arabs out of Oman and Persians from Basra focused first on the Persian Gulf and the Indian Ocean and then on the Horn of Africa. Of course, Gujarati, Hindu, and Serendip sailors had already been sailing these waters and trading with one another for centuries, and the Arabs built on their maritime experience. They also used their own knowledge of the movements of some forty-eight stars, the placement of thousands of coastal landmarks, and the seasonal shifting of winds to guide them on their way across the seas or along their coasts.[5] They established perma-

nent way stations and spice warehouses in the ports of Africa and Asia
that functioned much the way their caravansaries in the Arabian deserts
had always functioned.

It was in the ports along these coasts that they came on some species
of spices that were far more abundant and valuable than those growing wild in the desert interior. Although the populations of aromatics
of the peninsula were undeniably potent due to their desert upbringing, they were few and far between compared with those of India, Sri
Lanka, the Moluccas, China, Zanzibar, or Madagascar. These culinary
ingredients began to transform the simple cuisine of nomadic herders
into the Middle Eastern cuisines we know today: *laham mishwi*, skewers of spiced lamb or goat meat cooked over wood fires; *hays*, a mix of
dates, curds, and ghee; *tharīd*, unleavened bread crumbled into a simple
savory stew; *khazira*, thin meat broth laced with bran and herbs; and
sariq, a porridge of barley, durum, or emmer wheat.[6]

Thanks to imports from Asia and Africa, such dishes were soon "pep-
pered" with new herbs and spices, sweetened with honey and cane sugar,
and laced with the astringent juices of sour oranges and kaffir limes. In
addition, these newly abundant foodstuffs from other lands became perceived as so luxuriantly exotic that they dazzled nearly all those who
traded with the Omanis, and soon they were lavishly expensive in the
political and economic capitals of the Greek, Roman, Mesopotamian,
and Ptolemaic empires. It was as if the power mongers of Athens, Rome,
Alexandria, Lygos (Byzantium), and Babylon were uncontrollably smit-
ten by the potent aromas and flavors, if only for the enhanced status
they gained through the conspicuous consumption of the fashionable
imports. Today, it is hard to imagine how makeshift camps of herders or
small villages of peasant farmers were able to satisfy the demands of the
city-states for such luxuries and novelties for several centuries running.

The unquenchable thirst of the sedentary gave Omani seafarers more
than enough incentive to venture forth, to learn foreign languages in
order to negotiate directly with spice producers, and to advance their
navigating and provisioning skills so that they could survive months at
sea without suffering from scurvy or being buffeted by cyclonic storms.
Certainly by 100 BCE, and perhaps much earlier, they were regularly
acquiring Chinese goods, if not through purchases in China, perhaps by
meeting the Chinese themselves or their intermediaries on the Malabar
Coast, in Malaysia, or in the Moluccas. The Chinese did not distinguish among Persian and Arab ships when they first encountered them
near the Gulf of Tonkin; they simply referred to them as *shang-hu,* or

"foreign merchants." Black and white pepper, cassia and true cinnamon, nutmeg and mace, star anise and cloves all came into their hands and were stored in their holds. The geographic area from which they extracted aromatics expanded to include the farthest reaches of the known world.

Of course, by this time, various kinds of incense were no longer the only major product lines, nor even the ones determining exactly where most trade routes should run. Asian products such as silk, musk, and medicinal plants had become immensely valuable. Some of these traveled overland from Central Asia by camel to the southern or western ports of India.

Omani Arabs and even the Phoenicians had earlier traveled into the hinterlands by camel caravan to secure such products, but the ease of moving these goods as far as possible by sea began to trump other factors involving trade logistics and costs. Boats were built to be larger, stronger, and swifter; the caravans could never scale up in the same manner by simply increasing the size of load per animal or by recruiting additional donkeys, mules, horses, camels, or elephants. Beasts of burden did not become obsolete, however. Indeed, so-called camel bag teas can still be found in marketplaces today, because the long hours spent in the desert on the back of a camel imbue the tea leaves with an aroma unlike any other!

So it turns out that the question sometimes raised by the historically curious as to whether Arab and Jewish traders first got to China by land or by sea may not be that interesting or revealing. Many of the early (pre-Christian and pre-Islamic) traders from Oman probably used both means of transport on the same trip, as did their Asian counterparts. The trade crew likely included Arabs who practiced some rudimentary form of Judaism, along with others who remained polytheistic, whether guided by multiple gods or by shamanistic encounters with jinn.

The terms *Arab* and *Jew* were not used as mutually exclusive categories, for it appears that various Semitic groups, in addition to the Canaanites, had become followers of Moses (Moshe or Musa), the prophet who came out of Egypt and into Sinai, where he had his revelatory experience. Jewish sailors and traders remained integrated into Arab communities for many more centuries. With the advent of Islam, they, along with early Christians and Sabians, became known as the *dhimmi,* or People of the Book. The *dhimmi* were required to pay a tax to their Muslim hosts in exchange for right of residence and for protection that afforded the opportunity to practice certain rituals otherwise

✴ MAQLAY SAMAK ✴
Fried Fish on a Bed of Coconut Rice

Perhaps no food items give the sense of ancient trade across the Indian Ocean as clearly as spiced fish, rice, coconut milk, lentils, kaffir limes, and young ginger. Indeed, it is hard for newcomers to the Omani coast to know whether they are being served traditional Omani Arabic dishes or recently introduced fare from the many Indian and Pakistani guest workers currently engaged in the food-service industry in the sultanate. From a historical perspective, trade between the Arabian Peninsula and the Indian subcontinent in staple grains, legumes, fruits, dried fish, vegetables, and spices has been going on for so long that the definitions of what is traditional, endemic, or authentic to either landscape are ambiguous at best.

Maqlay samak, which translates simply as "fried fish" in Yemeni Arabic, calls for marinating fish in spice-laden lime juice, frying it, and then serving it on a bed of rice infused with coconut milk. Any coastal white fish, such as bream, mullet, or sea bass, can be used.

A simple side dish of baked eggplant slices marinated in olive oil or of baba ghanoush is a fitting accompaniment. *Serves 4.*

½ cup green lentils
¾ teaspoon fresh lemon juice
1½ cups basmati rice
    Olive oil for sautéing rice
4 cardamom pods, split
    Ghee for frying
1 tablespoon peeled and grated fresh ginger
3 cups coconut milk
1 cup water
    Sea salt
½ teaspoon freshly ground cumin seeds
1 teaspoon freshly ground cardamom seeds
1 teaspoon freshly ground cassia cinnamon
½ teaspoon ground turmeric
    Juice of 2 kaffir limes
1 fish, about 2 pounds, cleaned

In a bowl, combine the lentils with water to cover and stir in the lemon juice. Allow to soak at room temperature for about 7 hours. Drain, rinse, and reserve.

Put the rice in a bowl, add water to cover generously, and swirl the rice around with your fingers until the water is cloudy. Pour off the water, re-cover the rice with water, and swirl the rice again, then drain. Repeat until the rinsing water is clear, then drain the rice well. In a frying pan or wide saucepan, heat a spoonful or so of olive oil over low heat. Add the rice and sauté for a couple minutes, then remove from the heat and set aside. This step ensures the rice grains will not stick together as they cook.

In a dry saucepan, toast the cardamom pods until fragrant, then remove from pan. Add ½ teaspoon ghee to the same pan and heat over medium-high heat. Add the ginger and cook until fragrant. Add the reserved lentils and rice and stir well. Add the coconut milk, water, and cardamom pods and bring to a simmer. Season with salt, turn down the heat to low, cover, and cook until the liquid has been absorbed and the rice and lentils are tender, 30 to 45 minutes. Remove from the heat. Use a spoon to remove the cardamom pods before serving.

About 10 minutes before you put the rice and lentils on to cook, begin preparing the fish. In a shallow bowl large enough to accommodate the fish, combine the cumin, ground cardamom, cinnamon, turmeric, kaffir lime juice, and a pinch of salt and stir well. Let stand until the mixture thickens, at least 10 minutes. Rinse the fish, pat dry, and place in the bowl with the spice mixture, turning the fish to coat it evenly. Let marinate at room temperature for 30 minutes.

Place a frying pan or wok over medium-high heat and brush the surface with ghee. Heat until the ghee is sizzling, then remove the fish from the marinade, add it to the pan, and fry, turning as needed to prevent scorching, until well browned on both sides and the flesh just flakes when prodded with a knife tip, 10 to 12 minutes total. The timing will depend on the thickness of the fish.

Spoon the rice onto a platter, top with the fish, and serve.

Al Taie, Lamees Abdullah. *Al-Azaf: The Omani Cookbook*. Muscat: Oman Bookshop, 1995, pp. 161–62.

prohibited in Muslim communities. This special status of dhimmitude fostered tolerance over most of their shared history, and only began to erode with the rise of secularism in the seventeenth century.

While in Oman, I visited a UNESCO museum that celebrates the trade history of frankincense. There I was surprised to see a copy of an ancient manuscript written by one of the earliest documented Omani spice traders in the East. He was certainly not among the very first involved in the Sino-Arab trade I have just described, for such trade had begun centuries before he was born, but he had nevertheless arrived in China and written of his experiences there by 750, some five hundred years prior to the fanciful accounts of the illiterate Marco Polo, which were put down on paper by one of his prison mates, Rustichello.[7]

The name of Oman's own Polo-like hero has never become a household word in the Arab world, let alone in the West: Obeida bin Abdulla bin al-Qasim. It is not that Arabs refrain from honoring their heroes and pioneers, but rather that Arab scholars know that he was but one of thousands of traders who reached China prior to the arrival of any Europeans. The only reason to single him out, perhaps, is that his record of early China in Arabic has survived intact. But because it is not as captivating as accounts of Asian trade written centuries later by the erudite and immensely colorful Ibn Battuta, it has never been highly regarded outside of Oman. As I looked through the glass of the protective case that held this precious manuscript, I realized that most of the Arabs around me in the museum were not impressed by the document. Indeed, many of them likely considered it run of the mill. Any true Arab scholar of maritime history could probably name a dozen such accounts.

Although the first entry date remains conjecture, it is well established in documents written in second and third person that Arab seafarers from Oman and Yemen were regularly arriving in what we now call Malaysia and perhaps in China by 500, some 250 years before Abu Obeida wrote extensively of his experiences. In the briefer and more casual reports by earlier Arab seafarers, China is known as the Middle Kingdom, perhaps because the Mongols were known to be to the north of them. Well before the adoption and spread of Islam, Omani seafarers (including Jewish merchants) set off from Sohar or Muscat, stopped briefly in Basra near the apex of the Arabian Gulf, and then headed south to Siraf (in present-day Iran) or to Qays, farther south in the Persian Gulf, and on to the Malabar Coast. During this era, the Omani Arabs were not alone in combining overland trade with shipping by sea through the Persian Gulf and Indian Ocean.

The Phoenicians and Persians (or Parthians) were there early on, as were the Chaldeans and Gujaratis. Many of the ports on both sides of the gulf were in fact multicultural and excluded only the Greeks and Romans. Semitic languages, Farsi, and Hindi were all spoken. The caravansaries above harbors like the Chaldean port of Gerrha had to accommodate camels as well as elephants and drovers as well as sailors. Pearls were as common as purple dyes, and central Asian deer musk was as much in demand as Yemeni frankincense. Coriander, cumin, anise, and sesame came in from several directions.

The raw or toasted seeds of *Sesamum indicum* offer a pleasantly sharp, somewhat nutty flavor that favors their use as both a spice and a cooking oil. In fact, the seeds are 60 percent oil by weight, and the sesame plant may be the source of the world's first cultivated oil seed, having been domesticated on the Indian subcontinent well before the written records of all Eurasian and African civilizations. An annual herb with lovely tubular flowers, it produces small, teardrop-shaped seeds that come in all shades of white, beige, pale red, brown, and jet black.

Most of the wild relatives of sesame are found in Africa, but one particular wild ancestor, *S. orientale* var. *malabaricum,* is restricted to the Indian subcontinent. The oldest sesame seeds found in an archaeological context come from the Indus Valley site at Harappa, now in Pakistan, which dates back four thousand to forty-six hundred years. This discovery appears to indicate that sesame was domesticated more than four and a half millennia ago somewhere on the Indian subcontinent, and probably spread from there to Mesopotamia within five hundred years (2000 BCE). Sesame seeds were pressed into the only oil used by the Babylonians, and reached the Egyptians by 1500 BCE. By 200 BCE, sesame had been grown in China long enough to become a prevalent crop. Curiously, much of the remaining diversity of sesame's ancient varieties occurs between India and China. The many Chinese varieties spread westward into Central Asia along the Silk Roads. And of course, black sesame seeds coat many forms of sushi in both Japan and the United States.

My fellow ethnobotanist and long-time friend Dorothea Bedigian has called sesame a *wanderwort,* for various forms of its name became so widespread through early trade that it is difficult to establish its linguistic origin. Oddly, sesame seems to have come out of the Malabar Coast to reach Mesopotamia during the Early Bronze Age as *taila* or *tila,* a generic term in ancient Sanskrit that was used in northern India to refer to the oiliness of any seed. Along the same line, the Akkadian term *šamaššammû* means "oily" or "fatty seed." The later related Assyrian term *shaman shammi* may have given rise to the Aramaic *shumshema* (also written as *šumšêm*), the ancient Arabic *as-samn,* and the modern Arabic *as-simsim.* The Hebrew term, *sumsum,* is similar. All connote oily seeds.

Today's Modern Persian *konjed* is derived from the Middle Persian *kunjid,* which may have its roots in the classic Armenian *küncüt* or the Turkic *künji.* The related Hindi *gingi* may echo the rattle of the seeds in their dried capsules, as well. It may also be related to the ancient Arabic noun for "echo," *jaljala,* which undoubtedly gave rise to the Spanish *ajonjoli* and the Maltese *gulglien.*

In the eastern reaches of its historical range, the Chinese terms *hu ma*, or "foreign hemp," and *zhima*, or "oily hemp," have long been used. In Africa, *benne, benniseed*, and similar words are used in many dialects and languages, and in the southern United States, *benne* continues to refer to sesame plants as a cover crop and wildlife forage.

The nuttiness of the tiny waferlike seeds is intensified by toasting, and there are sesame oils for those who enjoy that intensity and those who do not. The oil pressed from the untoasted seeds is pale but fragrant and is good for baking and for stir-frying and other high-heat cooking because it has a high smoke point. Toasted sesame oil, which is amber and has a robust flavor, is ideal for dressing salads or for adding to already-cooked dishes. It is seldom used for frying, as it has a low smoke point. The third "oil" product from sesame is the viscous paste known as *as-simsim bi tahini* in the Arabic-speaking world and as tahini elsewhere.

One of my earliest memories is of watching my Lebanese grandfather carefully whip tahini together with lemon juice to coat some fish he was frying. When my grandfather died, my father took up this same ritual with equal diligence. Both men regularly gifted me the brittle but delicious candy made from toasted sesame mixed with caramelized sugar that was distributed by the Sahadi family out of Brooklyn, New York. My love for this candy was one of the motivations that prompted me to become a partner in farming sesame amid ten acres of heritage grains and beans in Amado, Arizona.

Crushed and sweetened sesame seeds are used for making another kind of paste that is dried and hardened into the popular confection known as halvah from eastern Anatolia through Lebanon, Syria, Jordan, and Palestine. That same term, however, is used for a broader

At some time prior to 140 BCE, the Chinese themselves had begun to arrive in these Indian and Chaldean ports to trade directly with the Arabs and Jews from Syria, Oman, and Yemen who congregated there. During the Han dynasty, from 206 BCE to 25 CE, Chaldea was known as T'iao-chih by the Chinese and was accessible by both land and sea, with the maritime route taking roughly one hundred days. The Chinese of this era were also familiar with Petra, which they called Li-chien. And yet, it appears that the Tang dynasty Chinese preferred the Semitic seafarers and traders to come to them, for they lamented that "there is something in the sea which is apt to make a man homesick, and several have thus lost their lives."[8]

range of confections—some with sesame and some without—from Egypt through Morocco.

Throughout the Islamic and Jewish worlds, sesame seeds are sprinkled on round breads made with bran—both leavened and unleavened—called *semit*, or in Spanish, *pan de semita*. They remain popular from Turkey through the Levant and to North Africa. During the Spanish Inquisition, the consumption of these breads was officially banned because of their cultural importance to Jews and Muslims in Spain as well as in its Latin American colonies. Of course, the bakers and their sesame bread went underground, only to reemerge in places as distant and divergent as San Antonio, Texas; Magdalena, in Sonora, Mexico; Santa Fe, New Mexico; and San Ignacio, in Baja California, Mexico.

Although Jewish historians have claimed that the presence of sesame-laced *pan de semita* in Mexico and the American Southwest is an indicator of crypto-Jewish presence, this bread could have also been introduced and sustained as a tradition by crypto-Muslims and Catholics descended from the heterogeneous populace of Andalusia. Indeed, one might argue that sesame seeds have accompanied Semitic peoples and others wherever they have migrated. Perhaps I am living evidence of that phenomenon. After occasionally growing a few sesame plants in my garden over the years, in 2011, I grew a small patch of sesame in southern Arizona, as just described, so that its seeds could be offered to artisanal bakers in my own adopted homeland.

Bedigian, Dorothea. "History of the Cultivation and Use of Sesame."
    Introduction to *Sesame: The Genus* Sesamum. Edited by Dorothea
    Bedigian. Boca Raton, FL: CRC Press, 2011.
Gambrelle, Fabienne. *The Flavor of Spices*. Paris: Flammarion, 2008.

What this brief commentary reveals is that while other cultures such as the Chinese may have had immense seafaring capacity as early as the Semitic tribes, they were more prone than the Omanis, Nabataeans, and Phoenicians to get in and get out, to return to their motherland, the seat of their culture and religion. In contrast, the Semitic sensibilities somehow allowed their merchants to establish satellite communities far from their holy places and shrines, to stave off any lingering sense of homesickness, and to adopt another tongue as their lingua franca, without a profound loss of cultural or personal identity. It seemed that they would adapt to any circumstance to ensure successful trade and have outstanding adventures to tell about later.

It was in the context of this trade network centered on the Persian Gulf and Indian Ocean that spice traders took the next big leap. According to the accounts in *The Periplus of the Erythraean Sea*, written between 50 and 60 CE, the Greeks began to sail directly across the open waters of the Indian Ocean both ways, by careful seasonal use of the monsoon winds. Others, including the Arabs, had either accomplished the same feat earlier, unnoticed by the Europeans, or had soon followed, leaving the shallows of the continental shelf for deeper, more dangerous waters. In both a physical and psychological sense, the seafaring spice traders were at last untethered, sailing for days beyond the sight of land with no shallow shoals beneath their rudders. They had achieved the maritime equivalent of leaving the earth's gravitational pull to depart for the moon or for other planets.

Once they had sped from the Arabian Peninsula across the entire Indian Ocean in less than forty days, it was only a matter of time before they passed the Land of Serendip (today's Sri Lanka) to thread the needle of the Strait of Malacca, where the greatly sought-after cloves, nutmeg, and mace awaited them. From Socotra or Yemen's port of Aden, they would quickly pass over to the Horn of Africa, but once south of the horn itself, they would take to open waters again. In time, these Omani seafaring dynasties would colonize the Lamu Archipelago near Kenya and the islands off the Spice Coast known as Zanzibar. Once they had arrived at Zanzibar and had begun to procure products from the strangely exotic flora, the Arab seafarers may as well have reached an altogether foreign planet. Life there was simply not created under the same constraints and conditions as those in the *nejd*, where the sky rarely rains and the ground can hardly be called soil.

The possibilities for extracting novel natural resources and taking them to distant markets suddenly seemed boundless, as if some Dr. Seuss-like creator had fashioned altogether-different suites of bizarre species for traders to carry from one continent or island to the next. (This experience of discovering exotic flora would be echoed later in history, when Christians, Jews, and Muslims reached the Caribbean islands and American continents and extracted previously unforeseen plant products from them for the Columbian Exchange.) The Old World had at last become one large shopping mall with a panoply of "factory outlets" providing access to a seemingly infinite variety of plant and animal chemicals to sniff, savor, and consume.

The dry, unopened floral bud of *Eugenia caryophyllus* looks like a reddish brown wooden nail, and so, as early as the Roman Empire, it was given the Latin name *clove*, or "nail." Its pungent but sweet flavor has been described as "intense enough to burn the palate," though many also find it to be a good oral anesthetic and an aphrodisiac.

Along with pepper, nutmeg, and mace, the cloves of the Moluccas played an important role in the history of world trade. The earliest records of their use in China come from the Han dynasty early in the second century BCE. It appears that the Chinese first received cloves through several cultural intermediaries, including Nusantao seafarers, who are among the putative ancestors of today's Filipinos. The spice reached India around the second century CE, where it was given the Sanskrit name *kalika-phala,* which diffused into Arabic-speaking lands as *karanful.*

Cloves had made it into both Greek and Egyptian markets by the first century, and over the next two centuries, Phoenician traders delivered cloves to all parts of the Mediterranean. Later, Radhanite Jewish traders assured their distribution throughout Europe.

It took until the publication of the journals of Marco Polo around 1300 for Europeans to become aware of the origin of cloves. The book describes how, on his way back to Europe, the Venetian learned about cloves in Hui Muslim and Han Chinese ports on the East China Sea. By 1421, the Hui Muslim naval commander Zheng He had cultivated the collaboration of Moluccan spice traders, who had already converted to Islam in order to renew links among Muslim traders who moved cloves along various trade routes. The Portuguese were latecomers to the spice trade, but by the early sixteenth century, they had developed a monopoly on the valuable spice, which lasted for about a century. Following the Portuguese, Dutch middlemen controlled clove commerce until 1662, when King Charles II forbid the purchase of cloves by Englishmen unless they came directly from the producers.

Green, Aliza. *Field Guide to Herbs and Spices.* Philadelphia: Quirk Books, 2006.
Katzer, Gernot. "Gernot Katzer's Spice Pages." http://gernot-katzers-spice-pages.com/engl/index.html. Accessed May 4, 2013.
Turner, Jack. *Spice: The History of a Temptation.* New York: Vintage, 2005.
Weiss, E.A. *Spice Crops.* Wallingford, UK: CABI Publishing, 2002.

FIGURE 9. Open-sea transport of spices catapulted regional delicacies into global markets. Cloves, once available only in the Spice Islands, began reaching India, China, and Rome. In the nineteenth century, Zanzibar became the world's leading producer of cloves, shown here spread out to dry. (Courtesy Library of Congress Prints and Photographs Division, www.loc.gov/pictures/item/2001705556.)

But the task that lay ahead of the spice merchants was still a daunting one: how to consolidate these far-flung sources of goods into a cohesive system of trade, with shared systems of currency, valuation, and taxation that would stretch from Madagascar to the Maghreb to the Middle Kingdom.

CHAPTER 5

Mecca and the Migrations of Muslim and Jewish Traders

It is a moonless night along the beaches that front the resort hotels of Abu Dhabi. And yet, I struggle to find any darkness at all in the desert itself as I speed across a stretch of the Arabian Peninsula. The land itself remains illuminated with as many foot-candles as crude oil can buy. There are roving spotlights, laser shows dancing across the bay, and blazing digital billboards. I glimpse concert halls and stadiums surrounded by parking lots with metal halide floodlights kept so bright that you could read a newspaper without any visual aids.

As I speed along the superhighway between Abu Dhabi and Dubai in a Lexus rented as a "shuttle" by my favorite airline, I am amazed by what I can see in the wee hours of the morning. One of the recently completed resorts, Palm Jumeirah, occupies an artificial island complex constructed of a half billion metric tons of rock and sand piled up in a silhouette of a date palm. In addition to roughly fifty miles of newly created beaches lining the Persian Gulf, there are over four thousand villas, apartments, and hotel rooms. These habitations surround a multimedia entertainment center for those who tire of swimming or sunbathing all day. A sheikh has built a giant racetrack there, where you can watch camels fight for the lead from the comfort of your air-conditioned box seat. Skyscrapers more numerous than those in Los Angeles, Tokyo, or São Paulo stretch along the horizon, an infantry of giants marching to the edge of the sea.

One need not succumb to cynicism or sarcasm to see Abu Dhabi and

Dubai as the ultimate expressions of globalization to have appeared on the planet toward the end of the twentieth century. Despite some arabesque motifs seen in hotel lobbies, the architecture is cosmopolitan and technology driven rather than culturally based. The food can rightly be called fusion cuisine, since Mexican, Pakistani, Indian, and Chinese ingredients and culinary techniques are used as much as anything locally sourced, traditionally prepared, or endemic to the Arabian Peninsula. And the economy is so global that Halliburton, one of the world's most powerful oilfield service corporations, which has its founding headquarters in Texas, has established a second headquarters in Dubai, to accommodate a business that now spans all continents.

But a couple of years after 9/11, when George Bush's U.S. government was close to awarding a security contract for twenty-two of its international shipping harbors to Dubai Ports World, the entire range of American politics—from the John Birch Society and Michael Savage to Hillary Clinton and Barack Obama—expressed anxiety. They feared that because Dubai Ports World was operated by a holding company controlled by Dubai's Sheikh Mohammed bin Rashid al Maktoum, who was also the prime minister of the United Arab Emirates (UAE), Arab terrorists could easily infiltrate its operations.[1]

As one observer familiar with Dubai explained to a National Public Radio show host, there are indeed terrorists based in Dubai, but expert counterterrorists are just as available for hire there. It is really an ideal place, he suggested, because if you pay the right price, you can purchase excellent intelligence information on terrorist activities and protect yourself from them. It didn't much matter whether the security-force employees are followers of Islam, Arabic speakers, and UAE natives, they will do the work required as long as you pay them well. Nevertheless, the U.S. Congress voted five to one against the Dubai Ports World contract, and the company quietly turned over four U.S. ports that it had already been managing to an American-owned firm. Nevertheless, its thirty thousand employees continue to manage maritime trade through over fifty ports that U.S. ships frequent in thirty-one countries, making the company as essential to the intercontinental movement of spices, perfumes, medicines, oil, and fiber today as other Arabs were in centuries past.

Although the ports of Dubai and Abu Dhabi may be the most prominent trade centers on the Arabian Peninsula today, fifteen hundred years ago, an altogether different kind of place began to emerge as the peninsula's most important hub for spice merchants. It was, in ways, a rather odd location for a trade center, for the site called Mecca was far inland from the great ports of its era. What's more, there were few spices or incense trees of any value that grew in the bleak and inhospitable uplands that surrounded the valley where Mecca was nested.

Even though a few Meccans served as guards or guides on one of the most ancient and frequently traveled Frankincense Trails that passed in or near their town,[2] Mecca was somewhat off the beaten path for most caravans moving along the major desert corridors running between Yemen and Syria. As one historian has put it,

> In the hilly areas of the Hijaz in western Arabia there were [a few] small commercial and agricultural towns, including Medina and Mecca, and it was the inhabitants of these small Hijazi towns who [became the trade-oriented] elite of the early Muslim empire. . . . The most important of these new trading centers seems to have been Mecca. Mecca is situated in a barren valley between jagged arid mountains, a very discouraging environment for a city, but it seems to have had a religious significance that attracted people. A shrine had grown up around a black meteoritic stone.[3]

If tens of thousands of Arabs and Jews could be captivated by an enigmatic black meteor believed to have been sent from the heavens—for it was merely one of thousands of meteor fragments that land on earth each year—then perhaps it was because they were rich in imaginative capacity, even though they remained poor in natural resources. Other than that luminous black stone called the Kaaba, venerated by pilgrims passing through the desert, nothing notable or even tangible seemed to occupy Mecca at that time, for it was more of a social and economic backwater than a crossroads.

Out of such an apparent void, however, there emerged a cadre of outrageously audacious and imaginative poets, prophets, and seers who performed and proselytized at nearby fairs, festivals, and celebrations. Keep in mind that "poetry was the sole medium of literary expression among the Arabs of the pre-Islamic period,"[4] and that the society believed poets to be endowed with spiritual, political, and promotional power not currently afforded to this calling by contemporary societies. They were the voices that cried out from the desert wilderness, ultimately demanding global attention. Curiously, these charismatic poets and prophets included both Arabs and Jews, and that ultimately led to a showdown between these two Semitic cultures.

Within a few miles of Mecca's center, three small villages had become renowned both for their markets and for what we might today call their poetry slams. These poorly populated outposts burgeoned with thousands of additional Bedouin tents a few times each year when trade fairs featured goods passed hand to hand, as well as stories and verses passed mouth to mouth from as far away as Yemen, Oman, Egypt, Syria, Chaldea, and Persia.

At these pre-Islamic fairs, various goods entered new hands without being taxed or even elaborated into value-added products. At the fabled trade fair in the meager marketplace of Ukaz, just outside Mecca, most of the local Bedouins simply bought fresh goat meat, bulgur wheat, raisins, and dates, and perhaps sold some of their own goat cheese, clarified butter, or medicinal plants. They also brought in huge piles of stiff rawhides and bags of unwashed wool, which were sent away to distant markets before the desert winds closed off the roads for a season. If they were lucky, they might be shown a few tantalizing pieces of silk and baskets of saffron, some clay pots dripping with sesame oil or packed with incense, modest pieces of onyx or little bottles of perfumes. Hawkers tended to offer a rather small quantity of these exotic items, so they encouraged a motley ensemble of Arab street poets to make the fair more memorable in order to pump up the enthusiasm and spending of the crowds. Occasionally, someone would recite a few verses of his own *saj'* composition, which might predict a disaster, foretell of a social schism, or rivet listeners with a satirical parable that would be remembered for decades.

About a millennium after the first poems in Arabic were recorded in the region, sometime between 500 and 600 CE, a loosely knit but rambunctious amalgam of Bedouin merchants and livestock breeders trickled into town, hoping to capitalize on trade in some of the precious metals that had recently been found in the hills of the Hejaz. Members of an Umayyad tribe known as the Quraysh, they first took possession of Mecca's sacred Kaaba stone and positioned themselves to capture most of the revenues from visiting pilgrims.[5] They gained some prominence in the short-distance distribution of goods across the peninsula known as transit trade as well as in camel breeding.

One of the few spices that they themselves brought into trade was called *al-sh/hēbā'*, a "grayish entanglement" that may have been either a lichen known in English as stone flower or a parasitic dodder.[6] Its bitter flakes were added to soups and stews that the Quraysh themselves were fond of eating, but stone flower soup never gained much currency with the Egyptians, Persians, Romans, or Greeks. The stone flower was nearly as perishable as manna and not as suited to long-distance trade and inflated prices as the Quraysh might have wished. In fact, the Arabs had yet to have much effect on European and Asian cuisines, except for their role in making some extra-local spices available to the royal and merchant classes.

To make a living with the scant natural resources at hand, the Quraysh merchants had to elaborate value-added products from the little that they could accumulate. They excelled at tanning goat hides with the acidic bark of desert shrubs and at cleaning and spinning sheep's wool. They would select their most highly bred camels and try to sell them off to the Persians and Syrians by elaborating fantastic stories of their feats. They were also engaged in the trade of finely cured and highly ornamented leather goods. But the Quraysh in the role of middlemen were never able to accumulate the wealth that their Nabataean predecessors had achieved. Their bulky, relatively low-value goods failed to make many of them rich.

So they played their hand in transit trade across the peninsula as best they could. Twice a year, Quraysh caravans brought incense originating in Indonesia, Yemen, or Ethiopia through Mecca, including *lubān jāwa* (Javanese gum Benjamin) from the benzoin tree and *darw* or *mastikā* (mastic) from wild pistachios, a widespread species. But the historic timing of their developing caravans out of Mecca was rather poor. By this period, most of the frankincense and myrrh was already being transported by boat across the "liquid roads" of the Red Sea and Persian Gulf rather than mounted on camels and tediously making its way along one of the many landlocked Frankincense Trails.[7] The merchants who had specialized in more valuable goods were now riding more ships than camels, using the Arabic term *rakaba markab* to claim that they were metaphorically "mounting the backs of the waves and galloping across the seas."[8] The 680 denarii cost per camel of running a caravan across the peninsula could easily be undercut by faster-sailing maritime caravans with larger hauling capacities.

In short, the Quraysh risked being in the wrong place at the wrong time. Mecca appeared to be an exceedingly unlikely location for the emergence of an intercontinental trading center, let alone a major religion. But a struggle would soon take place in the Hejaz between two eloquent men whose talents were not dissimilar: a poet and a prophet. Whichever visionary most entranced the "language-intoxicated" masses[9] of the Hejaz would become the winner who would take all. The poet was half Arab and half Jewish but recognized as an up-and-coming sharif among the Jews of Medina. The prophet was from a splinter

FIGURE 10. Salman the Persian (Salmān al-Farsi), a disciple of Muhammad, is shown meeting merchants from the Quraysh tribe. From *Siyar-i Nabi* (The Life of the Prophet), 1594–95. (Spencer Collection, New York Public Library, Astor, Lenox and Tilden Foundations.)

group of the Quraysh and had begun to chant some remarkable revelations that he had received in a cave just under two miles from the Arab settlement in Mecca.

The name of the half-Jewish poet, Ka'b ibn al-Ashraf, is one that few contemporary people, other than medieval scholars, can conjure up today, despite his infamy in the earliest Islamic era. The name of the prophet was, of course, Muhammad, who is known by most people living in the world today. The prophet's full name was Abu al-Qasim Muhammad Ibn Abd Allah Ibn Abd al-Muttalib Ibn Hashim. Once a spice merchant, he was mystically transformed into a spiritual messenger. In the very first line of his sura informally known as "1001 Nights," Muhammad straightforwardly identified his roots; his upbringing and surroundings were replete with the traders of spices and other goods: "I was a merchant among merchants."

Abd al-Muttalib, Muhammad's grandfather, was a prominent Quraysh trader and a guardian of the Kaaba. He was esteemed and loved by his peers and was a caring elder who took the little orphaned boy under his wing. He let the boy apprentice with his son and the head of the Bani Hashim clan, Abu Talib, who had once been a respected merchant banker but who had become so poor that he made the adopted boy herd sheep and goats for him. During this time of his life, Muhammad became content with the simple foods of the shepherd's camp, rustic dishes such as *tharīd*,[10] and never acquired the taste for more sophisticated or exotic foods. But when he was between nine and twelve years of age, Abu Talib took him on a camel caravan to Syria to expose him to the larger world, hoping he would learn the art of cross-cultural trading with Jews and Christians. Along the way, a Christian hermit noticed that as the caravan passed by, a sheltering cloud followed the boy wherever he walked or rode. This anchorite was named Bahira and was perhaps the first to recognize that Abu Talib's charge would emerge as a prophet.[11]

Once Abu Talib and Muhammad had arrived with their wares in Damascus, they undoubtedly haggled over prices with the speakers of Aramaic and Syriac who flocked into such cities as Damascus and Aleppo at that time. They probably carried camel hair, wool, and goat skins with them, as well as some spices or perfumes.

Damascus is where I enter my first Middle Eastern souk as well, accompanied by my brothers and my Lebanese uncles from the Bekáa Valley. I have been told that we are going to an open-air market, but the

✤ THARĪD ✤ GAZPACHO AL-ANDALUS
Soup with Unleavened Bread

This gazpacho is a descendant of *tharīd*, or *al-thurda*, a class of thick broth-and-bread recipes that goes back to the pre-Islamic era on the Arabian Peninsula. It was reputably the Prophet Muhammad's favorite dish, humble yet elegant and savory. There are many variants, most of which include soaking and crumbling unleavened flat bread, but a few stack the bread into a pyramid-like pile in a meat broth, puree, or soup. Some have vegetable purees—eggplant, cucumber, or tomato—and others do not. Classically prepared in a glazed porcelain basin called a *mithrad*, these dishes may be the precursor of Portuguese *açorda* soups, Andalusian gazpachos, and perhaps even the Mexican *sopa de tortilla*.

The following recipe derived from Inés Butrón is a typical gazpacho of al-Andalus that probably came to the Iberian Peninsula between the time of the arrival of Abd al-Rahman I and Ziryab. When tomatoes and bell peppers were introduced from the New World, these members of the nightshade genus were cautiously incorporated. At first, they were well roasted and salted and then pureed to remove any bitterness or toxins. In time, however, tomatoes became as much the base of this soup as the bread had been.

Serve with cucumber slices dressed with yogurt and dried mint. *Makes six to eight ½-cup servings.*

> 4 ounces unleavened or day-old leavened flat bread, cut into small dice
> ½ cup white vinegar, plus more if needed
> 2½ pounds vine-ripened red tomatoes, peeled, seeded, and cut into small dice, plus 1 firm tomato, seeded and minced
> 1 green bell pepper, seeded and minced
> 2 cloves garlic, minced
> ¾ to 1 cup olive oil
> 1 teaspoon sea salt
> 1 green onion, including tender green tops, finely chopped
> ½ cucumber, minced
> 1 egg, hard-boiled, peeled, and chopped
> 1 tablespoon mayonnaise, or ½ teaspoon anchovy paste
> 1 to 2 cups bread cubes from country-style loaf, toasted

In a bowl, moisten the flat bread by sprinkling it with the vinegar and then tossing it with your hands to distribute the vinegar evenly. Let the bread stand for a few minutes to soften, then crumble the bread with your fingers.

Transfer the moistened bread to a large mortar or wooden bowl. Add the diced tomatoes, bell pepper, and garlic and crush with a pestle or a wooden spoon while gradually adding the olive oil. Add only as much oil as needed to create a flavorful, slightly chunky puree. Alternatively, use a blender or food processor, working in batches as needed. Season with the salt, then taste and adjust the seasoning with more vinegar and salt if needed. Cover and place in the refrigerator or a cool cellar for at least 1 hour before serving.

Meanwhile, in a bowl, combine the minced tomato, green onion, cucumber, egg, and mayonnaise and stir to mix. Set aside to use as a garnish.

Ladle the gazpacho into small bowls, top with the garnish and bread cubes, and serve.

Butrón, Inés. *Ruta gastronómica por Andalucía*. Barcelona: Salsa Books, 2009.
Casas Delgado, Francisco. *La cocina andaluza Guadalquivir arriba: Charlas y recetas*. Seville: Alfar, 1992, p. 183.

walkways are sheltered from the blazing summer sun by all matter of cloths, plastic, and tarps. While my brothers look at Persian rugs from the nineteenth century that they hope to air-freight back to the United States, I set my sights on a trail-worn camel saddlebag with a pale geometric design woven into it, akin to those on the saddle blankets that my Navajo friends weave from the wool of Navajo-Churro sheep in the Painted Desert of Arizona. My Lebanese uncle Victor is assisting my brothers with identifying and evaluating the quality of some kilim carpets when he notices that I am ready to pay the shopkeeper for a camel saddlebag. The Syrian merchant is trying to talk me into purchasing two bags for a 10 percent discount on both when my uncle interrupts him.

"What price did you ask of that boy for that frayed, camel piss–stained piece of junk?"

The shopkeeper switches from English to Arabic and tries to calm my uncle down. And yet, when Victor hears the price, he is livid. He takes the camel saddlebag out of my hands, throws it on the floor, grabs me by the arm, and begins to escort me out of the shop, waving to my brothers to put the kilims down and to follow us. Then, once we are out in the walkway of the souk, he whistles to the shopkeeper and begins his ritualistic rant: "You offer those scandalous prices to my own blood and kin when I've known you since you were still sucking on your mother's breast? My father did business with yours on the old Damascus Road to Zahle, and yet you forget the ties we've had? Their grandfather Najim, their granduncle Ferhat, and my own father—bless his soul—helped defend you Syrians during the Ottoman war, and what do we get for it? Prices like we are tourists! Prices like we are foreigners! I will never allow another man from the Nabhan clan to set foot in this shop!"

The shopkeeper rushes up to my uncle and hugs him, kissing him three times on each cheek, and then holds his hand.

"Victor, I thought you were becoming an old man, but you still have your fire! Of course, I wasn't going to cheat your nephew. I was just offering this bearded one a second camel bag for free. Now I will give him both camel bags for free if one of his brothers offers me a fair price for the fine kilims I have on hand. I will make another discount and give them each a bottle of Syrian rose water or arak if both of the brothers buy kilims from me before noon."

At one thirty in the afternoon, after two hours of negotiation, each of my brothers leaves the shop with a giant kilim, and the rug dealer throws in both of my camel saddlebags gratis.

All of the passionate bickering and bartering that Uncle Victor and the Syrian shopkeeper engaged in was little more than a minor drama compared to that which young Muhammad probably witnessed as understudy to his uncle Abu Talib. Although he apparently gained some facility in such negotiations, there are hints that he found cross-cultural haggling to be distasteful and beyond his capacity for patience and tolerance at the time. Nevertheless, he was good enough at caravanning across the desert and delivering the goods that a distant relative of his, a widow named Khadijah bint Khuwaylid, asked the twenty-five-year-old man to make a few runs for her to trading hubs for a salary that was twice as high as what she paid others.[12]

Muhammad made good on her confidence in him in a manner that became like an economic golden rule for Muslims. This principle, loosely paraphrased, states that if someone is doubly kind to you, repay them twice over for the trust they invested in you. The profits that he returned to her after his first expedition to Damascus were indeed twice what she had anticipated, so she sent him off to Yemen the next winter with triple the usual commission. Again, he came back with profits greater than what Khadijah had expected. Although his entrepreneurial skills may have initially caught her eye, she soon noticed his passionate spirit as well, and before long she engaged him as her husband.

In Arabic narratives, Khadijah is regarded with considerable admiration, for she routinely fed and sheltered the poor, offered hospitality to foreigners, and parted with most of her wealth to promote the ideals of

Islam. Her wisdom and guidance helped nurture the best in Muhammad after their partnership began in 595. But perhaps she is loved as much for being the kind of enigmatic person who challenged and still challenges the Western stereotypes of Arab and Muslim women. It is clear that she held the purse strings, not only during her relationship with the younger Muhammad but also while managing the trade for her father and two earlier husbands.

And yet, it was not uncommon in those times for a confidant woman to be in fiscal control of expeditions that took men away from their home base for months at a time. That said, Khadijah was more than an operations manager. She was also a venture capitalist. She grubstaked young men to go out on the road with a certain range and quantity of goods and coached them on how to bring back the best financial dividends to be shared by all. This replicable pattern of mentors guiding younger men and women in how to set up franchises of their pioneering businesses in faraway places became a common thread in the blanketing of the world with what we now know as globalization.

While Muhammad took on the role of traveling salesman, or *al-tajir as-saffar*, Khadijah ran the other aspects of the business in Mecca, acting as head merchant in residence, or *al-tajir al-muqim*. Whether Muhammad or his colleagues set out on the Hejaz road to the Transjordan and Syria, one of the Frankincense Trails to Yemen, or the *nejd* road to Hira in what is now southern Iraq, Khadijah was back in Mecca both holding down the fort and planning future expeditions.

But after a few years of running caravans for Khadijah, Muhammad suddenly lost interest in living a merchant's life on the road. He became listless and began to spend more of his time meditating in the dark recesses of Gar Hira, a tiny cave that he found by climbing six hundred steps up above the desert floor of Mecca to the mountain Jabal al-Nour. Many of his friends and relatives feared that he was listening to some crazy jinn that had gotten inside his head, as they had with other poets and seers, and Khadijah, who was at first baffled, took him to be diagnosed (or exorcised) by a nearby Christian monk who lived among the Nestorians. The monk intuitively understood that Muhammad was already on a spiritual quest and assured him and his wife that his visions were "messages from the divine."[13] Khadijah stood by him. His prophesy painfully and laboriously spun itself out over several years, and yet it has become one of the world's most orally elegant and eloquent incantations. Its immense popularity has continued to grow over the centuries, so that today, it is recited daily by about one-third of the world's

✵ DAMASCUS ROSE ✵ ROSE OF CASTILE

If a single wonderfully scented flower can reveal more about the history of the spice trade than any other blossom, it is the Damascus rose (*Rosa* × *damascena*), with its sweetly persistent fragrance and flavor. This peculiar double-flowered rose is not known to exist in the wild anywhere on earth. Instead, it appears to have arisen as an accidental hybrid between the common wild rose of the Caucasus and one or two others, perhaps the Levant rose *R. phoenicia* cultivated by Phoenician women in ports of the Mediterranean.

No one is sure whether this hybrid was first recognized in present-day Syria or Turkey, but the history of *Rosa* × *damascena* has long been tied to the capital of Syria, the country once called the Land of Roses. Damascus is certainly where this rose has been cultivated for the longest stretch of recorded history. Called *al-warda* by the Levantine Arabs, its pink to pale reddish petals are rich in the aromatic oils geraniol, citronellol, and nerol, though one particular chemical, beta-damascone, provides its most distinctive fragrance. Herbalists everywhere steep its fragrant petals in spring water, olive oil, or alcohol to make "rose water," which they then use as a flavoring for *loukoumia* (Turkish delight), jams, jellies, and sauces.

When I was four or five years old, I had the impression that my Lebanese and Syrian grandfathers, all of my uncles, and my father naturally smelled of roses. Whenever they called me *habibi* and kissed me on both cheeks, as Arab men are fond of doing to children in their clan, I became overwhelmed by the fragrance of the Damascus rose. It was not until several years later when I went to a barber shop with one of my uncles that I witnessed how Rex the barber splashed an astringent mixed with rose water on my uncle's newly shaven skin and greased his hair with rose oil. Not too much later, I read the words *rose water* on a bottle my father kept in my parents' bathroom. However naively these early olfactory memories arose in me, they have had staying power.

A half century later, after spotting so many roses lining the bou-

population. The Prophet Muhammad's gift to the world from the poverty of that cave is called the Qur'an.

After his revelations became known, Muhammad had difficulty returning to camels, caravans, or trade in cumin. Nevertheless, over the rest of his illustrious life he saw no contradiction between the spiritual path he was promoting and the trail of trade that Khadijah and other businesswomen had sustained. As long as she and her kin took care of levards in Damascus, after tasting rose petals in the *ras el hanout* of Fez, after noticing that those same delicate petals were strewn on the walkways of the Alhambra in Granada, and after whiffing acres of roses in bloom on the terraced slopes of Jabal al-Akhdar in Oman, I realized that the Damascus rose could be found nearly everywhere I had traveled in the world. Nevertheless, I had always assumed that the rose of Castile displayed in Mexico during the Feast of the Virgin of Guadalupe was a flower of an altogether different origin. I was in error. These two roses of different names are one and the same.

Throughout most of its travels, however, this rose has kept its allegiance to the Syrian capital evident. From Japan and Russia to England and France, horticulturists and florists reaffirm that this rose hails from Damascus. In the Arabic- and Farsi-speaking stretches of the world, variations of the ancient Semitic *al-warda* remain more prevalent. The rose was likely taken to Morocco and Spain by the Umayyads fleeing from Damascus; the Abbasids who then took power dispersed it to their strongholds in Persia and Turkey and vainly attempted to monopolize its production. But the Damascus rose surreptitiously found its way into other gardens, oils, ointments, and dishes, until the Abbasids conceded that it could not be owned. When the great eleventh-century medical scholar and chemist Ibn Sīnā (Avicenna) devised an easy means of distilling rose water from the petals, its reach expanded once more.

Over the centuries, this venerable flower has infiltrated many cuisines, from Indian to Moorish to Latin American. Damascus rose oil, like mastic, contributes to the delightfulness of Turkish delight confections. It can also enrich a Moroccan *tagine* and a Spanish *picadillo*. I keep a bottle of rose water in my bathroom, and sometimes another in my kitchen, just to remember who I am.

Davidson, Alan, ed. *The Oxford Companion to Food*. Oxford: Oxford University Press, 1999.
Katzer, Gernot. "Gernot Katzer's Spice Pages." http://gernot-katzers-spice-pages.com/engl/index.html. Accessed May 4, 2013.

the poor and offered a portion of their wealth to sustain the religious endowments known as *waaf* funds, there was no inherent contradiction between making money and the spiritual precepts of Islam.

But Khadijah and Muhammad were careful to caution individuals or clans against accumulating so much wealth that they created greater disparities among communities of believers, and they endeavored to redistribute capital across clans and landscapes in ways that fostered cohesion among all these communities. More important, they forbid *riba*, or "usury," a custom common among Jews of charging exorbitant interest on loans to the poor, for such practices would sooner or later make indentured servants out of those who lacked capital. They proclaimed that wealthy trade brokers controlling harbors and caravansary outposts could not tax any practitioners of their faith. The only duty Muslims were required to pay was the *zakat* redistribution of wealth that provided charity for the poorest of the poor.

These mandates and constraints on how trade could be enacted did not sit well with the richest of the Quraysh in Mecca, nor among the Jewish moneylenders with whom they regularly dealt. Even though Muhammad was born into the Banu Hashim, one of the Quraysh tribes, the other Quraysh tribes forced him and his followers out of Mecca. Over the next decade, three major battles ensued among these factions. The Prophet himself barely escaped from several assassination attempts by the Quraysh. So Muhammad and his "new Muslims" took refuge in nearby Yathrib, now known as Medina (from Madinat Rasul Allah, the "Holy City"), where the Banu al-Nadir, a tribe of Jewish merchants, was in power.

The Banu al-Nadir Jews were just as wary as the Quraysh Arabs of the Prophet Muhammad's growing power. They also found his boycott of moneylenders engaged in usury disruptive and the militancy of his followers worrisome. But when they witnessed his followers' bloodthirsty attacks, not only on the Quraysh but also on some of their own, the Banu al-Nadir began to fear for their own lives. Muhammad had already ordered the killings of two lesser Jewish poets, but he was now vying to silence the voice of their greatest remaining bard.[14] The Jews were defiant, however. When they sent envoys to the Quraysh to leverage an alliance against Muhammad, one of those envoys was their poet-sharif Ka'b ibn al-Ashraf, who, by some accounts, was as charismatic as the Prophet himself.

When I was in Abu Dhabi, I had learned that the poet Ka'b was born into my own paternal tribe, the Banu Nebhani. But he soon became a leader in the tribe of his Jewish mother, the Banu al-Nadir, and for some reason, the fact that his father was a polytheistic Arab of the Banu Nebhani is rarely mentioned.

Upon discovering that I had a famed poet in my ancestry, I was at first elated. But when I came to understand how Ka'b's poetry had put a wedge between Muslims and Jews that has persisted for centuries, my enthusiasm evaporated. The Arabs claimed his cleverness and cruelty with words were evidence that he was under the spell of jinn if not Satan himself, for he used his power as a bard as a weapon in his struggle against Muhammad, challenging the Prophet's new moral, religious, and economic protocols.

To his credit, Muhammad had made some pacts with Jewish tribes other than the Banu al-Nadir, but he had clearly become wary of the economic power wielded by particular Jewish tribes in his area. They still profited by employing usury on the poor. They also taxed merchants like Muhammad's own wife, Khadijah, when she sold her goods in their privately owned markets. Such practices set up economic disparities to which Muhammad objected. When he considered building a utopian community (*umma*) in Yathrib for the supertribe he would coalesce under the banner of Islam, he dreamed of a mosque, a garden, a madrassa (school), a *haram* (sacred enclave), a *hima* (a land sanctuary or inviolate reserve of pasturelands), and last but not least, an equitable, communal marketplace where no form of usury would be allowed.[15]

So when he set his roots down in Yathrib, Muhammad wondered whether he could restructure the world of trade, employing ethical protocols that would be consistent with the spiritual precepts that had been revealed to him. Curiously, his first public action in his new hometown was to set up an unrestricted marketplace as a charitable endowment that would benefit the broadest range of participants possible, including the spice traders who had come with him from Mecca.[16]

It was an Occupy Wall Street sort of move into Jewish-controlled territory. In this public rather than privately owned market, no one could exclusively control cooking spaces or access to water, and traders were forbidden to have any merchandise earmarked for them as "futures" before they were delivered to the marketplace. This latter policy change allowed everyone to compete equally for the incoming spices, metals, or fibers without some participants receiving special deals in advance. Muhammad also mandated that taxes and bribelike payments could no longer be extorted from merchants and caravanners. His principle of *al-suq sadaqa* essentially allowed public markets to be duty-free zones along many transcontinental trade routes.

All of this began once Muhammad and his disciples roped off and occupied an area for the new Yathrib market, with the idea of establishing shops on the lower level and rentable sleeping quarters above, so that the souk would be structured like so many caravansaries he had frequented in his youth. But as soon as he began to implement his design, two problems quickly arose. First, he had chosen to occupy land that already belonged to Jews allied with the tribe of Ka'b ibn al-Ashraf, land that they had used in the past as a cemetery. Ka'b considered Muhammad's action to be a violation of sacred Jewish-controlled space.[17] Ka'b and his followers were also wary of the Prophet's economic reforms, for it meant that they might eventually lose their competitive edge.

Worse yet, Ka'b considered the new market to be in direct competition with one that three Jewish tribes, including his own, had long managed in Yathrib as one of their primary sources of income. Muhammad and Ka'b were suddenly on a collision course, as the chronicler Ibn Shabba reported at the time:

> The Prophet pitched a tent [for the market] in the Baqī al-Zubayr [cemetery], and said [to all comers, including his followers from Mecca]: This is your market. Then Ka'b b. al-Ashraf came up [to the area], entered inside [the roped-off area] and cut its ropes. The Prophet then said: Indeed, I shall move it into a place which will be more grievous for him than this place. And he moved into the place of the "Market of Medina"[which Ka'b's tribal allies had controlled]. . . . Then he said: This is your market. Do not set up sections in it [that will aggravate factionalism among you] and do not impose taxes for it.[18]

While Muhammad drew a line in the sand to distance Islam's economic activities from those routinely managed by Jews, Ka'b used his poetic talents to tell of the horrific massacre that had taken place at the hands of the new Muslims in the Battle of Badr. He wrote a eulogy that lamented the loss of Quraysh men at the hands of the Muslim warriors:

> O, how I wish that when these men were killed
> The earth beneath them could have opened its arms to caress them,
> Cradling them so that all their assassins, when they heard
> The news, would cower with fear, or be struck deaf and blinded.[19]

It became clear that the Hejaz wasn't big enough for two singer-seers as powerful as Muhammad and Ka'b. By some accounts, as soon as Muhammad heard Ka'b's eulogy for the Quraysh, he immediately sought out someone to kill the poet. Others claim that Ka'b was part of an assassination attempt against the Prophet. Still others claim that Muhammad was insulted and humiliated by Ka'b's satirical poems that made fun of his revelations. But what most Muslim historians contend is that Muhammad displayed patience until Ka'b ibn al-Ashraf crossed the line with a bawdy poem that defamed the honor and chastity of a young Muslim woman, Ummu'l-Fadl bint al-Harith.

PLATE 1. *Clockwise, from top left:* annatto, cardamom, melegueta pepper (also known as grains of paradise), dried frankincense gum, star anise, long pepper, sumac, turmeric, fennel, and coriander. (Photos by Lia Tjandra.)

PLATE 2. Frankincense gum oozing from a tree trunk in the *nejd* of southern Oman. This fragrant resin, popular as a spice and incense, was one of the most coveted objects in the early global aromatics trade. (Photo by the author.)

PLATE 3. Yemeni spice trader. (iStockphoto.)

PLATE 4. Depiction of a camel caravan from the Middle Ages. (Color lithograph by J. Coin from *L'Art arab d'après les monuments du Kaire,* 1877. Art and Architecture Collection, Miriam and Ira D. Wallach Division of Art, Prints and Photographs, New York Public Library, Astor, Lenox and Tilden Foundations.)

PLATE 5. Muslim women in Dushanbe, Tajikistan, selling local and imported vegetables, fruits, and spices. (Photo by the author.)

PLATE 6. View of the facades of tombs cut from the rock cliff in Petra, Jordan, a Nabataean trade hub that once received tons of spices annually. (Courtesy Library of Congress Prints and Photographs Division, www.loc.gov/pictures/item/2002698303.)

PLATE 7. Ships arriving for trade in the harbors of the South China Sea. (Photo by the author of an exhibit at the Quanzhou Maritime Museum.)

PLATE 8. Stand selling mole preparations from San Pedro Atocpan at the Flower Festival of San Angel, Mexico City, 2009. (Photo by Thelmadatter.)

PLATE 9. The "crafty" Arab is transformed into a taco vendor at a mobile food stand in the desert oasis of San Ignacio, Baja California Sur, Mexico. (Photo by the author.)

That indiscretion proved too much for the Prophet and his lieutenants to tolerate, so they commissioned a Muslim half brother of Ka'b named Silkan to set a trap for the poet in the fortress of the Banu al-Nadir. Around the time of the spring equinox in 625, after a night of reciting poetry with his half brother, Ka'b was in bed with a girl who warned him of trouble in the air.[20] Ka'b ignored her but soon found himself being dragged out of bed by his half brother, the Muslim convert. Silkan was then joined by Muhammad's most trusted guards and together they stabbed the poet to death. From then on, there was only one prophetic and poetic voice left to be heard in the Hejaz.

Nearly fourteen hundred years later, I find Muslims and Jews who still differ in how they read the series of events that led to Ka'b ibn al-Ashraf's death and the sparing of the Prophet Muhammad. I have met contemporary Jews who argue that these events initiated a lingering animosity among Muslims toward all people of the Jewish faith. For them, Muhammad did not place a death wish solely on a Jewish poet; he condemned all Jews. I have also met Muslims who feel that no Jewish poet or comic has the right to ridicule the Prophet. But this limited view fails to take into account the fact that Ka'b ibn al-Ashraf had Arab blood—more specifically, Nabhan blood—running through his veins. It is clear that this initial conflict was as much about the ethics of economic exchange as it was about religious and political dominance. Regardless of whatever else has been read into these incidents by revisionist historians of the Jewish or Islamic faiths, there were originally Jews and proto-Muslim Arabs on both sides of the argument. It remains contested ground to this day.

Contrary to what was written about Muslims in the historic texts of the West, Islam spread more by mutually beneficial trade relations than by the oppressive specter of the sword. A closer look at historical sources bears out the fact that Muslims and Jews have lived, for the most part, peaceably within the very same communities and maintained trade relations with each other since the Prophet's death five years after Ka'b's assassination. Jews as well as Christians were given special privileges in Muslim-dominated trading centers, for there was special status granted to the People of the Book. Nevertheless, special status is not the same as equal status. As noted earlier, almost from the start of Islam, Christians and Jews were mandated to pay an additional fee called *al-jizya*. While this gave them the privilege of living and working among Muslims, they could rightly contend that it was a tax differentially levied against them by a faith that claimed it would not tax or levy usury-like interest rates within their communities.

As such, it has been endlessly debated whether or not Khadijah's concern for the poor and hospitality for other cultures trumped Muhammad's apparent anger with Ka'b ibn al-Ashraf and the other satirical poets among the Banu al-Nadir Jews. Perhaps it was a mix of their sensibilities as a couple, even with all the inherent contradictions, that became embedded in early Islam's spirituality, ethics, and economy. But it remains clear that Khadijah herself strongly encouraged the nurturing of cross-cultural relationships as well as the reduction of economic disparities across all the landscapes through which their trade routes extended, and regularly included those of other faiths.

In fact, some historians claim that until their deaths, both the Prophet Muhammad and his first wife, Khadijah, remained socially and politically motivated to deal with the glaring disparities in wealth and well-being around them. They had personally witnessed these inequalities when traveling between desert landscapes endowed with widely varying capacities for producing natural and agricultural resources, and what they saw prompted them to forge the economic principles and ethics of Islam to address this dilemma directly. In the seminal work done on the economic origins and spread of Islam by economic historian Stelios Michalopoulos and colleagues, we can see the pattern that emerged in the years following the death of the Prophet. Islam was adopted precisely among those cultures that were historically located in agriculturally poor regions, for it offered the local inhabitants a safety net.

> Consistent with the hypothesis that Islamic principles provided an attractive social contract for populations residing along productively unequal regions, we find that Muslim adherence increases in the degree of geographic inequality. . . . Islam spread successfully among groups historically located in agriculturally poor regions featuring few pockets of fertile land. It was along these places that the Islamic institutional arrangement would be appealing to the indigenous populations.[21]

There was one particular aspect of Islam that especially fostered a more globalized mentality, first among the formerly disparate Arab tribes who had initially united behind the Prophet and then among all Muslims. It was the insistence that the Qur'an be recited only in Arabic and not subject to the kinds of tedious translations that might dilute the unifying power of the Prophet's holy poetry. Perhaps the near-exclusive use of Arabic in reciting the sacred verses was the first wave of linguistic colonialism to splash up on the shores of every continent. It had been preceded and then later followed, of course, with more secular and insidious forms of linguistic monoculture, first with Greek, then with Latin, Spanish, and Portuguese, and more recently with English. Sequentially, each of these few languages has become the lingua franca at the expense of some sixty-eight hundred other languages that barely remain in currency on the planet.

Linguistic monoculture ultimately removes most impediments to rapid globalization, since the adoption of the conqueror's language may disarm the cultural values, symbols, and rhetoric that otherwise allow an indigenous culture to resist imperialism. In other words, linguistic imperialism has often become a tool of ecological and culinary imperialism as globalization proceeds. (In keeping its slogan, "I'm lovin' it," in English in more than eighty-five nations, McDonald's is linking linguistic imperialism to culinary imperialism.) Although many cultures that embraced Islam still spoke their native language in the recesses of their village or home, the use of Arabic as a holy language certainly fostered its acceptance as a globalized lingua franca.

Even before the Prophet died in 632, in the arms of A'isha, the most beloved among his later wives, his troops had begun preparations to introduce Islam to Syria, just as they already had done across much of the Arabian Peninsula.[22] This task was accomplished in 635, as if to demonstrate to the world that the death of the Prophet would in no way impede Islam's momentum. Islam had begun to spread like wildfire from one tribe, one country, and one continent to another. And yet, it would be a mistake to attribute the rapidity of Islamic expansion solely to the existing trade networks that Arab merchants like Khadijah and Abu Talib had already nurtured.

Something altogether new was occurring: the coalition of many localized or regionalized transit trade routes into a cohesive globalized network system managed from end to end by Muslims. In the case of Egypt, Tunisia, Morocco, Andalusia, Sicily, Anatolia, the Balkans, and India, the sword was initially used to vanquish obstacles to the spread of Islam.[23] But over much of the Old World, the engagement of other cultures in a peaceful spice trade eventually led to their conversion to Islam. Spice traders who were recent converts often served as the "first wave" of Muslims who captured sequential control of various segments of ancient, lucrative trade routes and brought them into the fold. Nearly everywhere they went, they established the now-legendary *funduq,* a trading center with bargaining floors, spice warehouses, and camel liveries that became the precursor of the modern stock exchange.

Although it could not have been too surprising, itinerant Muslims soon found that some of the pre-Islamic trade routes, particularly those in North Africa, had already been worked for centuries by Berber, Phoenician, Greek, and Roman merchants, as well as Jewish traders. The first wave of Jews apparently arrived in Egypt and Ethiopia in ancient times, but most of those who immigrated to the Maghreb came immediately after the fall of the Temple in Jerusalem in 70 CE. The thirty thousand Jews taken as slaves to Qart Hadasht (Carthage) eventually freed themselves from their Roman captors and learned how to garner goods from across the Sahara as understudies to the Punic descendants of the Phoenicians. The majority of the newly arrived Jews to the Maghreb who became merchants seem to have stuck close to the more cosmopolitan ports of the coastlines, from Alexandria all the way to Mogador on the Atlantic. They generally functioned as brokers and bankers in the urban hubs and harbors.

Generalities, however, gloss over the most interesting anomalies in the globalization of Africa. There were indeed a number of more adventurous Jews who moved inland, marrying into the Berber tribes of the Sahara and converting them to Judaism.[24] By the time the first Muslims arrived in the Sahara, they were greeted by all-Jewish clans among both the Berbers and their kin to the south, the Tuareg or Kel Tamasheq. One of these Jewish clans of Tuareg, the Iddao Ishaak, later became legendary for leveraging trade between the ports of North Africa and the deeper reaches of West Africa. Other Jewish clans, perhaps those that had drifted westward from Ethiopia across the Sahel to Mali in ancient times, eventually settled in western and southeastern Nigeria.

Today, their descendants are called Igbos, or Igbo Benei-Yisrael Jews. They trace themselves back to particular Hebrew patriarchs who either forcibly or voluntarily left their homeland for Africa prior to written records of such movements.

Not surprisingly, when Muslim armies and merchant fleets arrived in their midst, the Jewish traders were worried. They had heard rumors from the East of the successes the Arab tribes had achieved in converting others to Islam; they also learned that Muslim traders had captured and consolidated trade routes that the Jews had previously accessed without much difficulty. And they were alarmed at how quickly the world they had known was being transformed into a world that chanted the Prophet's words.

PRECINCTS OF THE DWELLINGS OF THE GREAT MERCHANTS

FIGURE II. Sub-Saharan merchants such as these portrayed in Timbuktu in 1897 often formed collaborative communities to protect themselves from bandits or competing forces. (General Research and Reference Division, Schomburg Center for Research in Black Culture, New York Public Library, Astor, Lenox and Tilden Foundations.)

As Islamic adventurer and itinerant geographer Ibn Battuta later confirmed, these nomadic spice traders had expeditiously carried Islam westward, far beyond Mecca and Medina within a century after the Qur'an was revealed to the Prophet Muhammad.[25] Islam was embraced by many in Alexandria by 641, although Jews and Christians persisted there. After arriving in Tripoli by 647, in Carthage by 698, and in Tangier by 709, the sheer power of Islam rippled inland.[26] The Prophet's words then echoed all the way across the Sahara, into the areas where Jewish traders had gained a foothold.

Despite the presence of Jewish tribes, Berber and Tuareg caravans regularly recited the Qur'an as they navigated seven perilous routes across the sand seas to reach the Niger River basin. Centuries later, when Timbuktu became a trading hub for rock salt, African floating (deepwater) rice, and melegueta pepper, Islam expanded farther southward and westward into the watersheds of the Niger and Senegal rivers. The sedentary Songhai and Soninke embraced Islam and spread its customs and trading protocols throughout West Africa.[27]

Not every Berber, Tuareg, Songhai, or Soninke household fell under the spell of the Prophet Muhammad, however, and at times, Jewish-led

✦ MELEGUETA PEPPER ✦
GRAINS OF PARADISE

The reddish brown seeds of a perennial herb in the ginger family, melegueta pepper (*Aframomum melegueta*) may be what "preadapted" Africans to their predilection for tiny, fiery chiles. The crunchy texture of the seeds has been likened to the woodiness of cracked black pepper, with its gingerols leaving a slightly numbing piquancy in the mouth reminiscent of cloves. The exquisitely warm flavors of this native of the West African wetlands have been called peppery, spicy hot, gingery, and pleasantly bitter, with an aftertaste of lemon, cardamom, camphor, and cloves. The dozen chemicals already isolated from its essential oils suggest that it delivers a witch's brew of pungency.

The first peoples to recognize the value of the melegueta pepper were the foraging and farming tribes of West Africa, mostly from present-day Ghana, but also from Guinea, the Ivory Coast, Nigeria, and Sierra Leone. The most ancient name for this spice was rooted in a cognate that may have been *wiza*, since it is known as *awisa* or *awusa* by the Ewe, *wisa* or *wusa* by the Fante, *wie* by the Ga-Dangme, *citta* by the Hausa, and *eza* by the Nzema. In North African Arabic and Berber, it became *tin al-fil*, or "pepper fruit," and in Turkish it was known as *itrifil*, a condensation of terms meaning "African pepper."

Long before the Portuguese came to dominate maritime trade with West African tribes, Berber, Arab, and Jewish merchants were obtaining melegueta pepper from the Pepper Coast of present-day Liberia, where harvests from the outback arrived in the ports. Tuareg camel caravans carried this highly valued spice up across the Sahel and the Sahara and then across the continent through the Sudan. These Arabic-speaking traders integrated it into an aromatic spice composite termed *gâlat dagga*, which also included black peppercorns, cinnamon, cloves, and nutmeg, with cubeb sometimes substituted for the latter.

resistance temporarily halted the spread of Islam. The most remarkable episode of resistance in North Africa was led by a woman warrior reputed to be of Jewish descent (a fact many scholars dispute) who was born in an era when Algeria was part of the Byzantine Empire. Although the name given to her at birth was Damya, Dahya, or some similar variant, she became known throughout the Maghreb by the Arabic name al-Kāhinat, "the soothsayer," "seer," or "priestess." She was tall, wore her curly hair long, and was not afraid to wield a sword or prophesy doom for her enemies or for some of her own.[28] After her father died

Two other Arabic terms, *jouz as-Sudan* and *gawz al-Sudan,* probably reflected the sub-Saharan trade routes by which the spice entered the Arabian Peninsula and the Levant. Melegueta pepper also came across the Sahara on trade routes to the coast of present-day Libya.

Once the Portuguese trading fleets ventured south of Morocco and Mauritania, they began to gain more direct access to the spice, which then, as now, went by several names. The term *melegueta* has uncertain origin, but it may be somehow linked to *meligo,* Italian for "millet," or to Málaga, the ancient Phoenician port on the Andalusian coast across from Morocco. Another hypothesis is that it refers to the stinging and numbing sensations it produces, likening it to the effect one feels when stung by the *malagua,* or jellyfish, of coastal Africa. Curiously, the term *melegueta* was transferred to the tiny chiles that grew wild where the Portuguese established colonies of African slaves in Brazil.

Despite the wide acceptance of the spice elsewhere, the Portuguese must have felt that they needed to dress up its label for the European market (where it was only marginally known), so they gave it two new names, *sementes-do-paraíso* and *grãos-do-paraíso.* The notion of an exquisitely spicy seed straight from paradise took root among the French, Dutch, German, Hebrew, Hungarian, Italian, Chinese, and Romanian spice merchants. The Slovaks were holdouts, comparing its seeds to those of cardamom, as were the English, who called it Guinea grains or alligator pepper. It continues to be a popular addition to many dishes in West Africa; in Europe and the United States, it is primarily used to flavor boutique beers, ginger ale, and gin and as a substitute for peppercorns by some high-end chefs.

Green, Aliza. *Field Guide to Herbs and Spices.* Philadelphia: Quirk Books, 2006.

Katzer, Gernot. "Gernot Katzer's Spice Pages." http://gernot-katzers-spice-pages.com/engl/index.html. Accessed May 8, 2013.

Sortun, Ana, with Nicole Chaison. *Spice: Flavors of the Eastern Mediterranean.* New York: Regan Books, 2006.

in the early 680s, al-Kāhinat succeeded him as both a military strategist and a spiritual leader, rallying together the Jrāwa, Zenāta, and Lūwāta tribes of Berber Jews in the Aurès Mountains. She soon convinced the Tuareg and other Berbers to join together to resist Muslim expansion from Carthage westward into the rest of the Maghreb, or the Numidia of Ifriqiya, as Africa was then called. The Berbers feared that if control of Carthage was lost, they might be enslaved or taxed by the Arabs far worse than they had been by the Romans.

Carthage, the Roman capital of Numidia on the Gulf of Tunis, had grown into a trade center with perhaps as many as a half million people, its great port sending olive oil, grains, dried fruits, spices, pottery, and tax money back across the Mediterranean. While it was now a multicultural melting pot, its economic development had clearly been forged under Punic and Roman influences. A half century earlier, Muslim armies had swarmed into Alexandria, Barqa, and Tripoli to take these trade centers from their Egyptian, Punic, or Roman citizenry, but they knew that they had not yet tapped into the mother lode of the Maghreb.

So the Muslim caliph in Mecca dispatched Hasan ibn al Nu'man al-Ghassani, then an emir in Egypt, to take the Gulf of Tunis from the Romans and Berbers. Like many of his soldiers, Hasan was from a Yemeni tribe that had come out of the Syrian deserts to become part of the Umayyad elite that had made Damascus their capital. The caliph gave Hasan forty thousand troops and a fleet of ships to accomplish his task and, to strengthen his confidence, declared him general and *sheikh amin*, or "trusted elder."

When his troops and ships arrived at the Gulf of Tunis in 685, most of its Byzantine and Roman Christian protectors had already chosen to flee, leaving only the Berber peasantry to deal with the invaders. Kusaila, the Christian Berber military leader who had fathered one of al-Kāhinat's sons, was captured by the Arabs and forced to convert to Islam. It was the first time in nearly eight hundred years that the Romans lost their power base among the Berbers for extracting wealth from Africa.[29] Hasan's army and navy thoroughly looted the fine new harbor of Carthage of all of its riches. But when he did the same to the older harbor of Utica nearby, he learned that al-Kāhinat had been crowned the Queen of the Berbers and had defiantly gathered most of the Berber tribes together to block Hasan's army from passing into any more of their lands.

Their armies met face to face in what is now Oum el-Bouaghi Province in Algeria, a valley some distance inland from the Mediterranean. Just as the battle began, Kusaila, the supposed convert to Islam, betrayed the Arabs with misinformation that cost them their strategic advantage. Surprising Hasan with their resolve, al-Kāhinat's Berber troops so forcefully routed the Umayyad army that Hasan fled to Libya, where he stayed in hiding for the next five years. When al-Kāhinat captured and adopted a young Arab of high rank named Khaled ibn Yazid, she learned from him that the Muslims wished to secure all of the harbors on the Gulf of Tunis, from which they planned to control Mediterranean trade and eventually attack Rome.[30]

This prompted al-Kāhinat to go beyond resistance to the Arab army

and its efforts to convert Berbers to Islam. She decided to leave nothing in the Maghreb that would entice them to return. In a speech she
reportedly gave to Berber nomads and herders, the seer with long black
hair and wild eyes made assertions that, over the centuries, have been
paraphrased in this manner: "The Arabs only want Ifrīqīya for its cities
and gold and silver while we only want agriculture and flocks. The only
solution is the destruction [kharb] of the whole of Ifrīqīya so that the
Arabs lose interest in it and they never return again!"[31]

She then went on the warpath, torching every caravansary and oasis
outpost between Tripoli and Tangier, especially devastating those that
had aided and abetted Hasan's movements. Between her own siege and
the earlier attacks by Hasan, Carthage itself was left in such ruin that its
harbor was abandoned for another two centuries. While these actions
made most nomadic Berber tribes jubilant, the sedentary oasis dwellers and merchants were not pleased by the way the Jewish priestess had
scorched the earth around them. They silently pledged their support to
Hasan, should he ever return. Meanwhile, al-Kāhinat and her troops
went back to their stronghold in the wilds of the Aurès Mountains,
where they could effectively block the only routes from the plains of
Tunisia westward into Algeria and Morocco.

Around 698, Hasan did return, bringing not only his own troops
but also some twelve thousand Berbers who could no longer accept
al-Kāhinat's despotism and destructive urge. Just before their armies met
near Gabis, the seer apparently had a dream in which she foresaw her
own fate. The next morning she requested that Khaled ibn Yazid, the
Arab youth whom she had taken into her own family, take her sons back
with him to the Arab army in the hope that they would not be killed in
battle. The Muslim army overwhelmed her troops and sent her back
into the wilds of her Aurès refuge. Hasan pursued her and ultimately
defeated the Berber resistance north of Tobna, at a site now called Bir
al-Kāhinat. Although some claim that the enigmatic warrior-priestess
died fighting with a sword in her hand, other accounts suggest that she
drank poison to keep from being raped or killed by the Arab soldiers.

With al-Kāhinat's death, which most sources put in 702, the last of
the three Muslim invasions of North Africa had succeeded in securing a
strategic position on the Gulf of Tunis, directly across the Mediterranean
from Sicily and Italy. Her sons as well as most of her Berber followers converted to Islam from Judaism and Christianity. The jihad continued on with little difficulty for the next nine hundred miles, with
Muslims taking control of the entire Mediterranean shoreline all the

way to the Jabal al-Tariq, known today as the Rock of Gibraltar, which overlooks the strait of the same name. In 708, Muslim forces found no resistance when they entered the twin cities of Tangier and Ceuta, the closest African ports to the Iberian Peninsula. From there, they would later stage their entry into western Europe.[32]

By that time, Islam had already been embraced in much of East Africa as well. That was because some of the Prophet's original followers had fled Mecca to escape the wrath of the Quraysh clans against those who aligned themselves with the Prophet and Khadijah. They had quickly established trading hubs in Abyssinia, where Yemeni and Omani Arabs had been negotiating for myrrh, coffee, and other goods for centuries. After the conversion of the black African leader King Negus, Islam spread through the Sudan all the way to Ghana. The rapid coalescence of various legs of the East African spice trade into a single network was as remarkable as what soon happened in the Maghreb. The Lamu Archipelago near Kenya later became a colony for Omani and Yemeni spice traders, who took Islam along on their dhows. Zanzibar became another of their colonies, where in time the production of spices taken from Asia provided the Arabs with an alternative source when conflicts prevented their passage eastward. Still later, Madagascar was assimilated into their trade networks.

From that point, it would be Muslim caliphs, emirs, brokers, and merchants, not Jewish or Christian traders or bankers, who would decide who could trade along their routes, some of which now ran twenty-two hundred to three thousand miles long. Despite their avoidance of usury and oppressive taxation, the Muslims made sure that considerable wealth moved back toward Mecca, Damascus, and other places along their chain of command. Jews and Christians could place their aromatics and other wares onto caravans running through countries under Islamic control, but they could hardly afford to work independently of the Muslim trade networks.

Although some goods still moved surreptitiously through underground routes to black markets nearby, it would have been difficult for Jews or Christians to deliver many goods to more distant buyers clandestinely. Thus most Jewish and Christian spice traders sought allies within the Muslim mercantile class and negotiated with them for favors and privilege. Few of the People of the Book who were involved in globalized trade would ever again deny that Muslims had gained the upper hand. In a matter of a century, they had consolidated numerous fiefdoms into vast transcontinental networks throughout which most players adhered to the same economic principles. That fact alone made the minor economic experiments and expeditions first organized by Khadijah and Muhammad breakthrough moments in the history of trade, for their innovations and ethics emanated from Mecca and Medina to much of the rest of the Eastern Hemisphere.

While in the Moroccan port of Essaouira one spring, I slowly came to realize that Jews have not only survived for centuries in the Islamic Maghreb but have also thrived as partners with Arab traders there. Here, both practicing Jews and their descendants who became converts to Islam (called *la'louj* in Berber) have lived among Arabs, Berbers, Greeks, Phoenicians, Portuguese, and Gnawa Sufis descended from West Africans of Mauritania, Senegal, Mali, and Ghana for upward of two thousand years. Some scholars say the Jews first came to Essaouira, then known as Mogador, in pursuit of African gold but they ended up trading in salt instead. In time, they became esteemed as spice traders, jewelry makers, woodworkers, and blacksmiths.

While wandering around the ancient medina looking for spice markets, I came into the oldest part of the city, a quiet quarter known as the Mellah, "the place where the Jews reside." Here the Jews had their synagogue, schools, fountain, baths, and most of their homes, and I hoped to glimpse remnants of that past and evidence of their artisanship. But what struck me as I walked down the narrow corridors of the Mellah were the symbols carved into sandstone on the portals above the doors, icons that marked one's ethnicity, faith, and tolerance for other faiths.

When I saw a carving of the Star of David sitting by itself above an ancient doorway, I assumed that I was in a Jews-only sector of the city. But I soon noticed other doorways marked by the Star of David and a rose with four petals, an ancient symbol of Christian hospitality. Perhaps this house had belonged to a Jew who had married a Christian, or was a Jewish home that had welcomed Christian sailors staying over in the port. There were also doors with the Star of David juxtaposed with a rose of eight petals, the symbol of Arab Muslims. I saw other symbols as well, such as pomegranate blossoms, an Andalusian symbol of welcome, and an olive branch, a sign of peace welcoming all comers.

I had learned that many Jews had been brought to Essaouira as *tujjar al-sultan,* the merchants that Arab sultans enlisted to help them negotiate trade with both African and European Christians. I could now see how the city served as a gateway to the west coast of Africa, Portugal, and the Canary Islands. As I looked around me in the medina, I could

FIGURE 12. Cryptic symbols such as these, carved in stone above doorways in the Jewish section of Essaouira, Morocco, once guided travelers and traders to homes that accepted Jews, Christians, or Muslims as boarders. (Photo by the author.)

sense that Essaouira continues to host active exchanges among a multitude of faiths and ethnicities, as it always has.

But what I learned that impressed me the most was how even the most sedentary Jew in Essaouira could post messages on ships and camel caravans that would reach other Jewish merchants, not only in the nearby ports of Agadir and Azemmour but also inland at Marrakech. By passing messages through a network of ship captains, the Jews of Essaouira could communicate with merchants in Larache, Tangier, Tunis, Cyrene (or Libya), Alexandria, Gaza, Byblos (Lebanon), Aleppo, and Smyrna. By runner, donkey rider, and camel drover, their requests for spices and payment could be delivered to Meknes and Fez to the east, or Draa, Messine, and Sigil Massa to the south. Some of their messages and spice orders eventually made it to Damascus, Baghdad, and Aden.

While the Muslims were going about ruling and coordinating the wider world, Jews had found a vehicle on which they could piggyback their own interests. It was in Essaouira that I first imagined how a Jewish or Muslim trader there might have communication and influence as far away as the North China Sea, some sixty-two hundred miles to the east of their harbor on the western edges of the Maghreb. This is a phenomenon that becomes more evident as this story proceeds.

CHAPTER 6

Merging the Spice Routes with the Silk Roads

I am now following the waft of fragrances into the deserts and steppes of Central Asia. My wife, Laurie, and I are making our way up to the crowded entrance of a market known as Shah Mansur. We have been dropped off by our friend Jumbaboy on the corner of the Nissor Muhammad and Lahati Boulevards in Dushanbe, Tajikistan, and we pause by the market's gate to gulp down the aromas and take in the scene. Staged in a rather dingy, Soviet-era pavilion, this "green market" has been so sanitized and standardized by the Russians that it doesn't seem as Oriental as foreign visitors like us might hope it to be.

And yet Jumbaboy has assured us that since the Russians left, Shah Mansur has regained some of its informality and local color. As we step through its entryway and begin to wander down the aisles, the piles of blemish-free fruits and candied nuts lure us in. Behind them I spot the stalls where the spices have arrived from both directions of the Silk Road, as well as from spice routes trailing southward.

Perhaps Dushanbe today is as close as it gets to a true crossroads between the Silk Road and the spice routes that meander up from Afghanistan and Pakistan, India and Sri Lanka. Of course, no caravans of Bactrian camels alerted us to the fact that we were approaching such a crossroads, only old Russian Lada sedans and some recent Japanese and European imports. And this was clearly not a souk, bazaar, or khan of any antiquity, for the city of Dushanbe is not even a century old, and the pavilion of Shah Mansur is far younger than that. But as we move from booth to booth beneath the towering rain-shelter roof, we meet Tajiks and Turks, Uzbeks and Kyrgyz, Chinese and Kazakhs bringing in vegetables, fruits, spices, and fresh herbs from every direction.

Vendors from the west and northwest—from Samarkand, Bishkek, and Bukhara—carry dried peaches and apricots, fresh figs and pomegranates, wild pistachios and huge Persian melons. Their counterparts from the highland steppes to our east and northeast, the Fergana Valley and the shores of Lake Izzyk, have transported half a dozen apple varieties, pears, persimmons and pumpkins, and dozens of dried Chinese spices and medicines. From the northwest—the republics that formerly made up the heartland of the Soviet Union—come napa cabbages, beets, Bukhara peppers, horseradish, garlic, and peas, and from the southeast, through Afghanistan from India, Myanmar, and the Moluccas, arrive mace and nutmeg, cinnamon and cloves, saffron and turmeric. The medicinal plants—piles of them next to old bronze balances that weigh them out by the ounce or gram—have come from who knows where—perhaps India, Tibet, and China.

Vendors slip the produce we purchase into plastic bags, paper cones, and burlap sacks as the tinny sounds and surreal sights of Bollywood videos blast away above them. Despite such distractions, they remain true to what they do best, just as generations of their ancestors have done before them: "Is this your first time in the city? Here, try this sun-dried peach! It is all natural, no sulfur coating! It is from Samarkand. You know, the Golden Peaches of Samarkand, heh? Its flavor is unforgettable, you will see. Do you want only a half kilo or an entire kilo of them?"

For their displays, the vendors have set the dried fruits down in layers, like overlapping shingles on a perfectly assembled roof. I take a furry sun-dried peach and pop it into my mouth, closing my eyes. Its intense sweetness overwhelms my palate. I reopen my eyes just in time to see Laurie, her eyes still closed, experiencing the same burst of flavor. When we recover, the merchant comes close to us and whispers, "I noticed that you were looking at the saffron earlier on. Well, that saffron there is for anyone. Let me bring out for you the saffron of the highest quality in the world. It is fresher than the others. You know, just this year's crop, handpicked from tens of thousands of flowers by a friend of mine. It will brighten any dish of *oshi plov,* one of the best of Tajik pilafs. You will be proud to go home and make it for your family and dearest friends."

At neighboring stalls, other merchants are arranging their lemons

☙ OSHI PLOV ❧
Persian-Tajik Rice Pilaf with Quince

This is perhaps the quintessential meal of Central Asia's segment of the Silk Roads, from Baghdad through Bukhara and Samarkand to Dushanbe and Kabul. It is embraced by both the Bukharan Jews and the Ismaili Muslims of Badakhshan and was no doubt held in high esteem by the Zoroastrians of the region. The *pilav, pulao, palau,* and *plov* of Central Asia probably hark back to the earliest introduction of rice into the area, though bulgur wheat or couscous may well have been there prior to the arrival of rice. Variations emerge in the Middle East with *maqluba, khoresh-e beh,* and *kidra,* and in Spain with paella. In most cases, these dishes include an aromatic rice that has been partially cooked in a seasoned broth with caramelized onions, then steamed with other ingredients layered or buried in the rice. Like a paella, a *plov* is often prepared in huge quantities for festivities such as weddings or holidays, and each cook contributes his or her own distinctive flair to the dish.

In the fourth century BCE, Alexander the Great and his troops became so taken with Bactrian and Sogdian pilafs that they reportedly took the preparation back with them from the Sogdian capital of Marakanda (present-day Samarkand) to Macedonia. But the first detailed description of how to prepare a pilaf properly came to us during the tenth century from Ibn Sīnā, known to the Western world as Avicenna. Because of his enormous influence, Ibn Sīnā is considered by many culinary historians to be the father of modern pilaf preparation.

The foundation for the following recipe was offered to me by a Tajik man named Jumbaboy, whom I met in Dushanbe. He noted that the Tajik version of the dish was most often made in late autumn, just as the fruits were ripening on quince trees. To gain a more detailed perspective on proportions of fruits, nuts, and spices relative to the lamb, rice, and onion base, I have relied on Najmieh Batmanglij's Persian version in her fine book, *Silk Road Cooking: A Vegetarian Journey.*

Serve with a mixture of diced tomatoes, cucumbers, red onions, and capers marinated in cider vinegar or lime juice. *Serves 6 to 8.*

For the Rice
3   cups basmati or other long-grain white rice
4½ cups water
1   tablespoon sea salt
2   tablespoons butter

For the Broth
1½ teaspoons butter, ghee, or olive oil
1   white or yellow onion, thinly sliced into rings
8   ounces boneless lamb from shoulder, cut into small cubes (optional)

2 large carrots, peeled and julienned
5 cups water
½ cup turbinado sugar
1 tablespoon grated orange zest
2 cardamom pods, split
1¼ teaspoons freshly ground cumin seeds
Sea salt

To Finish
2 quinces, peeled, halved, cored, and cut into ½-inch cubes
1 tablespoon orange blossom water
½ teaspoon saffron threads, dissolved in 2 tablespoons hot water
2 tablespoons butter, cut into small pieces
½ cup slivered almonds, toasted
½ cup pistachios, toasted and salted

Put the rice in a bowl, add water to cover generously, and swirl the rice around with your fingers until the water is cloudy. Pour off the water, re-cover the rice with water, and swirl the rice again, then drain. Repeat until the rinsing water is clear, then add water to cover and let the rice soak for 30 minutes.

Meanwhile, make the broth. In a heavy stockpot, melt the butter over medium heat. Add the onion and sauté until tender and lightly caramelized, 5 to 7 minutes. Add the lamb (if using) and carrots and sauté until the carrots are just starting to become tender, 2 to 3 minutes. Add the water and bring to a simmer. Add the sugar, orange zest, cardamom, and cumin, then season with salt. Turn down the heat to medium-low and simmer for 15 minutes.

Drain the rice, transfer it to a nonstick saucepan, and add the water, salt, and butter. Place over medium-high heat and bring to a boil, then turn down the heat to low, cover, and cook until the liquid is absorbed, about 15 minutes. Let stand for 10 minutes, then stir. The rice should be fluffy and tender.

When the rice is ready, add it to the broth in the stockpot and stir well. To finish, using a large spoon, open a basin in the middle of the rice mixture. Put the quince in the basin and cover the quince with the rice mixture. Drizzle the orange blossom water and saffron water evenly over the surface, then scatter the butter and half each of the almonds and pistachios evenly over the top. Reduce the heat to low, cover tightly to prevent any heat from escaping, and cook until the quince cubes have "melted" into the rice mixture, about 30 minutes. (The covered pot can instead be transferred to a 350°F oven and baked for about the same amount of time.)

Remove from the heat and let stand, still covered, on a damp surface for 5 minutes, to loosen the rice crust that invariably forms on the bottom of the pot. The lightly caramelized crust that forms on the pot bottom adds texture and depth of flavor to the dish. Invert the pilaf onto a serving platter and garnish the top with the remaining pistachios and almonds.

Batmanglij, Najmieh. *Silk Road Cooking: A Vegetarian Journey.* Washington, DC: Mage Publishers, 2002, p. 166.

into geometrically elegant cylindrical pyramids, or stringing together yellow, red, and purple chiles into gorgeous wreaths. One of the wreath makers, a man in his midforties, waves me over while Laurie is looking at the lemons on the other side of the aisle.

"Come here, my friend. You are my elder, but if I may, let me give you some advice. I see you have a beautiful young wife over there. I see from the bags under your eyes that you are quite old—I do not know for sure, maybe sixty?—even though your face is young and your thoughts and desires are too. I have this herb for you. I will not talk about it when your wife comes close, but for men like you it is better than Viagra. You can mix it into your food when no one is looking . . ."

This polyglot of a spice trader smirks at me, but like his Arabian counterpart known as *al-tajir al-muqim,* he knows how to gain the attention of a potential customer. Such traders proceed easily at first. They use flavors, colors, shapes, and vocal tones to draw you in. And then, to seduce you, they tell stories that speak to your strongest desires, your highest hopes, and your darkest fears.

If only Central Asia's Bactrian camels and horses could tell this story. They have been the freighters of the desert, the carriers of cassia cinnamon, cumin, ginger, anise, musk, and silk for centuries. But these beasts were also kept close enough to the campfires at night to have heard the parables and poems, the legends and lies told by the Arab cavalrymen, infantrymen, imams, and merchants who traveled far beyond the bazaars where Arabic was spoken. They entered the khans and caravansaries where Turkish and Farsi instead of Arabic were used to describe the heady aromas, unusual flavors, and exquisite textiles that they, as beasts of burden, had carried along. They saw the feasts where Persian chefs and musicians brought out the best they had to offer, while the Arab, Turkish, and Indian poets from the south praised them with an honorific *ghazal.* On occasion, they scavenged and grazed on the left-

FIGURE 13. Herbal Viagra in a market in Dushanbe, Tajikistan. (Photo by the author.)

over onions, rice, lemongrass, and celery stalks found on the dry desert ground after the party was over.

The camels and horses knew all about what had come out of the desert like a whirlwind to stun the unsuspecting community or unprepared rival. They had carried that whirlwind on their backs.

The animals could not speak to me, of course, but as I visited the spice and silk markets of Asia, Muslim shopkeepers and bards all reminded me of the same fact. Following the rise of Muhammad, Islam had spread into Asia with astonishing speed. Indeed, according to old Chinese Muslim texts, even before Muhammad's death, one of his earliest converts, Sa'ad ibn Abi Waqqas, a military leader at the Battle of Badr in 624, had gone by ship all the way to Fujian Province in China to alert the emperor of the East of the new prophet in the West. There, in 616, he became the first Arab from Medina to spread the revelations found in the Qur'an.

He then played key roles in Islamic expansion in Asia, helping defeat the Persian forces from the Sassanid Empire on the Euphrates at the Battle of al-Qadisiyya in 637, and vanquishing the last Sassanid army in 642 at the Battle of Nihāvand.[1] As commander of Muslim troops in Iraq, he tried to motivate their pride with this encouragement: "You are Arab chiefs and notables, the elite of every tribe and the pride of those who follow you."[2] Finally, as a fifty-six-year-old elder, in 651, he returned to Asia with his son as a Muslim envoy from Caliph Uthman ibn Affan to Tang emperor Gaozong. That same son would one day build the first mosque in Han-dominated China.

Of course, it took more than fast horses and Bactrian camels to accomplish the expansion of the Islamic empire with such lightning speed. It took Arabs willing to spread their unshakable belief in the Prophet's compelling vision for the world. They had to be individuals capable of forming and managing a social organization that could allow such a vision to bear fruit.

The Prophet's relatives and disciples first drove into the heart of the Levant and of Mesopotamia early in 633. Within the next couple of years, they took Damascus, Antioch, and Homs. Over the following decade, the first Quraysh tribal converts to Islam recruited other related tribes to join their cause. Among these new allies were members of the northernmost Tayy tribe, who were living as Marsh Arabs in southern Iraq at the time. Together, they challenged neighboring Turks and Persians constrained by the Byzantine Empire to join them against the Christianized Roman rulers there.

When Sa'ad ibn Abi Waqqas and his Arab Muslims first stirred up the Persian dust in late 637, the locals did not immediately warm to them. For a time, it seemed as though fierce counterattacks by both Roman troops and the Persians themselves might stop the Arabs at the Zagros Mountains. Force—and fright—would be needed to break this log jam.

But Sa'ad ibn Abi Waqqas had a new innovation to employ in an assault on the Persian capital. He used twenty heavy artillery units with so-called sling beam engines, which were essentially catapults that shot missiles from slings.[3] The same weapons were used to breach the walls of Samarkand. They were successful in terrorizing their opposition and helping Islam gain the ground that the lure of trade could not muster.

With the final victory over the Persian troops in 642, Islam arrived at its most remarkable turning point in Asia. It could now reach far beyond the Arabic-speaking world into the land of Farsi speakers, of Persians, Sogdians, and the ancestors of the present-day Tajiks. That is how key portions of the Sassanid Empire began at last to fall into the hands of the Muslims: it was clear that this religion was not meant merely for the old Arabic-speaking tribes from the interior of the peninsula. From Medina, thousands of miles to the south, Caliph Umar ibn al-Khattab directed Sa'ad ibn Abi Waqqas and others to move their Arab troops on multiple fronts until the outlying stretches of Persia still under Sassanid control were conquered in 644 and then integrated into the emerging empire.[4]

In short, Islam had suddenly become the most pervasive economic power in the entire "known" world. It had stitched into a single cohesive quilt all of the isolated regions and cultures that had formerly been ragtag fragments of an imperfectly functioning network.

Within two decades after Muhammad's death, the Umayyad dynasty was formed by the Banu Umayyah clan of the Quraysh tribe. Its members recruited a broader amalgam of tribes, Arab, Persian, and Turkish, to become a single community under Allah. Curiously, newly converted Muslims began to call this collection of tribes by the name they already had for the northernmost Bedouin-like Arabs, the Tayy. Some of the chroniclers called this Arabized mix the Taits, or in Persian, the Tazik. But soon the name was being applied to Arabized Persians by their Farsi-speaking kin to the east. In time, the term *Tajik* was used for "Arab-influenced" tribes in general.[5]

As Islam marched eastward, the term came to embrace all Farsi-speaking Muslims as far away as Afghanistan, Uzbekistan, and present-day Tajikistan. Chinese traders and monks coming west over the many strands of the intercontinental cable now known as the Silk Road called these Arab-influenced Farsi speakers *dashi ren,* with the Banu Umayyah in particular called the white-robed *dashi ren.* As one Islamic envoy boasted to his kin back in Mecca during the seventh century, with their conversion to Islam, "all people would become Arabs."[6]

Wandering the city streets and market walkways of Dushanbe, I become obsessed with the hope or dream that I might meet a Tajik who clearly understands that he or she is descended from the Tayy. My dream arose out of just a few words I once read in an obscure manuscript, one for which I have unfortunately forgotten both the author and the title. It suggested that when the Banu Nebhani and Tayy tribes had come out of Arabia around 170, they were inextricably hitched at the hip. They were so intermarried that the two differently named tribes were genetically one and the same. I imagined that some of my Banu Nebhani ancestors had come north with the Tayy to live as Marsh Arabs along the Tigris and Euphrates. These Arab clans had converted to Islam and assisted the empire with its eastward march into the deserts and steppes of Central Asia. They had then settled down in a trading town in the Vakhsh River valley, adding Farsi to their repertoire of tongues.

Did they take on the role of cross-cultural traders in their newly found homes? Were spices, herbs, and incenses among the items that they moved between the West and the East? Perhaps I want too much from these distant relatives.

So it is not surprising that my hopes of finding these hypothetical long-lost kin are dashed. I learn from a scholar in Dushanbe that the only residual enclave of Arabic-speaking Muslims left in Tajikistan is located a couple of hundred miles to the south of the city. Their villages are on the Afghan border, in a zone known for its black-market trade in opium and firearms. Regardless of whether or not they stand in harm's way along one of the world's most volatile borders, I would be a sitting duck if I were to show up in their midst. My vainglorious dream of potentially discovering a few distant Nabhan kin hidden among the many Tayy Tajiks living there will have to wait.

The proposed spiritual, cultural, economic, and culinary makeover of Persians and Sogdians did not occur instantaneously, of course. The Umayyad dynasty established the Diwan al-Kharaj as a central council of revenue to manage the finances of the entire empire. It tried to jump-start the tedious process of consolidation by attempting to instill a shared ethic of sacred Islamic economics into all of its trading partners.

The Diwan al-Kharaj reaffirmed Islam's initial focus on socially responsible trading and investing, with no money made off goods forbidden by Qur'anic mandates. The Banu Umayyah hoped to distinguish themselves in significant ways from the Jews by upholding Muhammad's and Khadijah's ban on usury. When lending had to occur, the counselors of the *diwan* insisted on the provision that no interest could accumulate at the expense of the lendee. They placed a *zakat* tax on the harvest of crops only to the extent that it allowed a portion of the harvest to be reallocated to those who were hungry or otherwise in need. They also recommended that trade negotiations be guided by the concept of *gharar*, "the interdiction of chance," which cautioned traders in foodstuffs to share with farmers both the equity accrued during bumper crops and the costs of recovery after losses caused by droughts or other random events. In this manner, debts as well as rewards were spread among all partners, much as is done in community-supported agriculture today.

Through the Diwan al-Kharaj, the Umayyad leadership encouraged all Arab spice traders to select their business partners, even those who were neither of Arab blood nor presently of the Islamic faith, from those willing to nurture and support everyone along the entire spice supply chain. In this manner, the whole network of producers, middlemen,

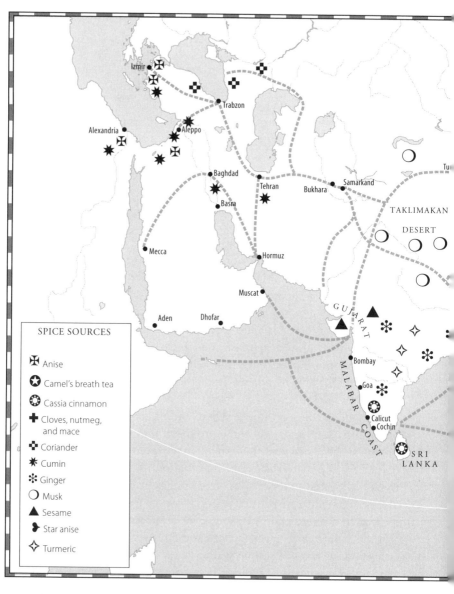

MAP 3. Spice trails of the Desert Silk Roads and Maritime Silk Roads

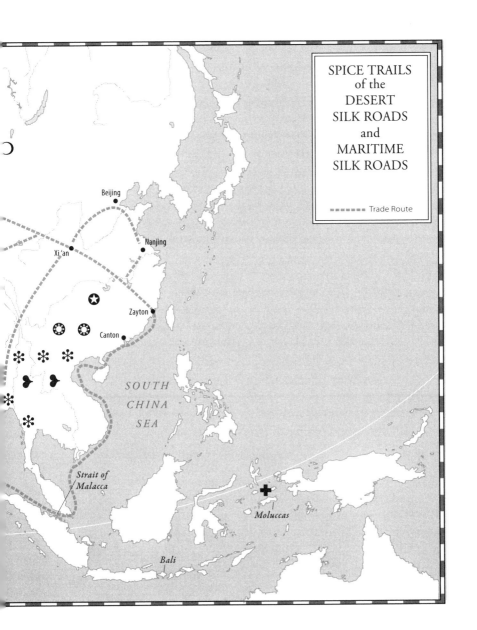

SPICE TRAILS
of the
DESERT
SILK ROADS
and
MARITIME
SILK ROADS

- - - - - - Trade Route

Beijing

Nanjing

Xi'an

Zayton

Canton

SOUTH
CHINA
SEA

Strait of
Malacca

Moluccas

Bali

brokers, and bankers was anchored in commonly held values. It developed rules for fiscal exchange between banking institutions located considerable distances from one another, so that funds could be transferred, loans could be paid off, and venture capital could finance projects throughout the Islamic world.[7]

Further, the Umayyad caliphs demanded that those who benefited from this system, especially Muslims, Buddhists, Hindus, Jews, Zoroastrians, and Nestorian Christians who traded in aromatics, horses, camels, precious metals, silk, and other textiles, were expected to direct a significant portion of their earnings back to the power base of the Umayyad dynasty. The Muslims were the network facilitators to some extent, but they acknowledged the knowledge and wealth of other players.

Protection could not and did not come without a price. The Umayyad elite of Quraysh descent accumulated fortunes for themselves and for their institutions by unilaterally setting that price. Some members of that Quraysh clan must have wondered why their grandparents back in Mecca had ever opposed Muhammad to begin with, for now they themselves were raking in the cash and feasting on far richer fare than the *tharīd* of unleavened bread soaked in broth that their humble Prophet had favored.[8]

Perhaps they remembered that their Arab ancestors from the deserts of the peninsula had never been able to accumulate much wealth. Instead, they had been constantly on the move with their caravans or herds, reinvesting whatever gains they accrued in more camels and horses. They had forked over pay-offs to petty sheikhs who offered them the privilege to pass through their territories.

After the Umayyad caliphs settled into their capital of Damascus, they could more easily compare themselves and their abodes to what they witnessed in Persian communities to the north and east. They realized that their newly acquired sedentary life in palatial settings both looked and tasted better than the life they had previously eked out in the searing heart of the Arabian Peninsula.

What Umayyad bureaucrats sooner or later had to learn, however, was that rules, regulations, and ethical aspirations were not enough to solidify their network into a stable empire. They needed something else to make their trading partners among the Persians, Parthians, Sogdians, and Turks want to become "good Arabs." It would take memorable meals, stories, and songs to forge a culture that was truly galvanized.

Once Persia and Arabia were spiritually, militarily, and politically united, they needed artistic, culinary, and poetic expressions to move their cultural synthesis beyond what either had achieved in the past. And so, perhaps unconsciously at first, the Umayyad dynasty fostered a highly expressive hybrid culture and fusion cuisine that would soon turn the heads of many astute observers.

Throughout the Golden Age of Islam, from 750 to 1257, Persian and Arab chefs, culinary journalists, and physicians generated more cookbooks in Arabic than were written in all of the other languages of the world during the same period.[9] This proliferation of recipes was not due solely to the broader range of staple foods and spices that had suddenly become available in Islamic kitchens. It emerged from something akin to hybrid vigor, in that it generated enhanced productivity among Arab and Persian chefs. In particular, the Umayyad court chefs began to experiment with sauces of fermented grains and fish, with steeping and marinating, with molding and layering meats and stuffing the layers with nuts and raisins, with coating fish in reductions of grape juice and honey, and with "cooking" fish not merely with heat and smoke but also with vinegar, lime, or sour orange juice. The culinary techniques and recipes that they perfected, such as *sikbāj*, the cooking of fish and fowl in sour juices and acidic vinegars, have endured in the Middle East, Maghreb, and Latin America to this day.[10] I see them in the desert borderlands of Mexico just south of my home, where *sikbāj* has been transmogrified into ceviche and *escabeche*, terms used in contemporary Mesoamerica by Spanish speakers.

Perhaps culinary invention in the world of Arab-Persian fusion, rather than military dominion over the heart of Central Asia, was the most lasting consequence of the Battle of Nihāvand. Over the following centuries, political boundaries and alliances shifted repeatedly, but the medieval Islamic interest in flavor and fragrance only intensified with time, and their culinary imperialism spread across space.

The Arabs themselves had finally reached into better-watered and more productive lands, places where their own food security was no longer in jeopardy from season to season. But they had also reached into foreign cultures with talents, skills, and imaginations that challenged their own. The more observant among these Arabs realized that they now had abundant incentives to merge their own culture with those of the Persians and Sogdians.[11] So the most upwardly mobile Arabs in Asia Minor encouraged these Farsi-speaking communities to help them put their collective portfolio of intellectual, artistic, and commercial assets at the disposal of the entire *umma*, the Muslim community as a whole, in order to form a truly creative, if not lucrative, Islamic empire.

In less than a decade following the conversion of the Persians and Sogdians, the newly labeled Tajik storytellers, singers, oud players, architects, sculptors, and chefs of the Islamic world had unprecedented support for artistic expression and innovation. They now had access to the finest materials and mentors that money could buy, since it seemed that nearly everyone attracted to living in Damascus, not just the Banu Umayyah elite, was out for entertainment.

They had, in short order, gained access to the entire range of culinary ingredients and cooking utensils available in every trading hub for staples and spices for one thousand miles to the east, as well as all of the technical knowledge harbored in every artisans' guild, school, and library. Muslim soldiers on the front line had already taken control of Merv and Herat by 650 and Balkh by 652. In the coming decades, they would voraciously consume whatever was available from Hind (India), southeast of them, and from Sin (China), northeast of them.

The extraordinary reach of the Central Asian Muslim spice traders made for both good eating and memorable stories. Their impassioned poetry and music became incorporated aesthetically into Muslim feasts across a wide geographic range, with Persian and Arab sensibilities and folk stories fused into masterworks like *One Thousand and One Nights*. Later, Sufi poets such as Rumi and Hafiz would spread the metaphor of the caravansary around the world, their feast of words inspiring spiritual pilgrims and spice merchants alike from many cultural backgrounds. The trading of both stories and recipes from all over the empire ensured that poetic and gastronomic innovation went hand in hand.

I have belatedly come to recognize that my Banu Nebhani ancestors are frequently mentioned in the Persian renditions of the corpus of stories known to Westerners as the *Arabian Nights,* although they are not always favorably portrayed. In several episodes, they come across as the nouveau riche from the Arabian Peninsula trying to buy or bludgeon their access to anything of interest in Basra or Mosul. Around the 640th night, the Banu Nebhani sheikh al-Hamal bin Májid, who had gained some wealth as a merchant of aromatics in the south, hears of the charms of a Persian emir's beautiful daughter, Madhíyah. He offers to bring her "great company" in immediate exchange for her hand, and then dumps extravagant gifts on her doorstep, including a hundred slave girls and a hundred female camels laden with loads of ambergris, aloe, camphor, and jewels, as well as the rare faunal aromatic we now call musk. Not amused, Madhíyah categorically dismisses him as a yokel. Infuriated, al-Hamal kidnaps her while the emir is away at a friend's wedding feast, killing many of her guards and forcing the others to flee.

Of course, al-Hamal ultimately had to pay for his arrogant and impulsive actions, and his meaty head ended up skewered by a sword as if it were no more than another kebab made for roasting. Madhíyah, the beautiful maiden, was freed to live out her days feasting, fasting, and praying among Persians and Arabs who respected one another.

In the regions to the north and east of their ancient peninsular homelands, the Arabs began to intermarry with the Persians who had fled from the sinking Sassanid Empire. Then, as they reached eastward into Central Asia, they established colonies and arranged marriages with other Farsi speakers, especially those Sogdian merchants who had already been dominating the trade among China, India, and Mesopotamia since the second or third century BCE. The musk that the Banu Nebhani sheikh had dumped at Madhíyah's feet in the *Arabian Nights* had likely come west by way of Sogdian caravans.

The Sogdians (who called themselves Turanians early on) have never been given much notice, let alone respect, by the Western world.[12] That is odd, for the Chinese have long acknowledged the pivotal role Sogdians played in Eastern trade over the course of a thousand years. They remind us, as do the Gujaratis, Hindus, Berbers, and Italians, that Muslims and Jews were not the only innovators in spice commerce. The Sogdians first appeared on the world stage in a bit part as sedentary inhabitants of the fertile valley flanking the Zeravshan River. But as the riverside crossroads of Samarkand and Bukhara began to flourish as trade centers in the semiarid lands we now call Tajikistan and Uzbekistan, the Sogdians moved into the limelight. When Bactrian camels made their historic debut on the Central Asian stage, the Sogdians took on the lead role of the *sabao*, or caravanner. It was then that they took their very good show on the road, impressing even the most-seasoned Arab trader of aromatics.

Like the Arabs, the Sogdians knew how to leverage global value out of some rather obscure product from the arid hinterlands. They drew on the Uighurs of the Taklimakan Desert, the Mongols of the Gobi, and the Tibetans of the high, dry plateaus to provide them with some of the world's most potent aromatics, such as musk, camphor, and Sichuan pepper. They knew how to conceal the origins of such treasures and poetically heighten their mythic power and appeal. Fortunately, they had recruited a capable and resilient ally who could help them transport these precious substances out of the hinterlands and into the bazaars of the Islamic empire. That ally was none other than the Bactrian camel. Wherever I have come across these two-humped wonders, from Izmir, Turkey, to Turpan, China, I have immediately sensed that they are a force to be reckoned with.

It would be difficult to overestimate how much the symbiosis of the Bactrian two-humped camel with Sogdian, Persian, and Arab caravanners changed the course of human history. The Bactrians do not simply carry one more hump than the dromedary of Arabia and Africa; they are stronger and sturdier and able to shoulder several hundred more pounds of goods. They are also highly adaptable and able to endure the extraordinary range of weather extremes, given that they evolved around the Gobi and the Taklimakan,[13] where temperatures have been known to shift by as much as eighty degrees in a single day. I have witnessed them nonchalantly sitting below sea level in the Gobi at the foot of the Flaming Mountains on a 106-degree day in July; six months later, those same camels might be crossing the snowbound passes of the Tian Shan range fifteen thousand feet above the barren desert floor.

Although they are named for the Bactrian region of present-day Afghanistan and Iran, it appears that they were first domesticated farther east around 2500 BCE. But as beasts of burden, Bactrian camels may not have been available as far west as the nursery grounds of the Bactrian and Sogdian peoples along the Zeravshan River for another millennium. Once the Sogdian traders and Bactrian camels joined forces, however, they were carrying loads twice as heavy and twice as far as the most durable dromedaries the Sabaeans, Minaeans, and Nabataeans had ever known. As camel historian Daniel Potts famously noted, if the Silk Roads became the bridge between the cultures and cuisines of the East and the West, the Bactrian camel became the locomotion across that bridge.[14]

With the logistical dilemmas of moving large loads for long distances lessened by the Bactrian camels, the Sogdians transformed their trading hubs in Samarkand and Bukhara into just two of the many links in the chain that erroneously became known as the Silk Road.[15] In truth, there were many paths that formed an interlinked network of corridors between the East and the West. No less than five camel routes led north or south of the Taklimakan and Gobi where they edge the Turpan Depression of western China. Along those stretches, the Sogdian *sabao* and their Bactrian camels may have carried more musk than silk or tea. Farther west, in the Sogdian heartlands, the Zeravshan became known as the River of the Sabao, and its sumptuous fruits became renowned as the Golden Peaches of Samarkand as far east as coastal China and Korea.[16]

As the Sogdians enlisted Persian and Arab capital to build and secure other caravansaries along the trade routes emanating from Central Asia, they used these strongholds for more than just occasional stays while passing through. They took to harboring colonies of Muslim, Orthodox Christian, Nestorian, and Bukharan Jewish merchants far beyond their original homelands. Regardless of who ruled the steppes at any particular moment, the Arab-Persian-Sogdian alliance stayed in charge of trade at least as far east as the Chinese capital of Chang'an. Now known as Xi'an, and still home to more than fifty thousand Muslims of Arab, Persian, and Sogdian descent, Chang'an served for many centuries as a terminus for the Silk and Musk Roads of the north, and tapped into the Tea and Horse Roads that began far to the southeast.

During the medieval era, Chang'an grew to be the largest city in the world.[17] By 742, when its thirty square miles of trading grounds engaged some two million inhabitants, no fewer than five thousand of its residents were foreign-born traders and caravanners called Franke. Most of them were Sogdians, with a handful of Persians, Indians, Arabs, and Turks in the mix. The foreigners from Asia Minor with eyes of blue, hazel, green, or gray were nicknamed the Simaren or Suma on account of their unusual eye color. Their odd appearance amused the likes of Hanshan, the great hermit poet of the Tang dynasty.

Of course, when compared with the Sogdians, the Arabs were latecomers to Central Asia. Centuries before Islam reached that far eastward, Sogdian merchants, who practiced Zoroastrianism, had become the primary go-betweens linking China, Mongolia, Central Asia, India, and the Middle East. Without a doubt, Arab merchants had much to learn from them.

By throwing their lot (and genes) in with the Persian and Sogdian merchants, Arab entrepreneurs rather suddenly gained access to, if not control of, most of the "interstate" commerce across half of Asia. Through a series of mergers and hostile takeovers, they wove together the many braids of the Silk Roads into one unbreakable network of trade.

In doing so, they not only promoted Islam and extended its power, but they also seeded their own magical stories of heavenly fragrances and flavors. They introduced their mercantile ethics and economic theories

The most potent and enduring aromatic in the world comes from a rare substance held in the scent glands of several now-endangered Asian deer species in the genus *Moschus*. Because musk deer bucks have no antlers (though they do have sharp tusks), they attract mates and repel competing bucks in a unique way: they mark their territory by dropping grainlike secretions onto shrubs at its margins from an abdominal pouch that protrudes not far from their genitals. In the wild, a one-and-a-half-year-old buck might produce and "paste" twenty to twenty-five grams of waxy, blood-colored musk grains onto shrubs each mating season.

When these pasty droppings are dried, they become charcoal black grains rich in the pheromone known to chemists as muscone. The fragrance of freshly harvested musk is so powerful that newcomers find it either repulsive or divinely pleasurable. After it has been diluted, musk has a warm, aromatic, earthy fragrance that some have likened to the scent of freshly cut wood or a baby's skin just after a bath.

There is some evidence that musk was traded extra-locally as early as frankincense was, around 3500 BCE. By the sixth century CE, musk had become the most widely sought-after and highly prized fragrance in the world, with a single kilogram of musk worth twice the value of an equal amount of gold. (Today, it is worth three to four times its weight in gold.) It has had many uses beyond its addition to perfumes and aromatic soaps. In India, it was valued as a cardiac cure for pulmonary diseases, and in Europe and Great Britain, it found culinary favor as an ingredient in baked goods, beverages, candies, ice creams, molasses, and puddings.

When Marco Polo described the collection of amber musk grains off the forest floor for trade westward, they were probably being gathered in the natural habitats of the Siberian musk deer (*M. moschiferus*) in either the Tian Shan or the Altai Mountains. This widespread musk deer species ranged from Siberia and Outer Mongolia southwestward across the trade routes of the Gansu Corridor and Xinjiang, and then all the way to Kazakhstan. Mongolian and Huigu (proto-Uighur) harvesters knew how to obtain the grains without killing the deer, and no doubt passed them on to Sogdian traders, who, starting in the fifth century, annually delivered as much as fifteen hundred kilograms of musk westward as far as Constantinople, Athens, and Rome.

But the demand for good-quality amber musk put pressure on nomadic hunters to kill and gut rather than sustainably harvest the deer. It took killing thirty to fifty sexually mature bucks to gather a kilogram of musk, and often yearlings and does were killed as well. By the nineteenth century, the range of the Siberian musk deer had contracted and the number of deer had declined dramatically. Today, the only surviving population in China remains in the most remote reaches of the Altai Mountains. By the time I reached the Gansu Corridor in search of musk deer, the situation was pathetic. The only known population remaining in the province was on the Xinglongshan Deer Musk Farm, where five hundred captive-bred bucks were offering up an average of only 8.8 grams of musk grains per year, less than one-third of what their wild counterparts formerly produced.

As primary sources of amber musk declined, harvesters turned to Tonkin musk from the black musk deer (*M. fuscus*) living in the Tibetan highlands. In time, its fragrance became even more highly regarded than that of amber musk, but the black musk deer population soon rapidly declined, as well. Finally, poachers, hoping to meet the continuing demand, ruthlessly began hunting a third species, *M. chrysogaster,* from farther south in the Himalayas, and its numbers have also fallen. Now, all three species are considered vulnerable to extinction, and the sales of their products are banned through international treaties on wildlife trade.

Nevertheless, an estimated two thousand kilograms of musk are traded on the black market every year. In the 1970s, a single kilogram fetched as much as forty-five thousand dollars. A recent report estimates a sixfold increase in the number of illegal musk hunters since then, implying that the black-market price per kilogram has continued to rise accordingly.

Curiously, the terms for musk and musk deer in the Far East are for the most part quite different than those used in the Middle East, Europe, and North Africa. This suggests that some intermediaries—first the Sogdian traders of Central Asia, and later the Persians and Arabs—took pains to conceal the geographic and cultural origins of the musk that they disseminated as a way to maintain control over the markets in the West.

She-hsiang is the Chinese term for "musk deer aromatic," and *she-fu* and *hsiang chang* refer to the deer that produce a "fragrant liquid." The Chinese term *she* alludes to the fact that the deer sprays the musky aroma as a spurt or squirt. The Tibetan term for the musk deer (*M. fuscus*) is *glaba* and the scent of the musk is *glartsi*. Mongolian boasts two terms for the deer (*M. moschiferus*), *küdäri* and *cigar.* In at least some Old Turkic dialects within the range of this same animal, the deer is called *kin* and the musk itself is *yipar*. The compound lexeme *kin yipar* appears on an ancient stele that was found in Mongolia and that I was able to see firsthand at the Xinjiang Provincial Museum in Ürümqi.

According to the fine Asian historian and lexicographer Anya King, none of these terms made it very far west of the Tian Shan, Hindui Kush, and Himalayan ranges. Historical documents attributed to Sogdian traders in Central Asia indicate that musk was referred to as *yys yaxs*, or *yxsyh* when selling it to Westerners. Another ancient term, *mus,* originated in either Sanskrit or a related ancient Iranian dialect, and then spread. In both the classic and new Persian spoken in Baghdad over the centuries, the term *musk* was used in trade; this same term was spelled *mwšk* in the pre-Islamic Pahlavi likely used through much of the Sassanid Empire.

Musk was clearly being traded to Arabs as far west as the emerging Islamic Empire of the seventh century. In ancient Arabic texts, several terms were recorded for musk, among them *mis, misk,* and *nafijat. Misk,* probably a loan word from Arabic, was used by Western Turks throughout the Ottoman Empire and remains in use in modern Turkish bazaars, such as the Spice Bazaar in Istanbul.

Well outside of Baghdad and Istanbul's bazaars, Armenians used the term *mus,* Syriac speakers used *muška,* and Ethiopians used *mesk,* suggesting that the Persian and Arabic terms were carried across their trade networks without much discontinuity. In Europe, the Russians called musk *muskus,* the Greeks called it *móschos,* and Latin speakers used *muscus.* In the Romance languages, this gave rise to the Spanish *musco,* the Italian *muschio,* and the French *musc.*

Although we now think of musk merely as one of many ingredients in secular perfumes that ostensibly function as sexual attractants, it has long been used in religious contexts as a fragrance associated with immortality and purity. This spiritual quality of musk, noted by the Prophet Muhammad himself, is attested to at the musk-scented Blue Mosque of Sultan Ahmed next to the Hagia Sophia in Istanbul, the Kutubia Mosque in Marrakech, and the Iparli (Safa) Mosque of Diyarbakir; their walls are said to emit a musky fragrance to this day. For the Iparli Mosque, a wealthy Muslim spice merchant took seventy loads of musk he had obtained through trade with kingdoms in western China and mixed it into the mortar for the walls.

Fagong, Kang, et al. "The Musk Production of Captive Alpine Deer (*Moschus chrysogaster*) from the Xinglongshan Musk Deer Farm of Gansu Province, China." *Acta Theriologica Sinica* 28 (2008): 221–24.

Garrett, Theodore Francis. *The Encyclopedia of Practical Cookery: A Complete Dictionary of All Pertaining to the Art of Cookery and Table Service.* Vol. 2. London: L. Upcott Gill, 1898.

Green, Michael J.B. and Bihaya Kattel. "Musk Deer: Little Understood, Even Its Scent." Paper presented at First International Symposium on Endangered Species Used in the Trade of East Asian Medicine. Hong Kong, December 7–8, 1997. http://archive.org/details/muskdeerlittleun97gree.

King, Anya H. "The Musk Trade and the Near East in the Early Medieval Period." PhD diss., Indiana University, 2007. www.gradworks.umi.com/32/53/3253639.html.

Vaissière, Étienne de la. *Sogdian Traders: A History.* Leiden, Germany: Brill, 2005.

Zhixiao, Liu, and Sheng Helin. "Effect of Habitat Fragmentation and Isolation of Alpine Musk Deer." *Russian Journal of Ecology* 33 (2002): 121–24.

into the archipelago of colonies stretching from the Empty Quarter of Arabia all the way to the Gobi Desert. But it was in the southern Gobi, along the Gansu Corridor, where their desert-adapted seeds germinated into the most lucrative economic opportunities. For the next several centuries, various Chinese dynasties demonstrated an almost insatiable appetite for all things Western, which for them implied the fashions and flavors of Persia and Arabia. The people of the Middle Kingdom became captivated by all the pretty horses, exotic spices, and fabulous ideas that visionaries from more westerly arid regions had to offer them.

Perhaps the most remarkable testament to this early fascination with the West comes not from a Tang dynasty poet or merchant but from a Buddhist monk. A contemporary of the Prophet Muhammad, Xuanjang was a young monastic apprentice and linguist when he took off from Chang'an, the terminus of the Silk Roads, in 629. He set out to learn whatever he could about the spiritual and secular presences looming on the western horizon. Before returning to China some sixteen years later to tell his tales, Xuanjang had covered more than ten thousand miles on foot, camel, and horse, surveying the people, spiritual practices, and landscapes of outposts in the countries now called Kazakhstan, Tajikistan, Uzbekistan, the Kyrgyz Republic, Afghanistan, Pakistan, and India.[18] Reaching as far west as the Zeravshan River and its trading center of Samarkand, he seemed less impressed by the military power held by the great khan of the Western Turks and more intrigued by the entrepreneurial skill of the Sogdians, Persians, and Jews he encountered: "The merchandise of [these] many countries was found and the craftsmanship of [their] artisans appeared superior to that of other countries."[19]

I catch a glimpse of the profile of Xuanjang, the spiritual pilgrim, carved in stone on the third tier of an ancient pagoda in Quanzhou, a city in Fujian Province that has as much Islamic history as it does Buddhist. I have seen where he traveled through the lost cities of the Turpan Depression below the Flaming Mountains on his way from Chang'an to Samarkand. I have hiked along the Yellow River up near its headwaters in the tawny-colored steppes of the Gansu Corridor, where Hui and Mongolian Muslims have traded with Tibetan Buddhists for many centuries. In the town of Linxia in Gansu Province, I have visited Islamic mosques and Buddhist temples adorned with many of the same sacred symbols: the napa cabbage, the dragon, the lotus, and the pomegranate.

All these encounters have made me wonder whether being among people of other faiths enriches rather than threatens that of our own.

FIGURE 14. Spices from Central Asia became regularly available to Muslim, Christian, and Jewish traders via Bactrian camel caravans and maritime trade routes. Shown here is a camel train in Mongolia, 1902. (Courtesy Library of Congress Prints and Photographs Division, www.loc.gov/pictures/resource/cph.3b03982.)

Why do some people, like the Hui Muslims or the Bukharan Jews, frequently choose to live with or near the more economically and politically dominant Han? Why have they persisted in the roles as vendors and traders of foodstuffs and spices, even when others around them have opted to become computer programmers, electricians, or plumbers? What do they inevitably gain by living as filter feeders on the very edge between desert and river, earth and sky, the Buddha and the Prophet? What do we ourselves miss by staying clear of these tension zones, these interfaces where new innovations frequently arise?

As I pondered such questions, I turned my attention to the ways in which Persian and Arab sensibilities had been united by Islam such that they began to generate intellectual curiosity about the East. Silk, musk, ginger, camphor, star anise, cinnamon, and blue ceramics now extended beyond China proper, into the Indian subcontinent, into Central Asia, and, on occasion, all the way back to Mecca on the Arabian Peninsula. Many cultures contributed to the mélange of spices reaching markets, but a few dominant groups had captured the role of catalyst in their global dispersal.

Just as the Chinese were led to believe by the Sogdians and Arabs that cotton could only be obtained by shearing an animal unique to the West, the Han of China had a few of their own secrets. Although trade in silk cloth had reached the Western frontier at Niya by 206 CE, and silk cocoons were produced at Astana in the Turpan Depression by 420, it took centuries for the knowledge of silkworm production to penetrate west of the Tian Shan. With some of the harshest deserts in the world physically isolating Europe and Asia Minor from China, traders teamed up to perpetrate myths and intrigue about the people living on one terminus of their trade routes to shock and awe those living at the other terminus.

This is the mix of fantasy, fact, and literary elaboration of true-life adventure familiar to anyone who has ever sat down to read the fables in *One Thousand and One Nights*. Perhaps this genre emerged more from Farsi oral traditions than it did from the stories told by speakers and singers of Arabic, but no matter. It served as the imaginative bridge between the East and the West—between the so-called Oriental and Occidental sensibilities—in ways that have continued to shape our impressions of "the other" through international policies and prejudices to this day.[20]

Perhaps that first century of Arabian-Persian-Sogdian intermingling brought about more unprecedented innovations in the arts, architecture, hydraulic engineering, agriculture, and cuisine than any other period in history. After the Banu Umayyah had relocated their caliphate from Mosul to Damascus, they enhanced the productivity of its irrigated fields and terraced orchards along the Barada River with knowledge that they had brought from visiting the Ma'rib oasis in Yemen. The recently converted Persians and Sogdians also introduced food-producing technologies to the mix. It appears that they fostered investment in the water harvesting, transfer, and storage technologies known as *qanat* and *qarez* among their Muslim allies. These techniques spread to the

❧ GINGER ❦

Believed to have been first recruited from the wild in southern China, ginger root (*Zingiber officinale*) has become a world traveler. Despite its popular designation as a root, it is actually a pale silvery green to ivory brown rhizome shaped like a fleshy hand with pudgy fingers. It has an unforgettably zesty, citrusy fragrance, an herbal sweetness, and a piquant bite that have made it a signature of Chinese regional cuisines since ancient times. Ginger powder, perhaps because it is dry, is less pungent but has more prevalent citrus notes.

The characteristic flavor of ginger is derived from a nonvolatile resin called zingerone that contains hydroxyaryl compounds. The same compounds are found in turmeric and galangal, two relatives of ginger. Zingiberene, the primary component of the rhizome's essential oil, imparts the fragrance we identify as gingery, and cineol and citral provide the hints of citrus. Curcumene, zingiberol, linalool, cineol, and camphene are also present in varying degrees in different strains.

The first written Chinese record on ginger, dated c. 500 BCE, is attributed to Confucius, who reported in the *Analects* that he was never without ginger when he ate. This spice may have first entered global trade networks through an arc of harbors reaching from Zayton (Quanzhou) in China through Southeast Asia all the way to Ceylon (Sri Lanka). Sometime after Confucius penned his observation, dried ginger was being traded from India to Arabia and then to Egypt. By the thirteenth century, Arabian ships carried either the rhizomes or potted plants down the east coast of Africa as far as Zanzibar. Ginger was popular in Morocco and Andalusia by the sixth century, and it is now propagated in tropical and subtropical climes far beyond Asia.

I have seen freshly harvested ginger prominently featured on the bamboo tables of predawn fruit and fish markets in Denpasar, Bali; in handwoven baskets of Amharic-speaking women on the edge of the Abay River in Ethiopia; and in the produce sections of Chinatown groceries in Honolulu and San Francisco. It has sailed across turbulent seas and climbed over snowy passes in the highest mountain ranges of Asia to find new homes.

Known as *jiang* in Chinese, ginger diffused southward along the Maritime Silk Roads via Champa traders from present-day Vietnam and Tamil traders from Ceylon and southern India. By the time the rhizomes reached the Indian subcontinent, they became known as *shringavera* in Sanskrit and *singivera* in several Indic languages; it has been speculated that these terms are derived from the Old Greek *zingiberis*. At the same time, Turkic-speakers such as the Uighur, who call it *sansabil,* aided its spread across Central Asia to Persia and the Middle East. Many of the terms used to label ginger may be cognates of this Turkic term, including *zanjabil* in Farsi, *zanjabil* in Arabic, and *sangvil* in Hebrew. (Although ginger is not mentioned in the Jewish Talmud or in the Christian Gospels, it does appear in at least one sura in the Qur'an.) The names for ginger in many European languages are ultimately derived from these same roots, including the Latin *zingiber* and the Modern Greek *dzindzer.* It is not surprising that the scientific name for the family that includes ginger, galangal, turmeric, and other spices became Zingiberaceae.

Ginger is often deployed in combination with other fiery spices, as in Chinese five-spice powder and Indian curry powders. In the West, fresh ginger is considered so potent that it is usually finely chopped or minced before it is added to meat, poultry, fish, or tuber or other vegetable dishes. In many regional Chinese cuisines, however, fresh ginger is cut into large slices, which are then slowly simmered in a broth to soften them or stir-fried in concert with other ingredients. One such dish in Fujian features veritable slabs of ginger with duck and sautéed amaranth greens in a hearty broth. Kung pao (or *gongbao,* literally "palace guard") chicken, a gingery favorite that also features chicken, peanuts, garlic, and chiles, is among the better-known stir-fried dishes of Sichuan Province. Pickled ginger is often served alongside sushi and sashimi in (and now far beyond) Japan. I frequently depend on pickled ginger to calm my nausea-prone stomach and keep a plastic pouch of its pinkish slivers readily accessible in my refrigerator.

Although ginger is included in the dishes of various European and African cuisines, it is perhaps more commonly used to spice up beverages. Ginger is now a rather minor ingredient of ginger ale compared with the fructose and carbonated water that goes into it, but ginger-flavored kombucha is becoming the rage in the United States and can be quite potent. It continues to be used to flavor beers, breads, and cookies throughout the West, with gingerbread men and gingersnaps still legendary among youngsters of western Europe, the United States, and Canada.

Gambrelle, Fabienne. *The Flavor of Spices.* Paris: Flammarion, 2008.
Green, Aliza. *Field Guide to Herbs and Spices.* Philadelphia: Quirk Books, 2006.
Katzer, Gernot. "Gernot Katzer's Spice Pages." http://gernot-katzers-spice-pages.com/engl/index.html. Accessed May 8, 2013.
Sortun, Ana, with Nicole Chaison. *Spice: Flavors of the Eastern Mediterranean.* New York: Regan Books, 2006.
Weiss, E.A. *Spice Crops.* Wallingford, UK: CABI Publishing, 2002.

desert mountains of Oman, where they are now known as *falaj,* and to the Gobi, where they are known as *kares.*

Damascus had become not only the gateway to the Fertile Crescent but also an experimental marketplace of ideas, technologies, and goods attractive enough to lure Persians, Sogdian, Indian, and even Chinese merchants to come for a quick look-see. In Damascus, the Diwan al-Kharaj of the caliphate had anchored its network of tithing and taxation in order to create a magnitude of wealth that dwarfed anything earlier Semitic peoples had witnessed either at the Ma'rib oasis or the stronghold of Petra.

With wealth pouring in from all directions, the Banu Umayyah elite surrounding the caliph no longer restricted themselves to living and eating as frugally as the Prophet had lived in Mecca and Medina.[21] Instead of merely enjoying the relative abundance of agricultural goods found in their islandlike oases amid the surrounding sea of austere desert scrub, the Banu Umayyah began to reshape and reclaim desert landscapes with larger and larger public works for water transfer and lavish irrigation of food crops. They transformed the once-arid landscape into their own image of paradise.

And so, the Barada River valley became dense with plantings of annual staple crops; prolific orchards of pomegranates, dates, stone fruits, and olives; aromatic gardens of Damascus roses and mints; lush pastures of dairy cattle, sheep, and goats; and vineyards heavily laden with muscat grapes. The feasts hosted by the Banu Umayyah royalty went far beyond what the Prophet himself might have consumed in his day, incorporating animal and vegetable delicacies and aromatic spices imported and transplanted from nearby Anatolia and Mount Lebanon, as well as from every other part of the Islamic world. Remarkably, lavish displays of Arabian-Persian-Sogdian cuisine were not restricted to the ruling class. Other Arab inhabitants of Damascus were exposed to them, as well.

The modest bread-and-stew diet of the Prophet became embellished beyond anything that the cave-dwelling hermit would have recognized. As Lilia Zaouali tells it, "Mu'awiya ibn Abī Sufyān, the first Umayyad caliph at Damascus, was little inclined to deny himself the pleasures of food. Having discovered the refinement of Syrian [and Persian] cooking, he was able, thanks to the wealth of his office, to give free rein to every wish. . . . The Arabs' predilection for Persian cuisine, evident since the pre-Islamic period, increased still more owing to their fondness for sweet desserts such as *falūdhaj,* a confection made from sugar, starch, and nuts and flavored with musk and rose water."[22]

Perhaps it was this very extravagance that led to the downfall of the Umayyad dynasty, for it bred jealousy and discontent in the hinterlands, where many of the Islamic faithful still struggled to put bread on their table and into the bowls of their humble *tharīd* stew. It was not simply that the Banu Umayyah had paid for their lush paradise at the Rusafa palace near Damascus with the taxes collected throughout the empire. Others had done that before them, and it would still be done after they were gone. What enraged the emerging corpus of dissidents was that *only* full-blooded Arabs were given first-class-citizen status in Damascus, despite the pretense that the Muslims were all alike under Allah.

The Arabs who had intermarried with Persians, Sogdians, and Turks had lost any special status they may otherwise have had and were taxed as though they were lower-class *mawali*, without a single drop of Arab blood in their veins. Finally, there was the sense that the ruling family was hypocritical about all of this, for the last Umayyad caliph himself had married a beautiful Berber woman from Africa's Maghreb.

This time, it was largely the mixed breed or hybrid culture of Persian, Sogdian, and Yemeni Arab traders from Central Asia that struck with lightning speed. Before the decadent rulers of Damascus knew what was happening to them, their last caliph, Marwan II, was chased out of town, hunted down, and killed in Egypt in 750. Not long after that, in the same year, an entourage of imposing dissidents from Central Asia arrived at the Rusafa palace to share a meal with the caliph's inner circle and ostensibly to put aside their differences.

Not a single Banu Umayyah adult left that dinner table alive. Abd al-Rahman, the only other mature male descendant of the last Umayyad caliph, somehow escaped the palace grounds with a few guards. He was then taken as far from Damascus as possible, while the Rusafa palace was sacked and then burned to the ground.

Within the coming years, the emerging Abbasid dynasty would attempt to redirect the destiny of Islam, return its control to descendants of the Prophet Muhammad, and better accommodate the formerly disenfranchised non-Arabs as well as the Shia in its inner workings. Once again, revolutionaries had spilled out of the arid and austere hinterlands to purge their society of its impurities. And so the Abbasids left the contaminated grounds of Damascus behind for good, first building up their power base in Haran, Turkey, and then founding a new capital entirely from scratch. Their newly planned circular capital would become known as Baghdad.

The only luxury they took with them from the Rusafa grounds was the Damascus rose, in the vain hope that they could retain exclusive control over its cultivation and use. But despite their efforts to control the intellectual property rights of this favorite fragrance, they eventually realized that a rose is a rose, and beautiful, aromatic flowers soon find their way into many hands in many lands.

It would take just a few years before the Abbasid caliphs would be accused of the same excesses that they had witnessed in the last days of decadence among the Umayyad rulers of Damascus. But one part of their revolution did stick.

Islamic civilization, including its trade in high-end aromatics, could never again be the exclusive domain of Arabs. Islam as a religious and economic system could no longer extend privilege to the founding families of Mecca and Medina at the expense of Persians, Sogdians, Turks, or Berbers, or, for that matter, Muslims of mixed blood. Eventually, another kind of capitalist elite called the *sahib al-mal* would emerge, but their members would not belong to a single bloodline. By the tenth century, these economic titans had formed an exclusive mercantile guild of spice traders who accumulated enormous wealth outside the control of the state. Neither genetics nor language guaranteed membership in the Karimi guild of traders, for it was reserved for those who fully understood how economic power could be further concentrated along the various spice trails, Frankincense Trails, Silk Roads, and maritime routes. Long before most Western European Christians could even articulate, let alone fathom, the notion of a world economic system, the Muslims and Jews, among others, had set one in motion.

CHAPTER 7

The Flourishing of Cross-Cultural Collaboration in Iberia

On a mountainside overlooking the city known as Gharnata in medieval times, I am immersed in the aromas of jasmine, lavender, roses of all colors and sizes, myrtle, and olive wood. I have pursued the promise of these fragrances throughout my travels on the way to the southern reaches of the Iberian Peninsula, and at last I have inhaled their intoxicating scents. Many kinds of citrus surround me, though the season for the release of their perfumes passed several months ago. Nevertheless, enough volatile oils are wafting through the air here to keep anyone mesmerized.

Just as I'm imagining that I have entered a garden designed by an obsessed aromatherapist, I realize that the many soothing sounds I hear are the work of human hands, as well. There is water rushing, dripping, gurgling, spraying, and puddling wherever I turn, in chutes and cascades, pools and fountains. Around these water features, leaves are rustling and some birds are chirping while others are gently mocking them.

I start to wonder whether this might be what paradise smells and sounds like. As my nostrils take in the heady aromas, my eyes move from the brilliant sun shining on the hills of Andalusia to the shadows, where flowing water enters cavelike grottos and sanctuaries, thickwalled hammams with bathing pools carved out of stone, and underground cisterns called *aljibes*. These are words that I've learned across the strait to the south of Andalusia in Fez, Morocco. They speak to the pragmatic as much as to the paradisaical.

I turn to look out over verdant terraces, each dedicated to a different group of useful plants: an evenly spaced plantation of roses, the petals of which are picked for syrups and scented waters; a grove of olive trees whose small green fruits will be pressed into oil the following autumn; vineyards of fresh table grapes, raisin grapes, and wine grapes for making vinegars; experimental gardens called *almuñias,* where specially selected artichokes, garlic, onions, and leafy herbs are being tested and tasted; and orchards loaded with loquats, apricots, medlars, figs, and pomegranates. These lands were planted with more than pleasure in mind. Some pragmatists knew how to replenish local larders with sun-dried fruits, vinegars, pickled vegetables, and more.

Wherever I wander, I also notice that pomegranate trees have also been shaped into hedgerows, windbreaks, and field borders. As I walk down from the grounds surrounding the sprawling structures of the Alhambra and from the gardens of Generalife, the old summer palace, I realize that I am also seeing the pomegranates cast in iron and copper nearly wherever I look: resting atop fence posts, on signposts, along stairway banisters.

I laugh to myself as I ponder the language attached to the much-repeated pomegranate. In ancient Latin, it was known as *malum punicum,* "the apple of the Phoenicians living in Carthage," or as *malum granatum,* "the multigrained apple."[1] In botanical Latin, it is *Punica granatum,* "the multigrained (fruit) of the Phoenicians." In the Berber spoken in medieval Morocco and in al-Andalus (the term used for parts of the Iberian Peninsula and France under Muslim rule from the eighth through the fifteenth century), the latter term was transformed into a brief linguistic telegram announcing the arrival of a tasty fruit, *gharnata.* As that term was polished and simplified for the Spanish tongue, it rolled out of the mouth as *granada.*

Granada, called the City of Pomegranates, might more properly be named the Orphanage for Pomegranates, for these intrepid wanderers have lost their parents and strayed far from home. As such, their own journey represents the one also taken by the descendants of some of the first Arab Muslims who carried those fruits here thirteen centuries ago.

Abd al-Rahman I, the highest-ranking survivor of the Banu Umayyah elite, rejoins our story here in the role of the Pomegranate Pilgrim. After escaping the subterfuge and slaughter at the Rusafa palace, he fled via what amounted to an underground railroad west to the Land of the Setting Sun, the Maghreb.[2] Barely evading assassinations in Syria, Egypt, and what is today Tunisia, he set out to take refuge among his mother's Nafza Berber tribe in what is now Morocco. Five years after the massacre of his father's Arab family, he came out of hiding in the Moroccan hinterlands to join his mother's kin near the city of Ceuta, which today joins the city of Melilla as the only Spanish territories on the African continent.

Ceuta was roughly fifteen miles across a strait from the small isle-like promontory called Jabal al-Tariq. In time, Jabal al-Tariq became known as the Rock of Gibraltar and acted as the stepping-stone for many Arabs and Berbers emigrating to al-Andalus in particular and to Europe at large.

In addition to a sizable Berber population that had conquered the region in 711, al-Andalus harbored a number of other peoples. They included Phoenician descendants; first wave Arab settlers (*baladi-yun*), mostly from the "old country" of Yemen and southern Oman; Arabic-speaking Christians later known as Mozárabes (from *musta'rib*, or "Arabized local"); and a new wave of diaspora Arabs (*shami-yun*), who were largely Syrian soldiers escaping to the Iberian Peninsula in 752, just two years after the Abbasids ushered in the Umayyad collapse.

Of course, far more Catholics than Muslims remained in the southern stretches of the Iberian Peninsula, so much so that Abd al-Rahman was unsure whether these Christians would accept him as the rightful heir to the Islamic empire in their midst.

Now known only as al-Dakhil (the Immigrant or Pilgrim), Abd al-Rahman was sequestered in Ceuta among his mother's relatives, savoring his last few weeks in the semiarid heath of the Tangier coastline before deciding whether to leave Africa's dry lands behind for the more lush and diverse Iberian Peninsula.[3] Meanwhile, his Greek companion Bedr had sailed ahead to al-Andalus to gauge the receptivity of the Muslims (and indirectly, the Catholics) to having an Umayyad emir make a new home base among them.

The response was mixed. Although most of the Syrian refugees had lived in Damascus and had been trading clients of his family, the Syrian military commander was loath to see a twenty-five-year-old from a defeated family usurp his power in Andalusia. The Berbers were clearly divided, since some were angry that Abd al-Rahman did not plan to remain in Morocco among his mother's people. In the end, it was the Yemeni old guard who told Bedr they would welcome Abd al-Rahman as an ally, in the hope that they could regain some of the political and economic power they had lost to the Syrian immigrants. At the same time, Christians and Jews were promised that they would not be forced

✤ POMEGRANATE ❧

Although you might not consider the succulent pulp and seeds of a fruit to be a spice, the seeds and syrup of the pomegranate (*Punica granatum*) can be used as a garnish, in a salad dressing, as a flavoring for sauces, and as a nutraceutical, much like many spices and herbs. Technically speaking, the pomegranate fruit is a leathery-skinned berry, and each of the many seeds in that berry is surrounded by a juicy, gelatinous aril. Some heirloom pomegranate varieties yield fruits that are exceedingly sweet and pleasant tasting; others run to sour, bitter, astringent, or tartly acidic but are widely used nonetheless. The juice is rich in oesterone, an antioxidant that is a potential anti-cancer agent.

The wild ancestors of domesticated pomegranates are likely of Central Asian origin, though some fruit historians pinpoint Persia as the place of first domestication, and others suggest a broad arc between the Caucasus and the Himalayas. Another *Punica* species now cultivated as an ornamental is native to the island of Socotra, which lies about 150 miles off of the Yemeni coast, but it did not directly contribute its genes to pomegranate domestication. Incidentally, the term *Punica* alludes to the pomegranate's association with the Phoenicians and Punic traders, who moved the fruits around the eastern Mediterranean.

The pomegranate had made it into the Levant by the Early Bronze Age, as evidenced by the carbonized skins found in ruins at Jericho. Many Biblical historians agree that the Tree of Knowledge of Good and Evil mentioned in Genesis was most likely the pomegranate and not the apple. Pomegranates are still grown in Jericho and Jerusalem, where I have seen their gorgeous scarlet blossoms being visited by Palestine sunbirds.

Quickly adopted throughout the Levant, from southern Turkey to the northern edges of the Sinai, pomegranates diversified greatly under cultural selection. The five hundred named domesticated varieties can be as large as a softball or as small as a tennis ball. Some have deep red interiors to their compartmented fruits, and others harbor pale translucent seeds among a pinkish cream gelatinous pulp of the arils. I have witnessed displays of diverse pomegranates in the markets of Istanbul that were the botanical equivalent of seeing Saint Bernards and Chihuahuas in the same dog show.

It appears that both Turks and Persians carried pomegranates eastward, southeastward, and northward along their trade routes. The Farsi name *anar* and Turkic name *nar* are echoed in loan words found in Armenian, Bulgarian, Dhivehi, Punjabi, Hindi, and even Kazakh.

When the pomegranate made it from Damascus to al-Andalus with

Banu Umayyah refugees, it was a big hit. The first cultivar in Spain was named *safarí*, and it persisted with that name for hundreds of years after its introduction around 755. But rather than retain the ancient Semitic term *al-rummân* for all pomegranates, the Moors and Syrians who immigrated to Spain instead chose the Latin-derived *pomum granatum*, which was Arabized and condensed to *gharnata* and then Hispanicized to *granada*. The latter, of course, also became the name of one of the three great centers of culture and agriculture in Moorish Spain during the era of *convivencia*, though I was disappointed to find few fresh pomegranates in its markets today.

Sephardic and Moorish Jews became just as fond of pomegranates as Arabs were and used the image of the fruit above the doorways of their homes throughout the West. From Spain, pomegranate cuttings, including the *safarí* variety, went on to the Canary Islands and then to the Americas.

Curiously, iconic pomegranate flowers set in silver have become known as squash blossoms in Navajo and Zuni Indian jewelry in the American Southwest, but no doubt hark back to Spanish-introduced designs that could ultimately be derived from Jewish or Muslim traditions that reached Spain. Pomegranates themselves made their way north from Mexico with Spanish missionaries, who took them as far as Havasupai villages in the Grand Canyon and isolated desert oases in Baja California. The Tohono O'odham of the Sonoran Desert along the United States–Mexico border still grow pomegranates around their homes, taking the Spanish loan word *granada* and making it their own: *galniyu*.

On the other side of the border in Coahuila and Nuevo León, it is likely that crypto-Jews played a role in elaborating the pomegranate-garnished dish *chiles en nogadas*, which was prominently featured in the best-selling novel *Like Water for Chocolate*, and in the film of the same name. The pomegranate seed garnish on the stuffed chiles echoes the seeds' use in the Middle East and the Maghreb on stuffed eggplants. Although this fact is never explicitly mentioned in the novel, at least some members of the de la Garza family of northeastern Mexico who were fictionalized in the book were conversos.

Katzer, Gernot. "Gernot Katzer's Spice Pages." http://gernot-katzers-spice-pages.com/engl/index.html. Accessed May 4 2013.

Mcnocal, María Rosa. *The Ornament of the World: How Muslims, Jews and Christians Created a Culture of Tolerance in Medieval Spain*. Boston: Little, Brown, 2002.

Musselman, Lytton John. *Figs, Dates, Laurel, and Myrrh: Plants of the Bible and the Quran*. Portland, OR: Timber Press, 2005.

to leave or to convert to Islam if they chose to live with the new emir's protection.

On August 15, 755, Abd al-Rahman set sail for the small port of Almuñécar, in the heart of what had been, just a few centuries before, the Phoenician-controlled coast of al-Andalus. His Berber relatives had tried to convince him to stay and even fought to detain him as his boat left the Ceuta harbor. But within a few hours, Abd al-Rahman had arrived on the shores of the Iberian Peninsula. There, over the next three decades, he would construct a world-class palace and mosque.[4]

But they were perhaps the least of his legacy. He and his descendants would soon transform what they called Qurtuba, today's Córdoba, into Europe's most sophisticated center for intercontinental trade, translation, and education; research in the arts, sciences, and letters; and agricultural, horticultural, and medicinal plant experimentation.[5] There he hoped to grow a little bit of paradise to salve the wounds of the last few years.

It is fitting that Abd al-Rahman's point of arrival in Spain was called Almuñécar, for the name echoes the classical Arabic term *munyah*, or "desire," which came to mean "farm" or "garden" in Moorish Spanish; *almunia* is still used in Spain today for the many private experimental gardens that the Immigrant emir fostered. He had set foot on new soil, and he spent the remaining years of his life cultivating that soil and that society. Both would bear fruit on an arguably unprecedented scale.

Abd al-Rahman and his descendants added another element to the phenomenon of globalization. They attempted to remake in perfect facsimile the entire world that they had known and loved in Damascus and that now lay thousands of miles away from their adopted home. Outside of Córdoba, Abd al-Rahman constructed an exact replica of the gardens and palace of Rusafa, the place from which he had fled just as he had come of age. He could no longer return to his original home, but he would do all he could to construct one of equal, if not surpassing, grandeur.

The meaning of this act of reconstruction has not been lost on historians such as María Rosa Menocal.[6] Abd al-Rahman was not only making a gesture of nostalgic longing for his birthplace but also boldly asserting dominion over the peoples and landscape of southern Iberia by creating a culturally and economically novel ecosystem in which they would all live. As Menocal sees it,

> He built his new Andalusian estate, Rusafa, in part to memorialize the old Rusafa deep in the desert steppes northeast of Damascus, where he had last

lived with his family, and also, no less, to proclaim that he had survived and that this was indeed the new and legitimate home of the Umayyads. Although it would be two more centuries before one of his descendants actually openly declared that Cordoba was the seat of *the* caliphate, al-Andalus was transformed and now anything but a provincial seat. . . . Just outside Cordoba, Abd al-Rahman built his new Rusafa . . . a botanical garden as well, a place where he could collect and cultivate the living things that had been so central to beauty and delight in Syria.[7]

When Abd al-Rahman heard that his son Sulaiman and a couple of his sisters had also escaped from Damascus and were still alive, he beckoned them to sail to al-Andalus. He hoped that they could reassemble as a family at the new palace he had under construction. To assure their safe passage, he dispatched one of his best Syrian men to return secretly to the Middle East and guide his family on to al-Andalus.

But one of his sisters declined to travel that far with the others. Instead, she insisted that the party carry back to al-Andalus a living gift from her to her brother. She urged the family's Syrian guide to sneak back to the ruined Rusafa palace and rescue any plant still surviving in the deteriorating gardens around it. He clandestinely dug up a few young date palms and grabbed several pomegranate fruits that had somehow survived. He boarded these treasures on the same ship that carried Abd al-Rahman's son and sister, hoping that they, too, could be newly established in al-Andalus.

The next episode of this story has been recorded and retold in heartbreaking detail over the ages. We can almost see the tears of joy in Abd al-Rahman's eyes when his family arrives and places a homegrown but somewhat overripe pomegranate in his hands. It had both the aroma and taste of his onetime home. As the famous historical geographer Ibn Said al-Maghribi later recalled to the Algerian-born historian Ahmed ibn Mohammed Maqqari,

> The monarch [Abd al-Rahman] held the unspoiled portions of the remaining pomegranate fruits [taken from al-Rusafa] and marveled at what was left of their beauty, for he had a strong desire to share with others. So he passed them on to a respected nurseryman who resided in the small *qariya* or hamlet of Reyo near Malaga and the port of Almuñécar. There the nurseryman named Safr b. Abd Allah undertook a *khabara,* or experimental treatment of the seeds, so that they would germinate. They produced "pippins," or seedling pomegranates, which he transplanted and cared for in his nursery. He then nurtured them along with ample water and nutrients so that they could be transplanted out into an orchard. They grew into trees that soon bore fruit, and he carefully protected some of the first fruits until they were ripe and ready to eat.[8]

Safr then selected a particularly beautiful fruit that had been kept in the shade (to prevent it from cracking open or spoiling from sunburn). With the help of his staff, he immediately carried it to Córdoba, so that it could be presented to Abd al-Rahman while it was still fresh.

When the emir received the fruit, the nurseryman asked him if he could confirm whether it was identical to or at least similar to those he had eaten as a child at Rusafa. The emir tasted it and quickly confirmed that it had the very same qualities of the fruit he had known as a boy. The emir then asked Safr how he happened to propagate it successfully.

Safr carefully explained his procedures, and the emir expressed his admiration for the nurseryman's horticultural skills. He was delighted that Safr had discovered how to propagate pomegranates from seed rather than from a cutting. The emir thanked him profusely and then generously compensated him for his work.

Over the following years, the emir showcased pomegranate seedlings at his Rusafa palace and also offered them for planting in other gardens and orchards in the Muslim community. He then distributed rooted cuttings of the variety to other Muslims all across al-Andalus, where it became known as the *safarí* pomegranate, in honor of the nurseryman who enabled it to survive.

Ironically, the name *safarí* also implied (by way of pun) that this pomegranate was a "traveler"—out on safari from the Middle East— just as the emir himself was. It is remarkable that the story of the *safarí* pomegranate endures with so many details still intact thirteen centuries after this horticultural rescue took place.[9]

According to horticultural historian D. Fairchild Ruggles, this is "the first reference to the deliberate and controlled acclimitization of an exotic species, and perhaps even to a botanical garden"[10] documented anywhere in the world. And yet the very fact that a single plant received such attention and acclaim hints at the longing that Abd al-Rahman must have felt to taste the finest fruit of his childhood once again. He clearly wished to share this experience with future generations of Muslims in al-Andalus. His emotional attachment also comes through in the short but poignant poem he composed about his introduction of a date palm variety to the West:

A palm tree stands in the middle of Rusafa
Born in the West, far from the land of palms
I said to it, "How like me you are, far away and in exile!
In long separation from family and friends
You have sprung from soil in which you are a stranger
And I, like you, am far away from home.[11]

And so it is clear that this Immigrant Emir, this Pomegranate Pilgrim found solace in living among "immigrant" plants. Once the plants were in hand, he and his descendants used them to reconstruct in al-Andalus a semblance of entire landscapes they had known back home. Dates, Damascus apricots, figs, olives, and pomegranates were planted everywhere that the Iberian soils could support them, and beneath or between their canopies sprouted capers, saffron, anise, and spearmint. Thus began the process of truly comprehensive ecological imperialism—the wholesale overhaul of the composition, structure, and function of cultural landscapes—that predated the ecological imperialism accomplished by the Spanish in central Mexico by some seven centuries.

Of course, many crops that had originated or diversified in the Middle East had already come westward with the Phoenicians and Berbers, by serendipity or otherwise. This is also true for many agricultural and industrial technologies later used in Spain. But Abd al-Rahman and his descendants fostered a deliberate process of plant introduction, agronomic evaluation, and propagation of the fruits, nuts, vegetables, grains, and aromatic herbs to determine which were best suited to the climatic constraints and opportunities of their adopted home. They encouraged Muslim farmers, bakers, and chefs to participate in the processes of agronomic and culinary evaluations of newly introduced food-crop varieties. More significantly, perhaps, they enlisted Jewish and Christian scholars to join together in documenting the historical origins of horticultural practices and disseminating the results of their shared agricultural, biomedical and culinary experiments. This scholarly collaboration of linguists, historians, and scientists from all three faiths is one of the hallmarks of the cultural intermingling now known as *convivencia*, or "coexistence." Although economic and political power was not equally shared during the era of *convivencia* that began in the eighth century, something fresh did begin to occur both cross-culturally and intellectually.

Within just a few decades of Abd al-Rahman's arrival in al-Andalus, Jewish and Christian families became Arabized in their use of language, in their behavior, in their land stewardship ethics, and in their cuisine. Both what came out of their mouths and what went in aligned more with the Islamic renaissance than with the lingering cultural doldrums we tend to associate with the Dark Ages in Europe.

Over the next seven centuries of Arab and Berber dominance in al-Andalus, the pluralistic collaborations among Muslims, Christians, and Jews resulted in both the transformation and diversification of the Iberian landscape and a profound influence on Europe as a whole.[12]

First, they established libraries and universities—for women as well as men—where everything from poultry science to agrarian poetry was taught. Next, they opened the School of Translators and commissioned teams of Latin-, Greek-, Arabic-, and Hebrew-speaking scholars to translate and print ancient agricultural classics from other arid and semiarid lands, in the hope that farmers and orchardists might be guided and inspired by the works.

Suddenly, a multicultural agricultural revolution emerged from the literate members of the farming community—a revolution that was possible because literacy rates in al-Andalus were far higher than those in the rest of Europe at that time. Whether Christian, Jew, or Muslim, these farmer-scholars instantly applied the ideas they found in agrarian classics such as the first century CE *De re rustica,* which codified the knowledge of farm management among the Phoenician and Roman farmers of Cádiz, and the eighth-century *Agricultura nabatea,* which rescued even older agricultural practices forged in the Negev.[13] Moreover, public discussion of these works initiated new agricultural and culinary innovation, as well as long-term commitment to these arts. The Arabs in particular realized that al-Andalus was better endowed with fresh water and arable land than most of the Middle East and North Africa. If they had arrived in a paradise blessed with ample moisture and fertile soil, they had best make the most of it.

The results of their labors, accumulated over the following decades, noticeably improved the quality, fecundity, and productivity of Andalusian fields, vineyards, and orchards. Notably, Christians as well as Jews and Muslims made significant contributions through these cross-cultural exchanges. Their successes were then compiled and interpreted by a number of farmer-scholars who themselves resided in the Andalusian countryside. Their fresh insights and evaluations of plant introductions culminated in the publication of some of the most important works on dry-land agriculture ever printed. Among the most timeless agricultural classics were *Kitāb al-Filāḥa* (*Libro de agricultura*) by Abu Zacaria Iahia, *Kitāb Mabāhiy al-Fikhar* by Yamāl ad-Dīn al-Afghani y Muhammad, and *Obra de agricultura* by Gabriel Alonso de Herrera. As my New Mexican mentor, the great Hispanic historian of agricultural diffusion Juan Estevan Arellano, has reminded us, these are the works that old Christians, conversos, crypto-Arabs and crypto-Jews carried with them several centuries later when they escaped Spain to resettle and farm in the New World.[14]

The works by Abu Zacaria Iahia and Gabriel Alonso de Herrera in particular underscore that the horticultural and culinary arts were not as isolated from each other in al-Andalus as they are in today's world. Iahia devoted an entire twenty-eight-page chapter to gastronomy in his "agronomy manual," detailing the best means of drying, curing, preserving, and cooking the various food crops he had personally grown as a farmer.[15] Herrera describes the taste and texture of plums introduced from Damascus, the medicinal qualities of a rosemary variety introduced from Jerusalem by a Moorish spice dealer, and the rumors associated with eggplants brought in from Morocco. In his birthplace of Talavera, Herrera dryly notes that, "It is common opinion that eggplants were brought to these parts by the Moors ... and that they brought them to kill Christians with."[16]

Whether Herrera meant that the labor that was required to grow them in Spain was enough to kill a Christian or that the plant was a member of the deadly nightshade clan is unclear. What we do know is that centuries later the Spanish and Italians were at first hesitant to eat another introduced nightshade relative referred to as a *pomo d'Moro* (fruit of the Moor)—the New World tomato.

What was the Andalusian populace to do with all of these newly accumulated staples and spices, these flavors, fragrances, and textures the likes of which few Europeans had ever experienced prior to the arrival of the Umayyad Arabs on the shores of Iberia? The locals clearly needed guidance on both growing this diversity of foods in Andalusian soils and preparing them for the Andalusian table.

Fortunately, the Umayyad rulers were able to attract to al-Andalus the greatest culinary artist in the world at that time, a man who appears to have been a culturally and racially mixed Arab African, just as Abd al-Rahman and his descendants had been. His nickname was Ziryab—the Blackbird—because of his thick black hair, his olive skin, his sleek profile, his hands fluttering on the strings of the oud, and his melodious voice.

The so-called Islamic agricultural revolution had reached western Europe by 760, but it took Ziryab's arrival from Persia sixty years later to jump-start the culinary revolution that forever changed European cuisines. Perhaps no single man or woman reshaped the aesthetics of an entire continent as much as Ziryab reshaped Europe's, not just through the culinary arts but also through gardening, music, fashion, and high-minded conversation.[17] By all accounts, the multicultural Andalusians not only respected Ziryab for his talents in the garden, kitchen, dining room, and parlor for performing arts but also because he brought

❧ BERENJENA CON ACELGUILLA ❧
Sephardic Eggplant with Swiss Chard

Rather remarkably, Sephardic Jewish historian David Gitlitz has uncovered a burlesque poem or song lyric that not only captures tensions in the converso community of Moorish Spain at the time but also describes an eggplant casserole served at Sephardic weddings of the era. The Spanish term for eggplant, *berenjena*, spelled *verengena* in Moorish Spain, is clearly derived from *bitengen*, a term used throughout the Middle East and Africa by many Arabs, Jews, and Berbers. It had become a favorite vegetable to serve at feasts in Moorish Spain, perhaps because the meaty flesh of this solanaceous fruit so wonderfully absorbs the flavors of spices. Similar eggplant dishes, known as *cazuelas* (a term derived from the Arabic word for bowl and used for both the casserole or stew and the earthenware pot in which it is cooked), have been made in the Middle East for centuries and are kin to the famous dish *imam biyaldi*, or "the priest faints with pleasure."

The following excerpt from a sixty-five-stanza *canción* was sung by the Sephardic Jewish poet Rodrigo Cota, who apparently wrote it in retaliation for being left off the invitation list by his converso kin for a fifteenth-century Cota family wedding in Segovia. The wedding feast was attended by conversos to honor the arranged marriage between a girl from the family of Cardinal Pedro González de Mendoza and the grandson of Diego Arias Dávila, a converso who at that time was the minister of finance in the court of the Castilian king Henry IV, also known as Henry the Impotent, who reigned from 1454 to 1474. The song-poem includes this verse:

> At this Jewish wedding party
> bristly pig was not consumed;
> not one single scaleless fish
> went down the gullet of the groom;
> instead, an eggplant casserole
> with saffron and Swiss chard;
> and whoever swore by "Jesus"
> from the meatball pot was barred.

The recipe reconstruction originally offered by David Gitlitz and his wife, Linda Kay Davidson, in their fine book *A Drizzle of Honey*, has been modestly modified to take into account the spices used with eggplant during that era. I have also recommended using smaller Asian eggplants, rather than a large globe eggplant, as I found them easier to combine with the chard. *Serves 6.*

2 pounds Asian eggplants or small globe eggplants
Salt
1 large bunch red Swiss chard
2 tablespoons unfiltered or extra-virgin Arbequina olive oil
Ample pinch of saffron threads
1 white onion, sliced
1 clove Egyptian red garlic or other garlic, crushed
½ cup water, vegetable broth, or almond milk
¼ teaspoon white pepper
1 teaspoon freshly ground cassia cinnamon
¼ teaspoon crushed whole cloves
¼ teaspoon freshly grated or ground nutmeg
3 tablespoons finely chopped fresh cilantro
3 to 4 tablespoons pine nuts, toasted

Peel the eggplants, then cut crosswise into ¼-inch-thick slices. Lay the slices in a single layer on a work surface, sprinkle the slices on both sides with 1 to 2 tablespoons salt, and let stand for 30 minutes. Rinse the eggplant slices, then pat dry with paper towels. Set the slices aside.

Cut the stems from the chard leaves. Cut the stems crosswise into 1-inch lengths and coarsely chop the leaves. Keep the stems and leaves separate.

In a large frying pan or *cazeula,* heat the olive oil and saffron threads over medium-low heat until the oil turns yellow from the saffon, 4 to 5 minutes. Add the onion, garlic, and chard stems and sauté until the stems and onion are nearly translucent, about 10 minutes. Add the eggplant slices and cook, turning occasionally, for 3 minutes longer, to soften the slices slightly. Add the water, pepper, cinnamon, cloves, nutmeg, and 1 teaspoon salt and stir well. Turn down the heat to low, cover, and cook until the eggplant slices are nearly tender, 15 to 20 minutes.

Add the chard leaves, stir to combine, re-cover, and continue to cook until the vegetables are tender, 5 to 7 minutes. Transfer to a platter, garnish with the cilantro and pine nuts, and serve hot.

Gitlitz, David M. *Secrecy and Deceit: The Religion of the Crypto-Jews.* Albuquerque: University of New Mexico Press, 1996, p. 478.
Gitlitz, David M., and Linda Kay Davidson. *A Drizzle of Honey: The Lives and Recipes of Spain's Secret Jews.* New York: St. Martin's, 1999, p. 46.

Muslims, Jews, and some Christians together through his style and tact. In a time when Muslims, Jews, and Christians in al-Andalus were still struggling to get along and keep conflicts from erupting, Ziryab made many of them forget their differences through the pure excitement he generated among all with whom he came in contact.

Ziryab was born Abu al-Hasan 'Ali ibn Nafi in or near Baghdad within just a few years of the death of Abd al-Rahman I in Córdoba. Even though he was a freed slave of multiethnic descent, he was groomed and trained in singing, stringed instruments, culinary arts, and botany among the Abbasid elite. At a young age, he became so talented at playing the oud that his mentor, Isaac of Mosul, became jealous of his rising popularity and had his name removed from the list of artists to be supported by Abbasid patronage and had him banished from the courts. Ziryab drifted off to the south, only to find Damascus still in disarray, and so he went west, seeking work simply as a musician.

He ended up playing music for a time on the stretch of the Tunisian coast known in medieval times as Ifriqqiya. There, he was invited to join the court musicians of the third Umayyad ruler, al-Hakam I. But by the time he arrived in Andalusia in 822, his sponsor had died. Now desolate and as far from his birthplace as he could imagine going, he grew despondent. Only through the intervention of the Jewish musician Abu al-Nasr Mansur did he get an audience with the new emir, Abd al-Rahman II. Fortunately, as soon as he heard Ziryab play the oud and sing, the young emir invited him to stay in his court. But that was not all, for as soon as he saw Ziryab perform, the young emir quickly realized that Ziryab had talents that extended beyond music.

From his time working among the rivals of the Banu Umayyah in the Abbasid court of Baghdad, Ziryab had gained an intimate understanding of what fashion and festivity should be in the hub of the Islamic empire. It was to the emir's political benefit to let Ziryab loose so that he could enhance the cultural sophistication of court life in al-Andalus. On behalf of the displaced Umayyad dynasty stranded on the westernmost edge of the Islamic empire, Abd al-Rahman II brilliantly pursued the agricultural, culinary, and other arts, hoping to attract attention away from the more economically powerful Abbasid elite. This may be why, in 955, within a hundred years after Ziryab's death, a Catholic sister from the Gandersheim abbey proclaimed that in Córdoba, "the brilliant ornament of the world shown in the West . . . it was wealthy and famous and known for its pleasures and resplendence in all things."[18]

In essence, Ziryab had begun to serve as the emir's minister of culture and soon had his hand in upgrading everything from hygiene and clothing among the local elite to establishing standards for table manners, designing place settings, planning dinner-course sequences, and offering rigorous training for court chefs and musicians.[19] His recipes were so beloved that a number of them survive until this day, including *ziriabí*, a dish of salted and roasted fava beans.[20] The Blackbird's innovations created a buzz and were heartily embraced by Muslims, Jews, and Christians alike. Just as the young emir had wished, Andalusia's sophistication made the rest of Europe seem intellectually stunted and aesthetically deprived.

Lilia Zaouali has deftly summed up Ziryab's influence in renewing the culinary arts of al-Andalus during his lifetime: "It was a curious route—from Baghdad to Córdoba, via the Mediterranean and North Africa—for 'Abbasid gastronomic fashion to have taken. It is entirely possible that with his precious lute, Ziryāb brought with him books of recipes and linen pouches filled with [cassia] cinnamon (*Cinamomum chinese*, known to the Arabs as *dārsīni*) and other spices. . . . One might well imagine him attempting to re-create the flavors he had tasted at a banquet held by [Abassid ruler] Hārūn al-Rashīd in addition to playing the melodies he had heard there [in Baghdad]."[21]

By the time Ziryab died in 857, there can be little doubt that the landed gentry of al-Andalus was growing and using a greater variety of aromatic herbs and spices on a daily basis than the rest of Europe combined. *Recetarios* from the *convivencia* era suggest that Arabs, Berbers, and Jews were regularly acquiring, sharing, and experimenting with sumac, saffron, cumin, cloves, coriander, garlic, nutmeg, mace, ginger, mint, oregano, rue, laurel, and limes, as well as bitter orange and rose water. What is obvious is how similar this mix of herbs and spices is to what would be found in nearly any kitchen in the Middle East during the same era.

But most remarkable is that many of these herbs and spices were now being grown in western Europe for the first time. It was not that European Christendom had been devoid of farming and cooking traditions or herbal variety until this time, but it can be argued that the fresh influx of ideas and flavors greatly enhanced these Western European traditions. Again, the relative "placelessness" as well as the cosmopolitan nature of Iberian Arabs and Sephardic Jews allowed them to be among the earliest peoples on the planet to shift not just the use of aromatic herbs and spices from one continent to the next but also their cultivation as crops. They refined and intensified the cultural and agro-

The burgundy red berrylike fruits of *Rhus coriaria* offer a bright, tangy, mouth-puckering punch up front, followed by a resinous, woody, citric combination of sweetness, tartness, and saltiness. The tanginess and fruitiness of sumac happily linger on one's lips for some time. Sumac fruits typically grow in cone-shaped clusters, which deepen in their blush as fall proceeds. Each berry has a thin outer skin that surrounds seeds so hard that they often need to be soaked before grinding them into a coarse powder. Sumac is cultivated from Afghanistan westward, across the Middle East and the Mediterranean and as far as the Canary Islands.

Sumac, or in Levantine Arabic, *simmaq,* is usually sold already ground, and the crimson powder is dusted on skewered meats immediately before grilling. I grew up thinking that the smeared blotch of lipstick red that sat in the middle of each bowl of hummus was a dusting of paprika with a squeeze of lemon. I later learned that it took only a scatter of sumac to get that distinctive color and lemony zing. In Iran, parts of Turkey, Lebanon, and Syria, sumac is among the primary spices used in rubs for all sorts of grilled and baked meats, fish, and fowl. It is also a key ingredient in some, though not all, *za'atar* spice mixtures used in Lebanon, Syria, Jordan, and Palestine.

I have often been frustrated by the fact that most of the sumac I find in Middle Eastern markets in the United States is far from fresh and lacks the vibrancy of what I regularly taste in the Middle East. To remedy this dilemma, I have taken to harvesting the red berries of *R. trilobata,* the most widespread sumac (also known as lemonade berry) in the semiarid West. The berries of this species have long been eaten by the Navajo, or Diné, the largest tribe in western North America, but one that shares some of its genetic history with Turkic-speaking peoples of Central and northeastern Asia. Because there is at least one edible sumac species in most states of the United States (in addition to several poisonous ones), it is a good idea to source this spice from native populations near where you live.

Gambrelle, Fabienne. *The Flavor of Spices.* Paris: Flammarion, 2008.

Hill, Tony. *The Contemporary Encyclopedia of Herbs and Spices.* Hoboken, NJ: John Wiley and Sons, 2004.

Katzer, Gernot. "Gernot Katzer's Spice Pages." http://gernot-katzers-spice-pages.com/engl/index.html. Accessed May 8, 2013.

Sortun, Ana, with Nicole Chaison. *Spice: Flavors of the Eastern Mediterranean.* New York: Regan Books, 2006.

ecological diffusion processes, which extended from Asia to Africa and then to southwestern Europe, the very same processes later erroneously labeled by historian Alfred Crosby as an altogether new phenomenon, the Columbian Exchange, when it reached the Americas.

Instead, it was simply a form of globalization that had begun in the deserts of the Arabian Peninsula as much as thirty-five hundred years earlier. By the tenth century, it had ensured that most saffron was grown in, rather than imported to, al-Andalus, where the spice became a signature ingredient in paella and couscous. To this day, more saffron is grown in Islamic-influenced Spanish landscapes than in any other terrain in Europe.[22] It was probably during this same era that Arab or Jewish traders introduced green aniseeds from the Middle East to Córdoba and Granada. Aniseeds quickly germinated on their own in Andalusian soils and soon escaped as weeds into wheat fields and vineyards of the region, where they persist as a naturalized and occasionally harvested invasive today.

Apparently, the concept of *terroir*—of food grown in a particular place—did not matter as much to the immigrant cultures of the Iberian Peninsula as accumulation of wealth and reliable access to their favorite foods did. Despite lip service about longing for a return to the Holy Lands, most Sephardic Jews and Arabs of al-Andalus were no longer wedded in any way to their ancestral landscape of the Middle East. Due to its excesses, the power base of the Banu Umayyah once again collapsed around 1031 and its members dispersed, although a few Arab Muslims maintained their trading activities in the region.

I walk down the mountain ridge and through an entrance gate high above the ancient city of Córdoba. Madinat al-Zahra, whose walls once held the largest complex of Muslim-designed gardens of any place in Europe, today feels haunted by ghosts from its Islamic past.

It is painful for me to tour this historic monument, promoted by a government that has hardly ever tolerated the people who conceived, designed, and built it. But that is a common feeling among many scholars and tourists wishing to see the vestiges of Moorish al-Andalus that are scattered around the Spanish region of Andalusia. Here the past is glorified even while being presented as antiseptically as possible: no contemporary Islamic presence, and few if any living remnants of the cultivated plants and domestic livestock that they raised. What commands my attention is the sterility of the walls, terraces, and tunnels. Descending from the highest terraces, where fortified buildings domi-

The tiny, aromatic, sage green fruits of this Old World herb (*Pimpinella anisum*) emanate a vaguely dusty, licorice-like scent. Their sweet ane-thole-based flavor has been confused with that of fennel, star anise, wintergreen, and even dill. Although some native Latin American herbs with similar taste profiles are called *yerba anís*, true anise (also known as aniseed) is native to the Levant. It was quickly dispersed throughout the Mediterranean region and Asia Minor, and was well established in Greece by the fourth century BCE. In ancient Rome, Pliny observed that "be it green or dried, it is wanted for all conserves and seasonings."

It was first brought to the Americas as a cultivated herb three cen-turies ago. Nowadays, it is a common flavoring in various anisette spirits in both the New World and the Old. In many countries, it is used as a digestive and as a culinary spice in pastries and sausages. If you have tasted a biscotto in Italy or a sugar-coated *saunf* dessert seed in India, you have likely tasted true anise.

The popularity of anisettes seems to wrap around the northern Mediterranean shores, ranging from *anís* and *anisette* in Andalusia; Pernod in southern France; *sambuca* in Italy; ouzo in Greece; raki in Turkey, Cypress, and Crete; and arak in Lebanon and Syria. My first taste of arak was offered to me by one of my Lebanese American uncles when I was still a teenager. He prided himself on having worked during Prohibition with the best Lebanese and Syrian American boot-leggers, who had maintained a steady stream of the spirit flowing into communities of Middle Eastern immigrants in the United States.

At the same time, he painfully recalled to me that when he was exactly my age, he had been jailed briefly for selling some of his own uncle's bootleg arak to a plain-clothes policeman! His father and my grandfather had grown up distilling the fermented juices of grapes in the Bekáa Valley and curing their distillate with aniseeds specially grown and harvested by Bedouins in the Houran region of Syria. To this day, Syria remains the largest producer of aniseeds in the world, as well as the place where wild anise is most valued.

Although some scholars have argued that most languages spoken in and near Europe share *anis* as a loan word from either the Latin

nate the scene, I can make out the ancient gardens and fountains that Abd al-Rahman III took forty years to design, construct, cultivate, and populate. The gardens were elegantly framed by the stone silhouettes of ornate *miradores,* the portals that opened up one panorama after another in stair-step-like succession. But what is revealed by the recon-structed *miradores* of today is not what Abd al-Rahman III's guests (*anisum*) or the Greek (*anison*), I would argue that its roots are older and in the Semitic languages. The Hebrew *anis* and the Arabic terms *anisun* and *yansun* are less likely to be loan words from Greek or Roman than the other way around. Farsi also uses *anisun*. In fact, the handful of the world's languages that do not use a variant of *anis* imply that anise is a sweet form of fennel, dill, cumin, or star anise. In south-central Asia, a few languages like Sanskrit refer to anise descriptively as "a hundred flowers," but the similarly spelled terms in Thai, Telugu, and Sinhala may also refer to dill.

In the Americas, several wild and semicultivated species are called *yerba anís*, but they are all botanically unrelated to the Old World anise, which belongs to the parsley family. The herbs most commonly called *yerba anís* in Mexico are more closely related to Old World tarragon and belong to the genus *Tagetes* in the aster family. To add to the confusion, the true anise introduced to the Americas by Spanish missionaries has gone feral and naturalized in the desert oases of northwest Mexico, where it is typically called *yerba anís del monte*. In Mexico, anise is used in the nonalcoholic beverage *atole de anís* and in various distilled beverages. *Aguardientes* flavored with anise are popular throughout the Spanish-speaking world, as are anisette liqueurs, including Cartujo in Venezuela and Anís del Mono in Spain.

Toasted aniseeds are popular among Latin American confectioners, who use them as the signature flavor in the Mexican wedding cookies found in northern Mexico and the US Southwest and in *picarones*, Peruvian fritters made with pumpkin or sweet potato. The presence of anise in some Spanish and Latin American desserts may hark all the way back to the arrival of Phoenician, Arab, and Berber recipes on the Iberian Peninsula a dozen centuries ago and are now thought of as Spanish. In the remote desert oasis of San Borja in Baja California, Mexico, I once found true anise being grown and used in much the same ways as it has been in the desert oases of Arabia and North Africa since antiquity. Like the flavor of dates, the flavor of anise is a signature taste of the desert oasis wherever that oasis may be.

Hill, Tony. *The Contemporary Encyclopedia of Herbs and Spices*. Hoboken, NJ: John Wiley and Sons, 2004.

would have seen. Gone are the pomegranates, figs, and quinces, the grapes and dates characteristic of the cultural landscapes of Moorish Spain. Instead, ornamentals—myrtle and jasmine, flowering shrubs, fan palms, and citrus—stand in their place.

The apricot and rose varieties that medieval residents here knew as *damascos* have been replaced by nonfragrant, inedible horticultural varieties whose only asset is indestructible perennial foliage. Although the third terrace once held field crops of herbs and spices and vegetables of every shape and color, it is now predominantly hardscape, for historic preservationists seem to love barren stone more than they love living plants. Even though the pamphlets, folios, and guidebooks claim that Spanish archaeologists will use the dead seeds and pits they have found in tunnels and storage caverns to design an intentionally renovated cultural landscape on the terraces, no such thing can yet be seen, sniffed, tasted, or touched. They may be awaiting resurrection, as if suddenly, someday soon, a rapture will come and all of the ghosts will reroot themselves in this dry but fragrant earth.

Disappointed, I descend to the heart of modern Córdoba some twenty miles below, hoping to find a few spice markets that feature Berber- and Arab-style spice mixtures. After a few hours of searching for an open-air market, I finally find Mercado Ciudad Jardín, where Manuel Ruiz tends the spice shop known as Casa Manola. But it appears that the complexity of Moorish spice mixtures has dwindled down to just a few composites of four to six herbs per bag. These herbs are premixed, then vacuum sealed and labeled in bulk quantities.

Manuel Ruiz shakes his head when I ask if any local food artisan still custom mixes freshly dried herbs and seeds for sale in the city. "No, not here, not now" he replies, "but they still may mix *especias morunas* in the Alpurrajas region high in the mountains east of Granada." I glance at all his other shrink-wrapped bags of single spices and think of the ghosts also trapped inside those packages. I envision their aromas escaping into the night air at the midnight hour, playfully, fragrantly mingling with one another until the shopkeepers return in the morning.

CHAPTER 8

The Crumbling of *Convivencia* and the Rise of Transnational Guilds

Once again in charge of Moorish Spain, the Berbers brought in a long series of Muslim emirs, princes, and generals to take the place of the Banu Umayyah. They maintained strong ties with their kin in Morocco, in case they should ever need to escape from Christian forces. Likewise, the Sephardic Jews forged more substantial trading alliances with other Jews in Portugal, Provence, Belgium, Sicily, Morocco, Tunisia, Egypt, and Turkey. They regularly negotiated for musk from Tibet, silk from China, and ambergris from the Atlantic coast of Africa, probably from Mauritania.[1] They likely perceived no risk at all in bringing in other "immigrants" (plants) to grow in their own territory that they received from distant lands, especially if this cultivation could offer them greater control over the trade in culinary resources.

After the collapse of the Umayyad dynasty, the more altruistic components of the *convivencia* era began to disappear. Although there was nominal coexistence, there was also considerable conflict and oppression of minority faiths. It is not surprising that following the demise of Muslim-Jewish-Christian commercial and scientific collaborations on the Iberian Peninsula, two mercantile organizations independent of the ruling classes took up the slack in the power dynamics of international trade, not just on the peninsula but all across the world. They were the Radhanite Jews and the multiethnic Karimi, and perhaps for the first time in economic history, groups entirely independent of and transcendent of nation-states controlled spice commerce. As emirs and empires quickly came and went, these two entities demonstrated their staying power for several centuries. They not only traded in spices and other aromatics but also moved just about every other major salable product—from gold to linen—from Spain to China.

The Radhanites, or Radaniyya, were a guild or a clan (that is, united by genetic kinship) of Jewish spice merchants that first appeared by name around 500 CE, but later gained prominence in both western Europe and Asia Minor as the major go-betweens for trade between Muslims and Christians. Their name may have come from the Persian *rad-han,* "the one(s) who know the way," although other historians associate it with place names in their trading hubs of northern Persia, Mesopotamia, and southern France. They rose to prominence after 800, when both Muslims and Christians were formally banned by leaders of their respective faiths from trading directly with each other. It appears that a multilingual, widely traveled group of Radhanite merchants gained extraordinary wealth by serving as a bridge between Christian and Muslim traders.

They may have first specialized in transcontinental trade of just four aromatics: musk, camphor, aloe wood, and cassia cinnamon.[2] For well over a century after the ban on Christian-Muslim trade in 800, the Radhanites were nearly solely responsible for every ounce of these four spices that reached southern Europe's city-states. Soon, however, they added other spices along with perfumes, precious stones, jewelry, silk, furs, and swords to their inventory. Although only a few documents describing their activities have survived, it appears that the Radhanites also became more and more engaged in slave trade as time went on. They apparently had no qualms about moving female slaves and eunuchs among faiths, countries, or continents.

The Radhanites were relatively few in number, but they moved extraordinary numbers of small packages of high-value goods through ports such as Constantinople, Smyrna, Aleppo, Beirut, and Alexandria, where other resident Jews harbored them during difficult times.

Unlike more sedentary Jewish merchants, the Radhanites did not restrict themselves to working out of a few ports. Instead, particular individuals are known to have traveled from the Rhône Valley to Córdoba in al-Andalus, across the Strait of Gibraltar to Fez and Alexandria, then on to Baghdad, Basra, Cochin, and Canton. One Jewish traveler and trader who may have been a Radhanite descendant, Benjamin of Tudela, left Spain in 1165 and visited over three hundred cities in Europe, Asia, and Africa before he returned to Spain in 1177.

Along the way, he stayed with Jews in Italy, Turkey, Syria, Lebanon, Persia, Egypt, and Morocco; all the while, his ties with other Jews from the Iberian Peninsula remained strong.

Benjamin of Tudela's travels along the spice routes came more than two centuries after the heyday of Radhanite dominance. Not long after 900, the Venetians and the Karimi broke the Radhanite monopoly on the movement of aromatics. There was a brief free-for-all among many players to regain control of the trade routes they had managed prior to the Radhanite reach, but it did not take long for the Karimi guild of traders to trump all others and gain exclusive jurisdiction over a vast trade network.

Today, centuries after the Karimi traders were active, historians remain humbled by how little they know about this guild, which kept details of how its organization functioned secret. It appears that the term *Karimi* came from the Tamil language of the Indian subcontinent, where it was used for people involved in business affairs. But by 1150, an elite group of "merchants of pepper and of other spices" assumed the name. Although the primary residences of individual Karimi traders ranged from Spain to China, the members collectively purchased protection for their activities from both empires and pirates. As the affluence they derived from their control of trade eclipsed even that of the Radhanites and Phoenicians before them, they became what financial historian William Bernstein has called "the medieval world's greatest source of concentrated wealth."[3]

The guild began as a small group of merchants—perhaps fewer than fifty individuals—a mix of Tamil, Hindu, Persian, Arab, and maybe even a few Egyptian Jewish entrepreneurs.[4] But by the Mamluk era, which began around 1250, most of those newly selected to be in the guild were Arab Muslims who followed Islamic commercial, ethical, and social protocols exclusively. From then on, elite membership in the Karimi group was largely passed on from father to son, so that the *funduqs* (lodgings), based in strategically placed trade hubs, remained in the steady hands of specific family dynasties. This stability through time provided Karimi traders with a kind of collective-bargaining power that was unprecedented historically, much the same way that the oil-producing member nations of OPEC have controlled the price and supply of oil since the 1970s.

It is probable that the Karimi families controlled much of the spice trade within their particular regions of origin, but their collective interests were transnational rather than tightly tied to any single political power. First, they had coalesced to secure control over sea trade in spices across the Red Sea, Arabian Sea, and Indian Ocean. They initially commanded most trade out of the ports of present-day Yemen and Egypt but later added the finest ports of India, Ceylon, and the Great Horn of Africa to their portfolio.

Soon their networks had agents, shipbuilders, and merchant marine fleets that worked the seas from al-Andalus and the Maghreb in the far west to the coasts of Sub-Saharan Africa and Madagascar in the south. By 1415, they were using the prosperous port of Ceuta to obtain hundreds of thousands of pounds of melegueta and other Guinea peppers (grains of Selim, West African pepper) from the African continent, which they passed on to Arab, Italian, and Iberian merchants.[5]

Because European Catholic merchants were still forbidden to trade directly with the Muslims in the Karimi guild, the remnants of the declining multiethnic *convivencia* in al-Andalus continued to facilitate the transfer of Karimi-controlled goods into western Europe. The Karimi guild also exerted considerable control across the overland routes by having its families or agents based in Mecca, Damascus, Aleppo, Baghdad, and Smyrna. Later, it brought them direct access to China through the old port of Zayton and other harbors on the East China Sea.

The guild had within its ranks its own equivalents of Aristotle Onassis, Edward H. Harriman, and Cornelius Vanderbilt—men outside of royalty but critically positioned to control the transactions and transportation involved in regional and international commerce. Unlike the Jewish businessmen who played complementary roles during the same era, the Karimi merchants did not engage in money lending, tax farming, banking, or commodity wholesaling. Perhaps the single richest man in the preindustrial world was not a banker or a king but the Karimi merchant Yasir al-Balisi, whose fortune reached 10 million dinars, the equivalent of 500 million U.S. dollars in today's currency.[6] Many Karimi families amassed fortunes of 1 million dinars (50 million dollars) over the space of one to three generations.

Thirteenth-century spice trader Muhammad bin Abd al-Rahman b. Ishmail al-Jaziri began his career with less than five hundred dinars and increased his assets a hundredfold by his death in 1302, a result of personally brokering the transfer of goods from the Karimi base at Souk al-Atarrin in Alexandria, to Cairo, Mecca, Damascus, Aleppo, Baghdad, Basra, and Muscat. In addition, he traveled to Zayton three times to maintain his business interests there.[7] When not physically present in one of these ports, he could use Karimi banking institutions to make loans or transfer funds from the Middle East to the Land of the Rising Sun (the Far East) or to the Land of the Setting Sun (the Maghreb).

On the Iberian Peninsula, the Castilians and other Spanish-speaking Christians, perhaps feeling that their roots were deeper and more genuine, began to treat the Arabs and Jews with ever greater suspicion. From the view of Spanish Catholics, the Muslims and Jews of al-Andalus were growing more intellectually and culturally influential and more politically and economically powerful. The Jewish bankers and moneylenders became easy targets for fear-mongering Spanish Catholics. And ever since the beginning of the Crusades in 1095, Spanish Catholics had become increasingly ambivalent about the Arab and Berber Muslims who lived on their southern doorstep. Once the Sublime Ottoman State had captured the trading hub of Thessaloníki from the Venetians in 1387, both Catholic and Orthodox Christians became worried that they were on the verge of another Islamic surge into Europe.

Two years later, in 1389, when Ottoman troops won the Battle of Kosovo, it was clear that the Vatican's worst fears had become reality. The Ottoman Empire had begun to expand into Europe from the East, and the independent state of the Nasrid dynasty based in Granada had gained complete control of all maritime trade going through the Strait of Gibraltar.

And yet, it was not some potential political or military power that Jews and Muslims might ultimately harness against them that the Spanish Catholics feared. Instead, it was the pervasive and effective control that these immigrants had exerted over nearly every aspect of trade between the "Spanish" city-states and almost every other cluster of city-states and empires in the world at that time, exercised through their unparalleled mastery of the science of navigation.

The kings and queens of Castile, Aragon, Catalan, and Genoa were particularly distraught when the Ottoman Empire cut off Silk Road trade to Europe through Constantinople in 1453, and they remained frustrated by the tight Muslim control of the Strait of Gibraltar. The Castilians tried in vain to gain control of the Strait of Gibraltar several times. In fact their king, Alfonso XI, had succumbed to the Black Death while attempting to take the strait by siege in 1349. Instead, it remained under Muslim Berber control until 1462, even though Islamic Spain had dwindled to a tenth of its former size by that time.[8] More important, no Islamic army ever invaded Spain again after that era.

It is not always easy for a culture of one faith to remember its intellectual, spiritual, and even economic debt to cultures of other faiths. Despite the fact that Catholic families' own fortunes could not have been accumulated without Muslim and Jewish scholarship in Iberian universities and Jewish and Muslim business prowess in trade with Africa and the Middle East, the Catholic cousins known as Ferdinand II of Aragon and Isabella I of Castile saw little reason to invest any more in these intellectual and financial engines. By the time they had married and joined forces to reunite the kingdoms of the Iberian Peninsula, they had already begun to extract enormous tribute taxes from the Jewish, Arab, and Berber merchants who brought in great quantities of spices and other goods from North Africa. The very wellspring of their power became a moot point to Ferdinand and Isabella. When they seized the keys of the Alhambra from the last Islamic emir of al-Andalus, the bumbling Boabdil, he supposedly lamented to Ferdinand, "Allah must love you well, for these are the keys to his paradise."[9]

An eight-hundred-year legacy of innovation engendered by Christian, Jewish, and Muslim interaction on the peninsula had finally been broken. Most Muslims departed immediately. The Sephardim had likely maintained some presence in Iberia for longer than that, but their status too was destined to change.

At first, Ferdinand and Isabella feigned respect for the defeated Muslims, bedecking themselves in Arab garb as they climbed the hills of Granada to take possession of the magnificent Alhambra in February of 1492. They immediately asserted that Muslim and Jewish merchants would still have access to their mosques and synagogues, markets and maritime trade routes. Further, they magnanimously blessed those who chose to immigrate across the strait to Ceuta or Fez and invited them to take their belongings with them. Boabdil, also known as el Zogoybi (The Unfortunate), took them up on the amnesty offer, leaving his token fiefdom in the cool highlands of Alpujarras for the desert heat of Fez and taking eleven hundred servants and former soldiers along with him.

But as early as 1481, when the first Inquisition in Spain began, Ferdinand had confided to the pope that he intended to forcibly expel all Muslims and most Jews from the peninsula. On March 31, 1492, Ferdinand and Isabella issued the Alhambra Decree, an edict that forced the expulsion of all unconverted Jews and Muslims left in their kingdoms on the peninsula. If this edict was not enough to drive a stake into the heart of the *convivencia,* Ferdinand and Isabella called on

FIGURE 15. *The Capitulation of Granada*, by Francisco Pradilla Ortiz, 1882, depicts the surrender of Boabdil (Muhammad XII) to Ferdinand and Isabella.

Fray Francisco Ximénez de Cisneros, a former Franciscan hermit, then the minister general of the Catalan order in Spain, to begin the new Inquisition as its inquisitor-general. Cisneros also served as Isabella's confessor, giving him unprecedented political access to the queen. In 1499, while visiting the once-great haven of tolerance now known as Granada, Cisneros cranked up the level of xenophobia among Spanish Catholics to what was likely an altogether unprecedented level. The fearful prelate wrote, "Since there are Moors [everywhere] on the coast, which is so near to Africa, and because they are so numerous, they could be a great source of harm [to us] were times to change."[10]

Once the Inquisition got rolling, less than 1 percent of the Jewish and Muslim families chose to remain in Spain, and many left the peninsula for good. Estimates vary widely, but somewhere between 180,000 and 800,000 practicing Jews and Muslims departed from southern Spain as quickly as they could. Even those Jews and Muslims who had converted began to flee for their lives, for any minor suggestion that they had retained their former faith might lead them to being burned at the stake. Cisneros initiated indictments that resulted in over 125,000 Iberian residents of Jewish, Berber, and Arab descent being investigated for crimes of belief. By 1533, some forty-four thousand judgments had been made. No fewer than twenty-two hundred Jews and Muslims were executed for maintaining family rituals that suggested Judaic or Islamic beliefs. But thousands more were killed without trial by Christian vigilantes, and untold numbers died of disease while in captivity, awaiting trial. In later years, some scholars estimated that the numbers of Muslims who were killed or died in prison may have been double that of the Jews. But regardless of scholarly debates over the correct numbers, both Jews and Muslims suffered greatly during this horrific era in ways that no statistic can relate.

The minuscule proportion of "former" Jews and Muslims who stayed in Iberia were careful to abandon any residual outward trappings of their earlier faiths, especially their deeply seated food habits. The Catholics not only forced these conversos (former Jews) and *moriscos* (former Muslims) to eat pork but also replaced the once-abundant flocks of sheep and goats of the Andalusian countryside with sounders of swine. Worse yet, the Spanish Catholics nicknamed the Jewish conversos *marranos* (hogs) to remind them that they now must acquire a taste for pork. Kashrut and halal butchering rituals could no longer be performed. The derogatory term *marrano* was also used by the Jews who fled Spain for their brethren who had abandoned their faith and ancient food taboos.

The baking and eating of *pan de semita* (unleavened bread made with bran or sesame) and *capirotada* (a bread pudding made with fruit and nuts)—long associated with Passover and Ramadan fasts—were officially banned. Before they died (in 1516 and 1504, respectively) Ferdinand and Isabella had extended their ethnic cleansing campaign to scour away all questionable foods from the root cellars, larders, kitchens, and feasts of the converts.

The very foods that had long reinforced their links with the Middle East could no longer be eaten by Sephardic Jews, Berbers, and Arabs anywhere in Spain.[11] Most of the spices long treasured by Spanish Jewry and Muslim clans like the Banu Umayyah, especially the warm, sunny spices from the Middle East brought to Spain by Ziryab, suddenly vanished from the Iberian landscape.

Naively perhaps, I went looking for these spices and other seasonings on my first trip to Andalusia, frequenting farmers' markets in Málaga, Granada, Córdoba, and other towns. I liked the fruits I found there, especially the many apricot and plum varieties, the medlars and quinces. I found it curious to see so many *pata negra* hams hanging from hooks and very little mutton or goat meat. I asked for fresh spices, but when

✣ SIBĀGH ✣
Abbasid and Andalusian Dipping Sauce

According to scholar Lilia Zaouali, *sibāgh*, or dipping sauces, "occupy a place of the first rank in classical Islamic cuisine." In this version, a sort of fruit-and-spice pemmican is stored until needed, then reconstituted with vinegar to serve as a sauce or marinade. Related to ceviche, a dish in which a sauce is used to "cook" meat, poultry, or fish, *sibāgh* can be likened to a Spanish or Mexican *picadillo*. *Makes about 30 disks.*

    5   cups pomegranate seeds
    5   cups raisins from Muscat grapes
    1   tablespoon black peppercorns, crushed
    1   tablespoon cumin seeds, crushed
        Cider vinegar for rehydrating

In a large, wide wooden bowl, combine the pomegranate seeds and raisins and crush them together with a pestle. Add the peppercorns and cumin and mix well. Using your hands, knead the mixture into balls about 2 inches in diameter. Flatten each ball with the pestle into a disk 3 to 4 inches in diameter.

Arrange the disks on a wire rack and cover lightly with a piece of parchment paper, cheesecloth, or fine-mesh screen to deter insects. Place the rack outdoors in a hot, well-ventilated spot, preferably out of the direct sun, until the disks are completely dry. Check the disks daily; the timing will depend on the intensity of the heat and the amount of humidity in the air. Or dry the disks in an oven set at the lowest temperature or in a dehydrator. Transfer the dried disks to an air-tight container and store in a cool, dry place.

When in need of a marinade (or sauce) for kebabs, place a disk in a wooden bowl, add about 1 tablespoon vinegar, and mash with a wooden spoon until the ingredients are rehydrated and a marinade (or sauce) forms. Add more vinegar as needed to achieve the desired consistency. Place skewers threaded with lamb, onion, eggplant, and fruit in the marinade and let them sit while you light coals for grilling. When the coals are ready, grill the skewers over the fire.

Zaouali, Lilia. *Medieval Cuisine of the Islamic World: A Concise History with 174 Recipes.* Translated by M. B. DeBevoise. Berkeley: University of California Press, 2007, pp. 129–30.

⚜ CORIANDER ⚜ CILANTRO

The tan, ribbed seeds of coriander (*Coriandrum sativum*) have a citruslike aroma complemented by notes of sage and freshly cut grass. Their pyrazine-rich flavors are warm and somewhat nutty, with floral undertones that have been likened to lemon or orange blossoms. Although the flat parsleylike leaves of the coriander plant are known as cilantro in much of the world today, they have an entirely different flavor, which some people, perhaps by genetic disposition, find agreeable and others repugnant. I once took an Italian member of Slow Food International to the Grand Canyon, where she could smell the fetid aliphatic aldehyde fragrance of cilantro rising from a Mexican restaurant more than two hundred yards away. She and many others insist that cilantro leaves exude a soapy smell that they liken to burnt rubber or stinkbugs (see linguistic evidence, below). Others find the aroma to be divine.

Curiously, manna is likened to coriander seeds in the Bible. Coriander was apparently first sown as a spice crop in the Anatolian region of present-day Turkey and spread to the Levant, Egypt, Armenia, southeastern Europe, and southern Russia early on. It is specifically named and described as a medicinal plant in an Egyptian papyrus dating from 2500 to 1550 BCE. It was also listed with just a handful of other spices for stews in some of the earliest surviving recipes, inscribed in Akkadian script on clay tablets found in Mesopotamia. The library of the seventh-century Assyrian king Ashurbanipal housed documents describing the cultivation of coriander. In my own experience of cultivating the plant for many years, I find that it is the only leafy green that will yield a harvest year-round in my warm, semi-arid climate.

The oldest name for coriander may be linked to a number of contemporary terms: *kisnis* in Western Turkic, *geshniz* in Farsi, *gashnich* in Tajik, *kashnich* in Uzbek, *kishniz* in Urdu, and *kinj* in Armenian. This suggests Turkic or proto-Farsi diffusion of the term across Central

meager amounts were presented to me, they were not nearly as fresh, as numerous, or as sought after by local shoppers as what I had seen in Moroccan souks some weeks earlier.

I compared medieval recipes from al-Andalus with those offered in contemporary Andalusian cookbooks. Coriander, historically the most frequently used seed spice in al-Andalus, is rarely used in the region's current portfolio of traditional recipes. The use of saffron in recipes

Asia and into the Indian subcontinent. The Farsi or Persian name was used in parts of China, which lends support to the hypothesis that the plant was introduced to China through Parthian or Sogdian spice trade before the founding of Islam. It is described in a chapter on leafy vegetables in a Chinese agricultural manual from the fifth century CE, indicating that cilantro greens, not just the ground seeds, were already valued.

The Arabic term *kuzbarah* is at best distantly related to these Central Asian names but may possibly be linked to Asian terms such as the Sanskrit *kustumbari,* Akkadian *kisburru,* Telegu *kustumburu,* Gujarati *kothmir,* and Urdu *kothamir.*

Virtually all of the great Greek and Roman scholars interested in natural history and agriculture wrote about this crop: Aristophanes, Theophrastus, Hippocrates, Dioscorides, Pliny, and Columella. Their enthusiastic promotion of coriander may have played a role in its widespread dispersal under the Greek term *koriannon* (from *koris,* or "stinkbug") and the Latin term *coriandrum.* The names for coriander in most Western European languages can be traced back to these cognates. The terms *cilantro* and *culantro* used throughout Latin America are also derived from these same roots; however, the latter name is also applied to *Eryngium foetidum,* an herb with a distinctive aroma commonly used in the Caribbean and Southeast Asia.

Today, coriander seeds are essential ingredients in Indian curries and garam masala, Yemeni *zhoug,* Ethiopian *berbere,* Moroccan *ras el hanout,* and *baharat* mixes throughout the Arabic-speaking world. The leaves also enter into a few mixtures, such as the green curry paste of Thai cooking and certain Mexican moles.

Green, Aliza. *Field Guide to Herbs and Spices.* Philadelphia: Quirk Books, 2006.

Katzer, Gernot. "Gernot Katzer's Spice Pages." http://gernot-katzers-spice-pages.com/engl/index.html. Accessed May 7, 2013.

Sortun, Ana, with Nicole Chaison. *Spice: Flavors of the Eastern Mediterranean.* New York: Regan Books, 2006.

has been reduced to roughly one-third of the frequency it enjoyed in medieval al-Andalus. The use of cassia cinnamon has declined, as well, as has the regional demand for cloves, ginger, rue, rose water, and almonds. Only black pepper and garlic have increased in the frequency of use over the centuries, and after the colonization of the Americas, red chiles quickly eclipsed the use of the less piquant melegueta pepper from Africa.

At the start of August 1492, the mountain roads winding down to the Mediterranean coast from the uplands of Andalusia were swarming with Jews and Muslims carrying loads on their backs and pulling small carts. They had left most of their belongings with their converso and *morisco* kin who had stayed behind in Seville, Córdoba, and Granada. Those who remained would become the ancestors of the one out of every ten contemporary Spanish Catholics who carry the genes of Berbers and Arabs, or the one in five today who carry the genes of Jews. Those Muslims and Jews who were simply unwilling to feign allegiance to another faith now had to find boats to carry them away.

Unfortunately, the major ports in Spain directly across the sea from Morocco had more refugees than berths on ships to take them across. The harbors of Cádiz and Málaga, in particular, were swamped with desperados ready to join the diaspora. Many of those who did ship out across the strait would die of famine later that year.

Not knowing that, of course, some of those rejected from Cádiz headed to the small port of Palos de la Frontera in the first days of August 1492. About that same time, a Genoese navigator named Cristóbal Colón—Christopher Columbus—came out of the nearby Franciscan monastery of Rábida to greet two men, Luis de Torres and Juan Rodríguez Bermejo de Triana, who would soon be traveling with him. Columbus believed that Luis de Torres, a converso born Yosef ben Ha Levy Haivri, would be of great value to him as a translator when they reached the distant lands of the Indies, for he spoke Hebrew, Arabic, Aramaic, and Portuguese. The second man, known also as Rodrigo de Triana, was the son of a famous *morisco* maker of trade pottery and a Sephardic Jewish woman renowned for her beauty. Bermejo de Triana was recognized as having a sharp eye for detail, so Columbus would employ him as a lookout to climb the mast of the *Pinta,* one of the three ships he would soon sail out of Palos.

As three small ships sailed westward from Palos on August 3, 1492, no one could have known that Islam would never regain its former grandeur or territorial reach anywhere in Europe. For a while, Jews fared somewhat better in northern Europe but, like the Muslims, they became the ghosts of Spain, their imprints everywhere but their bodies absent.

The Sephardic Jews who left Spain for good treaded water around Lisbon briefly before reassembling in small refuges in the trading centers of Antwerp, Amsterdam, Bordeaux, Bayonne, Fez, Alexandria, Cairo, Beirut, Aleppo, Smyrna, Goa, Pesaro, Pera, Tiberias, Constantinople, Ancona, Thessaloniki, and Venice. These Sephardic enclaves did not serve so much as self-contained communities as they did nodes within a network of trade that had diffused across three continents, and interacted with European, African and Asian merchants of many cultures.

When a Jewish family living in one of these nodes was ready to marry off a daughter, a suitor was sought from another of the nodes in order to strengthen the supply chain along the entire trade network.[12] Sight unseen, a marriage would be arranged, with dowries and contracts for economic cooperation among the families established or renewed at the same time. Soon, a Jewish man would arrive in one of the nodes of the network. Most of the young women who married these traders would live their entire adult lives as if exiled from Jerusalem, exiled from their natal grounds, and exiled from their nuclear families.

One of the earliest offspring born among the six hundred well-to-do Sephardic families given asylum in Lisbon was Beatrice de Luna, who was later known throughout the world as Gracia Nasi.[13] She would soon become the wealthiest woman in Europe, but more than that, she would come to embody every good and bad aspect of globalization. Gracia Nasi, her incestuous kin, and her colleagues achieved what Fernand Braudel called "success of a colossal scale."[14]

At age eighteen, Doña Gracia (whom her Jewish friends called Hannah) married her paternal uncle, Francisco Mendes (Benveniste), who was twenty-eight years older than his bride. Francisco and his brother had already become "among [King João's] most important merchants" in all of Portugal, so much so that the king himself admitted that they had "accumulated enormous wealth here."[15] Even that comment may be understated, for they were already wealthier than the king himself. In the last six years before Francisco died, he and his brother had amassed such an absurdly large fortune through trade with India that they made the largest deposit of silver—some nine thousand pounds— ever put into a bank in western Europe during that era.[16]

They were geniuses at maneuvering pepper, ginger, nutmeg, cinnamon, and cloves past their adversaries in various ports around the world. In particular, they had a stranglehold on the pepper trade from India to North Africa to southern Europe, where the spice was said to improve vision, eliminate liver ailments, cure dropsy, and mask the off flavors of rancid meats and oil. It was as if the House of Mendes could thread peppercorns through the eye of a needle, shipping and slipping them from the docks of Goa to the port of Alexandria, past Constantinople and Venice, and all the way to the warehouses in Lisbon and Antwerp. As vividly documented by food historian Michael Krondl,

Venice, Lisbon, and Antwerp had already emerged as the greatest cities of spice in Christendom—or at least in Europe—and they provided the House of Mendes with both collaborators and competitors.[17] From there, these sought-after spices reached kitchen tables, canteens, and cupboards of nearly every ethnicity in western Europe. According to Sephardic Jewish historian Andrée Brooks, the House of Mendes held hegemony over spice markets across Europe, which made Gracia Nasi and her in-laws "major players" in the global marketplace.[18]

By the time the widowed Doña Gracia had replaced her deceased husband, joining her brother-in-law, Diogo, at the helm of the Mendes trade network, the Mendes clan had cornered the trade in pearls and many of the most expensive aromatics in world commerce. To maintain control over these goods, the widow regularly bribed kings and military commanders with sums of money that dwarfed what any peasant made laboring continuously for twelve months; in fact, a single bribe might be fifteen to twenty times greater than what the House of Mendes annually tithed to the poor, or what another merchant might make over an entire year.[19] Moving from Lisbon to Antwerp, the undisputed center of spice trade in northern Europe,[20] Doña Gracia and her brother-in-law allied their trading house with the Affaitadi Company and received Portuguese fleets of 40 to 130 spice ships twice a year. Eighty percent of what the ships delivered to the House of Mendes was pepper, with ginger, galangal, gallnuts, nutmeg, mace, cinnamon, cloves, cubeb, cumin, and camphor making up the rest of the cargo.[21] Gracia Nasi began to use the profits from her spice sales to provide loans to warlords whose excesses chronically generated "cash flow" problems, and she soon had a number of kings, counts, and colonels at her beck and call. By maintaining a near-monopoly in the trading of four to five million pounds of dried spices into western Europe each year,[22] Doña Gracia and her brother-in-law soon amassed a fortune larger than her dead husband could have imagined, eventually trading in every imaginable aromatic, from ambergris to wormwood.

It was in the ports of Portugal that I began to feel profound estrangement from the legacy of trade in aromatics originally associated with the desert homelands once shared by Jewish and Arab spice traders. Perhaps I had expected too much from this small country: it had long ago made an enormous fortune off of pepper, ginger, cinnamon, sandalwood, and spikenard, so I imagined that it might still feature such luxuries. It has indeed remained a hub for finance, as it had been during the time of Gracia Nasi, but most of its transnational trade income today is generated by what is euphemistically called "the tertiary sector": refineries, steel mills, textile finishing, and money lending. Because it is located in such a stunning site along the Atlantic shore, Lisbon has burgeoned into one of the largest ports on the open Atlantic coast of Europe. Much of it is for repackaging goods grown or mined or manufactured elsewhere. As I looked out over one after another of the country's drab industrialized harbors—the ones that some scholars claim to be descendants of the pivotal ports of the Age of Discovery—I sensed that they had lost most of their originality, dynamism, and aesthetic value over the centuries.

Gracia Nasi, aka Beatrice de Luna, Lisbon's native daughter whom Sephardic Jews now call "a hero in any age and a role model for today,"[23] was by most accounts an egomaniac who connived her sister and niece out of their inheritance, who had a relationship with her son-in-law that lacked civil boundaries, who infuriated rabbis, and who manipulated and bribed sultans and popes to ensure that her economic empire continued to grow exponentially during an era when most of Europe was being devastated by famine. She lived as if she were above any societal rules—a woman without a country, one who shifted her name, her dress, her religion, and her political alliances without a moment's notice—while creating monopoly after monopoly for one spice after another.

The House of Mendes became the first transnational corporation to be free of any taxation; to pressure governments into giving them exclusive rights to transfer certain goods; to perform as if it were above the law of any country in which it worked; and to send heads of state and leaders of faiths scurrying for cover whenever Doña Gracia determined through her extensive intelligence network that they were attempting to constrain her.

As Andrée Brooks paraphrased one of Gracia Nasi's Jewish contemporaries, Rabbi Joshua Soncino, conversos such as those in the Mendes-Nasi clan had become "money-grubbing, amoral people."[24] If she were alive today, rather than being treated by her Jewish contemporaries as a hero or role model, she would be regarded by youthful activists in the Occupy movement as emblematic of the 1 percent responsible for the concentration of wealth in too few hands.

Gracia Nasi had become so adept at employing usury to gain political and economic favors that both her competitors and her debtors reacted to her rise in power with a mixture of fear and jealousy. When she refused to let her daughter marry a Christian nobleman from

Iberia—perhaps out of revulsion that her pure Jewish bloodline would be mingled with that of an "old Christian"[25]—the royalty in western Europe became convinced that she was a practicing Jew who had never really converted to Catholicism.[26] She decided to leave the Christian-dominated world she had lived in since birth, eventually relocating in Constantinople after sojourns in Venice and Ancona.

Because members of the European elite looked the other way when Gracia Nasi's spice smugglers were close at hand, they also overlooked that she had used her fortune and her European network of merchants to help hundreds of Jews and Muslims escape the Spanish Inquisition. Ironically, Isabella and Ferdinand nearly depleted their coffers, first by funding the Reconquista and then by bankrolling Columbus's attempt to reach the spices of the Indies by sailing west, while the Mendes spice dynasty, from a Spanish family of Jewish merchants that Ferdinand and Isabella had expelled from their kingdom, quickly became both wealthier and more powerful than the repressive monarchs.

After Gracia Nasi unseated her family's spice business from the Iberian Peninsula, she had the means to employ many of the conversos she had delivered from the hands of the inquisitors. By the time she arrived in Constantinople in 1553, she had placed a good number of them in strategic locations around the world so that they could retrieve aromatics and other goods from ever-more-distant lands. Some of them continued to work the ports of Spain and Portugal clandestinely, pulling smuggled goods out of the ballast of ships arriving from India, Africa, or the New World. These goods were quickly shuttled over to Morocco, and from there they traveled from one port to the next, brokered by Sephardic Jews at each stop, until they reached Constantinople, the last hub of the House of Mendes.

It is interesting to note that most of the New World's treasures did not enter into European commerce and cultural diffusion through Spain. Instead, they came in through Turkey. The long-term contribution of Catholic Spain and Portugal to the Columbian Exchange—a circulation of crops and livestock that was just one more phase in an already well-articulated process of globalization—has been overrated.[27] The Canary Islands, not Spain itself, offered most of the seeds, fruits, and livestock breeds that were transported to the Americas and the Caribbean.[28] Maize became known in parts of Europe as *grano turco*, the Turkish grain, and New World tobacco was called Turkish tobacco. Sunflowers, squashes, and chiles followed a similar trajectory. Whatever culinary curiosities and aromatics were brought back from distant lands, it is probable that the House of Mendes was responsible for introducing them to and controlling their trade within Europe. While Ferdinand and Isabella focused on the gold and precious metals arriving from the Americas, something far more precious and lasting in its influence was slipping through their hands and making its way to Turkey and from there into eastern Europe, North Africa, Asia Minor, and beyond. At the onset, Gracia Nasi's network had more to do with moving those novelties into the marketplace than did a hundred Catholic kings, cardinals, and popes.

CHAPTER 9

Building Bridges between Continents and Cultures

I have come to search for the old stone bridges of Zayton, an ancient harbor on the East China Sea now hidden within the concrete and steel structures that form the modern city of Quanzhou. My friends and I are being chauffeured around the sprawling metropolis by an impetuous Chinese taxi driver who becomes sullen when we ask him to leave the paved streets between the skyscrapers to search among industrial dumps for the bridges and the harbor they once supported. We see some egrets flying up to the right of us and decide to shadow them, hoping that they indicate that wetlands are close enough to prevent the taxi driver from expelling us from his vehicle before we arrive.

On a dirt road otherwise used only by dump trucks hauling rocky fill to a construction site, we meander between piles of rubble while the driver curses. At last, we catch a glimpse of a low bridge stretching over shallow wetlands choked with cattails, water hyacinths, tamarisks, and giant cane reeds. Above the cattails, we see single mothers pushing their infants in strollers along the bridge. Young men are jogging on it, teenagers are necking in the half-hidden niches of its way stations, and the elderly are practicing their tai chi on the open planks. All of this is taking place on an ancient bridge over troubled waters in which mirrorlike pools of motor oil reflect the high-tension lines marring the sky.

During the Song dynasty, the coastal flats around old Zayton were called the Land of Bridges, because 313 causeways and bridge complexes spanned water courses in this stretch of Fujian Province. But the Land of Bridges brand was metaphorical, as well. From the seventh to the fourteenth century, the entire economy and multicultural community here also functioned as a bridge between the Far East and the Middle East, between the Han Chinese on one hand and the Arab-Persian domain on the other.[1]

For several years, I had dreamed of making a pilgrimage to Zayton, the easternmost terminus of the Maritime Silk Road. I knew that it had been called "the emporium of the world," for it served as a major redistribution point for both loads of aromatics that had been sent eastward and loads about to head west across the seas.[2] I had imagined colorful exchanges among speakers of various dialects of Chinese, as well as those of Farsi, Arabic, Hebrew, and Hindi, as they bantered and bartered for silk, spices, incenses, and teas. Today, the Zuan Ziu dialect is what is primarily spoken in Quanzhou, although the street English of American rock and hip-hop can be heard at all hours.

There remains some debate over when, why, and by whom the harbor that predated modern Quanzhou had been given the name Zayton, but few historians deny the coincidence with a loan word from Arabic. There is some doubt that it was originally derived from *zeitun*, the same Arabic word that was Hispanicized into *aceituna*, the word still used for "olive" in most of Iberia and the Americas. Historians have found Chinese documents from the tenth century suggesting that the port was then called Zi-tong, but it is not clear whether this was a cognate with the Zayton term used by Persian and Arab traders who had arrived in the region by 758.[3] The name likely refers to the olive tree introduced from the Middle East—or at least to an olive branch as a sign of peace and multicultural prosperity. Of course, no one knew how long such peace and prosperity might be shared among people of very different races and faiths before they would wither.

As I walk across the Anping Bridge, I look in vain for remnants of olive trees—the ones for which Zayton may have been named—but see none along the edges of the tidal backwaters. A group of English-speaking tourists pass by me, and I hear one of them assert that Anping's bridge is the longest one built during the medieval era that remains standing anywhere in the world today. It was constructed of giant pink granite slabs around 1140, and those same slabs are still in place, though softened and stained by saltwater spray, oil, acid, and constant foot traffic. Each roughly half-meter-wide slab is fit tightly against the next one to make a bridge seven meters wide. Row after row of slabs was brought by boat from a nearby island and placed in the tidewater estuary until they spanned a stretch of water measuring 2,250 meters. Anping's historic structure is also called Wuli (or "Five Li"; a traditional *li* is 500 meters) by the Han Chinese, suggesting that its original span was nearly 2,500 meters. Of course, the Han was not the only ethnic population to have traversed the bridge during the twelfth century. On the very same slabs on which I walk, Arabs and Persians, Jews and Saracens, Tamils and Moguls, and Gujaratis and Cham (from present-day Vietnam) walked before me. When that steadfast pilgrim from Tangiers, Ibn Battuta, came here in the 1340s, some two centuries after the bridge was built, he claimed that nearly twenty thousand of the people who were milling around Zayton's harbor could be described as *semu ren,* or those [from the West] with colored eyes. He specifically mentioned the presence of several Persians there, including a Muslim dean, a judge, a merchant, and a Sufi sheikh.[4]

Among the *semu ren* were the *dashi ren,* Arabic-speaking peoples who had arrived in ever-increasing numbers since the eleventh century, when maritime commerce to China began to exceed overland trade.[5] They came with cargo from the port of Aden on the coast of Yemen; from Mecca in the interior of Saudi Arabia; from the Gulf of Hormuz; from al-Malighi in Persia; and from Bukhara in present-day Tajikistan. Some had sailed in boats across the Maritime Silk Road; others had journeyed along landlocked routes that edged sand seas and snow-capped mountain ranges. They first came for spices, medicines, and incenses and later for tea and silk. The merchants of Zayton had so much silk passing though their hands that the name of the harbor, in modified form, became synonymous with the silky feel of luxury: satin.

Yes, satin from a term that had already become widespread in the Middle East and North Africa for olive. The Chinese may have regarded olives as an exotic delicacy as much as the Arabs and Persians regarded silk as an exotic fabric. Not only did their marketable items change hands, but their words moved from one culture to the next, referring to altogether different things even though they possessed the same status. For example, jujubes, fruits native to Asia that look like small dried dates when mature, were called Chinese dates by the Arabs. It was believed that if you could afford such luxury in your home, a treasure that originated in some exotic place halfway around the known world, then you surely have become a member of the elite. Your power to extract resources from someplace else—a place that you have never seen—no doubt seemed limitless!

As I walk along the bridge, I begin to whiff a peculiar fragrance in the

FIGURE 16. The eastern part of the Anping Bridge, between the Shuixin Zen Temple and the Shuixin Pavilion. (Photo by Vmenkov. Courtesy Wikimedia Commons.)

air and look up from the pink granite slabs to see what it may be. I follow my nose some two dozen steps to a Buddhist temple where incense is being burned and the mantra *Om mani padme hum* is being chanted. My nostrils open to those fragrances, ones that enchant me with olfactory sensations of sandalwood, aloe wood, frankincense, and myrrh.

Other, more familiar fragrances are in the air, as well. As I glance around at the little island in the estuary on which the temple sits, I notice that rose bushes and citrus and pomegranate trees are in bloom. They are the same aromas that I have known from my time in the aromatic gardens of the Middle East. Although I fail to spot a single olive tree, I have no trouble smelling the Arab influences that have held on in Fujian.

Not far from Anping Bridge, another ancient bridge, the Luoyang, also still survives, standing at the edge of the tidewater estuary at Houzhu Harbor in Quanzhou Bay. There, sometime between 1239 and 1265, a 380-ton cargo ship sank into the mud. When the ship was discovered in 1973, and then unearthed from the tidal flats the following year, divers and excavators found that much of it had remained intact and that most of its storage chambers were remarkably free of water damage. Archaeologists carefully opened thirteen of its sealed chambers and found that two and a half tons of aromatics had been preserved for more than seven hundred years. These goods had apparently come in from ports on the Indian Ocean, the Persian Gulf, and the bays off of the Horn of Africa. Sorting through the cargo, the archaeologists easily recognized frankincense, ambergris, aloe wood, dragon's blood, and peppercorns. But there were bits of other spices and incenses that they could not initially identify with confidence by only smell or sight.

So the archaeologists asked Chinese historians if any documents had survived from the era of the ship that talked about what was being traded at the time, in the hope that they might contain information that would guide them in identifying the other aromatics. They were surprised to learn of still-extant ledgers that registered an astonishing diversity and abundance of items being traded in and out of Zayton during the medieval period.

The ledgers recorded the purchase and delivery of black cardamom, green cardamom, saffron, and fennel; of white pepper, long pepper, ginger, and cloves. They tracked the movements of cinnamon, cinnabar, cassia, and star anise and of hazelnut, betel nut, pine nut, and fenugreek. Although not often regarded as spices today, apricot, rhubarb, coconut, and hemp seeds were treated no differently than cumin or coriander. The ledgers affirmed transcontinental trade to China of aloe wood, sapanwood, frankincense, and myrrh and catalogued the uses of dragon's blood, sandalwood, aloe leaves, and osmanthus. And if these treasures were not enough to delight and awe the archaeologists, the ledgers also noted cargo ships carrying ivory from elephant tusks and horns from rhinoceroses.

At first glance, you might presume that the Han Chinese themselves had become the masters at managing maritime trade during the Song dynasty, with their own sailors and merchants exchanging goods with their equivalents from dozens of other nations. In addition, foreign sailors did drop off cargo, receive their payments from the Han, buy some Chinese-made goods, and then embark on another round-trip journey to exchange more items of value with Han Chinese merchants in Zayton. But elite groups other than the Han took primary responsibility for managing most of this maritime trade into China over the course of five centuries. These groups certainly included Muslims, largely of Arab, Uighur, Turkish, and Persian descent; probably a few Jews and

Although star anise (*Illicium verum*) contains the same sweetly warm, aromatic oils that true anise does, just about everything else about this eastern Asian spice could not be more distinctive from its western Asian analog. Its mahogany-colored pods, shaped like eight-pointed stars, are harvested from an evergreen tree before they reach full maturity. The essential oils that carry the flavors of anise, citrus, clove, pepper, and cassia for which star anise is known are found in the dried pulp of the pods' pericarp rather than in the seeds.

Native to southwestern China and northeast Vietnam, though no longer found there in a truly wild state, this tree is now cultivated throughout southern China, Laos, Cambodia, India, the Philippines, and as far from its natal grounds as Jamaica. The only populations outside of human management today are feral remnants of abandoned orchards. Some sources suggest that the cultivation of star anise in southern China dates back at least three millennia.

Throughout its range of cultivation in Asia, star anise is a key ingredient in making some of the world's most distinctive spice composites. In China, it is typically blended with ginger, cassia cinnamon, Sichuan pepper, cloves, and either fennel or licorice to make five-spice powder, or *wuxiangfen*, an aromatic blend characteristically used in marinades for rich meat dishes such as Peking duck. Star anise also finds its way into garam masala, the Persian-influenced seasoning used in the Mogul cuisines of northern India in sauces or marinades for meat and poultry. For this blend, it is usually combined with true cinnamon, fennel, cardamom, cloves, coriander, pepper, nutmeg, and bay. In southern Thailand, star anise adds a pleasant sweetness to iced tea.

Its name in both Mandarin (*bajiao*) and Cantonese (*baat gok*) refers to its eight-cornered star shape, but other, more descriptive terms in various Chinese dialects liken its flavor to that of fennel. Not surprisingly, as star anise was carried westward, most cultures created syllogisms that compared it to anise. But the term for this heady spice that is echoed most widely in other languages is *badijian*, its Farsi name: *badyani* in Urdu, *badijan* in Macedonian, *badián* in Spanish, *badyan* in Russian, *badjans* in Latvian, *badiane* in French, *badian* in German, and even badian anise in English. The similarity of these terms likely reflects the key roles that Farsi-speaking Sogdians and Persians played in moving Chinese spices along the Silk Road to their ultimate consumption and delight in Europe and elsewhere.

Green, Aliza. *Field Guide to Herbs and Spices*. Philadelphia: Quirk Books, 2006.

Katzer, Gernot. "Gernot Katzer's Spice Pages." http://gernot-katzers-spice-pages.com/engl/index.html. Accessed May 8, 2013.

Nestorian Christians; and perhaps some Hindu traders from Southeast Asia or the Indian subcontinent.

One thing is certain: even before Sa'ad ibn Abi Waqqas, Muhammad's maternal uncle, brought the first alert of Islam's growing power to the emperor Han Wudi in 616, his father and other relatives from Mecca and Medina had already organized trading expeditions to Fujian Province as early as 586. His father returned with other Arab traders in tow around 628. By 629, Han Chinese historians themselves were recording Muslim residents settling around the harbors of present-day Quanzhou. During the gap in his own visits, Sa'ad ibn Abi Waqqas was strategically assisting with the Central Asian expansion of the Islamic empire. But in 651, now recognized as an imam, he returned to Zayton with his son and was welcomed back by the Tang emperor, Gaozong, who had been born in the year before the imam's first arrival and had taken the throne just two years prior to his second (and presumably last) visit. His son and another pioneering saint of Islam were buried in the Lingshan Tombs just outside of Quanzhou's city limits, and that site has served as a major shrine and touchstone for seafaring Muslims ever since.[6]

Why did the emperor grant these outside groups trade privileges and allow the son of Sa'ad ibn Abi Waqqas to build the Huaisheng Mosque on behalf of the incipient Muslim community that had already congregated there? (The mosque has been rebuilt on the same site at least twice since then, and today it is also known as the Lighthouse or Guangta Mosque.) One theory is that the emperor sensed he could personally benefit from levying taxes and tribute on their goods, despite what it might cost him politically or economically to tolerate the Muslims living and worshipping in their own quarter of Zayton. And yet, the Han Chinese could not have been fully aware of how rapidly the Islamic empire was expanding, nor would they have believed assertions that Islam had gained more power than any other faith or kingdom in the known world. The Han playfully called the chants of the Qur'an the *Hui jiao*, or "teachings of the Hui," and referred to Islamic religious, social, and economic protocols as *dashi fa*, or "Arab law."

The first mosque did not hold the burgeoning Muslim population of Zayton for very long, and six more were built in the port town over the next few centuries. Between 1127 and 1350, Zayton had the largest populations of Arabs and Persians of any city in the Far East. When Marco Polo visited the city in 1292, it had nearly surpassed Alexandria as the most important port for spice trade in the world. Rustichello da

FIGURE 17. Qingjing Mosque in Quanzhou, the oldest surviving Arab-style mosque in China, is a reminder of the arrival of Arab spice traders in the port of Zayton during the time of the Prophet Muhammad. (Photo by the author.)

Pisa's recounting of the Polo family travels made Marco Polo's port of departure from China seem no less wondrous: "Zayton [is] *the* port for all the ships that arrive from India laden with costly wares and precious stones . . . it is also the port for all the merchants [sending goods out] of all the surrounding territory. And I can assure you that for every one spice ship that goes to Alexandria to pick up pepper for export to Christendom, Zayton is visited by one hundred."[7]

Members of Fujian's Muslim community (now called Ding Hui) were recruited to play bureaucratic and diplomatic roles in the Southern Song (1227–79) and Yuan (1271–1368) dynasties. Two of the Ding Hui families, the Xia and the Ding, claim to trace their descent to particular founding fathers from Persia, Borhan al-Dīn Kazerūni and Sayyet-e Ajall Shams-al-Dīn Bokārī, through centuries-old genealogies.[8] Another such family from this community, reputed to be of Central Asian origin, was called the Pu or Po clan. Its patriarch, Pu Shugeng, was appointed minister of foreign trade in 1274, and his son also played a long and effective role in mediating between Muslim traders and the Southern

Song government. Over subsequent generations, the Pu became the most influential Muslim family in maintaining trade relations with long-standing allies.[9]

Later, during Ibn Battuta's last few days of visiting Zayton in 1346, he affirmed that "its harbor [had grown to be] among the biggest in the world, or rather is the biggest," frequented not only by hundreds of Chinese junks but also by many more dhows from the Middle East that brought merchants to trade or permanently reside there.[10] The same year, the Franciscan brother Giovanni de Marignolli noted that Zayton's foreign-born residents were not exclusively Arab, Persian, and Turkish Muslims. Assyrian, Genoese, and Venetian Christians were living there as well, as evidenced by the three cathedrals that stood near the port. One Star of David inscribed in stone cut during this era has intrigued urban historians and archaeologists alike. It suggests a Jewish presence during some era of Zayton's history. In fact, in the *City of Light,* a tract of somewhat dubious origin, Jews as well as Saracens are noted as being present among Zayton's many traders.[11] In short, Persians and Arabs may have had the run of Zayton at that time, but the Han seemed to tolerate the People of the Book among them as much as the Muslims did. Perhaps it was the city's very plurality that allowed it to function as the emporium of the world, attracting merchants from over seventy foreign countries and eclipsing all other Chinese port cities in the magnitude of its trade.[12]

Then, around 1350—just four years after Ibn Battuta and Giovanni de Marignolli witnessed Zayton in all its multicultural glory—something altogether unprecedented began to occur there. Cross-cultural tensions emerged that irrevocably changed the relationship between the East and the West. It appears that the wealthiest of the Muslim traders became impatient with paying tribute to the Han, for they, not their Chinese hosts, were largely responsible for the economic prosperity of Zayton. The Arab and Persian merchants began to keep to themselves the riches they had accrued through maritime trade, and for a brief moment in time, Farsi became the lingua franca of all harbors in the East China Sea. One prominent Arab trader based in Zayton came to control one-fourth of China's entire revenue for external sources, virtually monopolizing the wealth gained from transcontinental spice trade. This phenomenon signaled another sort of structural advance for globalization: if a merchant could actually control more wealth than his political hosts, economic imperialism threatened to outflank both political and military imperialism.

ZALĀBIYA ⁑ SHAQIMA ⅋ BUÑUELOS
Deep-Fried Cardamom-Spiced Fritters Soaked in Saffron Syrup

One of the delights that the Han Chinese did not have in their repertoire until the Persians and Arabs arrived was fried pastries soaked in sweet sauces. The Chinese derivative of Persian fritters may be *shaqima*, the sweet fried pastry commonly served in Fujian and Guangdong Provinces. The pastry also traveled in the other direction, from Persia to al-Andalus, where a dough was formed into spheres or spirals, fried until golden, and then soaked in a saffron-infused syrup. It was known among the ancient Persians as *zoolbiya*, and the earliest written reference to it comes from a favorite cookbook of Persians and Turks, written by Muhammad bin Hasan al-Baghdadi during the Abbasid dynasty. It is known today as *ziebia* in Iran; *zalābiya* in Syria, Lebanon, and Egypt; and *zlabia* or *zlebia* in the Maghreb. Mogul traders apparently carried it to the Indian subcontinent, where it was first called *zoolbier*, which later transformed phonetically into *jalebi*.

As the pastry traveled westward, it became *lokma* among the Western Turks and *loukoumades* among the Greeks. Algerians apocryphally claim that their term for it, *zalabia*, is derived from the Berber version of Ziryab's name. In Morocco, *zalābiya* or *zlebia* is a favorite fast-breaking food at the nighttime festivals of Ramadan. In Spain and beyond, Sephardic Jews have called it by a set of related names: *bumuelo, binuelo, bermuelo,* and *bulema*. Once crypto-Jews and crypto-Muslims moved on to the Americas, their recipes lost a connection to saffron, but these same sweets have become known as *buñuelos* in Mexico and the U.S. Southwest. It is likely that crypto-Jews brought them to the area around Santa Fe, New Mexico, three centuries ago, where they remain exceedingly popular.

It appears that as this dessert strayed farther from its homeland, it also lost its signature flavor in the dough (cardamom) and its use of lime or sour orange juice and rose water in the syrup. However, New Mexican–style *buñuelos* often include aniseeds, cinnamon, and even raisins in the syrup. In the East today, the pastry often comes in fantastic shapes (spirals and pretzels). In much of the West, it is served like doughnut holes the size of Ping-Pong balls. Regardless of the shape, the texture of the deep-fried dough lies somewhere between chewy and crispy, with a crystallized, somewhat crunchy sugar coating surrounding it. *Makes 12 fritters.*

For the Pastry
1½ teaspoons active dry yeast
¾ cup warm water (about 110°F)
1½ cups pastry flour, sifted
1 teaspoon sugar
Seeds from 2 green cardamom pods, crushed

Pinch of salt
Safflower oil or rice oil for deep-frying

For the Saffron Syrup
1½ cups loosely packed brown sugar
Pinch of saffron threads, dissolved in 1 cup water
Grated zest and juice of 1 lime, 1 tablespoon sour orange juice, or 1 tablespoon rose water

To make the pastry, in a bowl, sprinkle the yeast over the warm water, stir gently, and let stand until foamy, about 5 minutes. Add the flour, sugar, cardamom, and salt and mix together until a smooth, wet dough forms.

Cover the bowl, set it in a warm spot, and let the dough rise until it has doubled in size, 1 to 2 hours.

Just before the dough is ready, make the syrup. In a nonstick saucepan, combine the brown sugar, saffron water, and lime juice. Place over medium heat and stir until the sugar dissolves. Bring to a boil, without stirring, then turn down the heat to medium-low and simmer gently until the syrup thickens slightly, 8 to 10 minutes. Remove from the heat, add the lime zest, and pour into a heatproof bowl. Cover to keep warm.

When the dough is ready, pour the oil into a deep, heavy saucepan or a deep fryer to a depth of about 3 inches and heat to 375°F, or until a drop or two of water flicked into the hot oil sizzles on contact. Have ready a bowl of water.

When the oil is hot, dampen your hands with the water, pick up a walnut-sized piece of dough with one hand, shape the dough into a ball between your palms, and carefully drop it into the oil. Shape more balls the same way and add them to the oil, being careful not to crowd them in the pan. Alternatively, scoop up the dough with a spoon and drop it into the oil. Dip the spoon into the oil before taking the next scoop to keep the dough from sticking. Fry the balls, turning them as needed to color evenly, until golden and crisp, 3 to 5 minutes. Using a slotted spoon, transfer the pastries to paper towels to drain. Repeat until you have fried all of the pastries.

If needed, rewarm the syrup. Arrange the warm pastries on a platter with the syrup alongside. Invite guests to dunk each fritter into the syrup before eating.

Butel, Jane. *Jane Butel's Southwestern Kitchen.* New York: HP Books, 1994, p. 28.
Shaida, Margaret. *The Legendary Cuisine of Persia.* New York: Interlink Books, 2002, p. 264.
Twena, Pamela Grau. *The Sephardic Table.* Boston: Houghton Mifflin, 1998, pp. 242–43.

Needless to say, this did not sit well with the Chinese, or even with the other ethnicities in the merchant class of Zayton. They began to chip away at this Muslim-run economic stronghold. While the poor became pirates and scavengers that robbed as much as they could from the Muslims, the Chinese bureaucrats tried to impound, tax, embezzle, or sabotage Muslim-controlled cargoes. Exasperated, the Muslim merchant class recruited two Persian mercenaries, Saif ud-Din and Anmir ud-Din, who formed the *espāh* (Persian) or *yi-si-ba-xi* (Chinese) militia to break the backs of bandits, bureaucrats, and black-market traders who were rebelling against Persian and Arab control of all capital in the city. (In Central and South Asia, as in Africa and Asia Minor, the terms *espāh* and *sipahi* were used for militias of mercenary soldiers, usually, but not necessarily, of the Islamic faith.) Not surprisingly, the Chinese ruling class, which still benefited from the wealth amassed by the Muslims, had been slow to respond to the people's outrage that foreigners had become the medieval equivalent of Wall Street's 1 percent. Believing that the emperor would not get in their way, in 1357, several thousand of the Muslim mercenaries went on the offensive and took full control of parts of Fujian Province, including Xinghua (today's Putian), Fuzhou, and the mercantile sector of Zayton's harbor.

When the imperial elite finally protested, the Arab and Persian Muslims not only asserted economic autonomy but also declared political independence, establishing the now-obscure sovereign Muslim state of Ishafran, which controlled all maritime trade in and out of Fujian. Although there is only limited documentation in European languages regarding the brief tenure of Ishafran, its rise and demise remain part of the oral history of the Hui.

Why the new state was called Ishafran is not well established. The word may be cognate with the Arabic term *'ishra,* which had been used to describe the longtime "mutually beneficial economic relationships established by Muslims" with various Asian, Arab, and African peoples.[13] If that is the case, perhaps the power structure of Ishafran was hoping to market its corporate takeover of Zayton as one that would eventually allow wealth to trickle down to all who played along with the new hierarchy.

What the Persians and Arabs attempted in Fujian was nothing less than audacious. They undermined the power of their hosts and declared their colony of venture capitalists a sovereign nation—not a satellite of Arabia or Persia but its own entity—in order to control globalized trade along routes back toward their homelands, which lay months of travel to the west of the East China Sea. It became known as the Ispah Rebellion.

Perhaps it was the moral equivalent of the British colonists in North America declaring independence from England at the same time that they were claiming economic and political sovereignty over lands and waters that clearly belonged to Native Americans. Or, we might consider as analogs some contemporary moves by transnational corporations to transcend (or skirt) the laws and mores of their host nations to achieve greater capital gains and more autonomy: the 2012 revelation that Wal-Mart may have bribed its way into becoming the largest source of food, beverage, and spice sales (as well as the largest private-sector employer) in Mexico, or, as noted earlier, Texas-based Halliburton establishing a second headquarters in a port of the United Arab Emirates, where taxes as well as moral scrutiny may be held to a minimum.

In retrospect, it proved an imprudent act for the thousands of Muslim mercenaries and merchants, given that they were surrounded by millions of Han Chinese and isolated from their own kith and kin by thousands of miles. The Chinese military acted swiftly, and by 1362, it had already weakened Muslim control of its ports. Then, in 1365, the Yuan General You-ding confronted the *sipahi* militia in a battle at Xinghua and massacred thousands of Muslim mercenaries.[14] When he arrived in Zayton, he wantonly slaughtered every single Muslim, Christian, or Jewish resident who had not immediately fled by sea or taken refuge in the hinterlands. The survivors tried to keep their identities hidden. By 1366, the Han Chinese had fully regained every one of its harbors for the Great Yuan Empire, and had dissolved the independent Muslim state, putting any remaining *semu ren* into more subservient positions.

The episode brought to a close the era of "free trade" in the Far East, along with any further colonization by Middle Eastern merchants. Remarkably, however, the Muslims and Christians who gradually trickled back toward Zayton were not arrested or deported, though many eventually resettled in the nearby township of Chendai. Instead, the Yuan emperor's bureaucrats worked to rehabilitate them, encouraging them to moderate and vary their roles in Chinese society if they were resolved to stay in the region. To avoid any further monopoly on trade by Muslim merchants, many of the Arabs and Persians were encouraged to become fishermen and cultivators of clams, professions that their descendants maintain to this day. Others became farmers and processors of Fujian's famous teas.

Of course, there were economic benefits as well as disadvantages to the Muslims rejoining forces with the Han Chinese. Both sides felt compelled to collaborate, since the international commerce that had long fueled the economy of Fujian had come to a complete standstill. And so, because foreign merchants were no longer arriving with goods to trade, some of Zayton's Muslims were invited by the Chinese to assist in regaining control of their part of the transcontinental spice trade.

Historical linguist and geographer Jesse Watson, my wife, Laurie, and I had heard much about the Quanzhou Maritime Museum, but when we arrive there, it seems as though something has gone awry, for parts of it are in disarray. I notice that curators are disassembling what must have been a rather large exhibit—large enough to have taken up an entire wing on the ground floor of the museum.

There, half in boxes and half on the floor, with interpretative signs stacked on a table nearby, are the objects and oral histories of ethnic Quanzhou residents once assembled by local folklorists. Much of what we see appears to be an inventory of stone markers found in the oldest quarters of Quanzhou. Back when the city was called Zayton, stone carvers living nearby used scripts and symbols to inscribe the words from a variety of cultures residing close to the harbor. Most, if not all, of the stones were unearthed when the last buildings of ancient Zayton were condemned to make room for the skyscrapers and shopping malls of modern Quanzhou.

There are gravestones and residence markers from the thresholds of entryways to houses built six to ten centuries before our own arrival. Some have inscriptions in Arabic, some in Farsi, and others in a mix of archaic Chinese scripts and Arabic. Some have no writing at all, just a Star of David or an iconic plant, much like the house carvings I had seen in Essaouira, Morocco.

Collectively, these stones are somehow touching, sitting there naked, the exhibit broken down for who knows how long. But before we are able to explore and reflect on the entire range of markers once assembled there, a security guard whisks us out of the room, explaining that it is formally closed to public viewing. Then, he adds, a few of the elements missing from this collection have recently been installed in a new Islamic culture museum next door. Jesse, Laurie, and I decide to depart from the dimly lit backwaters of the maritime museum and hurry over to see if the Islamic museum is open.

The Ding Hui Muslims of Fujian Province have used four galleries in a large building complex to document their history, from their involvement in the maritime spice trade six hundred years ago to their survival throughout Fujian Province today. The photos, drawings, objects, and oral histories tell of their work not only as multigenerational spice traders but also as bakers, clam cultivators, farmers, and fishers. Although the collection does not ignore the legacy of famous Muslim seafarers and caravanners, it focuses more fully on the history of ordinary individuals.

As I walk through the exhibits, from photo to photo and sign to sign, I notice that the locals did not outwardly refer to themselves as members of the ethnic Hui until relatively recently. Most of them appear to have adhered to the teachings of the Hanafi school of Sunni Islam, just as the Abbasids did. They knew that some of their relatives had originally come to China overland via the various Silk Roads, but they were not sure when or why. Others knew that their ancestors had been engaged in maritime trade with today's Vietnam or India, and that many had steadfastly held to Islam even when China's emperors had suppressed it. Following the Ispah Rebellion, many of these Muslims moved out of Quanzhou to avoid further persecution from the Han, so that the Chendai township has become the hub for people now known as the Ding.[15]

The photos and oral histories of this multiethnic minority strike me as both endearing and priceless, if only because they are seldom integrated into any "official" history of Fujian. The stories are less about heroes, statesmen, and military giants and more about blue- and white-collar workers going about their daily business and prayers.

One particular black-and-white photo from early in the twentieth century intrigues me. It straightforwardly shows thirty-five Ding Hui spice traders together at the Chendai mosque, coming out of prayer, gathered together as friends, coworkers, and relatives. There is a cohesiveness to the group, a sense that its members have strong affinities with one another, if not outright love and respect. These are not random individuals idly passing through the mosque on a particular day. This is community.

Now, at least, these Arab and Persian merchants are no longer abstractions to me. Their traditional profession in the spice trade had persisted for centuries, unbroken. It reminds me of similar photos I had seen in Fez and Jerusalem that recorded a century of shopkeepers tending their spices. I have even met families of spice traders who have continued working in the same souk for upward of four hundred years.

I am astounded and pleased that the culture museum's exhibits also feature one Ding Hui family whose members I had contacted at their offices in nearby Chendai. They are descendants of Pu Shugeng, the spice trader turned minister of foreign trade in the Southern Song dynasty. Many of them now live in a small fishing village nearby. Like a number of their Ding Hui neighbors, they have cultivated razor clams, worked in small factories where bags or sandals are woven, or grown poppies for harvesting opium. And yet, no less than six centuries after the Pu clan first became engaged in the spice trade, some of its members still work in herb, spice, and medicinal plant commerce and remain known for their strong trade relations, particularly with the Vietnamese. I am pleased to learn that today the Pu clan is regarded as one of the eight most prominent Muslim clans involved in plant trade in Fujian Province, along with the Hjin, Chen, Li, Huang, Yang, Wu, and Zhang clans. It reminds me of encountering a Banu Nebhani descendant still selling frankincense in an Omani souk. Some family traditions die hard, or not at all.

As I leave these exhibits behind, I realize how impressed I am that the Pu clan of Ding Hui has resided in one region for so long, even though nowadays not all of its members are carrying on the family's ancient trading profession. To stay in one place for at least six centuries swims against the tide of restlessness and wanderlust endemic to many Arab, Persian, and Jewish family histories. The yearning to see Mecca, Baghdad, or Jerusalem may still crop up in family lore, but how many descendants of these peoples of diaspora have moved back to the motherland when given a chance? Culture is something that they have carried with them like a peddler's croaker sack or an old leather suitcase. It lifts up and leaves their places of origin as easily as a corn is removed from a sore toe . . . after treating it with an herbal salve.

CHAPTER 10

Navigating the Maritime Silk Roads from China to Africa

The Arab, Persian, Sogdian, and Chinese use of the Silk Roads for spice trade was closed down for much of the last quarter of the fourteenth century, largely because of the growing power of the Turkic conqueror variously known as Timur, Timur-e Lang, Tarmashirin Khan, or in the Western world, Tamerlane. His multiregional dominance, like that of Kublai Khan and Genghis Khan in the centuries before him, had pervasively disrupted overland trade routes between the West and the East. Based in Samarkand, Tamerlane was particularly vengeful in his relations with the Han Chinese, for they had overthrown his Yuan cousins in 1368. By conquering modern-day Armenia, Georgia, Azerbaijan, and Iraq by the close of the fourteenth century, he had effectively terminated the landward flow of goods from China into the Near East and northern Europe. Consummate middlemen such as the Turks and Armenians were particularly affected. This shift resulted in the stimulation of maritime trade from Arabia and India through Southeast Asia and on to the Chinese ports along the South China Sea. It also encouraged Muslim traders other than Arabs and Persians to attempt the control of routes from Bengal and the Malabar Coast on into Southeast Asia. There, the Muslims from the Indian subcontinent had success in converting the dominant powers in various seaports to the ways of Islam, not just spiritual ways but economic ways as well.

At the same time, piracy proliferated in these regions, with maritime marauders hijacking shiploads of sandalwood, Sichuan and black pepper, nutmeg, and mace, and then reselling their booty for outrageous prices. By the time Tamerlane launched a massive campaign from Central Asia against the Chinese in 1404, the Han Chinese rulers painfully realized that they needed to secure control of Southeast Asia's sea routes in case their former overland trade routes remained out of their control indefinitely.

Tamerlane died a year later, but the fear of economic isolation still loomed large among the Han Chinese. So the Ming emperors decided to establish stronger and more pervasive trade and tribute relations with many of the countries along the Maritime Silk Roads. They developed the notion of formal regional trade policies that functioned, for their era, like the North American Free Trade Agreement served United States economic hegemony at the end of the twentieth century. Their policy explicitly allowed access for each trading partner to only one port of entry on the South China Sea, and funneled trade through only one ruling family in each of those countries, which then had to offer regular tribute contributions to the Ming emperor. In this way, the Ming could ensure a monopoly over all goods moving in and out of Chinese-controlled harbors.

By the time I tried to fathom these historic developments along the Maritime Silk Roads, I had become a halfhearted museum visitor, preferring to see what dynamically persists of a culture on the backstreets and in the souks rather than believing what has been frozen in time by some curator. I had hoped to be edified by the Quanzhou Maritime Museum, but I was saddened by how it mythologizes and markets its internationally acclaimed hero, Zheng He, as a "Chinese" globetrotter. It barely notes in passing his Central Asian (and possibly Arab) ancestry. Worse yet, it makes the Han Chinese fleet he commanded into the premier explorers and "discoverers" of the outer world. Following Gavin Menzies into pop history,[1] the exhibit claims that China discovered America and Antarctica and hints at circumnavigation of the globe, all to further honor Han Chinese ingenuity. I am momentarily dazzled by the exhibit on the evolution of boat construction through the ages, until I realize that most of it features river traffic and has little to do with true seafaring.

It is easy to be amused at how the museum signage makes frequent jabs at foreign imperialists, from the Japanese to the Dutch, ones that sidestep any consideration of the historic Han Chinese as an equally good example of economic, ecological, and even military imperialists. Unlike other imperialists, however, their goal was not so much to seize

The dried two-seed berries of a group of Asian citrus trees known as prickly ashes (*Zanthoxylum* spp.) provide one of the most piquant and sizzling taste sensations of any spice on earth. Sichuan pepper is so distinctive that its peculiar spiciness has a name of its own in Chinese, *ma*.

As I approached a fifteen-foot-tall prickly ash in an orchard terrace along the Yellow River, the tree's lemony aroma and wispy appearance initially reminded me of trees from which sumac fruits are harvested. I immediately spotted a cluster of berries that were turning from olive green to a dull blood red, ready for harvest. As I popped a single berry in my mouth, it had a crunchy texture and an initial taste that was limelike, followed by grassy, tannic, and oily aftertastes. But none of that prepared me for the next forty-five minutes of throbbing numbness hitting my lips, nor for the gush of saliva flowing like a flash flood off my tongue and down the back of my throat! I had been "bitten" by the zesty essence of *ma!*

Even the smallest nibble of the berry's pulp can trigger an anesthetic sensation that spice experts have called shocking, tingling, tickling, fizzy, and electrical in its intensity. This is a plant so loaded with a strange chemical brew of alkamides, alkaloids, flavonoids, lignoids, essential oils, and tannins that chemists regularly continue to identify additional components.

The prickly ash most commonly used as a spice is *Z. piperitum*, which ranges from central and eastern China through Korea and over to Japan; several other species are harvested in the Himalayas and Southeast Asia. The first encounter I had with this piquant "pepper" was the one described above, which took place in the semiarid foothills of the Gansu Corridor portion of the Silk Roads that once passed through western China. In late July, entire local families, both Han and Hui, move out into their orchards, where they climb trees and ladders to harvest berries for the next twenty days. They strip a dozen or so berries off of each prickly branch on trees fifteen or eighteen feet tall, drop them into wicker baskets, and then dump the baskets upside

territory. Instead, they aimed to secure and extend their trade networks and then bring the various participants in those networks into a broader tribute system that provided the Chinese with both wealth and stature as the dominant power in trade relations. But if the notion of "Han imperialism" were ever broached in the museum, would it be possible to admit on state-subsidized signage that the success of the 1405 to 1433 expeditions of Zheng He owes as much to the influence of the Hui, down onto mats and tarps, where they leave the berries for a full day to dry in the sun. Middlemen from Sichuan Province come around in early August to purchase truckloads of these peppers, paying the orchard keepers sixty to eighty yuan (ten to thirteen dollars) per kilogram for their dried berries.

The Chinese name that is generically used for the berries of all the prickly ashes that offer the *ma* sensation is *jiao*. The specific term for *Z. piperitum* is *shanjiao* in Chinese and *sansho* in Japanese, meaning "mountain pepper." In the highlands of Sichuan Province, these "peppercorns" are a key ingredient in the classic Sichuan-style five-spice powder, which is now employed throughout China in savory stews and condiments. When used at the family table, freshly toasted Sichuan pepper berries are typically the last ingredient to be sprinkled on a dish. It is what adds the bite to *shanjiao bao yangrou,* a dry-fried lamb, bell pepper, and chile dish that has gained popularity in the West, where it is known as three-pepper delight.

Because Sichuan pepper is so distinctive and identifiable, its names in languages of nearly every other culture outside the Far East are variants of "pepper from Sichuan (Province), China, or Japan." It may be that its diffusion beyond that area is a relatively recent phenomenon. In the late 1960s, its importation to the United States was prohibited due to the lamentable fact that it is a carrier of a bacterium that causes citrus canker, a major pathogenic threat to Florida's orange groves. For a while, the ban only encouraged Sichuan pepper traders to go underground, smuggling it into ports in California and the Pacific Northwest where Japanese and Chinese immigrants could hardly do without it. But in 2005, heat-treated (nongerminable) Sichuan pepper was allowed to pass through U.S. ports of entry, and the spice is now available in Asian shops and some spice shops, particularly on the West Coast.

Green, Aliza. *Field Guide to Herbs and Spices.* Philadelphia: Quirk
    Books, 2006.
Katzer, Gernot. "Gernot Katzer's Spice Pages." http://gernot-katzers-spice-
    pages.com/engl/index.html. Accessed May 8, 2013.

Persians, and other ethnicities in China and its outposts as it does to the Han? The Han Chinese seem to have difficulty admitting all the Arab, Persian, Tamil, and Gujarati influences on their own destiny.

I take one last look at the highly rated permanent exhibits of the Quanzhou Maritime Museum and then walk outside to look at the museum's recently constructed facsimiles of ancient spice trading ships. I should have already conceded that most museums have little room or patience for "messy" stories, and that's too bad, for the stories of long-distance seafarers and caravans are never black-and-white. Good cross-cultural history, perhaps like passionate lovemaking, is always messy, and sometimes a bit sticky as well.

By far the best-known character in Sino-Arabic relations, and one who frequently stayed among the Ding Hui of Zayton and Chendai, was Zheng He, the legendary admiral of the so-called Treasure Fleet of the Ming dynasty.[2] He was born into a Hui family in 1371, just six years after the collapse of the Muslim state of Ishafran, and lived ambiguously as a practitioner of both Buddhism and Islam as an adult. Zheng would bring these two sensibilities together in order to achieve some of the greatest maritime, mercantile, and diplomatic accomplishments their societies had ever engaged in.

Although he was first called Ma He by his family in the small town of Kunyang on the shores of Lake Dian in Yunnan Province, his ancestral roots were elsewhere. According to some sources, his great-great-great grandfather may have been a prominent Persian administrator in the Mongol empire and the appointed governor of Yunnan during the Yuan dynasty.[3] Ma He was also believed to be a descendant of a Bukharan king of lands in present-day Uzbekistan and of a soldier in the troops of Genghis Khan.[4] In short, many of his ancestors were likely Hanafi Muslims who had been scattered along the Silk Roads. Both his grandfather and great-grandfather had been on religious pilgrimages to Mecca from China, so the tradition of completing a hajj must have been strong in his family—a tradition that he would continue.

Despite his later accomplishments, Ma He's life got off to a rocky start during the last years of the Yuan dynasty. When Ma was eleven, his father, a minor official in Mongol-controlled Yunnan, was killed by the Ming army, which had come into the province to overthrow the last stronghold of Mongol power in China. Although the Ming army had alliances with Muslim warlords, they captured the fatherless boy and made him into a eunuch. Ma was first trained to be the personal servant of the young Prince of Yan, Zhu Di, but he ultimately became his most trusted adviser. When the prince launched a coup d'état against his nephew, the legitimate third emperor of the Ming dynasty, Ma played a key military role in installing Zhu Di on the throne. In July 1402, Zhu Di became known as the Yongle emperor. Two years later, the emperor bestowed the name Zheng He on Ma He, in recognition of his military exploits, and appointed him both the imperial director of the palace eunuchs and the chief envoy of the emperor for overseas missions.[5]

By all accounts, Zheng He grew to be an impressive man who departed in many ways from the eunuch stereotype of his era. Reputed to have walked "like a tiger," he was reported by contemporaries to be "seven feet tall [with] a waist about five feet in circumference. His cheeks and forehead were high and his nose was small. He had glaring eyes, teeth as white and well-shaped as shells, and a voice as loud as a bell."[6]

Afte establishing a foreign language training institute in Nanjing, Zheng He surrounded himself with literate colleagues conversant in other languages (such as his Arabic-speaking envoy and biographer Ma Huan and other Muslim translators and navigators). Zheng apparently used these translators to enhance his ability to deal diplomatically with others who thought differently from himself, a critically important skill in his capacity to forge trade agreements and gain tributes for his Yongle emperor. He himself was also well read, having studied both Confucius and Mencius. These attributes offered him the means to solve problems that the emperor himself, ensconced in his palace and isolated from other societies, was unlikely to have mastered. Zheng could readily draw on advice from allies from a handful of different cultures, as well as intellectuals and strategists within his own circle. His knack for being able to imagine just what to do in unprecedented circumstances allowed him to rise to the challenge of leading the largest naval campaign in history.

From 1405 to 1433, Zheng He would initiate and direct seven maritime expeditions with the explicit purpose of actively forging extensive new trade relationships and of renewing damaged trade and tribute relations with various partners. He brought the finest musk, various "peppers" (no doubt including Sichuan), porcelain, and cloth from China to renew or attract additional trade partners, whom in turn gifted him with spices, salt, ambergris, frankincense, precious stones, and a menagerie of animals, from giraffes, ostriches, and lions to Arabian horses and zebras.[7]

Historians have attempted to document the size and nature of the fleet, and it is easy to be awestruck by its magnitude. The consensus now is that when the Ming armada set sail on the Maritime Silk Road in July 1405, it was comprised of sixty-two treasure ships large enough to hold several hundred passengers each, as well as 193 smaller vessels that helped with scouting, surveillance, protection, and logistical sup-

FIGURE 18. China's ancient harbors were filled with mercantile ships similar to this three-masted junk. These small junks would have been dwarfed by Zheng He's enormous nine-masted treasure ships. (iStockphoto.)

port. A landlubber most of his life, Zheng He now commanded a fleet that included scores of the largest ships that the world had ever seen.[8]

Zheng made up for his lack of seafaring experience by drawing on the navigational charts, journals, and oral histories of Chinese, Persian, and Arab admirals and mercantile seafarers who had explored some of the same straits, bays, and open waters over the previous centuries. In fact, most of the routes taken by his armada had historically been traveled by other seafaring merchants. Hindis, Guajaratis, and people from other South Asian cultures had long been island hopping to accomplish transit trade of spices and many other goods. Zheng not only studied their charts but also corrected them, and he initiated a forty-page strip map, completed and published many years later by others, that covered the waterways from China to Africa. Nearly two hundred years after his death, Zheng He's charts were included in the Chinese military encyclopedia known as *Wubei Zhi* and continue to be studied as classic navigational works today.

On most of the expeditions, the Treasure Fleet sailed from Nanjing in China to Champa (the port of Qui-Nor, in what is today central Vietnam) and on to the island of Java. It might stop at Gresik on Java or Palembang in southern Sumatra to load up on spices, incenses, and woods, but would then hurry on to Malacca, the pivotal port for the nutmeg, mace, sago, and cloves of the Moluccas, or Spice Islands.[9] From there, if the timing was not right, the fleet sometimes ran into the doldrums of the Indian Ocean before it reached a port near Colombo on present-day Sri Lanka, or else it ran into them immediately after leaving Colombo. The season of the voyage might allow the ships to venture down to the Maldives, or to sail directly on to several Indian ports, including Quilon, Cochin, Calicut, Pahang, and Lambri. The fleet then made its way up the Arabian Sea to the port of Hulumosi in the Gulf of Hormuz. There, as in other bazaars, Zheng He's chronicler, Ma Huan, made copious notes on the herb, spice, and incense inventories in the local markets. But Ma Huan also made more general social and economic assessments of each ethnic souk in the harbor of Hormuz: "Foreign ships from every place and foreign merchants traveling by land all come to this country to attend the market and trade; hence the people of this country are all rich."[10]

From the Gulf of Hormuz, the fleet's various expeditions followed different routes. At least once, it continued down the coast of present-day Oman, stopping at Dhofar or Muscat for incense, then entered present-day Yemen. On the fleet's first visit to Yemen, which occurred during its fifth expedition, it was stopped at the port of Aden by an army of over seven thousand foot soldiers and cavalrymen. The confrontation was short-lived, however, and the visitors were later presented with exquisite and exotic gifts as tribute by the sultan of the ruling Rasulid dynasty. In Aden, Ma Huan documented how globalized the cuisines of the Middle East had already become. He inventoried "husked and unhusked rice, [fava] beans, barley, wheat and other grains, sesame and all kinds of vegetables. For fruit they have . . . Persian dates, pine nuts, almonds, raisins, walnuts, apples, pomegranates, peaches and apricots."[11]

After stopping at Aden, the final three expeditions crossed over to the Horn of Africa. There, the fleet stopped at a number of African harbors, including Mogadishu, Barawa, Pate (in the Lamu Archipelago), and Malindi, all of which had been frequented and even colonized by Arab traders in the tenth century. On one voyage, the fleet likely reached Zanzibar and possibly Madagascar, but there is little to support the claims that Zheng himself or his understudies ventured farther.[12] It is probable that he died en route home from Calicut in 1433, and his body was ceremoniously buried at sea. A lock of his hair and other belongings were later placed in a tomb just outside Nanjing.[13]

Not long before his death, Zheng He was given the Muslim name

Hajji Mahmud Shamsuddin, because he had initiated a hajj on his final voyage. As was customary and permissible during his era, the last leg of such a journey was fulfilled by proxy. While Zheng He waited in Calicut, his envoys Ma Huan and Hong Bao sailed to the Arabian coast on a ship navigated by Arabs or Indians, and then traveled overland, carrying Chinese musk to the Muslim leadership at Mecca as a gift from both Zheng He and the Yongle emperor.

Perhaps inaccurately characterized as an explorer, discoverer, and conqueror of new lands, Zheng He was more fully engaged in revitalizing the tribute relations and spice trade once enjoyed by China's dynasties.[14] To do so, he forged military as well as religious alliances to secure control of intercontinental commerce that would ultimately benefit Zhu Di and his Muslim trade partners. As proof of his mercantile intent, one need only compare the list of ports in which Zheng chose to harbor with those where Muslim spice merchants were known to be active: Malacca, Gresik, Colombo, Cochin and Calicut, Hormuz, Muscat and Dhofar, Aden, Mogadishu and Jumbo, possibly Madagascar, and Malindi, Mombasa, and Pate off the Kenyan coast. It is telling that where Zheng ran into initial resistance was in ports like Palembang and Aden, where the transnational Muslim mercantile class had recently lost control of its portions of the spice routes. Zheng He was sent to "reconnect the dots."

In this latter capacity, some historians have claimed that Zheng He played a reinforcing role in "the development of Islam in Indonesia and Malaysia."[15] First, in the Strait of Malacca, Zheng sought out and destroyed the pirate ships of Chinese marauder Chen Zuyi, whose raiders had gained control of the commerce in Palembang, the Sumatran hub for spices from all parts of Indonesia. From his base in Palembang, Chen and his pirates had been intercepting incense, spices, and copper coins that were being sent to Zhu Di by the numerous Chinese Muslim merchants who had set up residence in the Javanese harbor of Gresik around 1410.

Zheng He's fleet found a way to stop this piracy by going upwind from Chen Zuyi's fleet of seventeen pirate ships. The fleet then showered the pirates' vessels with flaming arrows, poison-soaked hand grenades, and gunpowder-propelled missiles until ten of the ships burned and sank as Chen fled. Zheng's men later caught the pirate chief, who was executed in 1407, thereby allowing Chinese-Muslim trade to reopen for one more fleeting moment in history.

Once the pirates were out of the way, Zheng brought Chinese

❧ DAJAJ GDRA BIL-LAWZ ❧
Spiced Chicken in Almond Sauce

What did Zheng He eat when he arrived in the Muslim-dominated harbors of Hormuz, Aden, or Malindi in the fifteenth century? No one knows, but it is clear that he would have been offered the high cuisine of his era, which fused elements of the Persian, Arabic, and Moorish kitchens. He may have tasted an Old World precursor to the chicken moles of southern and central Mexico, the remnants of which still reside in North Africa (farther than he himself traveled), along the Strait of Gibraltar in Morocco. In my mind, the closest recipe to a mole still found among Berber and Arab populations is this spiced chicken with almonds cooked in the large pot, or *gdra,* that forms the lower chamber of a *couscousière.* It can also be made in a small *tagine,* the clay cooking pot with a cone-shaped lid that is used on the Moroccan brazier known as a *kanoun.*

I think of this dish as an ancestor to the sixteenth- and seventeenth-century moles of Mexico because of its four elements: poultry, in the form of chicken or turkey, to provide both a rich broth and meat; a coloring, such as saffron, turmeric, chile, or achiote, to brighten the broth; nuts or another thickener, like almonds, sesame seeds, peanuts, walnuts, or even chocolate, to give the broth body and flavor; and a medley of spices, such as cumin, cinnamon, and coriander, to impart a chorus of warm, savory tastes to the dish. A variant of this dish is made in Morocco with chestnuts instead of almonds, demonstrating the interchangeability of ingredients as long as they serve one of the four essential functions.

Serve over couscous. *Serves 4.*

  1 chicken, 3½ to 4 pounds, cut into 4 to 6 pieces
  2 large or 4 medium white onions, finely chopped
  1 tablespoon sunflower or sesame oil
  2 tablespoons butter or ghee
  2 cups water
    Ample pinch of saffron threads
  1 teaspoon ground ginger
  1 teaspoon freshly ground cumin seeds
  1 teaspoon freshly ground coriander seeds
  1 teaspoon freshly ground cassia cinnamon
  1 teaspoon freshly ground allspice berries or melegueta pepper
  1 tablespoon paprika or ground cayenne pepper
  1 bay leaf
    Black pepper
1¾ cups almonds, finely ground
    Sea salt

1 tablespoon honey
2 cloves garlic, minced
¼ cup fresh flat-leaf parsley leaves, chopped
  Juice of 1 lemon or lime

Place the chicken pieces, half of the onions, the oil, the butter, and the water in a *gdra* or other large cooking pot. Add the saffron, ginger, cumin, coriander, cinnamon, allspice, paprika, bay leaf, a few turns of the pepper mill, and the almonds, place over high heat, and bring to a rolling boil. Turn down the heat to low, cover, and simmer gently, turning the chicken pieces once or twice, until the chicken is tender, 30 to 45 minutes.

Remove from the heat. Using a large slotted spoon, transfer the chicken pieces to a plate to cool slightly. Season the cooking liquid with salt, add the honey, and stir well, then add the remaining onions, the garlic, and two-thirds of the parsley. Return the pot to medium-low heat and simmer uncovered until the onions and garlic are soft and the cooking liquid has thickened into a savory reduction, about 15 minutes.

Meanwhile, when the chicken pieces are cool enough to handle, bone them, discard the bones, and cut the meat into 1½-inch pieces. When the cooking liquid is ready, return the chicken pieces to the pot and heat through.

To serve, using the slotted spoon, transfer the chicken pieces to a platter. Spoon the almond sauce over the chicken, sprinkle with the remaining parsley, and squeeze the lemon juice over the top.

Roden, Claudia. *Arabesque: A Taste of Morocco, Turkey, and Lebanon.* New York: Knopf, 2006, pp. 88–93.
———. *The New Book of Middle Eastern Food.* New York: Knopf, 2000, p. 219.
Salloum, Habeeb, and James Peters. *From the Lands of Figs and Olives: Over 300 Delicious and Unusual Recipes from the Middle East and North Africa.* Brooklyn: Interlink Books, 1995, p. 135.

Muslim merchants from Gresik to Palembang, and then offered support to help their community build a historic mosque. According to historian Tan Yeok Seong, "These early Chinese settlements were populated by Chinese Muslims who had created a sphere of influence for themselves with the co-operation of Cheng Ho [Zheng He]. Religion and trade then went hand in hand. . . . Through Islam the Muslims, in spite of their racial differences became masters of trade; while, on the other hand, successful maritime trade helped to spread Islamisation."[16]

Of course, well before the spread of Islam, Arab sailors from Oman and Yemen learned to use the northeast monsoons to sail one way across the Indian Ocean between December and March, and back the other way with the southwest monsoons between late April and August. But if the summer monsoons arrived late or the Treasure Fleet arrived too early, the commander had the tough choice between staying in port or suffering through the doldrums out at sea before the sails caught the wind that would propel the ships across the Indian Ocean.

Not far from Java and Sumatra, I am sitting as still as I can be in a forty-foot sloop stuck in the Indian Ocean. In other words, because there is no wind, the sailboat is not moving at all. I look out across the Badung Strait toward the small island of Nusa Lembongan and not a swell or whitecap is in sight. The calm waters all around me are the color of a deserted sky, a pale, cloudless blue. A stark desert to the eye, a low pressure area to the ear, this is what the ancient mariner in Samuel Coleridge's poem recognized as "the doldrums":

> Day after day, day after day,
> We stuck, nor breath nor motion,
> As idle as a painted ship;
> Upon a painted ocean.[17]

As I sit on the edge of the sloop with my feet dangling over the lee side, I wait for the captain to decide whether he will turn on the back-up engine and get us out of here. But for now, I have time to think of the Muslim admiral of the Chinese Treasure Fleet that came through this region six hundred years ago. He sailed his ships into a swath of the world known as the Intertropical Convergence Zone, where the prevailing heat surrounding the equator creates a belt of low pressure. Sometimes the winds disappeared for days, and with them went the gulls and the frigate birds, the flying fish and the sea turtles. The area took on the appearance of a dead zone, where boats without motors moved more slowly than desert tortoises crossing a dry, sandy plain.

Despite the sophisticated navigational abilities of his crew and the enormous sails strung on masts made from the largest fir trunks ever taken out of China, on some days Zheng He could do little more than scan the horizon, for he was not convinced that his ships had actually moved. A landlubber like me for much of his life, Zheng was not at all accustomed to the doldrums; he was likely a man of action, not a man who could sit still for very long.

It is a lovely irony: the enormous fleet of the Yongle emperor—the vanguard of globalization for its era—would venture farther than any flotilla had gone up until that time, and yet there were some days when all of its ships sat still, as if treading water. They suffered from the doldrums day and night, sometimes for weeks. The seafarers' most difficult moments may not have been when they suddenly arrived, unannounced, in distant lands completely unlike their own, but when they did not move at all. As Saint Jerome once said, such a desert, whether it is on land or at sea, loves to strip you down. It may strip you down psychologically until there is nothing at all left of you.

There was a moment in 1409, on his return from the doldrums of the Indian Ocean, when Zheng He chose to make a gesture of tangible engagement in the acquisition of aromatics, rather than simply serving as an orchestrator of their globalized commerce. He ordered some sailors on his second expedition to go ashore to a small island so that they could personally harvest one of the very products that was widely sought everywhere from the East China Sea to the Atlantic Ocean. He wanted his men to get their hands dirty and to participate directly in finding and extracting a mother lode of incense that was reputed to occur nearby.

The fleet lingered near the island of Pulau Sembilan off the Strait of Malacca until the sailors were sure that they could reach a site nearby where the legendary agarwood (or eagle-wood) could be found. Many of Zheng's sailors and merchants had likely smelled the incense before, since its fragrance was well known for centuries by Buddhists, Hindus, Jews, Muslims, and Christians alike. Its Chinese name, *chenxiang,* means "sinking incense" or "heavy incense,"[18] so-named because it comes from the dense wood of a tropical lowland tree (*Aquilaria malaccensis*) infected with a fungus that makes the wood moldy but intensely fragrant.[19] As Zheng He's shipmate Fei Xin reported the incident in 1409,

> In the seventh year of Yongle, Zheng He and his associates sent the Emperor's troops ashore to cut incense on the island (then known as Jiuzhoushan). They encountered a dead tree from which they obtained six massive logs, each eight or nine chi in diameter [nearly three meters] and six or seven zhang in length [or eight to twenty-one meters in length]. Their aroma was pure and powerful enough to range far from the tree. The pattern of the wood we cut was black with fine striations embedded in it. When they saw the fine logs that we had selected and carried through their settlement, the

people of the island opened their eyes wide and stuck their tongues out in astonishment. Referring to our achievement, the locals told us that we were true soldiers of the Heavenly Court, and that our prowess was awe-inspiring, like that of the gods.[20]

Today, agarwood incense has been so depleted from the coastal forests of Malaysia and Indonesia that its host is now considered a threatened or vulnerable tree throughout its range. Although the biological depletion of incense and spice resources is difficult to link to a particular cultural era, this brief passage reminds us that globalized trade in aromatics has not been achieved without long-term ecological costs.

Whatever trophies were gained and publicly promoted reasons were articulated for mounting these expensive and time-consuming maritime expeditions, they were less about making a quick profit from teas and incenses than they were about renewing long-term trade options for the Ming dynasty. But the restoration of trade and tribute networks could hardly be done without forging stronger alliances with Muslim spice merchants and sultans that offered assistance in sustaining maritime trade when and if overland trade was once again disrupted by Mongols and Turks. It has been hypothesized that these alliances were initiated to accomplish tasks that the emperor and his imperial eunuch director may not have been able to reveal fully to the Han Chinese at the time. Although the evidence to support this hypothesis is scant and difficult to confirm, it is a tantalizing reminder that the policy decisions of nations or empires are sometimes guided by personal, familial, or religious reasons that are not disclosed to the general public when they happen.

What was not widely known during their lifetimes was that Zheng He and the Yongle emperor were linked to each other more deeply than through the ties that security, military, or political alliances typically develop. One of Zhu Di's descendants, Yusuf Chang, a Chinese Muslim from Taiwan, has recently revealed that both the Hongwu emperor and his fourth son, the Yongle emperor, were crypto-Muslims in Buddhist robes.

According to Yusuf Chang, who admittedly has a Muslim lens on historical events, several generations of his family have believed that Empress Ma, the consort of the Hongwu emperor and mother of Zhu Di, was a Muslim, as her Hui name suggests. Family oral histories passed on to Yusuf Chang suggest that Empress Ma was the only person allowed to prepare food or tea for the men of her family, and that she did it in

✿ TUOCHA PU-ERH ✤ CAMEL'S BREATH TEA

There is an ancient form of fermented brick tea that consists of loose tea leaves, stalks, and dust pressed into the shape of a small bird's nest, hockey puck, or melon. A thousand years before Westerners had ever heard the word *cha,* tea growers in southern China, starting with lightly oxidized green tea known as *maocha,* had begun to dry, roll, and then ferment the foliage and buds of a species of tea plant with particularly broad leaves (*Camellia sinensis* var. *assamica*) with the help of *Aspergillus* and *Penicillium* molds and various yeasts. After a half year of fermentation, the cured *pu-erh* tea was pressed into bricks of various shapes.

Indigenous mountain dwellers of China's Yunnan and Fujian Provinces have been cultivating this broad-leaved variety in terraced tea gardens for upward of seventeen hundred years. But it was the tea growers near the ancient *pu-erh* trading post in Yunnan Province who began to press aged black tea into doughnut-shaped bricks for storability and transportability. *Pu-erh* bricks soon became the primary form in which tea was consumed and distributed beyond the Yunnan and Fujian highlands, up until the Ming dynasty in the late fourteenth century.

The doughnut-shaped bricks became known as *tuocha,* named for the Tuo River that marked the beginning of the ancient trade route. For easy transport by camel caravans, the bricks were strung together on ropes and loaded onto the animals. The result was that the flavors of the bricks were further enriched by their postfermentation ride to other regions of China and beyond under the saddles of Bactrian camels. According to legend, the *tuocha* bricks developed a distinctive fragrance and flavor that became known by the quixotic name "camel's

accordance with halal principles. In addition, not only was wine banned from the royal chambers, but the Hongwu emperor banned its consumption throughout his empire, even though Han Buddhists were fond of it. Curiously, Yusuf Chang's ten indicators that the imperial Ming family was crypto-Muslim read much like those that contemporary Judaic scholars tentatively use to identify crypto-Jews in the Americas.[21]

Zhu Di's father was indeed known to have constructed a mosque and to have written poetry in praise of the Prophet Muhammad. And yet, like Zheng He, Zhu Di may have also practiced Buddhism when necessary, to show his Han Chinese supporters his solidarity with them. According to legend, Zheng was instructed to make a pilgrimage to Mecca on his master's behalf. (Perhaps the already-described journey that Ma Huan breath." It is now impossible to determine whether it was the sweat or the breath of the camels that imparted such an earthy taste to the aged tea when it was rehydrated in boiling water, but we do know that the bricks yielded a dark, intensely flavorful, full-bodied beverage. One aficionado has discreetly called the flavor "sturdy," and another has boldly claimed that it has the same "kick-ass" qualities as a syrupy espresso. Although *tuocha* bricks are still made today, they are nest or bowl shaped and lack the center hole, ending the possibility of stringing them together on a rope.

After the Ming dynasty, brewing loose-leaf tea became the fashion. That meant that *pu-erh* brick tea became less common, particularly in the tea trade beyond the Great Wall. But a recent resurgence of interest in *pu-erh* tea bricks by tea connoisseurs in Europe and the United States has raised their prices to astronomic levels.

I have recently seen *pu-erh* tea bricks proudly displayed in beautifully colored paper wrappings everywhere in China from Beijing and Quanzhou in the east to Ürümqi in the west. Although camel's breath tea is too rare to appear in every tea shop, I did find it along one of the old Silk Roads, in a store on the steppe that edges the Tian Shan range in western China. I have also sampled it in a similar landscape halfway around the world, on the short-grass prairies below the Front Range of the Rockies near Boulder, Colorado. Whenever I encounter a brick of the tea, I hold it up to my nose, close my eyes, and smell the camel caravans passing by.

Ahmed, Selena, and Michael Freeman. "Pu-erh Tea and the Southwest Silk Road: An Ancient Quest for Well-being." *HerbalGram* 90 (2011): 32–43.
Hohenegger, Beatrice. *Liquid Jade: The Story of Tea from East to West.* New York: St. Martin's Press, 2007.

and Hong Bao took to Mecca on behalf of Zheng He actually satisfied the desire of both Zheng and the emperor to complete the hajj.)

It is clear that the emperor sanctioned Zheng to reestablish alliances with Muslims and even to offer support for mosques in ethnic Muslim communities that had been scattered across the seas, sometimes becoming so isolated that they had stopped making pilgrimages to Mecca and had fallen out of the spice-trade networks earlier influenced by the Islamic empire. Zheng found a way to renew these connections by offering generous gifts to their leaders in return for the promise of tribute contributions for the emperor. These Southeast Asian Muslims may well have seen their part of the exchange in much the same way today's merchants assume that sales taxes are a customary cost of doing business.

Some contemporary Southeast Asian Muslims claim that Zheng left Hanafi Muslim sailors to work in these communities and used Ming resources to finance some of the first openly public mosques constructed in the harbors of Sumatra, Java, Malacca, the Philippines, and India. Some of his sailors may have also erected the shrines still found on Pate Island in the Lamu Archipelago off the coast of Kenya, though admittedly the shrines are of uncertain religious affiliation.[22] Today, in many of these places, Zheng He is regarded as a special Muslim saint.

After Zheng returned from his first expedition's encounter with Arab Muslims along the Malabar Coast, it appears that he urged Zhu Di to draw up a landmark edict regarding religious tolerance. The edict, released on June 16, 1407, while Zheng He was on his second expedition, not only protected all Muslims in the practice of their faith but also safeguarded their mosques throughout China from religious intolerance. Transcribed onto a tablet placed on the garden wall outside the Ashab Mosque in Zayton, it praises the Muslim inhabitants of China as loyal, sincere, and capable subjects of the empire "most deserving of commendation."[23]

According to a recently translated stone inscription found at Lingshan (Miracle Hill) in Quanzhou, Zheng He took time out in 1417, before his fifth voyage, to burn incense and pray on a grassy knoll at a Muslim cemetery there.[24] It is claimed in Hui oral tradition that Zheng He also went out from Zayton to the coastal Muslim villages near Chendai, where he recuperated in between his expeditions among the Ding Hui, who continue to revere him as a Muslim saint today.

Even before the death of the Yongle emperor in 1424, there were moves to curtail the voyages of Zheng He, which many courtiers deemed too costly. Despite their efforts, in 1431, Zheng began one last voyage, this time under the leadership of Emperor Zhu Zhangji, Zhu Di's grandson. As noted earlier, the expedition apparently returned to China two years later without much of Zheng He, beyond a shock of his hair, a few of his personal items, and the memories of his confidants, mercantile envoys, translators, soldiers, and sailors. His death marked the end not only of the Treasure Fleet but also of state-sponsored large-scale naval exploration and trade for centuries. Modest commercial trade and black market smuggling between China and India continued, so China never retreated into full isolation as some historians have suggested. But direct contact between the Ding Hui of the eastern seacoast of China and the larger Islamic world would be curtailed for much of the next five hundred years.

CHAPTER II

Vasco da Gama Mastering
the Game of Globalization

It is a long way from Zayton, the Chinese port town that was once associated with olive branches, to Lisbon, the Portuguese metropolis where olives, known as *azeitonas,* still grow along the boulevards. And there was just as much psychological distance between their favorite sons, Zheng He and Vasco da Gama. It is difficult to imagine two "explorers" and fleet commanders more dissimilar in their personal and diplomatic styles.

Vasco da Gama missed encountering Zheng He off the coast of East Africa by only about seventy years. The Portuguese spice and slave traders had begun to work their way down the coast of West Africa in the 1440s, less than a decade after Zheng He's death, but da Gama himself did not reach the harbors of East Africa frequented by Muslim spice traders until 1498.[1] As historical geographer Louise Levathes has asked aloud, "One wonders what would have happened if they had met. Realizing the extraordinary power of the Ming navy, would da Gama in his eighty-five to hundred-foot vessels have dared continue across the Indian Ocean? Seeing the battered Portuguese boats, would the Chinese admiral have been tempted to crush these snails in his path, preventing the Europeans from opening an east-west trade route?"[2]

Perhaps the combined Chinese, Buddhist, and Muslim presence would have nipped Portuguese colonialism in the bud, or at least tempered the zealotry of young Vasco da Gama, who believed himself to be on a holy crusade against Islam's economic and spiritual dominance along the spice routes.[3] We will never know exactly why Manuel I, also known as Manuel the Fortunate, chose young da Gama to lead a major expedition around the Horn of Africa in 1497, since he had little experience on the open seas and no diplomatic training, and was already known for his hot temper and quarrelsome behavior. He was an anomaly, not really representative of seasoned Portuguese sailors, or even of Western navigators of his era. As Fernández-Armesto once quipped, "Once he got to sea, he made almost every possible error."[4] As a teen, he may have fought alongside other youths from the town of Évora in a brief skirmish in Morocco. This may have impressed the young Manuel, a politically incompetent but fanatically religious Catholic who, on marrying the daughter of Ferdinand and Isabella of Spain, decreed that any Sephardic Jews who did not convert to Christianity and all Andalusian Muslims would be expelled from Portugal.[5]

The prices for spices reaching western Europe had soared during the fifteenth century, and the Portuguese were desperate to circumvent the middlemen that stood between them and India—wherever exactly that was—because they had been receiving adulterated saffron and black pepper for more than a half century. The king may have also wanted to expedite dominance over the Spice Islands to halt a growing anti-spice lobby among Portuguese moralists and economic conservatives. These groups disapproved of the hedonistic desire among Europe's elite for expensive aromatics, claiming that such demands were draining the treasuries of Christian nations while allowing the Muslims to prosper.[6]

Outfitted with four well-equipped ships and instructed to head southward around Africa, da Gama promptly appointed his more level-headed brother Paulo as his right-hand man and then set out from Lisbon. They were charged by the king not with conquering new lands but with contacting Christian nations in the East who might become Portugal's allies in wresting control of the spice routes away from the Muslims. Perhaps because the king was envious of his in-law's apparent success in helping Christopher Columbus discover "some place" beyond the world charted by European mapmakers, the stakes had been raised. It was critical for the Catholic world to ensure it had control of what were actually the Spice Islands, as it was believed that trade from there had fueled Islam's growing wealth and power.

And yet, even with some of Portugal's best navigators aboard, including a number who had sailed south with Bartholomeu Dias to the Cape of Good Hope at the tip of Africa in 1488, da Gama almost did not make it to the reaches of the cape. His tiny ships had been badly battered during the four months in which they bore the brunt of the powerful waves moving across the southern Atlantic. Even before the crews had actually passed the cape, they made a stop on the coast of southern Africa and terrified a band of residents. Within three days, the coastal community became so incensed with the behavior of the Portuguese that some of its members wounded da Gama and several of his men with arrows.

After several other trials and miscommunications with coastal Africans, da Gama and his seasick crew finally passed the Cape of Good Hope and entered the waters of the Swahili Coast, which was lined with ports unknown to earlier Portuguese navigators. By Christmas Day 1497, da Gama's scurvy-infested crew was finally approaching the trade routes long controlled by Arab seafarers and merchants. And yet it took them two more months of slowly sailing the waters between the southern tip of Africa and Madagascar before they were finally presented with foodstuffs laced with spices that they recognized: "a jar of bruised dates made into a preserve with cloves and cumin."[7] Perhaps, they hoped, the Spice Islands were close at hand.

Along the way, da Gama donned the garb of an Arab to win an audience with a local sultan and his family, but then failed to offer his hosts tribute gifts fit for royalty. His inability to fathom the importance of presenting such dignitaries with valuable items as tribute—a custom of the greatest importance throughout Africa and Asia—soon became the unifying theme of the expedition.

Before departing the southern reaches of the Swahili Coast in March 1498, the three Portuguese ships did add Arabic-speaking black guides to their crews at Mozambique. But da Gama soon became so convinced that they were serving as spies for the "White Moors," or Arabs, that he began torturing two of them by dripping hot oil onto their bare skin to get them to confess.[8] His tactics were disastrous, for both men squirmed loose and jumped overboard to their deaths.

Left without local speakers to serve as their pilots and intermediaries, the Portuguese fell short on supplies before they could reach Mombasa, and they took to looting Arab cargo ships. Muslim merchants in their seaworthy dhows had already come to view da Gama and his crew as little more than pitiful pirates, so once they did enter the port of Mombasa, they were immediately forced out. They drifted northward toward Malindi, where the local merchants were in competition with those of Mombasa. That rivalry ensured that da Gama received a better reception, and he ceremoniously signed a treaty of cooperation

Cumin (*Cuminum cyminum*) has merited inclusion in the title of this book exactly because it is so demonstrative of culinary globalization: it has been cultivated, utilized, and traded for so long that no botanist or archaeologist is sure where it originated. Although the broad-brush-stroke answer to its place of origin is western Asia, various historians have suggested Palestine, Syria, Lebanon, Turkey, Greece, Ethiopia, and even Southwest Asia as the locus of its domestication. There may be scant agreement as to when, where, or by whom it was domesticated, but there is little doubt as to why it began to be harvested, then managed, and finally cultivated. When toasted and ground, its khaki-colored seeds are so strongly aromatic that few can resist their lure. The cuminaldehydes in its oil have a warm, earthy aroma with a lingering pungency and a flavor that is pleasingly bitter at first, before melting into an aftertaste of sweetness. Cumin flavors are fitting complements to the flavors of many legumes, from garbanzo beans and lentils in the Old World to lima, pinto, and tepary beans in the New World.

Many scholars have established that cumin was harvested and used in the Levant during the earliest Biblical times. Written records describing its inclusion in gardens and fields indicate that it was already well entrenched in the Tigris-Euphrates region when the Mesopotamian and Egyptian civilizations emerged. It appears that Arab spice traders first took it to India, Phoenicians carried it westward through their North African colonies to the Iberian Peninsula, and Berbers transported it across trans-Saharan trade routes into the semiarid Sahel.

The origin of the English term *cumin* lies in the Semitic languages, including the Amharic *kemun*, Akkadian *kamûmu*, Aramaic *kamuna*, Arabic *al-kamoun*, Old Hebrew *kammon*, and Egyptian *kamnini*. The Old Greek *kyminon* and Latin *cuminim* are clearly derived from the Semitic cognate and not the other way around. Most Romance languages retain some variant of these ancient terms, including *cumino, comino, cominho,* and *cumin*. In Chinese, cumin is *kuming* except

with the sultan of Malindi. The sultan then offered da Gama a supper of six lambs, which were likely richly cooked in the same spices that were given to the Portuguese as special gifts: allspice or nutmeg, cloves, cumin, ginger, and pepper.[9] Again, the ease of access to some of the world's most expensive spices must have made some of the crew assume that their destination was near.

But it was already April 1498 and da Gama knew that he had gained no real knowledge of how to get to the Spice Islands or how far away when speaking of herbal medicine. Then cumin becomes *xiao hui xiang*, which likens it to fennel, just as in some other languages it is confused with caraway. In and near the Indian subcontinent, it appears that most names are rooted in the Sanskrit *jri*, which means to "digest," or "ferment." Indeed, cumin seeds are used as a digestive in many parts of the world.

Once it has been introduced into a new land and culture, cumin has a way of insinuating itself deeply into the local cuisine, which is why is has become one of the most commonly used spices in the world. When an Israeli student whom I was hosting told me that cumin was the signature spice of *hummus bi-tahini* in Tel Aviv, I was taken aback at first, since at that time I believed it was primarily a Mexican spice! Ask chefs in southern India to imagine garam masala without toasted cumin, and they might tell you that *jira* has been in their spice kit since Indians began to cook! Its use in China is championed among the Turkic-speaking Uighur of Xinxiang Province, who likely first received it from Sogdians, Persians, and Arabs traveling the Silk Roads. Cumin is essential to complex savory spice mixtures such as the Berber *ras el hanout*, Georgian *svanuri marili*, Yemeni *zhoug*, and Arab *baharat*. It is also a key ingredient in Cajun spice mixes, seven seas curry in Malaysia, and Indian masalas. It has made the fewest inroads in Europe, where it is largely limited to flavoring cheese, such as Gouda and Leyden. In fact, in Finnish, *juusto* means "cheese," and cumin is called *juustokumina*.

Gambrelle, Fabienne. *The Flavor of Spices*. Paris: Flammarion, 2008.

Green, Aliza. *Field Guide to Herbs and Spices*. Philadelphia: Quirk Books, 2006.

Katzer, Gernot. "Gernot Katzer's Spice Pages." http://gernot-katzers-spice-pages.com/engl/index.html. Accessed September 3, 2011.

Sortun, Ana, with Nicole Chaison. *Spice: Flavors of the Eastern Mediterranean*. New York: Regan Books, 2006.

Weiss, E.A. *Spice Crops*. Wallingford, UK: CABI Publishing, 2002.

they were. So, he took one of the sultan's diplomats as a hostage and told the sultan that he would exchange him for an expert navigator. Presumably, the sultan agreed to the deal or conceded that he had no choice but to be blackmailed. According to a consensus at a 2012 forum of Gujarati historians and journalists, the talented pilot was most likely a Gujarati originally from the Indian district of Kutch, but whether he was a Muslim or a possible convert from Islam to Christianity is still debated.[10] His name, according to the same scholarly group, was Kanji

Malam, and he was a seafaring trader of indigo and cotton[11] who may have been trained by the Arab nautical genius, Ahmad ibn Majid of Julfar (today's Ras al-Khaimah), on the Omani coast.[12] Kanji Malam had probably crossed the Indian Ocean before, carried maps, and knew how to time a ship's departure to take advantage of monsoonal winds.

Thanks to the guidance of this experienced navigator, Vasco da Gama arrived a few miles from the port of Calicut, India, in May 1498, and quickly claimed to have discovered India for the West. As we now know, an itinerant Portuguese named Pêro da Covilhã had come by land to the very same harbor almost a decade earlier.[13] To da Gama's dismay, his second day in port was spoiled by the arrival on his ship of two Spanish-speaking Tunisians! They were Muslims from the Barbary Coast who had arrived in Calicut via Cairo and the Red Sea, and they regularly traded with the local merchants.[14] The Tunisians passed word of da Gama's arrival to the overseer of India's great spice emporium, and soon da Gama was welcomed by the hereditary ruler of the Malabar Coast, the *samudra-raja* or *samuthiri,* whom the Portuguese called the *zamorin.* At that time, the *samuthiri* was a rather timid Hindu puppet lord for Muslim merchants who truly ruled the harbor of Calicut, but later rulers became the worst rivals the Portuguese warlords encountered along the Indian Ocean.

The Portuguese could immediately see that Calicut, which had been the cornerstone of both maritime spice trade around southern Asia and overland trade from the hinterlands for well over two hundred years, was endowed with enormous wealth. As the Portuguese Renaissance historian Fernão Lopes de Castanheda later chronicled, the bazaar was loaded with "all the spices, drugs, nutmegs, and other things that can be desired, all kinds of precious stones, pearls and seed-pearls, musk, sanders [sandalwood], aguila [eagles], fine dishes of earthen ware, lacquer, gilded coffers, and all the fine things of China, gold, amber, wax, ivory, fine and coarse cotton goods, both white and dyed of many colors, much raw and twisted silk, stuffs of silk and gold, cloth of gold, cloth of tissue, grain, scarlets [dyes], silk carpets, copper, quicksilver, vermilion, alum, coral, rose-water, and all kinds of [fruit] conserves."[15] This was in fact the mother lode of pepper, the Malabar Coast that the Christians of western Europe had been waiting to mine for a very long time.

When da Gama offered the *samuthiri* a few petty gifts in exchange for building a trading post there with exclusive rights to send spices westward, the Muslim merchants who had previously enjoyed a similar agreement with the Hindu ruler took offense. Da Gama's tribute to

FIGURE 19. Vasco da Gama shown delivering the letter of King Manuel of Portugal to the *samuthiri* of Calicut. (Courtesy Library of Congress Prints and Photographs Division, www.loc.gov/pictures/item/92513908.)

the ruler of the greatest spice emporium on the subcontinent—the one whom he had waited so long to see—amounted to only one case of cane sugar, two barrels of olive oil, two casks of honey, twelve pieces of striped cloth, four scarlet hoods, six hats, four strings of coral, and six brass basins. The *samuthiri* himself soon saw da Gama's impropriety, when the Portuguese commander claimed he had brought so few goods along because he had been instructed by his king only to make discoveries.[16]

The *samuthiri* and his advisers denied him exclusive rights and demanded that the Portuguese pay custom fees for trading in his kingdom. He then kidnapped da Gama and three other men and sent a notice to his brother Paulo that they would not be released until a ransom was paid. Paulo loaded up a dory with all of the most valuable goods from Europe still on the ships—other than statues of the Virgin and crosses—and paid the ransom. Frustrated and annoyed, Vasco da Gama instructed some of his men to remain in Calicut as the main conduits to their hosts on the Malabar Coast in case the *samuthiri* became more open to trade negotiations over the following weeks. Da Gama then took off with what he hoped were just enough exotic goods to be able to justify his long and expensive trip to King Manuel. Just before departing from Calicut, he kidnapped a few locals just to show his belligerence. When he reached Portugal, he displayed enough black pepper and hyperbole to be declared a hero.

Portugal's Fourth Armada to India in 1502 was prompted by a report that in the intervening years, a few of the trusted colleagues that da Gama had left in Calicut had been massacred by Muslim traders. The command post of the new armada was originally offered to Pedro Álvarez Cabral, the Portuguese discoverer of Brazil and leader of the second and third armadas to India. But just a few days before the armada departed, Cabral was replaced by da Gama, whom Manuel I titled Admiral of the Seas of Arabia, Persia, India, and all the Orient. He first put in at Cochin to gain support for his cause and then arrived in Calicut with sixteen heavily armed ships. He demanded that the *samuthiri* expel all Arab Muslim traders from the city and hoped that the same might be done in other ports along the Malabar Coast. When his request was denied, he bombarded the city until the ruler surrendered. Later, Portugal was given exclusive trading rights to all spices coming into ports of the Malabar Coast. For da Gama, this was the crowning moment of his personal crusade: to break the back of Islam by usurping its role in the spice trade. It also set the stage for the more disturbing elements of the next five centuries of globalization, in which economic, spiritual, and military imperialism went hand in hand.

After his arrival in Calicut, da Gama exacted revenge for the earlier deaths of his colleagues by capturing an unarmed Arab ship, the *Mīrī*, which was traveling between Calicut and Cochin. It was filled with nearly three hundred Muslims, including at least ten of the wealthiest spice traders from Calicut, all of whom were returning from the hajj. The group's leader, Jauhar al-Faqih, was not only a prominent spice merchant but also the diplomatic counsel to Calicut for the sultan of Mecca. He tried to negotiate with da Gama, offering him a wealth of spices and other treasures, if the Portuguese would spare his family and friends. But da Gama ordered his men to rob them of all of their gold, kidnap all of the children, and then set the ship on fire. After a five-day struggle, da Gama watched as nearly 250 passengers—the ones who had not already jumped overboard—were killed.

On witnessing this incident, a Portuguese companion of da Gama's, Gaspar Correia, called it an act of unequaled cruelty in the history of his people.[17] Centuries later, an Indian historian of the incident, Sanjay Subrahmanyam, suggested that it was a turning point in the history of maritime trade, for it introduced the systematic use of violence at sea.

Subrahmanyam controversially claims that such methodical genocide was first executed at the hands of Portuguese Christians on an unsanctioned crusade to devastate the Islamic world.[18]

Given the title of viceroy by John III, Manuel I's son and successor, da Gama set out on his third voyage to India in 1424. Within a few months of his arrival, he died in Cochin, after having squirmed for days with inexplicable pain. It is said that he suffered to the end from hard boils festering at the base of his neck, ones that propelled him into "great fits of irritation, [and] with the heavy burdens that he felt on account of the many things which he had done and had yet to do, [the pain] of his illness was doubled."[19]

Da Gama continued to travel without much rest for centuries. He was first buried in silk garments in a humble Franciscan church in Cochin, where Gaspar Correia reported that a couple of Portuguese mercenaries grieved for having lost "so honored a father, and [for having to lay him to rest] in such a desert of a place, of all the places in the entire kingdom of Portugal."[20] In 1538, his bones were repatriated to a convent in Vidigueira, Portugal, where the title of count had been bestowed on him in 1419. In 1880, they were supposedly disinterred and reburied at the Jerónimos Monastery in the Belém harbor, on the edge of Lisbon. But it was discovered some years later that the wrong set of bones had been transported. Not long after that accident was revealed, officials had what they hoped were da Gama's true bones moved to the monastery and then held a discreet celebration to commemorate the transition.[21]

Today, the tomb of Vasco da Gama sits alongside those of kings in the monastery on the Lisbon waterfront. The explorer rests within spitting distance of the tomb of his benefactor, Manuel I.

During my only week-long visit to Lisbon, the first thing I did after putting my bags down in my hotel room was begin the slow walk down from the coastal hills to the shores of the Tagus River where it widens into a bay. There, in the parish of Belém, the Jerónimos Monastery sits a few hundred yards from the waterfront.

As I walked into the monastery's cathedral and read on a multilingual sign that Manuel I had built the complex to celebrate Portugal's role in what we now call the Age of Discovery, my head began to reel. Da Gama's tomb, which stands just inside the entrance, was surrounded by a spiral of tourists waiting to get close to it. When I finally stood before the gilded tomb, I tried once more to read about the man who is known as the first count of Vidigueira, an admiral and viceroy of India, and an esteemed member of the Order of Christ. As the crowd pressed in behind me, I began to feel claustrophobic, and I quickly turned and left the cathedral without seeing the tombs of the other famous men interred there.

Each day I was in Lisbon, I would walk the streets seeking neighborhood spice markets, but had little luck finding anything of significance. But the fourth day, while walking along the waterfront, I met a resident of Lisbon whom I asked to direct me to a typical outdoor marketplace where I might see some fresh produce and spices. He looked at me quizzically and rather than recommending that I visit the Mercado da Ribeira, a 125-year-old indoor fish, cheese, produce, herb, flower and meat market of considerable proportions but of little historic significance, he directed me to the oldest extant marketplace in Lisbon, back up in the hills overlooking the Tagus.

I climbed and climbed, spiraling up narrow roads until I came to the address the man had given me. There I saw what *feira,* or "market," has come to mean for most Portuguese. It was what Americans might call a flea market or a swap meet for the poor. Although a few drinks and some fresh watermelons were sold by a couple of vendors, the rest of the merchandise was made up of piles of cast-offs from the last half century of Western civilization. No aromatic herbs, not even a cheap aphrodisiac. Why look for such a thing when there are pornographic videocassettes and piles of CDs? There were cell phones and electric mixers, transistor radios and boom boxes. There were stalls full of fake leather accessories—belts, collars, and bracelets—and heaps of used auto parts, battered motorcycles, and scooters.

So, other than some *piri piri* hot sauce, cumin, and coriander, this is what globalized trade has ultimately provided to the Portuguese? These are the treasures that da Gama bestowed on his people by freeing the trade routes from the hands of the evil Muslims.

Fortunately, da Gama was followed by a man who was less brutal and more of a naval strategist. Afonso de Albuquerque first arrived in the Indian Ocean in 1503. It was about the same time that the last Banu Nebhani, a poetry-writing ancestor of mine named Sulayman ibn Sulayman al-Nebhani, was ruling Oman. He heard through the grapevine that Omani dissidents dissatisfied with his reign had begun clandestine negotiations with the Portuguese to overthrow him, and within a year's time of the rumors, the 350-year control of Oman's spice-trading ports by my Banu Nebhani tribe had collapsed.[22] It was an earlier season of Arab Spring.

By 1507, de Albuquerque had closed off the Gulf of Hormuz so that Persian and Arab ships could not easily reach India. He soon closed off all of the spice trade by other nations between the Atlantic, Mediterranean, and Red Sea on one side, and the Persian Gulf, Indian Ocean, and Pacific Ocean on the other. With less blood spilled than what da Gama had exacted, he had taken control of the ports of Muscat and Sohar from the resident Omani Muslims and Jews, and without incident had pressured Dhofar into surrender and into signing a treaty. In less than a decade, he turned the Indian Ocean into a *mare clausum* in which the Portuguese exclusively controlled the trade that the Turks, the Radhanites, and the Karimi had previously managed.

He stormed into Malacca—the central port for the Spice Islands and the westernmost reach of Chinese sailors—shot a few elephants, and sent the Muslim sultan running for his life. He dispatched ambassadors to Siam and to Canton, the far reaches of the known world.[23] The bridge between the Muslims of the Far East and of the Middle East had been closed on the overland routes of the Silk Roads by the Ottoman Empire around 1380, but it took more than another century for the bridge across the seas to come tumbling down. The pivotal role in the transcontinental trade of aromatics that my own tribe had been engaged in for centuries had apparently come to a close.

As I have learned recently, however, some of the Banu Nebhani tribe had moved on from Oman not long before the fall of their dynasty there. In the fourteenth century, an heir to the Nebhani mercantile fortune in Muscat and Bahla absconded with some of his inheritance and established his own nation-state in the Lamu Archipelago off the coast of Kenya. His name was Sultan Ahmad Abu Bakar Nebhani and he called his new kingdom and spice trading colony Akhbar Pate (or Patta).[24]

Native Kenyans as well as archaeologists who have visited Pate Island tell me that the prehistoric ruins from the era of Akhbar Pate continue to be impressive. On the eastern edge of the island are the remains of Shanga, a city built on white coral that was abandoned in the fourteenth century. Today, the site is littered with pottery shards and half-broken statuary that archaeologist James de Vere Allen believes came from Asia.[25] At its center are the ruins of a large mosque and a strange stone tomb with fluted pillars decorated with green celadon bowls. Similar fluted-pillar tombs are found not only on Pate but also up and down the Kenyan and Somali coasts wherever ancient harbors of the spice trade once stood. One such tomb can be found amid the ruins of the centuries-old town of Gedi, between Malindi and Mombasa, the two greatest spice-trading towns of the East African coast.

But what is even more curious than the archaeological sites on Pate are the appearance and customs of its current inhabitants. Community members of a fishing culture on Pate called the Bajuni were described by anthropologist Nello Puccioni in 1935 as having "a physical type absolutely different from other people of the region. The skin is rather light, in some, slightly olive. And in the men you can spot flowing beards; and the women part their hair in the middle and weave it into two side braids."[26]

Although no published genetic studies exist that confirm the probable multiple origins of the Bajuni people, linguists suggest that remnants of their dialect can be found in coastal Somalia and Kenya, and that they include loan words or grammatical structures from Somali, Arab, Indian, Persian, and possibly Southeast Asian languages.

Customs and language point strongly toward multiple origins of the Bajunis of Shanga, though scholarly work in the past conjectured that they came directly from Shanghai and remain a relatively pure example of an early Chinese diaspora.[27] Genetic evidence to date cannot confirm that. My own favored hypothesis, for a hybrid origin of coastal African peoples, with Arab, Persian, Indian, and Chinese traders, is at least as viable. It speaks to the fact that spice trade over millennia drove not only the structure, ethics (or lack of them), and culture of globalization but also brought various genetic populations back together again into a "rainbow" human family. The Lamu Archipelago on which my ancestors lived six centuries ago may have been inhabited by as many genetically mixed individuals from various continents as a place like Hawaii is today. Perhaps the ongoing underwater archaeological excavations in the Lamu Archipelago of a Chinese ship sunk roughly six centuries ago—when my Banu Nebhani kin were still on Pate—will eventually tell us something of that lost hybrid world, another island of convivencia where multicultural exchanges were perhaps virtuous for a while.

CHAPTER 12

Crossing the Drawbridge over the Eastern Ocean

It was almost too outrageous to record when it occurred at two o'clock in the morning on October 12, 1492, in the misty seascape surrounding a scattering of islands. On that now-legendary expedition westward led by Christopher Columbus, who was bankrolled by the fervently intolerant Catholic monarchs Ferdinand and Isabella, the very first man to catch sight of previously undiscovered land was not a Catholic Spaniard but a converso, one whose father was a *morisco* hidalgo. It is not clear whether Rodrigo de Triana had become a voluntary convert, or *cristiano nuevo*—what other Jews called a *meshummadin* in Hebrew or *marrano* in vulgar Spanish—or an involuntary convert, known as *anusim* in Hebrew. As for his Moorish father, he may have taken on a Christian pseudonym in order to be recognized as a descendant of nobility, or hidalgo, a term derived from *hijo de algo*, "a son of someone (of stature)." But to get on one of Columbus's three ships that departed from Palos earlier that year, the man born in Seville in 1469 at least had to feign being a Christian.

A few days after spotting what were likely some American golden plovers and Eskimo curlews that were presumably heading toward land, Rodrigo de Triana was up in the crow's nest when he caught a good glimpse of the islands that we now call the Bahamas. The first spot of land he saw was quickly named San Salvador, and by a leap of faith, Rodrigo "discovered" what were soon to become known as the West Indies and the Americas.

Yes, it was the same Rodrigo de Triana whom Columbus knew back in Spain as Juan Rodríguez Bermejo de Triana, the man whom he had personally selected for his expedition to the Indies because of his sharp eyes and broad training. But on this October morning, Columbus gave him no mind. Instead, he quietly recorded in his own journal that he himself had seen the first evidence of land the day before, thereby qualifying for the cash reward of ten thousand maravedíes that his sponsors had put up as an incentive for the discovery of a shortcut to the Spice Islands.

When Rodrigo later realized the fiction that his commander had perpetrated, he left the Catholic faith "because Columbus did not give him any credit, nor did the King give him any recompense for his having seen light in the Indies before any other man in the crew."[1] So troubled was de Triana that, on his return to Spain, he did not reconcile himself with his mother's Judaism but instead embraced Islam. De Oviedo, the expedition's chronicler, claimed that de Triana immediately moved off the Iberian Peninsula to live in North Africa, probably in coastal Morocco.[2] Remarkably, there is some evidence that he sailed with other Muslims to the real Spice Islands (the Moluccas) in 1525, before dying and being buried in the traditional fashion of a certain Muslim tribe of Moors called the Mudarra. He died with another bitter taste in his mouth, as well, for the Catholics had burned his *morisco* father at the stake for trading with Jews.

This odd set of occurrences reminds us how intertwined the fates of Jews and Muslims were in the days immediately following the onset of the Spanish Inquisition. Although in some ways they were treated differently, both groups were targeted in the edicts and decrees of expulsion emanating from the prejudicial policies of Ferdinand and Isabella, through what followers of Harvard psychologist Gordon W. Allport have come to call the "rejection of out-groups."[3] But the eight hundred thousand to one million Jews and Muslims who left Spain to escape the Inquisition did not all slink into North Africa and the Middle East to live out their days as their ancestors had done. Instead, some extended their spice-trading network by traversing the Atlantic Ocean, as if a new drawbridge had suddenly been firmly lowered onto American soil. By some scholarly estimates, at least one-fourth of the European settlers of Mexico prior to 1545 were Jews (and no doubt Muslims as well) escaping the Inquisition.[4] Few of these immigrants to the Americas became directly engaged with the spice trade, but there is little doubt that many of them craved the aromas and flavors of their homeland.

Muslim historian Saulat Pervez has said it simply and succinctly: "Columbus' 1492 expedition coincided with the fall of Granada, the very last Muslim stronghold in Spain. This led to some very harsh times for Spanish Muslims [and Jews], culminating in the Spanish Inquisition. This turn of events encouraged many displaced Muslims [and Jews] to go [first to the Canary Islands and then] to the New World in the hopes of freely exercising their religion once again."[5]

In short, they quickly got as far away from Rome, Madrid, Barcelona, Seville, and Granada as possible. In 1497, Portugal began to expel Jews and Muslims from its soil, and its own inquisition started in 1506. Because the Canary Islands had been filled to capacity, escape to the recently named West Indies seemed more inviting.[6] An estimated five thousand Jews and an equal number of Muslims fled to South and Central America as soon as they were able, that is, within just decades of Columbus's first voyage from Spain.[7]

That the Americas and the islands in the Caribbean were inhabited largely by indigenous peoples with strong place-based religions was probably of no immediate consequence to these religious and economic refugees. They could hardly imagine anything worse than the surge of religious intolerance and economic disruption that their Jewish and Muslim communities had recently experienced. As noted earlier, like Rodrigo de Triana, Luis de Torres, a Jew who had been born Yosef ben Ha Levy Haivri, traveled with Columbus on his first expedition. He had converted to Christianity just a few days before leaving Spain and then remained in Hispaniola, where he became the first Jewish-born converso to live in the New World. Joining the first expedition to the New Spain mainland undertaken by Hernán Cortés, Sephardic Jews and Muslims helped secure Mexico for Spain in 1521. Within seven years, a merchant named Hernando Alonso became the first of Cortés's company to be burned at the stake for Judaizing.[8]

But did these Jews and Muslims play a significant role in establishing the trade in spices between the New World and the Old World? It is odd that we know that Christopher Columbus and his crew had chiles in their hands by the last days of 1492, but historians do not agree on how chiles moved from the Antilles and the Americas to Africa, Asia, and Europe in less than fifty years after Columbus first wrote about them on January 1, 1492.[9] Nor are there shipping records to verify chiles, vanilla, allspice, and cacao coming through the hands of merchants of Jewish or Muslim ancestry in the first decades after 1492. But is there other evidence?

It is ironic that Christopher Columbus accidentally encountered chile peppers on his first expedition to the New World, a trip in which he searched in vain for the East Indies and the black pepper and other aromatics the islands promised. The irony comes from the fact that the five domesticated *Capsicum* species soon eclipsed black pepper as the most widely cultivated piquant spices in the world, and perhaps the most widely traded as well.

Archaeologists confirm that Columbus could have encountered one or perhaps two species of *Capsicum* on Hispaniola that had been domesticated on the American mainland. Chiles had reached what is now El Salvador at least nine hundred years and Hispaniola at least a century before the arrival of Columbus, probably through trade with farmers on the Yucatán Peninsula or with seafarers from the northern coast of South America. When I worked with geneticists, archaeologists, linguists, and geographers to pinpoint the origin of chiles, we estimated that *Capsicum annuum* was first domesticated in or near the Sierra Madre Oriental range in central Mexico between 5,800 and 6,500 years ago. According to linguistic analyses accomplished by my friend and colleague Cecil Brown, prehistoric gardeners and farmers in the Oto-Manguean language family, then spoken in the indigenous communities in the sierras of Puebla and adjacent Mexican states, likely domesticated it.

The first cultivated chile was not used as a vegetable, but rather as a spice to complement staples such as maize, which had been domesticated for at least a millennium before the chile. But the harvesting, protection, and management of wild chiles as a dried spice, condiment, vermifuge, and medicine may have gradually begun several hundred years before that. As soon as chiles were domesticated in Mexico, they became associated with the *molcajete,* the three-legged stone mortar used to mash fresh or dried chiles, salt, epazote, wild oregano, tomatillos, and onions together to create the precursor of salsa. When rubbed onto meats as a marinade, this pungent mixture, rich in antioxidants, helped keep the meats from spoiling.

Diego Álvarez Chanca, a physician who accompanied Columbus on his second expedition to the New World, may have been the first European to take chiles back to the Old World to grow and study them for their medicinal properties. Soon after that, official reports of their transport as a spice to Europe become scarce, perhaps because they were far too pungent for Western Europeans to use with food. As Flemish physician and botanist Charles L'Écluse would write in 1564, the ferocity of chile peppers amazed Europeans, who feared that their "sharpness would burn the jaws for several days."

Chiles appear to have been rapidly adopted by the Berbers and

Arabs of Ceuta, however, perhaps because they were already accustomed to the pungent melegueta pepper that had been part of their trade with West Africa for centuries. How chile pepper seeds arrived in Morocco in 1514—so soon after Columbus's expeditions to the West Indies—is anyone's guess, but mine is that crypto-Muslims and crypto-Jews like Rodrigo de Triana took seeds or pods with them when they fled the tyranny of Ferdinand, Isabella, and Columbus. From the ports of Lisbon and Cádiz, larger quantities of chiles and their seeds could have been smuggled in the ballast of ships headed to Ceuta on the other side of the Strait of Gibraltar. Once in North Africa, chiles would have little problem being diffused along Arab and Sephardic Jewish trade routes to countries where pungent spices were already welcomed, including Algeria and Tunisia, Egypt and Syria, Yemen and Turkey, Persia and India.

Amazingly, chile peppers made it to the Malabar Coast of India as early as 1542. As a possible explanation of this, my late, great friend Jean Andrews offered the following hypothesis in *The Pepper Trail:* "It could have been that these first Columbian [i.e., American] foodstuffs, including capsicums, came to Turkey from Spain via the Ottoman contacts with exiled Spanish Moors or expulsed Spanish Jews, who conceivably distributed them throughout North Africa all the way to Egypt" (21). From there they traveled Arabian caravan routes to India.

Although she ultimately preferred another hypothesis—that chiles reached most of Europe through Turkey, after entering Old World trade routes from the ports of India!—Andrews did claim that one element was common to both hypotheses: "By whichever route, Aleppo [Syria] was a key point. In 1600, Venice operated sixteen trading posts and a consular office in Aleppo . . . [and] European traders rarely went beyond the cities at the edge of the desert. . . . The realm of caravans was dominated by Moslem traders" (22).

Halaby fulful, one of the first distinctive chile varieties developed in the Old World, originated in and near Aleppo. Perhaps nurtured by the Sephardic Jewish spice merchants in Aleppo (Halab) and the Arab farmers near the Mediterranean coast, the coarsely ground, sun-dried Aleppo pepper receives high marks today from chefs on both sides of the Atlantic. Its flavor has been described as having a "deliciously deep, cumin-like earthiness and sweetness," and a "complex, slow, gentle heat" that is followed by a "pleasant warmth" or "a lingering ting of sweet and sour."

Virtually all terms for chile in Asian, African, and European languages are derived from the previously existing terms for black pepper or for various peppers or pepperlike fruits in general (melegueta, long, Sichuan, and so on). Most, though certainly not all, are cognate with one another: *pilpili* (Swahili), *felfel* (Farsi), *felfel* (Maltese), *feferon* (Croatian), *biber* (Western Turkic), *berbere* (Amharic), and *bghbegh*

(Armenian). There is a break in the use of these cognates when you arrive at the Indian subcontinent, suggesting to me that chiles did *not* diffuse into Turkey and eastern Europe from the Malabar Coast: *mirch* (Hindi), *marichiphala* (Sanskrit), *marchum* (Gujarati), and *murgh* (Pashto). Most European languages use variants of the words *pimento* and *paprika* for the sweeter vegetable peppers that developed later and for mild chile powder.

Andrews, Jean. "Around the World with the Chile Pepper: The Post-Columbian Distribution of Domesticated *Capsicums*." *Journal of Gastronomy* 4 (1988): 21–35.
———. "Towards Solving the 'Anatolian' Mystery: Diffusion of the Mesoamerican Food Complex to Southeastern Europe." *Geographical Review* 83 (1993): 194–204.
———. *The Pepper Trail: History and Recipes from Around the World.* Denton: University of North Texas Press, 1999.
Kraft, Kraig H., Cecil H. Brown, Gary Paul Nabhan, Eike Luedeling, José Luna Ruiz, Robert J. Hijmans, and Paul Gepts. "Multiple Lines of Evidence for the Origin of Domesticated Chili Pepper, *Capsicum annuum*, in Mexico." Proceedings of the National Academy of Science (U.S.). Forthcoming.
Perry, Linda, et al. "Starch Fossils and the Domestication and Dispersal of Chili Peppers (*Capsicum* spp. L.) in the Americas." *Science* 315 (2007): 986–88.
Wright, Clifford A. "The Medieval Spice Trade and the Diffusion of the Chile." *Gastronomica* 7 (2007): 35–43.

Columbus had gone looking for a westward route from Europe to find the mother lode of black pepper but had accidentally discovered chiles instead. When he declared them to be potentially "more valuable than either black or melegeuta pepper," he had trusted Jewish and Muslim conversos in his presence, ones whose families had already played a role in the spice trade for centuries, if not millennia.

When Columbus returned to Spain, some of those Jews, Arabs, and Berbers stayed on in the New World, establishing colonies that later attracted others of the same ethnicities or faiths. While their early presence as immigrants in the Americas is unquestionable, that fact alone does not assure that they played roles in restructuring spice trade and other commerce similar to those they had assumed in Europe, Africa, and Asia. The question that has hardly been asked in any history of the spice trade is this: could crypto-Jews and crypto-Muslims have played critical roles in taking chiles, chocolate, and other aromatics back to the Old World and then disseminating them? If not, why were they accused of the "sins of chocolate and chiles" by the Mexican Inquisition?[10]

At first glance, it is indeed curious that early Jews in Mexico and New Mexico were accused by New Spain's Catholic clergy of drinking "inebriating" chocolate beverages on Christian fast days and of hanging wreaths of dried chile peppers over Christian crosses. But those scandalous acts do not, in and of themselves, suggest that immigrants of Jewish and Arab ancestry controlled the trading of these goods. They simply used them in a manner that piqued the curiosity and wrath of the Spanish-speaking Catholic establishment. To answer this question more deeply, we must ascertain the roles Jews, Moors, and Arabs played not only in Mexico and what is now the U.S. Southwest but also in the Caribbean and Central and South America. And we must remember that the Aztec, Toltec, Mayan, and Incan empires had independently advanced their own forms of culinary imperialism, taxation, and tribute that preceded the arrival of the Spanish and Portuguese by centuries. The Aztecs, in particular, had engaged traders known as *pochteca* in the long-distance transport of spices and other aromatics. Clearly, European spice merchants who emigrated to the Americas were not entering "virgin" territory with regard to long-distance spice trade; they were simply opening up new markets for neotropical plant products for which there were already in place sophisticated means of harvesting, processing (including fermentation), extra-local distribution, and ritualized consumption.

To be sure, trade networks began to shift when itinerant merchants or descendants of major transcontinental spice-trade dynasties of Jews, Moors, and Arabs clandestinely entered the New World on the ships of the Spanish and Portuguese. They came to harbors near major spice production, and at least a few began to function as merchants there. Sephardic Jews reached the Yucatán Peninsula by the 1570s, Suriname by 1630, and Ashkenazi Jews may have joined them there as early as 1652. What is now the oldest continuously active Jewish congregation in the Caribbean was established in Curaçao by 1651. Fortuitous circumstances led me to first look at Jewish and Moorish (Mudejar) influences in Mérida, Yucatán, which in many ways is as much a part of the Caribbean as it is a part of Mexico. As early as 1575, the Mexican Inquisition contended that Cristóbal de Miranda, then dean of the Mudejar-style cathedral in Mérida, was a *judaizante* (Judaizer). Other Jews of Miranda's cohort were already in control of the slave trade from Yucatán back to Spain, causing resentment (if not jealousy)

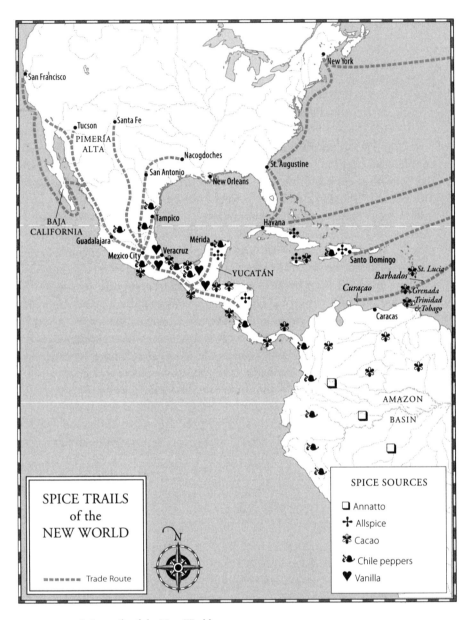

MAP 4. Spice trails of the New World

among less economically successful Catholics in Mérida. And just as early, many immigrants from Andalusia were accused of maintaining Muslim beliefs and ritualized practices of consuming or fasting from certain foods and beverages. In the 1570s, Diego de Landa Calderón, the bishop of Yucatán, ordered the torture of over forty-five hundred men and women convicted for their religious beliefs and the whipping, fining, or public humiliation of another sixty-three hundred suspects. Many of them had Jewish or Muslim ancestry. He was also known for forcibly converting Mayans to Christianity and for destroying their centuries-old codices.

Because my first visit to Mérida occurred 430 years after Bishop de Landa's death, I was not quite sure if any remnants of Arab or Jewish influences would remain in the city or its surrounds. At first, I tried to orient myself to the natural wonder of the Yucatán Peninsula, rather than trying to probe into the shadows of its past cross-cultural conflicts.

My daughter, Laura, and I watch as flamingos lope ahead of us. They are taking refuge in the backwaters of the ancient harbor of Yucalpetén, just off the Gulf of Mexico and about twenty miles from Mérida, the Spanish colonial trade center founded in 1542 and the capital of the state of Yucatán. Yucalpetén is a harbor like many others in tropical Mexico and the Caribbean—one that saw Spanish galleons for centuries before tourism became more lucrative than the spice trade. We head to Progreso, a modern beach town about four miles from Yucalpetén, where we decide to take a canoe out into the nearby mangrove lagoons, swatting mosquitoes and smelling brine and sulfurous muds as we skim along the water. We are surrounded on all sides by vestiges of ancient salt-drying ponds where the Mayans had once obtained this essential mineral, this geological spice. It feels just as I had always imagined it would: so humid that I can hardly tell my own sweat from the drizzle pervading the air and dampening my clothes; and sweltering hot until a sky strewn with dark purple clouds lets loose with a thunderstorm that cools down the air to a tolerable temperature.

We bus back into downtown Mérida, a *centro* filled with buildings that reflect the Mudejar architectural tradition of the Moors.[11] There we visit the giant market pavilion where Mayan vendors in brightly colored booths sell spices, vegetables, and fruits of all kinds. They carry both native seasonings, like epazote, habanero chile, achiote, chocolate, and vanilla, and introduced ones, like cinnamon, cloves, cumin, and lime juice. We eye the piles of complex spice mixtures and pastes called moles

The crimson pigments and sharply perfumed, earthy flavors of annatto emerge from the pulp that surrounds the seeds, which are secreted in spiny, scarlet heart-shaped pods. The pods grow in clusters that stand out above the broadly fingered leaves of this widely distributed tropical shrub or small tree (*Bixa orellana*). The seeds are best known by two names, *annatto,* from indigenous Caribbean languages, and *achiote*, from the Uto-Aztecan language family, with the latter derived from the Nahuatl term *achiotl*. The plant, also known as annatto, is believed to have originated in the lowlands of South America and then, perhaps with the aid of early cultivators, spread northward to the Yucatán Peninsula and the West Indies.

Currently surpassing saffron, turmeric, and paprika as the world's most widely used food colorant, annatto seeds, when soaked in water, deliver both yellow-orange and bright red pigments. The seeds are also used for achiote paste, which originated in the Yucatán and is made by grinding the seeds with other spices and flavorings. For *manteca de achiote*, a popular cooking fat in much of Latin America, the seeds are heated with oil or lard until the liquid turns a beautiful orange, then the seeds are discarded.

I first saw cultivated annatto plants in the dooryard gardens of the Ecuadorian Amazon, where the Jivaro, Tsáchila, and other local tribes still plaster their hair with the brilliant dye derived from the seeds; hence the tribes' nickname Colorado, or "reddish colored." The Aztecs added annatto to their thick, syrupy chocolate drinks to strengthen the brilliance of their brews, and today in the Caribbean, particularly in Jamaica, it is used to flavor and color codfish cakes.

The early Spanish, Berbers, Arabs, and Jews who immigrated to the Yucatán Peninsula used yellow-orange achiote as a substitute for turmeric and saffron in their *recaudos*. These marinades and pastes typically combined achiote with more savory and pungent spices in

and *recaudos* that blend plants of the East and West together in a single pot of native turkey broth.

Laura walks me down winding streets until we reach the Alameda, where Mayan street-food vendors are selling ground lamb and vegetables wrapped in tortillas, a snack they call *quibbe*. The smells of wood smoke, lamb fat, grilled onions, cinnamon, cumin, and allspice pervade the air around the food carts. One man I ask about *quibbe* says it is *una comida típica* for the Mayans of the Yucatán; Laura and I smile at each other, aware of its centuries-old link to the Middle East. We walk a few vinegar or in sour orange or lime juice. The blends, influenced by the newcomers' own culinary traditions, eventually evolved into the sauces and pastes that brighten such Mayan-adapted dishes as *cochinita pibil* and *múkbil pollo.* In Mayan villages I have visited on the Yucatán Peninsula, the crimson, pink, and green profile of the annatto tree brightens the walkways of nearly every dooryard garden, doubling as both an ornamental and a kitchen staple.

Crypto-Jewish spice merchants who helped to colonize Mexico may have been the first traders to send the seeds into the Old World spice networks, for achiote moved along the same trade routes that had long been managed by Sephardic Jews and Arabized Berbers. Traders in Martinique appear to have passed what they called annatto on from Portuguese, French, and Dutch colonies to Europe, Africa, and Asia, which is reflected in the fact that loan-word cognates of achiote are far less common in Old World languages than are cognates of annatto and *bija,* both derived from the Caribbean language family. *Urucul,* another indigenous term for annatto, may have originated in the Amazon Basin. It is likely the root of *ruku,* the term now used in Curaçao for annatto oil, an ingredient that is commonly combined with blue Curaçao liqueur in mixed drinks and marinades.

Today, annatto enjoys a pan-tropical distribution, being cultivated as far away from its natal grounds as China, Vietnam, India, and the Philippines. Once valued primarily as a hair dye, aphrodisiac, and digestive, the utility of annatto as a colorant, in everything from lipsticks, cheeses, sun screens, and red sun dresses and shawls to chewing gums, now trumps all of its other uses.

Green, Aliza. *Field Guide to Herbs and Spices.* Philadelphia: Quirk Books, 2006.
Hill, Tony. *The Contemporary Encyclopedia of Herbs and Spices.* Hoboken, NJ: John Wiley and Sons, 2004.
Katzer, Gernot. "Gernot Katzer's Spice Pages." http://gernot-katzers-spice-pages.com/engl/index.html. Accessed May 4, 2013.

blocks farther to Café Siqueff, a restaurant owned by a twentieth-century Lebanese immigrant. It has a hint of Mayan influence in its menu, since Jorge Siqueff Febels has Mayan as well as Lebanese kin.

There on Don Jorge's menu, the *quibbe* is spelled *kibi,* the *fatayer* (meat pie) is Hispanicized as *eftoyer,* and the yogurt has returned to its ancient Arabic name of *labneh.* The signature dish of the Siqueff dynasty, *huevos motuleños,* was first prepared at Café La Sin Rival in Motul in response to a request for "something different" for the breakfast of Yucatán governor Felipe Carrillo Puerto sometime before his

death in 1924. I look at its ingredients: eggs, black beans, ham, tortillas, bananas, peas, cheese, and chives. It is as much a transcontinental
hybrid as any dish I have ever eaten, part of what is sometimes called
Lebanese-Mayan fusion cuisine.

I once imagined that Spanish colonization of places such as Yucatán
would have resulted in colonies with cultural sensibilities much like
those of the imperialistic colonizers. In Mérida, I could see the flaws in
my own earlier assumptions. Many of the people who came from the
Iberian Peninsula in the sixteenth and seventeenth centuries were not
attempting to advance the Spanish empire; in fact, they were fleeing from
it. The people who had lost the most and who were the most threatened
by the ongoing Inquisition were among those who were driven to take
refuge elsewhere, including the brave new world that Rodrigo de Triana
had glimpsed. And once relocated on an island or the mainland of the
Americas, the newcomers reinitiated the livelihoods that their families
had championed over the centuries, including the trading of spices.

But first, the traders had to get off of the Iberian Peninsula and on
their way. Fortunately, despite the ongoing Inquisition, passage was not
too difficult to negotiate, because sympathetic Christians had formed an
underground railroad to help Muslims and Jews leave the peninsula. At
a major port in Spain with ships headed for the Canary Islands, it was
common knowledge that "whoever wants to purchase a license to pass
to the West Indies can do so on his own at the port of San Juan y la de
Santestevan. Look for the road that leaves for Tudela, at the end of the
stone bridge, and there on the street you can ask for Francisca Brava
or Nicolás Losada the cleric, who will sell you a license to travel to the
West Indies."[12]

By the end of the sixteenth century, more than nineteen thousand
individuals from Andalusia alone had legally emigrated from Spain to
the Americas, while others secretly arrived bearing pseudonyms and
false credentials fabricated in places such as the Canary Islands.[13] Of
course, Andalusia was the region of the Iberian Peninsula where most
of the crypto-Muslims and a good many of the crypto-Jews originally
resided. The emigrants included not only laborers but also many skilled
and educated professionals: doctors, lawyers, notaries, pharmacists,
shoemakers, blacksmiths, accountants, slave traders, and, of course,
spice traders.

Many Andalusians were among those who had left for Portugal or for
the Canary Islands, before taking the final leap to harbors in the West

Indies. Some of them later found ways to reach the Greater and Lesser Antilles, the Bahamas, and finally the American mainland, particularly through Mexico. The best indication that so many Jews and Muslims came early to the New World can be found in accounts of the belated— and mostly futile—attempts by the Spanish government to curb the flow. At first, Spanish bureaucrats established a whole set of laws and regulations to prevent Muslims and Jews from even entering the Americas. Portugal, of course, followed in proliferating its own anti-Semitic laws and regulations. Even though Portugal had granted one hundred thousand Jews asylum for the eight months following their expulsion from Spain in July 1492, the Portuguese later withdrew the right for any Jew to live and work legally in its lands on the Iberian Peninsula or in any of its American colonies. But it was too late. And once these new immigrants had arrived in the Caribbean or on the American mainland, they undoubtedly took notice of what spices, herbs, and other aromatics their new home offered. Of immediate interest were allspice, achiote, five species and scores of cultivars of chiles, chocolate, several kinds of oregano, copal incense, and vanilla.

Not surprisingly, most of these aromatics traveled the same route out of the New World that the diaspora Jews and Muslims traveled to get there. The spices and other goods most often went out through the ports of Veracruz and Mérida in Mexico, Spanish Town and Port Royal in Jamaica, Havana in Cuba, and through other ports in the Lesser Antilles and on the islands of Barbados, Cayenne, Curaçao, and Martinique. These are exactly the places where crypto-Jews and crypto-Muslims who had nominally become *cristianos nuevos* went when they fled Cádiz, Jerez, Palos de la Frontera, and Lisbon in droves.[14] Once they had gotten the dried plants into American and Caribbean ports, they did not necessarily declare all of them as cargo, but may have hidden many of them in the ballast of the ships. From there, they set off for the Canary Islands before reaching Europe. In the ports of the Canaries, these items could have easily and surreptitiously been unloaded and slipped onto ships leaving for Morocco, not Spain.

Soon, they saw which plants could enter the very same trade routes in Europe, Asia, and Africa that their forefathers had employed, and then, beginning along the southern shores of the Mediterranean, they found ways to get an entire set of New World aromatics across the ocean and into those routes. Shipping records? What smugglers keep such things?

In 1520, the Catholic Church, realizing that emigrated Jews and Muslims were now not only practicing their faiths but also controlling

Profoundly aromatic, the small, brownish, seedlike fruits, more commonly known as berries, of the allspice tree (*Pimenta dioica*) offer a sharp piquancy followed by notes of cinnamon, clove, and nutmeg—a heady mix that some Americans recognize as pumpkin pie spice. The clovelike fragrance and flavor arise from the presence of eugenol, methyl eugenol, and beta-caryophyllene, three key chemical compounds present in the essential oil of the berries. Although ground allspice has become the mostly widely used form of the spice, the foliage and wood of *P. dioica* are still used throughout the tree's Caribbean area of origin. The leaves, which are employed in marinades and in stuffings for meats, carry far less of the clovelike flavor than the berries do. Wood pruned from the trees is used as fragrant fuel for traditional barbecues.

In the Mayan lowlands of the Yucatán Peninsula in Mexico, allspice, chiles, and vanilla regularly flavored ritually consumed chocolate beverages. When I have had the opportunity to drink Mayan-style unsweetened chocolate drinks that include allspice, I have been struck by how well the two flavors complement one another, perhaps more so than even chocolate and vanilla.

Allspice was first noted by Columbus on his second voyage to the West Indies, but it didn't catch hold in Europe until the seventeenth century. It appears that Sephardic Jewish refugees living in Santiago de la Vega (Spanish Town) and Port Royal in Jamaica shipped allspice to other Jewish traders residing in Old World ports, such as Constantinople, Venice, Genoa, Amsterdam, and London. When it arrived in London, the English named it newspice and became its most fanatic consumers in the Old World, using it in pickling brines for vegetables and for flavoring stews. Because the bulk of its commercial production continued to come out of Jamaica, allspice became known as Jamaica pepper in many of its new destinations. It also grows on other West Indian islands, including Cuba and Barbados.

The natural range of allspice extends over to the coast of the Yucatán Peninsula in Mexico, Belize, and Guatemala and then southward into Central and South America, where I have witnessed robust trees fifteen to twenty feet tall. The Yucatecan allspice berries that I have sampled have an altogether different flavor complex from Jamaican berries, though they are in no way inferior to the island's harvests. Within the tropical and arid subtropical climes of Mexico, allspice has been known as *pimienta gorda* or *pimienta de Tabasco* and traditionally traded throughout the country. The latter name may in fact be the origin of the term *Tabasco pepper,* which was introduced to the United States around the time of the Civil War by a Confederate soldier who mistakenly applied it to a particular chile.

In Jamaican jerk pastes and rubs for meats, allspice is the key ingredient that complements black pepper, chiles, cinnamon, garlic, lime juice, and vinegar. It appears that Arabic-speaking *moriscos* and conversos in Mexico and the Caribbean may have also been involved in the allspice trade, since it became one more kind of "pepper" on the Old World trade routes. In fact, the majority of language groups to which allspice was introduced initially described it as just that: one more kind of pepper (*piment, piperi, pjerets, pepe, Pfeffer*), with allusions to it being a sweet pepper in its Arabic (*filfil infranji halu*), Mandarin Chinese (*ganjiao*), and Cantonese Chinese (*gam jiu*) names. The Berbers in Algeria call it *fulful mexik,* or "Mexican pepper," suggesting that it may have entered the Maghreb through early Mexican exports to Andalusia and Morocco. Bulgarians and Georgians simply treat it as one more Turkish- or Arab-introduced spice (*bahar*) suitable for adding to spice mixes such as *baharat* and *ras el hanout*.

Bengali and Hindi cooks view allspice as a spice-rub ingredient for Chinese kebabs (*kabab chini*) that was originally accessed through Silk Road trade with Muslims from western China. It is also used by my cousins in Lebanon in their rubs and marinades for various kebab, kibbe, and *kefta* preparations. In fact, in much of the Middle East, allspice from the New World is now so completely integrated into the local cuisines that it is easy to presume that it is native to the region. Today it is also present in ketchups, meat marinades, pickles, rum cocktails, and spice cakes around the world.

Gambrelle, Fabienne. *The Flavor of Spices.* Paris: Flammarion, 2008.
Green, Aliza. *Field Guide to Herbs and Spices.* Philadelphia: Quirk Books, 2006.
Hill, Tony. *The Contemporary Encyclopedia of Herbs and Spices.* Hoboken, NJ: John Wiley and Sons, 2004.
Katzer, Gernot. "Gernot Katzer's Spice Pages." http://gernot-katzers-spice-pages.com/engl/index.html. Accessed May 4, 2013.
Sortun, Ana, with Nicole Chaison. *Spice: Flavors of the Eastern Mediterranean.* New York: Regan Books, 2006.

a good deal of commerce in their new homes, appointed Pedro de Córdoba, a Dominican missionary, to be the first inquisitor of the West Indies and, by default, Mexico. Following his death in 1525, no new inquisitor was named, though for the next five decades, the reigning bishop of Mexico typically assumed inquisitional powers. In 1539, the Spanish government, alarmed by reports about the *cristianos nuevos* from its representatives in the colonies, issued a decree that explicitly prohibited "the transfer to the West Indies [including Mexico] of sons or grandsons of persons of Muslim or Jewish ancestry." Just four years later, as if acknowledging that these strategies to keep recent Jewish and Muslim converts to Christianity from going to New Spain had largely failed, Charles V ordered the expulsion of such converts, particularly Muslim-born Christians, currently living in the Americas. Then, in 1571, Pedro Moya de Contreras was named the first inquisitor of New Spain and immediately began to investigate the conversos who had already become prominent in managing trade between the ports of Veracruz and Cádiz.

By that time, the inquisitors would be lucky to find Jews or Muslims overtly practicing their faith in the Americas at all, let alone find enough of their neighbors willing to cooperate in the effort to deport them. In short, most were well integrated into the society of New Spain as merchants, bankers, doctors, or community leaders. We cannot be sure how many were of Muslim or Jewish descent, but at least one-third of all of the "Spaniards" emigrating to the Yucatán Peninsula in the first two centuries after 1492 came from families in Andalusia.[15] The Sephardic Jews and Mozarabic Muslims were widely scattered across the Caribbean and the Americas, and some of them were already re-engaged in the trading of spices, herbs, and other flavorings. It is my hypothesis—still no doubt to be tested—that they not only took on pivotal roles in moving chiles, chocolate, and vanilla across the ocean to integrate them into well-established trade routes but also may have captured the processing and trade of these spices among European American populations rather than let them stay under the control of indigenous peoples.

With a few exceptions, such as the trials of Jewish chocolate hedonist Doña Teresa Aguilera y Roche, historical documents from the fifteenth and sixteenth centuries reveal little about the lives of crypto-Jewish and crypto-Muslim merchants or spice traders in the New World.[16] We learn that a group of Jews thought to be conversos settled in Jamaica in 1530, in the harbor first christened Santiago de la Vega and later known as Spanish Town. By the time these traders moved to nearby Port Royal,

FIGURE 20. Cacao plants were successfully introduced to the West Indies at the end of the seventeenth century. This photograph from 1909 shows the processing of the cacao pods. (General Research and Reference Division, Schomburg Center for Research in Black Culture, New York Public Library, Astor, Lenox and Tilden Foundations.)

their community was not only flourishing but Judaism was also clearly being practiced once more. They exported Jamaica's fine allspice berries and moved chiles, cocoa, cochineal, and vanilla from Mexico.[17] They had become multilingual spice merchants just as their Jewish ancestors had been, but they were now plying their trade sixty-eight hundred miles to the west of the Souk al-Attarin in the Old City of Jerusalem.

The demand for vanilla, like chocolate, began to grow beyond its natural range. By 1655, the Jews of Jamaica had a monopoly over the shipping of vanilla to Europe and began to recruit other Jews to obtain either chocolate or vanilla from elsewhere in the Caribbean and from the northeast coast of South America. And so, in late 1658, two conversos, Josua Nuñez Netto and Joseph Pereira, settled in the Dutch plantation colony of Pomeroon, now part of Guyana. They encouraged settlement there by other crypto-Jews, who learned the Arawak dialects of the tribes along the Pomeroon River in order to find out how to extract vanilla from the orchids. One particular Jewish speaker of Arawak, Salomon de la Roche, mastered the entire traditional extraction process by watching his Arawak workers, and then worked with them on innovations that modernized the process to obtain higher yields.

Unlike most of the orchids of commerce, the vanilla orchid (*Vanilla planifolia*) emits a rather slight scent. Nevertheless, the vanillins in its long, thin pods and oily black seeds offer a flavor intensity that rivals that of saffron and an aroma that outdistances that of cardamom in its complexity. The taste of fermented vanilla has been described as sweet, smoky, and caramel-like, though it is so potent and enigmatic that a single drop in a carbonated beverage is sufficient to elevate the name of the drink to "vanilla flavored" and to command a higher price.

The economic value of this tropical vine was well established in the pre-Columbian era of Mesoamerica, with vanilla pods already a recognized form of currency in prehistoric Mexico. The conquistador Hernán Cortés witnessed Aztec rulers demanding vanilla pods as a tax from the Totonac people, who were the primary harvesters of the pods along the Mexican coast of Veracruz. Vanilla vines historically ranged though the wet tropical forest habitats of eastern Mexico, Guatemala, Belize, Honduras, and Costa Rica, but most of these have been logged, fragmented, and degraded over the last three centuries, so much so that wild vanilla orchids are listed as critically endangered. The native bee (*Euglossa viridissima*) that serves as their most allegiant pollinator is also of concern to conservationists.

It was the indigenous people of eastern Mexico rather than those of Central America who initiated the management and harvesting of vanilla orchids and the diffusion of their dried pods to others as a high-value culinary and medicinal product. It appears that the Totonacs were the first to bring this orchid out of the rainforest and cure its pods, calling them *xa'nat*. Their extra-local trade to the Aztecs was facilitated by *pochteca*, long-distance traders and merchants who saw the value in mixing *tlilxochitl* (vanilla) with *kakaw* (chocolate) for a luxurious after-dinner drink enjoyed by the Nahuatl-speaking elite of Tenochitlán.

Not until it arrived in Spain during the reign of Philip II did this spice take on the name *vainilla,* which refers to the slender or diminutive pods (*vainas*) of the orchid. The first written announcement of vanilla released in the Old World described it as a black-flowered orchid. It appeared in a 1651 natural history of herbs that was initiated by the Castilian court physician Francisco Hernández, who had been sent to Mexico to document the local flora, but was written and published by others long after his death. Eight decades after Hernández's visit, a Portuguese Jewish immigrant to what is now Guyana learned the traditional techniques for vanilla harvesting, extraction, and drying from Arawak-speaking natives of the Pomeroon River basin and began to modernize the process for higher yields of better quality. Dried vanilla pods were soon being sent across the Atlantic. For decades, this intercontinental trade was facilitated in part by crypto-Jews in Mexico City, the port of Veracruz, and Port Royal in Jamaica who had retained contacts with Sephardic Jewish refugees in major trading ports in Europe, Asia, and Africa. By the end of the eighteenth century, vanilla and cocoa were regularly being shipped from Mexico and Jamaica to Old World bakers and confectioners.

Given its high value, its habitat specificity, and its rarity, it is no wonder that horticulturists soon endeavored to cultivate vanilla in the Old World. Although live plants were carried from Mesoamerica to European gardens and greenhouses, they did not immediately flower or set seed. It was not until 1806–07 that vanilla vines finally flowered in Charles Grenville's greenhouse in England. This singular event triggered widespread dissemination of his cuttings to other greenhouses, most of them in southern Europe. However, it was the handful of cuttings from Grenville's plants that eventually made it to the island of Réunion that changed the trajectory of vanilla production forever. There, on the plantation of Féréol Bellier-Beaumont in 1841, a slave named Edmond Albius accomplished the first quick, practical means of cross-pollination of vanilla orchids by hand, thus eliminating the need to have *Euglossa* bees present to ensure the fertilization and full development of vanilla pods. By 1898, vanilla production on Réunion and nearby Madagascar and the Comoros Islands had far outstripped that of Mexico, and today there is also cultivation of a distinct vanilla orchid in Tahiti. Although the production of Mexican vanilla continues, the orchids are more likely to be tended by Italian immigrants than native Totonacs. What is harvested in its homeland competes in the global market with the pure vanilla extract from many other tropical nations, as well as with many imitation vanilla flavorings.

Gambrelle, Fabienne. *The Flavor of Spices*. Paris: Flammarion, 2008.
Ecott, Tim. *Vanilla: Travels in Search of the Ice Cream Orchid*. New York: Grove Press, 2004.
Hill, Tony. *The Contemporary Encyclopedia of Herbs and Spices*. Hoboken, NJ: John Wiley and Sons, 2004.
Rain, Patricia. *Vanilla: The Cultural History of the World's Favorite Flavor and Fragrance*. New York: J.P. Tarcher, 2004.

Other multilingual Jews began to move vanilla for de la Roche out of Cayenne (now French Guiana) and Martinique, then on to Jamaica, where it was destined for Jewish traders and confectioners in Amsterdam, Hamburg, Bordeaux, and Bayonne. But so much of the vanilla production for export became dependent on de la Roche that when he died in 1683, vanilla trade nearly came to an end. Fortunately, it was revived by one of his understudies.

At about the same time, another Jew, Benjamin d'Acosta de Andrade, played a similar pivotal role in the cocoa trade.[18] A half century later, yet another Jewish cocoa merchant, Nathan Simpson, regularly moved 150,000 pounds of chocolate through Curaçao every three months. Fluent in Dutch, Hebrew, Portuguese, and Yiddish, Simpson was known to manage twenty-three shipments of spices in and out of Curaçao over a fifteen-month period.[19] Although many of these Jewish traders advanced the globalization of trade in spices of American origin, some of them were also involved in the selling of their harvesters of cocoa or vanilla into slave markets. The cruelty of these traders prompted uprisings among enslaved Africans, who then killed their owners.

As multilingual money changers and maritime merchants, the New World traders coordinated the flow of spices and other flavorings, dyes, and cane sugar from Jamaica, Barbados, Saint Thomas, Veracruz, Mérida, and Curaçao on the western side of the Atlantic with Jews working in Genoa, Venice, Amsterdam, London, Constantinople, and the Indian ports on the Malabar Coast. Jews in Cochin and other Malabar ports would then disperse these same goods farther eastward.

Not all of these shipments were above board. Oral histories passed down among Sephardic Jews hint that many of the items entered Spanish and Portuguese ports hidden among the ballast in the hold of ships returning from the Americas. Once the "official" goods were offloaded and most of the crew had dispersed, the remaining crew members with ties to the Jewish or Muslim merchants moved the secreted goods into the hands of those who could smuggle them across the Strait of Gibraltar to Morocco.[20] We know that chiles made it back to Ceuta by 1514, only about a decade after Columbus's own physician took them to Spain. By 1542, Jewish purveyors of American-grown chiles may have facilitated their trade along Sephardic Jewish shipping routes and Arab camel caravan routes all the way to Goa. Of course, by that time, chiles had arrived there through the hands of the Portuguese.

Old World spices flowed in the opposite direction. Soon, Jamaican and Mexican Jews and Muslims were demanding black pepper, corian-

Although a web-based fable gently jokes that chocolate was discovered by an Arab Muslim scholar named al-Khakolati, it is clear that the cacao tree (*Theobroma cacao*) is native to the Americas. Most wild members of the genus *Theobroma* appear to have evolved in the tropical lowlands of South America, but only *T. cacao* seems to have spread northward, traveling from the Amazon Basin up to and across Central America and into Mexico. Some botanists suggest that the cacao tree arrived in eastern Mexico and adjacent areas of the Yucatán Peninsula on its own; others claim it came through cultural diffusion and was independently domesticated there as well as in South America.

My good friend and fellow ethnobotanist Charles Miksicek identified the oldest wood remains from cacao trees in Mesoamerica at the Cuello site in Belize, where they were estimated to be at least twenty-nine hundred years old. Cacao plant artifacts have also been found among archaeobotanical remains in Honduras that date back to 3100 BCE.

In prehistoric times in South America, the theobromine-rich pulp was made into a fresh, fruity beverage or fermented into a mildly alcoholic one. There, cultivated varieties were initially selected for their edible pulp, while selection for the seeds was stronger in Mesoamerica. Cacao pulp is still used to ferment alcoholic beverages and vinegar in Panama and perhaps in Colombia as well. Depictions of cacao pods on Peruvian pottery vessels have been tentatively identified and dated as being twenty-five hundred years old. Cacao seeds were not used to make caffeinated beverages there, perhaps because other South American beverage plants, such as yerba maté, *guaraná,* and *yoco,* pack a much more potent punch of caffeine.

In contrast, Mesoamericans greatly valued the effects of both the caffeine and theobromine in the seeds of their four prehistoric cacao varieties. The Nahuatl-speaking Mexica tribe also used the larger pods of three of the varieties as a form of currency. After the arrival of Europeans and Africans in Mexico, the two gene pools of cacao were hybridized, so that both the edible pulp and seeds found in cultivated cacao have qualities not found in their wild and semicultivated precursors. Nevertheless, it was the indigenous peoples of Mesoamerica who devised elaborate means of fermenting and extracting chocolate from cacao seeds that underlies how cacao is processed today.

Kakaw, the oldest known term for this plant and its products, appears to have come from the ancient Mixe-Zoque languages now spoken in the Mexican states of Chiapas, Oaxaca, Tabasco, and Veracruz. From there, it diffused into many languages, including those in the Mayan family. *Choko-atl,* the rather problematic Nahuatl term, was not recorded until the sixteenth century and may not have been used in pre-Columbian Mesoamerica at all. It is also unclear when chocolate became one of the signature ingredients in the sauces for meats that evolved into moles, which have peculiarly Old World formulas and ingredients, as discussed elsewhere in this book.

Remarkably, it has been recently confirmed that the Anasazi of Pueblo Bonito at Chaco Canyon, New Mexico, which reached its peak as a trade center between 900 and 1300, were ritually consuming chocolate-based drinks in Mayan-style cylindrical pottery vessels thousands of miles north of where chocolate naturally occurred. That means that chocolate may have entered the cuisines of the southwestern United States by 1000 to 1125, well before the use of domesticated chiles there, which may not have occurred until after 1450.

It appears that once Jews immigrated to Mexico and Central and South America, they quickly understood the medicinal, culinary, and even psychotropic value that chocolate had to offer. By the seventeenth century, Jewish merchants in Mexico and Jamaica were among the primary merchants moving cocoa to other Jewish spice traders in Amsterdam, London, and Lisbon. They also played critical roles in modernizing and diversifying chocolate processing. Among these innovative immigrants was Benjamin d'Acosta de Andrade, a Portuguese-born Jew who founded the first of several chocolate-processing operations on Martinique in the Lesser Antilles in the mid-seventeenth century. Later, in the last decades of the eighteenth century, American Jews such as Aaron Lopez and Levy Solomons, both living in the northeastern United States, developed chocolate processing and trade with Europe's most accomplished confectionaires, many of whom first advanced artistry with chocolate in the Netherlands.

Crown, Patricia L., and W. Jeffrey Hurst. "Evidence of Cacao Use in the Prehispanic American Southwest." Proceedings of the National Academy of Sciences 2009: www.pnas.org_cgi_doi_10.1073_pnas.0812817106.

Grivetti, Louis E., and Howard Yana-Shapiro. Chocolate: History, Culture, and Heritage. New York: Wiley & Sons, 2009.

MacNeil, Cameron L., ed. Chocolate in Mesoamerica: A Cultural History of Cacao. Gainesville: University of Florida Press, 2006.

Minnis, Paul E., and Michael E. Whalen. "The First Prehispanic Chile (Capsicum) from the U.S. Southwest/Northwest Mexico and Its Changing Use." American Antiquity 75 (2009): 245–58.

der, aniseeds, cloves, cinnamon, and sesame, among other items, from across the Atlantic. These were sometimes incorporated into the spice rubs of chile and allspice that Carib- and Taino-speaking natives of the Caribbean used on the fish, fowl, or game they smoked over racks of freshly cut wooden sticks called coa. Once beef, pork, and goat were introduced and prepared in a similar manner, the term *barbacoa* spread throughout the Americas as the name for marinated meats and fish cooked over a wood fire outdoors.[21]

Perhaps the most inspired mixture of New World and Old World spices anywhere on earth is mole, which emerged from the Puebla and Oaxaca regions of Mexico. The best-known version is *mole poblano,* though Oaxacans claim seven equally fine examples. Some food historians have conjectured that this dish originated with the Aztecs, but there is no historical evidence to substantiate the claim.[22]

The term *mole,* however, comes from *molli,* an ancient Nahuatl word that the Aztecs and others used for sauces made by grinding dried spices or mashing fresh chiles and herbs in a small stone mortar. The three-legged stone mortar, or *molcajete* (from the Nahuatl term *mulcazitl*), commonly seen throughout Mexico today dates back at least fifty-five hundred years in the Sierra Madre Oriental range, which runs from the Texas border to the state of Puebla. Just as moles and guacamoles in Puebla and Oaxaca have long been prepared by mashing spices, herbs, or fruits in a *molcajete,* other kinds of moles and *recaudos* have been prepared in a similar fashion on the Yucatán Peninsula. The Yucatecan sauces and marinades typically share one ingredient that hints of a linkage with the *ras el hanout* and *baharat* spice mixtures of al-Andalus and North Africa: the juice of citrus (typically lime or bitter orange) to help "cook" the meat, fish, or fowl to which the spice mixture is applied.

In addition to chiles, the predominant ingredients in traditional moles are largely Old World herbs and spices: almonds, aniseeds, bay leaves, cinnamon, cloves, coriander, cumin, garlic, marjoram, onion, peppercorns, raisins, thyme, sesame seeds, and walnuts. Of course, a number of New World herbs are used in moles as well, such as allspice, avocado leaves, chocolate, epazote, *hoja santa,* peanuts, pecans, and pumpkin or squash seeds, but they are not used in the same pot of mole as their Old World counterparts.[23] As noted by many Mexican food historians, from Sophie and Michael Coe to Rick Bayless, chiles, chocolate, or pumpkin seeds are typically the most conspicuous flavors in any mole. But they appear to be "add-ons" to a mixture of Old World spices that have been used together for more than two millennia, including cumin, coriander, black pepper, cinnamon, garlic, cloves, and sesame seeds.

When I began to structurally compare the moles and *recaudos* of Mexico with the more ancient *ras el hanout* and other *baharat*-style spice mixtures of North Africa and the Middle East, I immediately noticed that they all share several key elements. First, each has one

❧ POLLO EN MOLE VERDE DE PEPITA ❧
Spiced Chicken in Green Pumpkin Seed Sauce

Compare this recipe with the Moroccan-spiced chicken in almond sauce on page 223 and you will see the continuity among complex Moroccan, Andalusian, and Mexican sauces. It is true, as Diana Kennedy reminds us, that prior to the arrival of the Spanish, various Mayan communities were harvesting squashes and pumpkins for their seeds, which they mixed with chiles, tomatoes, and herbs to flavor stews made with turkey. But there is surely something that echoes Berber sensibilities in the mixture of spices found in some of the *mole pipián* versions prepared in the states of Puebla and Michoacán, or in *mole verde de pepita*, as it is called in Oaxaca. Substitute almonds for the pumpkin seeds and chicken for turkey or duck and you have something that looks very much like the savory *tagine* or *gdra* pot stews of Fez or Marrakech. I prefer the white seeds of green-striped cushaw squashes over the seeds of true pumpkins. Cushaws are grown as much for the meatiness of their seeds as for their dense, yellow flesh.

As a side dish, prepare a quickly sautéed succotash with fresh baby lima beans, diced red bell pepper, pearl onions, cubed summer squashes such as pattypan or zucchini, and corn kernels freshly cut from the cob. *Serves 4 to 6.*

- 6 boneless chicken thighs, about 2 pounds, cut into 2-inch pieces
- 1 large white onion, thickly sliced
- 5 small cloves garlic, chopped, plus 5 small whole cloves
- 2 bay leaves
- 1 teaspoon dried Mexican oregano or thyme
  Sea salt
- 4 cups chicken broth
- 1½ cups raw cushaw squash or pumpkin seeds
- 4 serrano or jalapeño chiles, coarsely chopped
- 10 tomatillos, husks removed, rinsed, and quartered
- 8 fresh *hoja santa* or avocado leaves, coarsely chopped or torn
- 3 tablespoons freshly ground cumin seeds
- 4 whole cloves, ground
- 4 allspice berries, ground
- 6 black peppercorns, ground
- 4 leafy sprigs fresh epazote, chopped
- 1 small bunch fresh flat-leaf parsley, chopped
- 1 cup hot water

6   tablespoons *masa harina*
2   tablespoons lard or sunflower oil

In a large pot, combine the chicken pieces, half of the onion, the chopped garlic, the bay leaves, the oregano, a pinch of salt, and the broth. Place over medium heat and bring to a simmer. Cook until the chicken is cooked through and tender, about 10 minutes.

Using a slotted spoon, transfer the chicken pieces to a plate and set aside. Strain the broth through a fine-mesh sieve and discard the solids. Reserve the broth. You should have about 3½ cups.

To toast the squash seeds, place a dry heavy frying pan over medium heat. Add the seeds and toast, stirring often to prevent scorching, until they are golden and you hear them pop, about 5 minutes. Transfer the seeds to a paper towel and let cool. Set aside ½ cup of the seeds for garnish.

In a blender or food processor, combine the remaining 1 cup cooled squash seeds, the remaining onion, the chiles, tomatillos, whole garlic cloves, *hoja santa,* cumin, cloves, allspice, pepper, epazote, and parsley. In a bowl, stir together the hot water and *masa harina* until a smooth paste forms, then add to the reserved broth. Add 1½ cups of the broth to the blender and blend until a smooth puree forms.

In a large, heavy saucepan, heat the lard over medium-high heat. Pour in the squash seed puree, bring to a simmer, and cook, stirring constantly, until thickened, about 10 minutes. Stir in 2 more cups of the broth and simmer until the mixture begins to thicken again, another 20 minutes.

Return the puree to the blender, let cool slightly, then blend until it is once again smooth. Return the puree to the pan, add the reserved chicken, and season with salt. Place over medium heat, bring to a simmer, adjust the heat to maintain a gentle simmer, and cook until the chicken is well coated with the sauce, 5 to 10 minutes.

Using a slotted spoon, transfer the chicken pieces to a platter, then ladle the sauce over the chicken. Decorate with the reserved squash seeds and serve.

Bayless, Rick, with Deann Groen Bayless and Jean Marie Brownson. *Rick Bayless's Mexican Kitchen: Capturing the Vibrant Flavors of a World-Class Cuisine.* New York: Scribner, 1996, p. 276 and pp. 316–17.
Kennedy, Diana. *The Art of Mexican Cooking.* New York: Bantam Books, 1989, pp. 226–27.
———. *The Cuisines of Mexico.* New York: Harper & Row, 1982, pp. 204–6.

ingredient that offers brilliant color as well as flavor. In the Old World, this is typically turmeric or saffron, and in the New World it might be chocolate, chile, achiote, or pumpkin seeds. Second, all of them have an oily matrix, shaped by sesame seeds, almonds, walnuts, pistachios or olive oil from the Old World, or by peanuts, chocolate, or pumpkin or squash seeds from the New World. Third, they share a truly "biting" peak flavor, whether from black pepper, Sichuan pepper, melegueta pepper, ginger, or chile. All of them also have undertones of warm savory herbs and spices, such as allspice, cassia, cloves, cinnamon, coriander, epazote, and oregano, that harmonize the entire mixture. And finally, in the aftermath of the Columbian Exchange, nearly all of these Mesoamerican "spice composites" carry the currents of onions, garlic, chives, or shallots from the Old World in their streams of flavors. All in all, these foods are straightforward indicators of a culinary imperialism and gastronomic globalization of major proportions. Blood, tears, and trauma are hidden within their legacy of flavors.

I once had a chance to spend time among Mexican cooks as they prepared their homemade sauces and home brews for the Feria Nacional de Mole, held that summer in the Nahuatl-speaking village of San Pedro Atócpan, high above Mexico City. Around the fairgrounds, maize and amaranth were flowering in the nearby milpas, and on the edges of the fields, giant prickly pears and enormous agaves lined the stone terrace walls. Elderly women meandered down the rows of agaves and gathered their sap, known as *aguamiel,* just as New Englanders might tap the sap of maple trees for making syrup. I followed them back to their field houses and watched as they prepared the *aguamiel* for selling at the fair. Their product was not some sugary syrup sold in jars, but the fermented beverage known as pulque, which they flavored with herbs or fruits.

I helped them carry their pots and vats over to the fairgrounds. We arrived just as the booths and tents had been set up and the ollas of *mole poblano, mole pipián,* and a dozen other variants had been set atop wood fires. Next to them, ollas filled with purple *ayocote* (runner) beans flavored with epazote and cumin simmered over the same fires. Many of the mole pots had chickens embedded in their thick, savory sauces, while others had turkey meat from heritage breeds soaking up the flavors of a heady mix of herbs and spices.

I wandered around with a small notebook, trying to record all of the variations in mole making, not only the ingredients themselves but also the various sequences in which they are combined. As I interviewed some of the best home-style cooks from all over southern Mexico, their husbands would hand me clay cups filled with pulque, then tip their hats and urge me to drink.

As I slowly became inebriated from drinking cup after cup of the viscous, mildly alcoholic brew, I desperately tried to tally up all of the spices and chile varieties that I had recorded. My list grew longer and gradually less intelligible. At one point, I looked down at my notebook, now stained and smeared with mole sauce, and realized I could no longer read any of what I had written. So I gave up on the research and just stayed around for another two hours, savoring sips of mole sauce and consuming beans with tortillas to try to counteract the buzz from the pulque and the pungency of what I was eating.

Near sundown, as I stood before the only pot of *mole poblano* that I had yet to sample, I realized that the history of mole could not be written, because it could only be known through the mouth and the nose, the lips and the tongue. It no longer mattered to me whether the first recorded making of mole was in the seventeenth century when it was prepared for the visit of an archbishop to the Santa Rosa convent in Puebla or for the arrival of some government dignitary to the same city.

I no longer worried whether mole was invented by Sister Andrea, or by Brother Pascual, whose sous chefs accidentally spilled all of the spices into an open *cazuela* when a windstorm wreaked havoc in their outdoor kitchen. (*Cazuela*, I did remember, was from the Arabic *qasūla*.)[24] All of those legends of local origin suddenly seemed equally apocryphal and completely irrelevant. What mattered was whether the spices themselves in each pot of mole could speak to me, hinting of the many places and cultures from which they have historically derived.

With my eyes half shut from the warm light of sundown and the prolonged effects of the pulque, I tasted one last spoonful of mole. It began to whisper a litany of places and spices: allspice from Jamaica, aniseeds from Syria, chiles from Puebla and Oaxaca, chocolate from the lowlands of Mexico and from Brazil, cloves from the Moluccas, cinnamon from Sri Lanka, coriander from Egypt and Sudan, onions from China, peanuts from the Brazilian Amazon, and sesame seeds from India.[25]

Long ago, some exiled Muslim and Jewish traders had brought a near-complete world of flavors and fragrances with them to the highlands of Mexico, where they encountered a few others that made perfect complements to their treasure trove of fragrances. The descendants of the Aztecs liked what they smelled and tasted. In fact, they liked them so much that they made them their own.

Epilogue

Culinary Imperialism and Its Alternatives

At first glance, the political ecology of the spice trade today seems far different from what it was during other eras over the last four millennia. As I write this, the economic downturns in southern Europe and the United States have dovetailed, and China seems to be ascending as a global economic power once again. Nations in North Africa and in parts of the Middle East are struggling to see what "season" may follow the Arab Spring. And although both business acumen and wealth are well represented in the Middle East, neither Israel nor any single Arab country appears to be *the* galvanizing power in the world of trade, in the same way that communities of Jews and Muslims once were. The richest man in the world today, Carlos Slim Haddad Helú, is of Lebanese descent but was born in Mexico, and is apparently not descended directly from Phoenician or Karimi traders.

Despite the resurgence of piracy on the open sea, most spices move between continents by ship, or across a continent by rail or road. Camels can still be seen browsing along the edges of desert highways from the Gobi to the Sahara but are seldom used for the transport of spices, except between remote gathering grounds and the desert oases where the goods are loaded on trucks. The movements of these cargo-carrying vehicles are now tracked by global positioning systems and instantly mapped on computers. Any potential difficulties with meeting the anticipated date of arrival for delivery are quickly communicated by e-mail or text message. If a ship, train, or truck is targeted by a suicide bomber who blows himself or herself up and snuffs out the lives of innocent contemporary spice traders in the blast, people of a half dozen faiths in some sixty to one hundred countries almost instantly hear of the destruction.

But wherever we are on this planet, whether we are devout believers in a specific faith or remain faithless, and whether we are engaged in business or stuck in a homeless shelter, we breathe the vapors of globalization and culinary imperialism nearly every waking moment of our lives. These vapor trails are in the air all around us and began to develop long before the industrial revolution, with the burning of incense in a desert cave some four thousand years ago. And while camel caravans no longer transport cumin and dhows no longer carry cloves, nutmeg, and mace, we are still benefiting from—and beleaguered by—the processes of gastronomic globalization first elaborated by Minaeans, Nabataeans, Arabs, Jews, Phoenicians, Persians, and others from the backs of camels or the decks of dhows.

This book has been a long and winding road that takes us back to the roots of globalization—roots that were put down more than three millennia before the era that fine scholars such as Charles C. Mann and Felipe Fernández-Armesto claim was the onset of the globalized, capitalized world that we know today. But that world clearly did not "begin" around 1492, nor did the processes of ecological imperialism made famous by Alfred Crosby as the Columbian Exchange. If this wayward journey chronicles anything, it is that both the virtuous and scandalous processes that we now refer to as globalization emerged centuries and millennia before the so-called Age of Discovery, whose recorded heroes, Christopher Columbus and Vasco da Gama, simply borrowed on the capital assets generated by Sephardic Jews and Arab Muslims over many centuries before these famed navigators went to sea.

Many of the socioeconomic processes and biocultural behaviors that we now associate with globalization were field-tested by desert-dwelling Semitic cultures that pioneered the ancient human pursuit we now call the spice trade. Certainly, other cultures contributed significantly to the globalization process, from Greeks, Romans, Egyptian Berbers, and Han Chinese to Sogdians, Persians, Venetians, Turks, Ethiopians, Armenians, Portuguese, Dutch, and Mayans. But what Mann, Crosby, and Fernández-Armesto view as a new beginning was actually just an extension of gastronomic globalization through spice trade to two additional continents—an effort that utilized the same cultural, economic, and ecological processes that had been employed on other continents

❧ PREHISTORIC MANSAF ❧
Kid and Lamb Stew with Yogurt, Root Crops, and Herbs

At the end of this book, I thought it appropriate to return to the oldest recorded recipes in the world, written in Akkadian cuneiform script on Mesopotamian clay tablets that are reputedly thirty-seven hundred years old. It reminds us that however far we have "progressed," there remains a lamb stew found in both Mongolia and northern Mexico. This recipe is adapted from one of these tablets and may be the precursor of the Bedouin stew called *mansaf,* still popular in Jordanian and Palestinian kitchens. The Arabic term *mansaf* connotes "an explosion" of flavors. As my friend Cecil Hourani has eloquently stated, "*Mansaf* is the national dish of Jordan because it represents the culinary fusion of Bedouin and village cooking, which is the defining characteristic of the traditional Jordanian kitchen."

Archaeologist Jean Bottéro made the initial effort to give these ancient dishes a cultural context within Middle Eastern culinary traditions. More recently, Laura Kelley has done linguistic detective work to identify some of the plant ingredients in them. This particular recipe reveals considerable sophistication in combining meats, vegetables, nuts, fermented dairy products, and spices during the era that Arab traders first came out of the peninsula to Asia Minor. In particular, it uses dehydrated, defatted goat's milk yogurt, which is fermented in goatskin and then reconstituted with water to make *jamīd makhīd,* a yogurt sauce. The sauce is seasoned with *baharat,* a spice mix that combines cumin, turmeric, cinnamon, and saffron with other spices in a manner that varies from household to household. The dish is typically topped with chopped fresh greens. Today, it is served atop flat bread, rice, bulgur, or couscous. Reconstructing this dish in an urban American kitchen may be tough, given that blood from a kid goat and yogurt dehydrated in goatskin are not easy to find. Nevertheless, goats do abound in parts of the country, so sourcing the ingredients could lead to new adventures.

Serve with cold glasses of arak mixed with water and with cold fresh figs. *Serves 6–8.*

2½   pounds bone-in kid goat, cut into 2-inch pieces

2   pounds bone-in leg of lamb or young ewe, boned, trimmed of excess fat, and cut into 2-inch cubes, with bone reserved

3   quarts plus 1 or 2 cups water

1   cup rendered lamb fat or clarified butter

2   Egyptian walking onions, peeled but left whole

1   head garlic, peeled but left whole

1   cup semolina flour

2   cups dehydrated defatted goat's milk yogurt, or 3 cups Greek yogurt

1 teaspoon freshly ground cumin

1 teaspoon ground turmeric or saffron threads, or a mixture

1 teaspoon freshly ground cassia cinnamon

1 teaspoon sea salt

½ cup goat's blood (or 1 tablespoon cornstarch or 1¾ teaspoons arrow-root mixed with ½ cup cold water to make a slurry)

2 or 3 parsnips, lotus roots, turnips, or red carrots, peeled and sliced

Handful of watercress, chopped

Handful of fresh anise or fennel leaves, minced

1 cup pine nuts, toasted

6 pieces flat bread such as pita, *marquq,* or *saj*

Put the goat and lamb pieces in a large pot, add the lamb bone, then pour in 3 quarts of the water. Place over high heat and bring to a boil, skimming off any foam that forms on the surface. Add the lamb fat and turn down the heat to low. Place the onions and garlic on a piece of cheesecloth, bring the corners together, and tie securely with kitchen string. Add the onion bundle to the pot along with the semolina flour and stir well to dissolve the flour. Bring to a simmer and cook, stirring occasionally, until the liquid begins to thicken, about 20 minutes.

Meanwhile, if using the dehydrated yogurt, in a saucepan, combine the yogurt with the remaining 2 cups water over low heat and heat, stirring, until loosened and gently combined. Remove from the heat and reserve. If using the Greek yogurt, spoon it into a bowl, add only 1 cup water, and stir until combined.

To make the *baharat* spice mix, combine the cumin, turmeric, cinnamon, and salt and stir well. Set aside.

Remove and discard the lamb bone. Add the blood or the cornstarch slurry, the reconstituted yogurt, the parsnips, and the spice mix to the meat, stir well, and simmer over low heat, stirring occasionally, until the meat is tender and the mixture has thickened, about 1 hour. Retrieve the cheesecloth bundle from the pot and discard.

To serve, transfer the stew to a large, deep platter or a shallow bowl and garnish with the watercress, anise leaves, and pine nuts. Pass the flat bread at the table.

Bottéro, Jean. *The Oldest Cuisine in the World: Cooking in Mesopotamia.* Chicago: University of Chicago Press, 2004.

Hourani, Cecil. *Jordan: The Land and the Table.* London: Elliot & Thompson, 2006, p. 77.

Kelley, Laura. "Some Mesopotamian Ingredients Revealed." *Silk Road Gourmet,* March 16, 2010. www.silkroadgourmet.com/some-mesopotamian-ingredients-revealed.

in earlier times. Yes, completely new species such as chiles, chocolate, vanilla, and allspice were brought into the warehouses, and entire landscapes were made over as Eurasian and African crops and weeds entered American landscapes. But similar environmental and nutritional impacts had occurred in the past, as traders intentionally and accidentally made their mark on other cultures, cuisines, and biotic communities.

There were winners and losers wherever that trade extended. For many centuries, the winners were the branches of the Semitic language family known to us as Arabs, Jews, Phoenicians, Nabataeans, and Minaeans, for these cultures played disproportionately large roles in managing and controlling trade in aromatics. Of the more than sixty-eight hundred linguistically encoded cultural world views that have emerged on this planet, why have only a handful enabled and driven the trajectory of the worldwide spice trade? Or, why have the three monotheistic faiths of Judaism, Christianity, and Islam played such dominant roles in cultural, ecological, and culinary imperialism? I have no answer to these crucial questions and I believe that it will take a long time and many minds to resolve them. But one tenet in which I do believe is that this trio of monotheistic religions and our modern economic structures emerged from the same ideologies, and that even today, they are not that far removed from one another.

Curiously, it was risk-taking desert peoples who first actively played their hands in the global gamble to move aromatics from sparsely populated and vegetated hinterlands into cities of splendor and wealth. They magnified and mythologized the value of lightweight incense, dried herbs, powdered spices, and musk through their fantastic stories, perhaps because they had so few other resources to rely on. In doing so, they became less dependent on *place*—that is, they no longer relied on the sacredness of particular ancestral landscapes or on the mores of national sovereignty and rooted faith. It is not to say that they were free of nostalgic-filled yearnings to visit Jerusalem, Bethlehem, Mecca, or Medina. But their very identity and their sense of the sacredness of place were no longer tethered to living in a specific locale.

Today, climate change is making a larger proportion of humankind into desert peoples, and geopolitical conflicts are making more of us into diaspora peoples. But, as in the past, we tend to ignore the lessons of history by insisting that the future will be a game changer—a new normal where the old rules will no longer apply. Moral threads continue to weave their way back through the centuries of trading spices, however, and the more that we try to pretend that we are freeing ourselves from what has gone before, the more obvious it becomes that we are destined to be stuck dealing with the very same ecological and social consequences that have dominated past human actions.

The ethical debate about the benefits and negative consequences of globalization no doubt began in the first communities that struggled to deal with the onslaught of goods from someplace else and the risks they posed to local economies and ecologies. These imported goods and the Faustian bargains negotiated to obtain them were likely seen as threats to what was intrinsically unique to the cultures and the places.

To paraphrase the late great poet John Hay, the entire sweep of human history can be summarized this way: we are making one place just like every other. The culinary correlate is how the fusion cuisines of wraps replacing tortillas, chapatis, and pitas have tended to make one fast-food meal more or less like every other.

My friend Woody Tasch, founder of the Slow Money movement, reminds us that many thresholds are crossed in the ever more entangled processes of the globalization of capital, culture, and cuisines, not merely those that occurred during the thirty centuries prior to 1492 that I have traveled in this book:

> Every 200 years or so, it seems, we arrive at a threshold moment in the history of capital and culture. In 1600, two men in Amsterdam stood on a bridge over a canal, designing the joint stock company, minimizing risk to capital, and galvanizing the flow of investment in exploration, conquest, and export. . . . In 1800, two men in New Amsterdam stood under a tree on the cow path that would become Wall Street, designing a stock exchange that would create hitherto unknown degrees of financial liquidity and, so, galvanize the flow of capital in support of exploration, extraction, and manufacture. . . . In 2000, we are entering a period of urgent postindustrial, post-Malthusian reassessment and reconnoitering. We find ourselves on a new threshold, signals of systemic unsustainability proliferating alongside those of ever accelerating capital markets and technological innovation. . . . It falls on us to undertake a new project of system design: the creation of new forms of intermediation that catalyze the transition from a commerce of extraction and consumption to a commerce of preservation and restoration.[1]

What Woody Tasch and many others suggest is that this moment cannot be one in which we fold our hand, throw in our cards, and succumb to the fatalistic notion that globalization is an inexorable process that no single individual or organization can either halt or even redirect. There remain many ways that we can collectively shift globalization's trajectory in another direction, to not only make it humane but also more responsive to the needs of many cultures. One of those ways is to rethink and redesign the forms of intermediation that spice traders and their kindred spirits have played out in societies for thousands of years. As Slow Food founder Carlo Petrini has said, we must imagine a more virtuous form of globalization in which "there's a just and true commerce to help small farmers,"[2] spice and incense foragers, and fishers and ranchers, instead of the brokers of commerce exacting such high prices from producers. We must pursue it with the discipline, tenacity, and moral courage shown by characters such as Zheng He, Ziryab, Gracia Nasi, and Ibn Battuta. We must track its scent as faithfully and ferociously as a dog with a bone.

We must wake up and smell the incense—the kind that pervades the air where we live, among those for whom we care.

Acknowledgments

First and foremost, I wish to thank my daughter, Laura Rose, and my wife, Laurie Monti, not only for engaging with me in the fieldwork for this book but also for adding their insights and perspectives to the endeavor. Laura Rose accomplished her own fieldwork on Lebanese and Arab influences in the Yucatán Peninsula, guided me around Mérida, and accompanied me to Lebanon and Egypt. Laurie traveled with me to western and coastal China, Kazakhstan, Tajikistan, Lebanon, Oman, Egypt, Italy, and Spain, paying particular attention to aromatics with both medicinal and culinary uses. I admire them for their unflagging curiosity about the world, for their superb language abilities, and for their tenacity when traveling under tough desert conditions. In addition, my greatest mentor, Agnese Haury of Tucson, Arizona, a Near Eastern studies scholar and human rights activist, provided countless observations, references, leads, and resources that helped push this project toward fruition. I will be forever grateful to these three women, who deserve unparalleled recognition for their contributions.

Near Eastern geographer Michael Bonine, who recently passed away, encouraged and informed me in innumerable ways over the last three decades. I am also indebted to Juan Estevan Arellano, the remarkable historian and farmer of Rio Arriba in New Mexico, for inspiring this journey with his own remarkable scholarship. And thanks to my longtime friend and editor Blake Edgar, who offered encouragement and ideas from the start, but then patiently waited for the strands to be woven together into a cohesive story. No press in the world has done as much to help us understand the history of spices and their cultural contexts as the University of California Press. It is an honor to be part of its community of writers and photographers. Special thanks to extraordinary editors Dore Brown and Sharon Silva for their insights as well.

Some others who journeyed with me not only joined in the fieldwork but also offered travel support. In particular, I wish to thank Diane Christensen and Dr. Ken Wilson of the Christensen Fund of San Francisco, Chris Merrill of the International Writing Program at the University of Iowa, Kareema Daoud Akguc of the United States Embassy cultural programs in the Middle East, and Dr. Emile Frison, director general of Bioversity International in Rome. Many others accompanied me on portions of my journeys through souks and spice-growing areas, including Jesse Watson of the University of California at Berkeley; Dr. Sulaiman Al-Khanjari of the University of Nizwa in Oman; Ali Masoud Al-Subhi of Sultan Qaboos University in Oman; David Cavagnaro of the Seed Savers Exchange; Father David Denny of the Desert Foundation; Ogonazar Aknazarov of the Desert Research Institute of Tajikistan; Karim-Aly Kassam of Cornell University; Kraig Kraf, formerly with the University of California at Davis, now with The Nature Conservancy in Nicaragua; chef Kurt Friese of *Edible Iowa River Valley;* Shibley, Norman, and Douglas Nabhan; and Rafael, Kanin, and Cody Routson. I have been particularly influenced by the works of Mohamud Haji Farah, my colleague at the University of Arizona, as well as by Gene Anderson, Tomás Atencio, Michael Krondl, Stanley Hordes, Clifford Wright, Gernot Katzer, Rick Bayless, Diana Kennedy, Lilia Zaouali, Charles Perry, Paul Buell, Jesus Garcia, Enrique Lamadrid, chef Moshe Basson, Abbie Rosner, chef Ana Sortun, Cecil Hourani, Janet Liebman Jacobs, and my dear friend and traveling companion, the late Jean Andrews.

I have been blessed with generous support over the years from the Agnese Haury Fund at the Southwest Center, the W.K. Kellogg Foundation, the Christensen Fund, the CS Fund, and projects or residencies associated with Slow Food International, the International Writing Program at the University of Iowa, and the United States Embassy cultural and scientific exchange program for Palestine. I thank them all for their work and their generosity.

No spice plants were injured in the making of this story.

Notes

INTRODUCTION

1. Charles C. Mann, "The Dawn of the Homogenocene: Tracing Globalization Back to Its Roots," *Orion* magazine 30 (May/June 2011): 16–25.

2. Alfred W. Crosby, *The Columbian Exchange: Biological and Cultural Consequences of 1492* (Westport, CT: Greenwood Press, 1973), and *Ecological Imperialism: The Biological Expansion of Europe, 900–1900* (New York: Cambridge University Press, 1986).

3. Gary Paul Nabhan, *Arab/American: Landscape, Culture, and Cuisines in Two Great Deserts* (Tucson: University of Arizona Press, 2008), 32.

4. Felipe Fernández-Armesto, *1492: The Year Our World Began* (London: Bloomsbury Books, 2009).

5. William J. Bernstein, *A Splendid Exchange: How Trade Shaped The World from Prehistory to Today* (New York: Atlantic Monthly Press, 2008); see pp. 20–21 for copper, pp. 58–59 for spice and incense.

6. Walter W. Skeat, *An Etymological Dictionary of the English Language* (Oxford: Oxford University Press/Clarendon Press, 1946).

7. Adina Hoffman and Peter Cole, *Sacred Trash: The Lost and Found World of the Cairo Geniza* (New York: Nextbook Schocken, 2011).

8. Paul D. Buell and Eugene N. Anderson, eds., A *Soup for the Qan: Chinese Dietary Medicine of the Mongol Era as Seen in Hu Szu-Hui's Yin-Shan Cheng-yao* (London and New York: Kegan Paul International, 2000).

9. Cleofas M. Jaramillo, *New Mexico Tasty Recipes* (Layton, UT: Gibbs Smith, 2008).

10. Stanley Hordes, *To the End of the Earth: A History of the Crypto-Jews of New Mexico* (New York: Columbia University Press, 2005).

11. Darío Fernández-Morera, "The Myth of the Andalusian Paradise," *The Intercollegiate Review* 41, no. 2 (Fall 2006): 23–31.

1. AROMAS EMANATING FROM THE DRIEST OF PLACES

1. Herodotus, in George Rawlinson, *Histories* (London: Wordsworth Classics, 1996), bk. 1, chap. 17.

2. Gary Paul Nabhan, *Desert Terroir: Exploring the Unique Flavors and Sundry Places of the Borderlands* (Austin: University of Texas Press, 2011).

3. Lilia Zaouali, *Medieval Cuisine of the Islamic World: A Concise History with 174 Recipes*, trans. M.B. DeBevoise (Berkeley: University of California Press, 2007), 145.

4. Beta diversity is the rate at which species accumulate as a plant or animal collector moves in a straight line away from any particular point. See Michael L. Rosenzweig, *Species Diversity in Space and Time* (New York: Cambridge University Press, 1995), 33.

5. Anya H. King, "The Musk Trade and the Near East in the Early Medieval Period" (PhD diss., Bloomington: Indiana University, 2007).

6. Patricia Crone, *Mecca Trade and the Rise of Islam* (Princeton, NJ: Princeton University Press, 1987).

7. Francesco di Balduccio Pegolotti, "The Practice of Commerce," trans. from Italian, in *Medieval Trade in the Mediterranean World: Illustrative Documents*, ed. Robert S. Lopez and Irving W. Raymond (New York: Columbia University Press, 2001), 109–14.

8. Pliny the Elder, *Natural History*, trans. H. Rackham (Cambridge, MA: Harvard University Press/Loeb Classic Library, 1942), vol. 10, bk. 43, p. 64.

9. Mohamud Haji Farah, "Non-Timber Forest Product (NTFP) Extraction in Arid Environments: Land-Use Change, Frankincense Production and the Sustainability of *Boswellia sacra* in Dhofar (Oman)" (PhD diss., University of Arizona, 2008), 45.

10. Ibid., 45–46.

11. Gary Paul Nabhan, *Singing the Turtles to Sea: The Comcaác (Seri) Art and Science of Reptiles* (Berkeley: University of California Press, 2003).

12. William J. Bernstein, *A Splendid Exchange: How Trade Shaped the World from Prehistory to Today* (New York: Atlantic Monthly Press, 2008), 53; and R.P. Evershed, P. F. van Bergen, T.M. Peakman, E.C. Leigh-Firbank, M.C. Horton, D. Edwards, M. Biddle, B. Kjølbye-Biddle, and P.A. Rowley-Conwy, "Archaeological Frankincense," *Nature* 390 (December 18, 1997): 667–68.

13. James P. Mandaville, *Bedouin Ethnobotany: Plant Concepts and Uses in a Desert Pastoral World* (Tucson: University of Arizona Press, 2011).

14. Lamees Abdullah Al Taie, *Al-Azaf: The Omani Cookbook* (Muscat: Oman Bookshop, 1995).

15. Caroline Singer, "The Incense Kingdoms of Yemen: An Outline History of the Southern Arabian Spice Trade," in *Food for the Gods: New Light on the Ancient Incense Trade*, ed. David Peacock and David Williams (Oxford, UK: Oxbow Books, 2007), 20–21; and Bernstein, *A Splendid Exchange*, 62–64.

16. Hilde Gauthier-Pilters and Anne Innis Dagg, *The Camel: Its Evolution, Ecology, Behavior, and Relationship to Man* (Chicago: University of Chicago Press, 1981).

2. CARAVANS LEAVING ARABIA FELIX

1. Peter Matthiessen, *The Tree Where Man Was Born* (New York: Collins / Picador, 1972).

2. "Land of Frankincense," UNESCO, whc.unesco.org/list/1010/; and "Al Baleed 2009," Lilian and Jan Schreurs, www.home.kpn.nl/~janm_schreurs/AlBaleed.htm. Both accessed April 21, 2011.

3. George Fadlo Hourani, *Arab Seafaring in the Indian Ocean in Ancient and Early Medieval Times* (Beirut, Lebanon: Khayats, 1963), 6.

4. William J. Bernstein, *A Splendid Exchange: How Trade Shaped the World from Prehistory to Today* (New York: Atlantic Monthly Press, 2008), 26–28.

5. Stelios Michalopoulus, Alireza Naghavi, and Giovanni Prarolo, "Trade and Geography in the Economic Origins of Islam: Theory and Evidence," Working Papers 700, Department of Economics (Bologna, Italy: University of Bologna, 2010), www.feem.it/userfiles/attach/2010631044NDL2010–075.pdf.

6. Hourani, *Arab Seafaring*, 4–5.

7. Paul Shepard, *Nature and Madness* (San Francisco: Sierra Club Books, 1982), 51.

8. Abraham Joshua Heschel, *The Sabbath: Its Meaning for Modern Man* (New York: Farrar, Strauss and Young, 1951), 4 and 16.

9. Patricia Crone, *Mecca Trade and the Rise of Islam* (Princeton, NJ: Princeton University Press, 1987).

10. Caroline Singer, "The Incense Kingdoms of Yemen: An Outline History of the South Arabian Spice Trade," in *Food for the Gods: New Light on the Ancient Incense Trade*, ed. David Peacock and David Williams (Oxford, UK: Oxbow Books, 2007), 12–13.

11. Ibid., 11.

12. Vicenzo M. Francaviglia, "Dating the Ancient Dam of Mar'ib (Yemen)," *Journal of Archaeological Science* 27, no. 7 (July 2000): 645–53.

13. Ibid.

14. Albert Hourani, *A History of the Arab Peoples* (Cambridge, MA: Harvard University Press, 2010).

15. John Noble Wilford, "Ruins in Yemeni Desert Mark Route of Frankincense Trade," *New York Times*, January 28, 1997.

3. UNCOVERING HIDDEN OUTPOSTS IN THE DESERT

1. Berta Segall, "The Lion-riders from Timna," in *Archaeological Discoveries in Southern Arabia,* ed. Richard LeBaron Bowen and Frank P. Albright (Baltimore: Johns Hopkins Press, 1958), 155–75.

2. John Lloyd Stephens, *Incidents of Travel in Egypt, Arabia, Petræa, and the Holy Land* (New York: Harper and Brothers, 1837), 241.

3. Ezra Marcus, "Early Seafaring and Maritime Activity in the Southern Levant from Prehistory through the Third Millennium BCE," in *Egypt and the Levant: Interrelations from the 4th through the Early 3rd Millennium B.C.E.,* ed. Edwin C.M. van den Brink and Thomas Evan Levy (London: Leicester University Press, 2002), 403–17.

4. Jane Hornblower, *Hieronymus of Cardia* (Oxford: Oxford University Press, 1981).

5. Stanley Mayer Burstein, ed., *Agatharchides of Cnidus on "the Erythraean Sea,"* Hakluyt Publications, 2nd ser. (London: Hakluyt Society, 1989), 172.

6. Ofra Rimon, preface to *The Nabateans in the Negev,* by Renate Rosenthal-Heginbottom et al. (Haifa: Hecht Museum, 2003). Exhibition catalog.

7. Charles Perry, foreword to *Medieval Cuisine of the Islamic World: A Concise History with 174 Recipes,* by Lilia Zaouali, trans. M.B. DeBevoise (Berkeley: University of California Press, 2007), xi.

8. Diodorus Siculus, *Library of History,* bk.2, trans. Charles Henry Oldfather (Cambridge, MA: Harvard University Press, 1935).

9. Walter M. Weiss and Kurt-Michael Westermann, *The Bazaar: Markets and Merchants of the Islamic World* (London: Thames and Hudson, 1998), 27.

10. Herodotus, cited in Andrew Dalby, *Dangerous Tastes: The Story of Spices* (Berkeley: University of California Press, 2002), 113.

11. Nelson Glueck, *Rivers in the Desert: A History of the Negev* (London: Weidenfeld and Nicolson, 1959).

12. Stephens, *Incidents of Travel in Egypt, Arabia, Petræa, and the Holy Land,* 237.

13. Michael Evenari, Leslie Shanan, and Napthali Tadmor, *The Negev: The Challenge of a Desert,* 2nd ed. (Cambridge, MA: Harvard University Press, 1982), 23.

14. Douglas Comer, "Monumental Tether: Why Nomads Built Petra, One of the Greatest Monuments in the World," unpublished manuscript cited in Douglas C. Comer, ed., *Tourism and Archaeological Heritage Management at Petra: Driver to Development or Destruction?* (New York: Springer, 2013).

15. Charles Perry, foreword to *Medieval Cuisine of the Islamic World,* xi.

16. Chris Arsenault, "Glencore: Profiteering from Hunger and Chaos," *Al-Jazeera News,* May 9, 2011, www.aljazeera.com/indepth/features/2011/05/2011572314985212o.html.

17. Edward Henry Palmer, *The Desert of the Exodus: Journeys on Foot in the Wilderness of the Forty Years' Wanderings* (Cambridge, UK: Cambridge University Press, 1871).

18. Nelson Glueck, *Rivers in the Desert* (London: Weidenfeld and Nicholson, 1959).

19. Berel Aisenstein, "The 'Kahrez,' An Ancient System of Artificial Springs," *Journal of the Association of Engineers and Architects of Palestine* 8, no. 5 (1947).

20. Evenari, Shanan, and Tadmor, *The Negev,* 178.

21. Jack D. Elliot Jr., "The Nabatean Synthesis of Avraham Negev: A Critical Appraisal," in *Retrieving the Past: Essays on Archaeological Research and Methodology in Honor of Gus. W. Van Beek,* ed. Joe D. Seger (Winona Lake, IN: Eisenbraums, 1996), 47–60.

22. Charles Perry, foreword to *Medieval Cuisine of the Islamic World,* x.

23. William J. Bernstein, *A Splendid Exchange: How Trade Shaped the World* (New York: Atlantic Monthly Press, 2008), 62.

24. Jack Turner, *Spice: The History of a Temptation* (New York: Vintage, 2004), 58–67.

25. Ibid., 79–80.

26. Brent Landau, *Revelation of the Magi: The Lost Tale of the Wise Men's Journey to Bethlehem* (New York: HarperOne, 2010), 118–19.

4. OMANIS ROCKING THE CRADLE OF CIVILIZATION

1. Aruna Shaji, "Seafaring and Trade in Omani History: The Call of the Sea," *Oman Observer,* February 17, 2002.

2. Gary Paul Nabhan, *Arab/American: Landscape, Culture, and Cuisine in Two Great Deserts* (Tucson: University of Arizona Press, 2009).

3. Vincenzo M. Francaviglia, "Dating the Ancient Dam of Ma'rib (Yemen)," *Journal of Archaeological Science* 27, no. 7 (July 2000): 645–53.

4. Albert Hourani, *A History of the Arab Peoples* (Cambridge, MA: Harvard University Press, 2010).

5. Shaji, "Seafaring and Trade in Omani History."

6. H.D. Miller, "The Pleasures of Consumption: The Birth of Medieval Islamic Cuisine," in *Food: The History of Taste,* ed. Paul Freedman (Berkeley: University of California Press, 2007), 136.

7. John Larner, *Marco Polo and the Discovery of the World* (New Haven, CT: Yale University Press, 1999).

8. George Fadlo Hourani, *Arab Seafaring in the Indian Ocean in Ancient and Early Medieval Times* (Beirut, Lebanon: Khayats, 1963), 16.

5. MECCA AND THE MIGRATIONS OF MUSLIM
AND JEWISH TRADERS

1. Adam Davidson, "Company's Takeover of U.S. Ports Raises Security Concerns, National Public Radio, February 14, 2006, www.npr.org/templates/story/story.php?storyId=5205334.

2. Daniel Peterson, *Muhammad: Prophet of God* (Grand Rapids, MI: Wm. B. Eerdmans Publishing, 2007), 15.

3. Hugh Kennedy, *The Great Arab Conquests: How the Spread of Islam Changed the World We Live In* (Philadelphia: Da Capo Press, 2007), 43–44.

4. Peterson, *Muhammad: Prophet of God,* 16.

5. Ibid.

6. James P. Mandaville, *Bedouin Ethnobotany: Plant Concepts and Uses in a Desert Pastoral World* (Tucson: University of Arizona Press, 2011).

7. Patricia Crone, *Meccan Trade and the Rise of Islam* (Princeton, NJ: Princeton University Press, 1987).

8. George Fadlo Hourani, *Arab Seafaring in the Indian Ocean in Ancient and Early Medieval Times* (Beirut, Lebanon: Khayats, 1963), 53.

9. Peterson, *Muhammad: Prophet of God,* 17.

10. Lilia Zaouali, *Medieval Cuisine of the Islamic World: A Concise History with 174 Recipes,* trans. M.B. DeBevoise (Berkeley: University of California Press, 2009).

11. Peterson, *Muhammad: Prophet of God,* 43.

12. Ibid., 44.

13. Michael Hamilton Morgan, *Lost History: The Enduring Legacy of Muslim Scientists, Thinkers, and Artists* (Washington, D.C.: National Geographic Society, 2007), 9.

14. Peterson, *Muhammad: Prophet of God,* 106.

15. Ibid., 93.

16. Ahmad Ghabin, *Hisba, Arts and Crafts in Islam* (Wiesbaden, Germany: Harrassowitz, 2009).

17. W.N. Arafat, "New Light on the Story of the Banu Qurayza and the Jews of Medina," *Journal of the Royal Asiatic Society of Great Britain and Ireland* 15 (1976): 100–107.

18. M.J. Kister, "The Market of the Prophet," *Journal of the Economic and Social History of the Orient* 8 (1965): 272–78; quotation is from p. 273.

19. This poem fragment is my free translation. For a more conventional translation into English, see Karen Armstrong, *Muhammad: A Western Attempt to Understand Islam* (London: Orion Publishing, 1991), 182.

20. Peterson, *Muhammad: Prophet of God,* 108.

21. Stelios Michalopoulos, Alireza Naghari, and Giovanni Prarolo, "Trade and Geography in the Economic Origins of Islam: Theory and Evidence" (draft dated May 22, 2010), 2; http://ssrn.com/abstract=1613303.

22. Peterson, *Muhammad: Prophet of God,* 159–60.

23. Karen Farrell et al., TED Case Studies 5: "Arab Spice Trade and Spread of Islam" (June 1996): 4, www1.american.edu/ted/spice.htm.

24. Natalie Zemon Davis, *Trickster Travels: A Sixteenth-Century Muslim Between Worlds* (New York: Hill and Wang, 2007).

25. Ross E. Dunn, *The Adventures of Ibn Battuta: A Muslim Traveler of the Fourteenth Century* (Berkeley: University of California Press, 2005).

26. Hugh Kennedy, *The Great Arab Conquests: How the Spread of Islam Changed the World We Live In* (Philadelphia: Da Capo Press, 2007), x–xi.

27. S.M. Ghazanfar, "Capitalist Tradition in Early Arab-Islamic Civilization," History of Economics Society Conference (Exeter, UK: University of Exeter, 2007).

28. Nigel Cliff, *Holy War: How Vasco da Gama's Epic Voyages Turned the Tide in a Centuries-Old Clash of Civilizations* (New York: Harper, 2011).

29. Kennedy, *The Great Arab Conquests,* 217.

30. Marc Eliany, "A Brief Social History of the Jews in Morocco: A Synthesis of Oral and Documented Accounts," in *Mind and Soul: Jewish Thinking in Morocco,* www.artengine.ca/eliany/html/mindandsoulinjewishmorocco/historyofjewsinmorocco.html.

31. Kennedy, *The Great Arab Conquests.*

32. Ibn Abd al-Hakam, "The Mohammedan Conquest of Egypt and North Africa," trans. Charles Cutler Torrey, in *Biblical and Semitic Studies,* vol. 1 (New York: Charles Scribner's Sons, 1901), 279–330; and Ahmad ibn Yahya al-Baladhuri, *The Origins of the Islamic State* [Kitāb futāh al-Buldān], vol. 1, trans. Phillip Khuri Hitti (London: P.S. King & Son, 1916).

6. MERGING THE SPICE ROUTES WITH THE SILK ROADS

1. Christopher I. Beckwith, *Empires of the Silk Road: A History of Central Eurasia from the Bronze Age to the Present* (Princeton, NJ: Princeton University Press, 2009).

2. Hugh Kennedy, *The Great Arab Conquests: How the Spread of Islam Changed the World We Live In* (Philadelphia: Da Capo Press, 2007), 63.

3. Kennedy, *The Great Arab Conquests,* 61.

4. Beckwith, *Empires of the Silk Road.*

5. V.V. Bartold, "Tajiks: Historical essay," in Korzhenevsky, N.L., ed., (1925) *Tadzhikistan: sbornik stateĭ (Tajikistan:)* Obshchestvo dlia izucheniia Tadzhikistana i iranskikh narodnosteĭ za ego predelami, Tashkent, pp. 113–150, OCLC 21620342, in Russian; republished in a revised version as A.A. Semenov and V.V. Bartold (1944) *Material'nye pamiatniki iranskoĭ kul'tury v Sredneĭ Azii* Gosizdat pri SNK Tadzhikskoĭ SSR, Stalinabad, OCLC 30576295, in Russian.

6. Beckwith, *Empires of the Silk Road.*

7. Subhi Y. Labib, "Capitalism in Medieval Islam," *Journal of Economic History* 29, no.1 (1969): 79–96.

8. Lilia Zaouali, *Medieval Cuisine of the Islamic World: A Concise History with 174 Recipes,* trans. M.B. DeBevoise (Berkeley: University of California Press, 2007); and Tamim Ansary, *Destiny Disrupted: A History of the World through Islamic Eyes* (New York: PublicAffairs, 2009).

9. Charles Perry, foreword to Zaouali, *Medieval Cuisine of the Islamic World,* xiv.

10. Ibid., and Zaouali, *Medieval Cuisine of the Islamic World,* 188n52.

11. Ansary, *Destiny Disrupted,* 80.

12. Beckwith, *Empires of the Silk Road.*

13. R. Ji, P. Cui, F. Ding, J. Geng, H. Gao, H. Zhang, J. Yu, S. Hu, and H. Meng, "Monophyletic Origin of Domestic B Camel (*Camelus bactrianus*) and Its Evolutionary Relationship with the Extant Wild Camel (*Camelus bactrianus ferus*)," *Animal Genetics* 40, no. 4 (2009): 377–82.

14. Daniel Potts, "Bactrian Camels and Bactrian-Dromedary Hybrids," in "The Silk Road," ed. Daniel Waugh, *Silk Road Journal* 3, no. 1 (2005).

15. Beckwith, *Empires of the Silk Road.*

16. Edward H. Schafer, *The Golden Peaches of Samarkand: A Study in T'ang Exotics* (Berkeley: University of California Press, 1963).

17. Beckwith, *Empires of the Silk Road.*

18. Sally Hovey Wriggins, *The Silk Road Journey with Xuanjang* (Boulder, CO: Westview Press, 2004).

19. Ibid., 38.

20. Edward W. Said, *Orientalism* (New York: Vintage, 1994).

21. Ansary, *Destiny Disrupted,* 81.

22. Zaouali, *Medieval Cuisine of the Islamic World,* 37.

7. THE FLOURISHING OF CROSS-CULTURAL COLLABORATION IN IBERIA

1. Gernot Katzer, "Pomegranate (*Punica granatum* L.)," http://gernot-katzers-spice-pages.com/engl/Puni_gra.html. Accessed May 18, 2013.

2. Richard Fletcher, *Moorish Spain* (Berkeley: University of California Press, 1993), 28; and María Rosa Menocal, *The Ornament of the World: How Muslims, Jews and Christians Created a Culture of Tolerance in Medieval Spain* (Boston: Little, Brown, 2002), 6.

3. Ulrich Deil, "Vegetation Cover and Human Impact: A Comparison of the Almarchal Region (Campo de Gibraltar, Spain) and the Tangier Hinterland (Morocco)," *Lagascalia* 19.1–2 (1997): 745–58.

4. Menocal, *The Ornament of the World*, 28 and 6.

5. Mahmud Ali Makki, "Balance global de la cultura de al-Andalus y su contribución universal," in *Al-Andalus Allende el Atlántico*, ed. Mercedes García-Arenal, Jerónimo Páez López, Federico Mayor, Camilo Alvarez de Morales y Ruiz-Matas, UNESCO, Legado Andalusí (Granada, Spain: El Legado Andalusí, 1997).

6. Menocal, *The Ornament of the World*, 64.

7. Ibid., 9, 64.

8. My adaptation of a passage presented in D. Fairchild Ruggles, *Gardens, Landscape, and Vision in the Palaces of Islamic Spain* (Philadelphia: University of Pennsylvania Press, 2008), 17.

9. Ahmad ibn Mohammed Maqqari, *The History of the Mohammedan Dynasties in Spain*, ed. Pascual de Gayangos, vol. 1 (London: W.H. Allen, 1849), 387.

10. D. Fairchild Ruggles, *Gardens, Landscape, and Vision in the Palaces of Islamic Spain* (Philadelphia: University of Pennsylvania Press, 2008), p. 17.

11. Alnoor Dhananik, "Andalusia: The Shrine of the Revealed Faiths," *Ismaili Magazine USA*, 2003, www.iis.ac.uk/view_article.asp?ContentID=105848. Accessed May 20, 2011.

12. Jonathan Lyons, *The House of Wisdom: How the Arabs Transformed Western Civilization* (New York: Bloomsbury, 2009).

13. Toufic Fahd, "Agricultura y botánica en al-Andalus y sus aportes al nuevo mundo," in *Al-Andalus Allende el Atlántico*, ed. Mercedes García-Arenal et al. (Granada, Spain: El Legado Andalusí, 1997), 181–205; and Thomas F. Glick, introduction to *Obra de agricultura* (1513) by Gabriel Alonso de Herrera (Valencia, Spain: Artes Gráficas Soler, S.A., 1979), 21.

14. Juan Estevan Arellano, introduction in Gabriel Alonso de Herrera, *Ancient Agriculture: Roots and Application of Sustainable Farming* (Salt Lake City: Gibbs Smith, 2006).

15. Expiración García Sánchez and Esteban Hernández Bermejo, eds., *Libro de agricultura, su autor el Doctor excelente Abu Zacaria Iahia* (Córdoba, Spain: Ministerio de Agricultura, Pesca y Alimentación de Andalusia, 1988).

16. Herrera, *Obra de agricultura*, 58.

17. Fletcher, *Moorish Spain*, 43–44.

18. Menocal, *The Ornament of the World*, 32–33.

19. Robert W. Lebling Jr., "Flight of the Blackbird," *Saudi Aramco World*, 2004,

www.saudiaramcoworld.com/issue/200407/flight.of.the.blackbird.compilation; and Lucie Bolens, *La cuisine andalouse, un art de vivre: XIe–XIIIe siècle* (Paris: Albin Michel), 28–31.

20. H.D. Miller, "The Pleasures of Consumption: The Birth of Medieval Islamic Cuisine," in *Food: The History of Taste,* ed. Paul Freedman (Berkeley: University of California Press, 2007), 145.

21. Lilia Zaouali, *Medieval Cuisine of the Islamic World: A Concise History with 174 Recipes,* trans. M.B. DeBevoise (Berkeley: University of California Press, 2004), 42.

22. Sally Schneider, "From the Saffron Fields of Spain," *Saveur,* March 23, 2007, www.saveur.com/article/Travels/From-the-Saffron-Fields-of-Spain.

8. THE CRUMBLING OF *CONVIVENCIA* AND THE RISE OF TRANSNATIONAL GUILDS

1. Fletcher, *Moorish Spain,* 92.

2. Anya H. King, "The Musk Trade and the Near East in the Early Medieval Period" (PhD diss., University of Indiana, 2007).

3. William J. Bernstein, *A Splendid Exchange: How Trade Shaped the World* (New York: Atlantic Monthly Press, 2008), 128.

4. S.D. Goitein, "New Light on the Beginnings of the Karimi Merchants," *Journal of Economic and Social History of the Orient* 1 (1958): 182–83.

5. Michael Krondl, *The Taste of Conquest: The Rise and Fall of the Three Great Cities of Spice* (New York: Ballantine Books, 2007), 115.

6. Subhi Y. Labib, "Capitalism in Medieval Islam," *Journal of Economic History* 29.1 (1969): 93–94.

7. S.M. Ghazanfar, "Capitalist Traditions in Early Arabic-Islamic Civilization," http://muslimheritage.com/topics/default.cfm?ArticleID=1029.

8. Fletcher, *Moorish Spain,* 160; and Menocal, *The Ornament of the World,* with maps on p. 38 and p. 48.

9. Felipe Fernández-Armesto, *1492: The Year the World Began* (New York: HarperOne, 2009), 38.

10. Translation adapted from Fernández-Armesto, *1492: The Year the World Began,* 40.

11. Janet Liebman Jacobs, "Women, Ritual and Secrecy: The Creation of Crypto-Jewish Culture," Society for Crypto-Jewish Culture (2000), www.cryptojews.com/WomenRitual.htm; see also Janet Liebman Jacobs, *Hidden Heritage: the Legacy of the Crypto-Jews* (Berkeley: University of California Press, 2002).

12. Colette Rossant, *Apricots along the Nile: A Memoir with Recipes* (Cairo: American University of Cairo, 2000).

13. Andrée Aelion Brooks, *The Woman Who Defied Kings: The Life and Times of Doña Gracia Nasi, a Jewish Leader during the Renaissance.* (St. Paul, MN: Paragon House, 2002).

14. Fernand Braudel, *The Mediterranean and the Mediterranean World in the Age of Phillip II* (New York: Harper & Row, 1972), 578.

15. H.P. Salomon and Aron de Leone Leoni, "Mendes, Benveniste, de Luna,

Micas, Nasci: The State of the Art (1532–1558), *Jewish Quarterly Review* 88.3–4 (1998): 185–211.

16. Brooks, *The Woman Who Defied Kings*, 62.

17. Michael Krondl, *The Taste of Conquest*.

18. Brooks, *The Woman Who Defied Kings*, 55.

19. Ibid., 164.

20. Cecil Roth, *The House of Nasi: Doña Gracia* (New York: Greenwood Press, 1948), 21.

21. Florence Edler de Roover, "The Market for Spices in Antwerp, 1538–1544," in *Revue Belge de Philogie et d'Histoire* 17.1–2 (1938): 214.

22. Edler de Roover, "The Market for Spices in Antwerp," 218.

23. Fayne Ericon, back cover of Brooks, *The Woman Who Defied Kings*.

24. Brooks, *The Woman Who Defied Kings*, 359.

25. Cecil Roth, *The House of Nasi*, 44.

26. Brooks, *The Woman Who Defied Kings*, 179.

27. Toufic Fahd, "Agricultura y Botánica en al-Andalus y Sus Aportes en el Nuevo Mundo," in *Al-Andalus Allende el Atlántico*, ed. Mercedes Gracia-Arenal et al., 181–205.

28. Gary Paul Nabhan, "Fruit Comes from the Archbishop for the Table and the Soul," *El Palacio* 117 (winter): 60–65; and Emily J. McTavish, Jared E. Decker, Robert D. Schnabel, Jeremy F. Taylor, and David M. Hills, "New World Cattle Show Ancestry from Multiple Independent Domestication Events," *Proceedings of the National Academy of Sciences of the United States of America*, March 25, 2013, www.pnas.org/content/early/2013/03/19/1303367110.abstract.

9. BUILDING BRIDGES BETWEEN CONTINENTS AND CULTURES

1. Ralph Kauz, *Aspects of the Maritime Silk Road from the Persian Gulf to the East China Sea* (Weisbaden, Germany: Harrassowitz Verlag, 2010).

2. Angela Schottenhammer, *The Emporium of the World: Maritime Quanzhou 100–1400* (Leiden, Germany: Brill, 2001).

3. Chen Da-sheng, "Chinese-Iranian Relations. VII. Persian Settlements in Southeastern China during the T'ang, Sung, and Yuan Dynasties," *Encyclopaedia Iranica*, www.iranicaonline.org/articles/chinese-iranian-vii; accessed July 9, 2013.

4. Ross E. Dunn, *The Adventures of Ibn Battuta: A Muslim Traveler of the Fourteenth Century* (Berkeley: University of California Press, 2005), and Chen Da-sheng, "Chinese-Iranian Relations."

5. Kauz, *Aspects of the Maritime Silk Road from the Persian Gulf to the East China Sea*.

6. Dru C. Gladney, "Muslim Tombs and Ethnic Folklore: Charters for Hui Identity," *Journal of Asian Studies* 43.3 (1987): 495–513.

7. Marco Polo, *The Travels of Marco Polo*, trans. Ronald Latham (London: Penguin Classics, 2005).

8. Chen Da-sheng, "Chinese-Iranian Relations."

9. Louise Levathes, *When China Ruled the Seas: The Treasure Fleet of the Dragon Throne 1405–1433* (New York: Oxford University Press, 1991), 201.

10. Dunn, *The Adventures of Ibn Battuta,* and Xiao Jia Go, "Muslims of Quanzhou," *New Statesman,* December 18, 2006, www.newstatesman.com/node/155179.

11. Jacob D'Ancona, *City of Light: The Hidden Journal of the Man Who Entered China Four Years before Marco Polo,* trans. David Selbourne (New York: Citadel Press, 2003).

12. Chen Da-sheng, "Chinese-Iranian Relations."

13. Dru C. Gladney, *Muslim Chinese: Ethnic Nationalism in the People's Republic* (Cambridge: Council of Eastern Asian Studies, Harvard University Asian Center/Harvard University Press 1996).

14. Chen Da-sheng, "Chinese-Iranian Relations."

15. Gladney, *Muslim Chinese.*

10. NAVIGATING THE MARITIME SILK ROADS FROM CHINA TO AFRICA

1. Gavin Menzies, *1421: The Year China Discovered the World* (London: Bantam Press, 2003).

2. Louise Levathes, *When China Ruled the Seas: The Treasure Fleet of the Dragon Throne 1405–1433* (New York: Oxford University Press, 1994).

3. Edward L. Dreyer, *Zheng He: China and the Oceans in the Early Ming Dynasty, 1405–1433* (New York: Pearson-Longman, 2007), 11.

4. Levathes, *When China Ruled the Seas,* 61–63.

5. Dreyer, *Zheng He,* 23.

6. Levathes, *When China Ruled the Seas,* 20.

7. Dreyer, *Zheng He,* 88, 186.

8. Ibid., 8, 51.

9. Giles Milton, *Nathaniel's Nutmeg: How One Man's Courage Changed the Course of History* (London: Hodder & Stoughton, 1999).

10. Paul Lunde, "The Admiral Zheng He," *Saudi Aramco World* 56.4 (July/August 2005), www.saudiaramcoworld.com/issue/200504/the.admiral.zheng.he.htm.

11. Ibid. For a more extensive inventory, see Ma Huan, *Ying-Yai Sheng-Tai: The Overall Survey of the Ocean's Shores* (1433), ed. J.V.G. Mills (Cambridge: Cambridge University Press for the Haklyut Society, 1970).

12. Menzies, *1421: The Year China Discovered the World.*

13. Dreyer, *Zheng He,* 182.

14. Ibid., 176–82.

15. Rosey Wang Ma, "Chinese Muslims in Malaysia: History and Development," in *Chinese Studies of the Malay World: A Comparative Approach,* ed. Ding Choo Ming and Ooi Kee Bey (Singapore: Eastern Universities Press, 2003).

16. Tan Yeok Seong, "Chinese Element in the Islamisation of Southeast Asia," in *Admiral Zheng He and Southeast Asia,* ed. Leo Suryadinata (Singapore: Institute of Southeastern Studies and International Zheng He Society, 2006,) 70.

17. Samuel Taylor Coleridge, *Complete Poems,* ed. William Keach (New York: Penguin Publishing, 1997), 498–99.

18. Dreyer, *Zheng He*, 65.

19. Lilian Swee Lian Chua, "Agarwood (*Aquilaria malaccensis*) in Malaysia," NDF Workshop Case Studies (Mexico D. F.: CONABIO, 2008).

20. Dreyer, *Zheng He*, 64–65.

21. Yusuf Chang quoted in "The History of Ming" (Beijing: China Scientific Book Services, n.d), www.hceis.com/ChinaBasic/History/Ming/htm. Stanley Hordes, *To the Ends of the Earth: A History of the Crypto-Jews of New Mexico* (New York: Columbia University Press, 2005).

22. Janet Liebman Jacobs, "Women, Ritual and Secrecy: The Creation of Crypto-Jewish Culture," Society for Crypto-Jewish Culture (2000), www.cryptojews.com/WomenRitual.htm.

23. Levathes, *When China Ruled the Seas*, 198–200.

24. Chen Da-sheng, "Chinese-Iranian Relations. VII. Persian Settlements in Southeastern China during the T'ang, Sung, and Yuan Dynasties," *Encyclopaedia Iranica*, www.iranicaonline.org/articles/chinese-iranian-vii; accessed July 9, 2013.

11. VASCO DA GAMA MASTERING THE GAME OF GLOBALIZATION

1. Jack Turner, *Spice: The History of a Temptation* (New York: Vintage, 2005), 14–15.

2. Louise Levathes, *When China Ruled the Seas: The Treasure Fleet of the Dragon Throne 1405–1433* (New York: Oxford University Press, 1994), 148–49.

3. Ronald Watkins, *Unknown Seas: How Vasco da Gama Opened the East* (London: John Murray, 2003).

4. Felipe Fernández-Armesto, *Near a Thousand Tables: A History of Food* (New York: Free Press, 2002), 158.

5. Levathes, *When China Ruled the Seas*, 21.

6. Nigel Cliff, *Holy War: How Vasco da Gama's Epic Voyages Turned the Tide in a Centuries-Old Clash of Civilizations* (New York: HarperCollins, 2011).

7. E. G. Ravenstein, ed., *A Journal of the First Voyage of Vasco da Gama, 1497–1499* (London: Hakluyt Society, 1898), 28.

8. K. G. Jayne, *Vasco da Gama and His Successors 1460–1580* (New York: Barnes and Noble, 1910).

9. Cliff, *Holy War*.

10. Sanjay Subrahmanyam, *The Career and Legend of Vasco da Gama* (Cambridge: Cambridge University Press, 1997).

11. Vinod K. Jose, "The Emperor Uncrowned: The Rise of Narendra Modi," *The Caravan*, March 1, 2012.

12. Watkins, *Unknown Seas*, 229–30.

13. Cliff, *Holy War*.

14. Alison Stark Draper, *Vasco da Gama: The Portuguese Quest for a Sea Route to India* (New York: Rosen Publishing Group, 2003).

15. Fernão Lopes de Castanheda, quoted in 2:346–347 of *A General History and Collection of Voyages and Travels,* ed. Robert Kerr (Edinburgh, Scotland: William Blackwood, 1811).

16. Cliff, *Holy War.*

17. Gaspar Correia, quoted in *Lendas da India,* ed. R.J. de Lima Felner (Lisbon: Archivos Real, 1858–1864).

18. Sanjay Subrahmanyan, *The Career and Legend of Vasco da Gama.*

19. Cliff, *Holy War,* 505.

20. Gaspar Correia, quoted in R.J. de Lima, ed., *Lendas da India.*

21. Cliff, *Holy War,* 505.

22. Hasan M. al-Naboodah, "The Banu Nabhan in the Omani Sources," in *New Arabic Studies,* ed. G. Rex Smart, J.R. Smart, and B.R. Pridham (Exeter: University of Exeter Press, 1997), 181–98.

23. Cliff, *Holy War.*

24. Gary Paul Nabhan, *Arab-American: Landscape, Culture and Cuisine in Two Great Deserts* (Tucson: University of Arizona Press, 2008), 80–81.

25. Levathes, *When China Ruled the Seas,* 201.

26. Nello Puccioni, "Anthropological Studies of the Bajuni," *Giuba o Oltre-giuba: Itinerary of the Mission of the Italian Academy, 1935* (Florence: Sansoni-Editore, 1937), 110.

27. Levathes, *When China Ruled the Seas,* 198–203. See also Menzies, *1421.*

12. CROSSING THE DRAWBRIDGE OVER THE EASTERN OCEAN

1. J.M. Carrillo Castillo, ed., *Gonzalez Fernandez de Oviedo: Oviedo on Columbus* (Turnhout, Belgium: Brepols, 2000).

2. Ibid.

3. Gordon Willard Allport, *The Nature of Prejudice* (New York: Basic Books, 1979).

4. Seymour B. Liebman, *The Jews in New Spain: Faith, Flame, and the Inquisition* (Coral Gables, FL: University of Miami Press, 1970).

5. Saulat Pervez, "Latin America: Historical Legacy," www.whyislam.org/muslim-world/latin-america-historical-overview; accessed July 9, 2013 (bracketed interpolations mine). See also Habeeb Salloum, "Arabs in Latin America: Cuba's Disappearing Arab Community," *Alminbar* 14 (1987): 14.

6. Luis Alberto Anaya Hernández, *Judeoconversos e Inquisición en las Islas Canarias* (Las Palmas de Gran Canaria: Universidad de Las Palmas de Gran Canaria, 1996).

7. Pamela Grau Twena, *The Sephardic Table* (New York: Houghton-Mifflin, 1998), 17.

8. Norman Finkelstein, *The Other 1492: Jewish Settlement in the New World* (New York: Charles Scribner's Sons, 1989).

9. Clifford A. Wright, "The Medieval Spice Trade and the Diffusion of Chile," *Gastronomica* 7 (2007): 35–43.

10. Frances Levine, " 'So Dreadful a Crime': Doña Teresa Aguilera y Roche Faces the Inquisition for the Sin of Chocolate Consumption," *El Palacio* 117 (Winter): 52–59.

11. Rafael López Guzmán, *Mudéjar Hispano y Americano: Itinerarios Culturales Mexicanos* (Granada, Spain: Fundación El Legado Andalusí, 2002).

12. My translation from Spanish of material from Lourdes Diaz-Trechuelo

Lopez-Spinola, ed., *La emigración Andaluza en America, Siglos XVII y XVIII* (Seville: Junta de Andalucia, 1990), 21.

13. Lopez-Spinola, ed., *La emigración Andaluza en America, Siglos XVII y XVIII*, 27.

14. David M. Gitlitz and Linda Kay Davidson, *A Drizzle of Honey: The Lives and Recipes of Spain's Secret Jews* (New York: St. Martin's Press, 1999); and Joyce Goldstein, *Saffron Shores: Jewish Cooking of the Southern Mediterranean* (San Francisco: Chronicle Books, 2002).

15. Mercedes Garcia-Arenal et al., ed., *Al-Andalus Allende el Atlántico* (Granada: El Legado Andalusi, 1997).

16. Levine, "So Dreadful a Crime," 55–56.

17. "Jews in Jamaica," *Wikipedia,* http://en.wikipedia.org/wiki/Jews_in_Jamaica, last accessed September 4, 2011. See also Liebman, *The Jews in New Spain.*

18. Patricia Rain, *Vanilla: The Cultural History of the World's Favorite Flavor and Fragrance* (New York: J.P. Tarcher, 2004), 56–58.

19. Louis Grivetti and Howard Yana-Shapiro, *Chocolate: History, Culture and Heritage* (Hoboken: John Wiley, 2009), 34.

20. Joyce Goldstein, *Saffron Shores.*

21. Gary Nabhan, introduction to *The Slaw and the Slow Cooked,* ed. James R. Veteto and Edward McLain (Nashville, TN: Vanderbilt University Press, 2011).

22. Sophie D. Coe and Michael D. Coe, *The True History of Chocolate* (London: Thames and Hudson, 2006), 216–17.

23. Diana Kennedy, *Oaxaca al Gusto: An Infinite Gastronomy* (Austin: University of Texas Press, 2010), 50, 151, 243; and Rick Bayless with Deann Groen Bayless and Jean Marie Robinson, *Rick Bayless's Mexican Kitchen: Capturing the Vibrant Flavors of a World-Class Cuisine* (New York: Scribner's, 2006), 276–84.

24. Camilo Alvarez de Morales, "Medicina y alimentación: Andaluces y Moriscos," in *Al-Andalus Allende el Atlantico,* ed. Mercedes Garcia-Arenal et al. (Granada, Spain: El Legado Andalusi, 1997).

25. Adapted from Ricardo Trujillo, "Mexican Mole Poblano: A Culinary Clash of Cultures," *Articles Base,* May 5, 2008, www.articlesbase.com/food-and-beverage-articles/mexican-mole-poblano-a-culinary-clash-of-cultures-404435.html, accessed March 4, 2013. See also Aliza Green, *Field Guide to Herbs and Spices* (New York: Quirk Books, 2006).

EPILOGUE

1. Woody Tasch, *Inquiries into the Nature of Slow Money* (White River Junction, VT: Chelsea Green Publishing, 2008), 3–4.

2. Amanda Hesser interview with Carlo Petrini, "Endangered Species: Slow Food," *New York Times,* July 26, 2003, www.mindfully.org/Food/2003/Slow-Food-Carlo-Petrini26July03.htm.

Index

Page numbers in bold refer to text boxes.

Al Maktoum, Mohammed bin Rashid, Sheikh, 106
almonds, 191, 265, 266; Dajaj Gdra Bil-Lawz (Spiced Chicken in Almond Sauce), 223–24
aloe wood, 182, 202
Al Taie, Lamees Abdullah (*Al-Azaf: The Omani Cookbook*), 19–20, 31, 81
Altai Mountains, 150–51
Álvarez Chanca, Diego, 246
amber musk, 150–51. *See also* musk
Americas. *See* New World *entries; specific places and peoples*
amomon, 54–55
Amomum subulatum, 54–55
Anasazi, 264
Anatolia, 142–43*map*
al-Andalus, 162, 166–71; after fall of Umayyads, 181–82; agricultural and culinary innovations in, 169, 170–71, 174–75, 177; Berber tribes in, 163, 175; Christians and Jews in, 163, 166, 169–70, 175, 177; *convivencia*'s decline, 184, 185–86; cultural pluralism in, 163, 169, 171, 174; eastern plant introductions, 167–69, 175, 177; Madinat al-Zahra, 177–80; Ziryab in, 171, 174–75. *See also* Iberia; Spain
Andalusia, author in, 161–62, 177–80. *See also* al-Andalus
Anderson, Eugene, *A Soup for the Qan*, 6, 7, 10
Andrade, Benjamin d'Acosta de, 262, 264
Andrews, Jean, 247
anise, 9, 98, 169, 177, 178–79, 179, 264, 265; trade routes, 58*map*, 142–43*map*
Anmir ud-Din, 209
annatto (achiote), 250*map*, 252–53, 255, 268
Anping Bridge, 199–200, 201*fig.*
Antwerp, 193–94
apricot, 169, 179, 202
Aquilaria malaccensis, 226
Arabian Nights, 146–47
Arabian Peninsula, 16–18, 33*map*, 58*map*; aromatics in, 17–18, 20–21; food and foraging, 42, 43; migration from, 20–21, 57–59, 93–94; oasis agriculture, 53–57; water storage and management in, 75. *See also specific places and peoples*
Arabian Sea, 33*map*. *See also* maritime trade; *specific ports*
Arabic alphabet and calligraphy, 69
Arabic language, 122–23
Arabic literature and poetry, 107–8, 146–

47, 155; cookbooks, 145. *See also* Ka'b ibn al-Ashraf
Arabs: as spice traders, 5, 13, 15, 274. *See also* Arabian Peninsula; *specific peoples and places*
Arab Seafaring in the Indian Ocean in Ancient and Early Medieval Times (Hourani), 48
arak, 9, 178
Arawak people, 259, 261
Arellano, Juan Estevan, 11, 170
aromatics, 3, 4, 19, 20–22, 23–24, 80, 84, 147–48. *See also* spice *entries; specific spices and incenses*
Ashab Mosque, 230
Ashurbanipal, 190
Asia: trade with, 94–95, 97–98, 100–102, 142–43*map*. *See also specific places and peoples*
Atencio, Tomás, 11
Avicenna, 117, 135
Aztecs, 249, 252, 260, 265

Bactrian camel, 147, 148. *See also* camel caravans
Bactrian people, 135, 148
Baghdad, Abbasid caliphate, 159–60, 174, 175
Bahamas, 243, 255
baharat, 272, 273
Bahira, 111
Bajuni people, 242
Balduccio Pegolotti, Francesco di, 24
al-Balid, 40–42, 41*fig.*
Bani Nabatu, 69
banking, 184. *See also* money lending
Banu al-Nadir, 118, 122. *See also* Ka'b ibn al-Ashraf
Banu Hashim, 118
Banu Nebhani, 23, 47, 118, 140–41, 146–47; in Arabian Peninsula, 45–46, 52, 91, 93, 240–41; in Lamu Archipelago, 241–42
Banu Umayyah, 140. *See also* Umayyads
barbacoa, 264–65
Barbera, Giuseppe, 87
barley, 41–42
Basra, 33*map*, 98, 142–43*map*, 146, 184
Basson, Moshe, 85
Batmanglij, Najmieh, 81, 135
bay leaf, 203, 265
Bedigian, Dorothea, 99
Bedouins, 18, 38, 55, 61, 66–68, 75, 178; Bedouin cooking, 272. *See also* Quraysh; Tayy

CALIFORNIA STUDIES IN FOOD AND CULTURE

Darra Goldstein, Editor